Introduction to

METAPHYSICS

The Fundamental Questions

Edited by

Andrew B. Schoedinger

 **Prometheus Books**

59 John Glenn Drive
Amherst, New York 14228-2197

Published 1991 by Prometheus Books

Inquiries should be addressed to
Prometheus Books
59 John Glenn Drive
Amherst, New York 14228–2197.
VOICE: 716–691–0133, ext. 207; FAX: 716–564–2711
WWW.PROMETHEUSBOOKS.COM

07 06 05 04 03   6 5 4 3 2

Library of Congress Cataloging-in-Publication Data

Introduction to metaphysics : the fundamental questions/ edited by
    Andrew B. Schoedinger.
        p.   cm.
    Includes bibliographical references.
    ISBN 0–87975–622–5
    1. Metaphysics. I. Schoedinger, Andrew B.
BD111.I48   1991
110—dc20   90–26687
                                                               CIP

Printed in the United States of America on acid-free paper

Contents

INTRODUCTION   9

PART ONE: THE QUESTION OF UNIVERSALS

Introduction   15

1. The Categories (Chapters 1–5)
   Aristotle   17

2. On Universals
   Peter Abelard   24

3. Of the Signification of Words, and General Terms
   John Locke   35

4. First Principles of Human Knowledge
   George Berkeley   41

5. Universals
   D. F. Pears   53

6. Universals and Family Resemblances
   Renford Bambrough   65

7. Empiricism, Semantics, and Ontology
   Rudolf Carnap   72

Select Bibliography   89

PART TWO: THE QUESTION OF CAUSATION

Introduction   99

8. Of the Idea of Necessary Connection
   David Hume   101

9. Of the Law of Universal Causation
   John Stuart Mill   108

10. On the Notion of Cause
    Bertrand Russell   119

11. On the Nature and the Observability
    of the Causal Relation
    C. J. Ducasse   133

12. On the So-Called Idea of Causation
    R. G. Collingwood   145

13. Law Statements and Counterfactual Inference
    Roderick M. Chisholm   163

14. The Metaphysics of Causation
    Richard Taylor   172

Select Bibliography   192

PART THREE: THE QUESTION OF PERSONAL IDENTITY

Introduction   199

15. On Thinking Things and the Soul
    René Descartes — 202

16. The Body, the Soul, and the Person
    John Locke — 212

17. Of Personal Identity
    Joseph Butler — 222

18. On Personal Identity
    David Hume — 227

19. Personal Identity and Memory
    Sydney Shoemaker — 233

20. The Soul
    Anthony Quinton — 246

21. Persons
    P. F. Strawson — 262

Select Bibliography — 286

PART FOUR: THE QUESTION OF FREE WILL AND AGENCY

Introduction — 291

22. Determinism
    Alasdair MacIntyre — 294

23. Willing
    A. I. Melden — 303

24. Basic Actions
    Arthur C. Danto — 311

25. Causal Power and Human Agency
    Richard Taylor — 326

26. Actions, Reasons, and Causes
    Donald Davidson   341

27. Intentional Action
    Alvin I. Goldman   356

28. Beliefs, Wants, and Decisions
    Andrew B. Schoedinger   371

Select Bibliography   376

PART FIVE: PROBLEMS OF ARTIFICIAL INTELLIGENCE

Introduction   383

29. Elements of a Theory of Human Problem Solving
    Allen Newell, J. C. Shaw, and *Herbert A. Simon*   385

30. The Compleat Robot: A Prolegomena to Androidology
    Michael Scriven   407

31. The Imitation Game
    Keith Gunderson   426

32. On Consciousness in Machines
    Arthur C. Danto   438

33. The Feelings of Robots
    Paul Ziff   444

34. Minds and Machines
    Hilary Putnam   450

35. Love in a Machine Age
    Paul Weiss   460

Select Bibliography   465

Introduction

The word 'metaphysics' is derived from the two Greek words *meta* and *physica*, and literally means "beyond physics." The Ancient Greeks were very much interested in understanding the workings of the world around them. Hence, in the most general of ways, they sought an understanding of physics. This is most clearly evident in their preoccupation with the notion of change. What happens, they wondered, when a log burns and turns to ashes? How is it that the color of a tree's leaves change? Answers to these and other questions led some to conclude that the world must be composed of fundamental elements, i.e., atoms (the Greek word for unbreakable units), and that the world must function according to the law of conservation of energy (though they didn't express it in this formal way). Along with their quest for an understanding of physics came the realization that an in-depth explanation of the physical workings of the world required going beyond the physical in order to explain it adequately. Concepts with no physical referents are necessary in order to account for that which is physical. Consequently, metaphysics constitutes the foundation upon which the physics *qua* physical rests.

The notion of "property" is a good case in point. If we were to inquire of a scientist if physical things possessed properties, he would undoubtedly respond in the affirmative. Such a response would commit him to the existence of properties. But what is a property? The concept of a property is that of something nonphysical. A little reflection will determine that we cannot account for anything physical without making reference to its properties or characteristics. Yet when going beyond the specific properties of a physical thing to analyze the concept of a property, all reference to the particular

9

(physical) thing disappears. At that point, we have gone beyond physics and enter the realm of metaphysics.

Reference has just been made to two key areas of metaphysical concern: (1) the nature of characteristics, which is rooted in the problem of universals, and (2) the problem of causation. These two subjects constitute the first two parts of this volume.

Note should be taken here of the intimate relationship between metaphysics (theories of reality) and epistemology (theories of knowledge). These two areas of inquiry constitute the core of philosophy as a discipline. It should be understood that, to a great extent, where we begin determines where we end up. In other words, if our initial interest is primarily epistemological in nature, then that will have a determining effect with respect to our metaphysical views, and vice-versa. This is most evident when addressing the question of personal identity. Consider, for example, the different epistemological starting points of René Descartes and David Hume and the respective conclusions they draw concerning the nature of personal identity. This intimate relationship between metaphysics and epistemology is also evident when problems of artificial intelligence are discussed. For example, the metaphysical criteria with which we begin to identify a mind (it is important to understand that we *must* begin with *some* criteria) determines whether or not noncarbon machines can possess them and, consequently, whether or not such machines can think and therefore possess the unqiue kinds of knowledge indicative of carbon machines (i.e., human beings). The questions surrounding personal identity and artificial intelligence constitute parts three and five respectively.

Part Four addresses the questions involved when discussing free will and agency. Historically, such discussions have been attempts to salvage free will from an onslaught of evidence in support of the view that human behavior is determined and hence not free. A commitment to the view that there is only one legitimate model of causation has undermined proponents of free will. However, casting the discussion in terms of agency has greatly contributed to a resurrection of free will. Consequently, our discussion of the problem in this book takes that direction. We might well query: "So what's the big deal if all behavior is determined?" Historically, it has been of major concern to moral theorists; for if there is no free will, assignment of any and all moral culpability for human action is rendered vacuous. Again, we might ask: "Why should this matter to us, from the point of view of metaphysics?" The answer concerns a quest for the truth of the matter spurred on by an unwillingness to accept the possibility that human beings have no control over their behavior and, therefore, no control over their individual destinies.

The study of metaphysics forces us to analyze phenomena that most people take for granted as fundamental. That all happenings, for example, presuppose causation is as fundamental as *can be*. It is this fundamental nature of metaphysical questions that demands investigation. In going beyond the physics, we discover the conceptual prerequisites that make the physical world possible. A knowledge of these prerequisites is (a) valuable in itself and (b) necessary for an understanding of ourselves as thinking human beings, the world around us, and the relationship between the two.

Part One

The Question of Universals

Introduction

Few people doubt the existence of particulars or *concrete entia;* those things which possess spatio-temporal coordinates. They are the things we see, feel, smell, hear, and taste. Such particulars are distinguished from one another either (a) by possessing characteristics and participating in relationshps with other particulars, or (b) by human observers who predicate characteristics and relationships of particulars.

If (a) is the case, particulars classify themselves; that is, pigs are pigs and parrots are parrots and never the twain shall meet. The characteristics are inherent in the things that possess them. If characteristics are inherent in things, then they must be as real as the things themselves, for it is by the possession of characteristics that particulars are what they are, namely, pigs or parrots. Characteristics and relationships among particulars are called *universals* since they are *shared by many particulars.* If characteristics and relationshps, e.g., "being north of," are real, then a genuine metaphysical problem presents itself. Universals are *nonconcrete entia.* We cannot pick up the characteristic "pig" as we can a rock or a textbook. Neither can we toss around the relationship "is north of." The problem is this: if universals are real but, at the same time, do not possess spatio-temporal coordinates, then just what sort of things are they or in what sense are they real? The desire to answer this question has inspired many philosophers' theories concerning the nature of universals. Those theorists who hold to the view that universals possess some sort of real status, independent of human conception or ability to classify the particulars that are perceived, have come to be known as *realists.*

Some philosophers have argued that a commitment to any real, and therefore independent, status for universals is a metaphysical wild goose chase.

No pig is like any other pig. "Everything is what it is and not another thing" as Joseph Butler maintained. It is human beings who, for whatever reason, possess a need to classify particulars, and in so doing they create and employ common names. Universals are common nouns, predicates of whatever functions as the subject in a sentence. Hence, philosophers of this persuasion construe universals as linguistic entities and, thereby, avoid a treasure hunt for the beast "universal" existing out there, its nature to be discovered. Rather, universals are right before our very eyes, making themselves known by way of the common noun. This anlaysis of universals is called *nominalism.*

Alternatively, some philosophers believe that there must be more than a mere common noun that warrants the ascriptions of a common noun to a group of things. After all, such a group of things must have something in common, otherwise someone would have no good reason to employ a common noun in the first place. It's much like what comes first, the chicken or the egg? Is there something real "out there" that provides the basis for a common noun, or is the phenomenon of classification a peculiarly human enterprise? Those philosophers who feel uncomfortable with realism or nominalism traditionally have opted for *conceptualism,* which is the position that universals have no real and independent status apart from the human ability to conceive and manipulate them. Nor are universals as arbitrary as mere words assigned to groups of particulars at the whim of people. Rather, human beings possess the unique ability to abstract from the many particulars they perceive the common characteristics that certain particulars share. The nature of such abstractions are concepts. Universals are therefore concepts.

Nevertheless, there must be some real basis enabling human beings to make such abstractions. After all, there must be something "out there," i.e., inherent in the particulars perceived by humans, that provides the basis for ascertaining elements of commonality by means of sense experience. If so, we come full circle to realism. And the debate goes on. One thing is for certain: regardless of the nature of universals, human beings must presuppose their existence, whatever the nature of that existence is, in order to make sense of the world.

1

The Categories

(Chapters 1-5)

Aristotle

1. Things are said to be named "equivocally" when, though they have a common name, the definition corresponding with the name differs for each. Thus, a real man and a figure in a picture can both lay claim to the name "animal"; yet these are equivocally so named, for, though they have a common name, the definition corresponding with the name differs for each. For should any one define in what sense each is an animal, his definition in the one case will be appropriate to that case only.

On the other hand, things are said to be named "univocally" which have both the name and the definition answering to the name in common. A man and an ox are both "animal," and these are univocally so named, inasmuch as not only the name, but also the definition, is the same in both cases: for if a man should state in what sense each is an animal, the statement in the one case would be identical with that in the other.

Things are said to be named "derivatively," which derive their name from some other name, but differ from it in termination. Thus the grammarian derives his name from the word "grammar," and the courageous man from the word "courage."

From *The Oxford Translation of Aristotle*, translated by E. M. Edghill, edited by W. D. Ross, vol. 1 (1928). [*The Basic Works of Aristotle*, edited by Richard McKeon (Oxford: Clarendon Press, 1941), pp. 7–14.] Reprinted by permission of Oxford University Press.

2. Forms of speech are either simple or composite. Examples of the latter are such expressions as "the man runs," "the man wins"; of the former "man," "ox," "runs," "wins."

Of things themselves some are predicable of a subject, and are never present in a subject. Thus "man" is predicable of the individual man, and is never present in a subject.

By being "present in a subject" I do not mean present as parts are present in a whole, but being incapable of existence apart from the said subject.

Some things, again, are present in a subject, but are never predicable of a subject. For instance, a certain point of grammatical knowledge is present in the mind, but is not predicable of any subject; or again, a certain whiteness may be present in the body (for color requires a material basis), yet it is never predicable of anything.

Other things, again, are both predicable of a subject and present in a subject. Thus while knowledge is present in the human mind, it is predicable of grammar.

There is, lastly, a class of things which are neither present in a subject nor predicable of a subject, such as the individual man or the individual horse. But, to speak more generally, that which is individual and has the character of a unit is never predicable of a subject. Yet in some cases there is nothing to prevent such being present in a subject. Thus a certain point of grammatical knowledge is present in a subject.

3. When one thing is predicated of another, all that which is predicable of the predicate will be predicable also of the subject. Thus, "man" is predicated of the individual man; but "animal" is predicated of "man"; it will, therefore, be predicable of the individual man also: for the individual man is both "man" and "animal."

If genera are different and co-ordinate, their differentiae are themselves different in kind. Take as an instance the genus "animal" and the genus "knowledge." "With feet," "two-footed," "winged," "aquatic," are differentiae of "animal"; the species of knowledge are not distinguished by the same differentiae. One species of knowledge does not differ from another in being "two-footed."

But where one genus is subordinate to another, there is nothing to prevent their having the same differentiae: for the greater class is predicated of the lesser, so that all the differentiae of the predicate will be differentiae also of the subject.

4. Expressions which are in no way composite signify substance, quantity, quality, relation, place, time, position, state, action, or affection. To sketch my meaning roughly, examples of substance are "man" or "the horse," of quantity, such terms as "two cubits long" or "three cubits long," of quality, such attributes as "white," "grammatical." "Double," "half," "greater," fall under

the category of relation; "in the market place," "in the Lyceum," under that of place; "yesterday," "last year," under that of time. "Lying," "sitting," are terms indicating position; "shod," "armed," state; "to lance," "to cauterize," action; "to be lanced," "to be cauterized," affection.

No one of these terms, in and by itself, involves an affirmation; it is by the combination of such terms that positive or negative statements arise. For every assertion must, as is admitted, be either true or false, whereas expressions which are not in any way composite, such as "man," "white," "runs," "wins," cannot be either true or false.

5. Substance, in the truest and primary and most definite sense of the word, is that which is neither predicable of a subject nor present in a subject; for instance, the individual man or horse. But in a secondary sense those things are called substances within which, as species, the primary substance are included; also those which, as genera, include the species. For instance, the individual man is included in the species "man," and the genus to which the species belongs is "animal"; these, therefore—that is to say, the species "man" and the genus "animal"—are termed secondary substances.

It is plain from what has been said that both the name and the definition of the predicate must be predicable of the subject. For instance, "man" is predicated of the individual man. Now in this case the name of the species "man" is applied to the individual, for we use the term "man" in describing the individual; and the definition of "man" will also be predicated of the individual man, for the individual man is both man and animal. Thus, both the name and the definition of the species are predicable of the individual.

With regard, on the other hand, to those things which are present in a subject, it is generally the case that neither their name nor their definition is predicable of that in which they are present. Though, however, the definition is never predicable, there is nothing in certain cases to prevent the name being used. For instance, "white" being present in a body is predicated of that in which it is present, for a body is called white: the definition, however, of the color "white" is never predicable of the body.

Everything except primary substances is either predicable of a primary substance or present in a primary substance. This becomes evident by reference to particular instances which occur. "Animal" is predicated of the species "man" therefore of the individual man, for if there were no individual man of whom it could be predicated, it could not be predicated of the species "man" at all. Again, color is present in body, therefore in individual bodies, for if there were no individual body in which it was present, it could not be present in body at all. Thus everything except primary substances is either predicated of primary substances, or is present in them, and if these last did not exist, it would be impossible for anything else to exist.

Of secondary substances, the species is more truly substance than the genus, being more nearly related to primary substance. For if any one should render an account of what a primary substance is, he would render a more instructive account, and one more proper to the subject, by stating the species than by stating the genus. Thus, he would give a more instructive account of an individual man by stating that he was man than by stating that he was animal, for the former description is peculiar to the individual in a greater degree, while the latter is too general. Again, the man who gives an account of the nature of an individual tree will give a more instructive account by mentioning the species "tree" than by mentioning the genus "plant."

Moreover, primary substances are most properly called substances in virtue of the fact that they are the entities which underlie everything else, and that everything else is either predicated of them or present in them. Now the same relation which subsists between primary substance and everything else subsists also between the species and the genus: for the species is to the genus as subject is to predicate, since the genus is predicated of the species, whereas the species cannot be predicated of the genus. Thus we have a second ground for asserting that the species is more truly substance than the genus.

Of species themselves, except in the case of such as are genera, no one is more truly substance than another. We should not give a more appropriate account of the individual man by stating the species to which he belonged, than we should of an individual horse by adopting the same method of definition. In the same way, of primary substances, no one is more truly substance than another; an individual man is not more truly substance than an individual ox.

It is, then, with good reason that of all that remains, when we exclude primary substances, we concede to species and genera alone the name "secondary substance," for these alone of all the predicates convey a knowledge of primary substance. For it is by stating the species or the genus that we appropriately define any individual man; and we shall make our definition more exact by stating the former than by stating the latter. All other things that we state, such as that he is white, that he runs, and so on, are irrelevant to the definition. Thus it is just that these alone, apart from primary substances, should be called substances.

Further, primary substances are most properly so called, because they underlie and are the subjects of everything else. Now the same relation that subsists between primary substance and everything else subsists also between the species and the genus to which the primary substance belongs, on the one hand, and every attribute which is not included within these, on the other. For these are the subjects of all such. If we call an individual man "skilled in grammar," the predicate is applicable also to the species and to the genus to which he belongs. This law holds good in all cases.

It is a common characteristic of all substance that it is never present in a subject. For primary substance is neither present in a subject nor predicated of a subject; while, with regard to secondary substances, it is clear from the following arguments (apart from others) that they are not present in a subject. For "man" is predicated of the individual man, but is not present in any subject: for manhood is not present in the individual man. In the same way, "animal" is also predicated of the individual man, but is not present in him. Again when a thing is present in a subject, though the name may quite well be applied to that in which it is present, the definition cannot be applied. Yet of secondary substances, not only the name, but also the definition, applies to the subject: we should use both the definition of the species and that of the genus with reference to the individual man. Thus substance cannot be present in a subject.

Yet this is not peculiar to substance, for it is also the case that differentiae cannot be present in subjects. The characteristics "terrestrial" and "two-footed" are predicated of the species "man," but not present in it. For they are not *in* man. Moreover, the definition of the differentia may be predicated of that of which the differentia itself is predicated. For instance, if the characteristic "terrestrial" is predicated of the species "man," the definition also of that characteristic may be used to form the predicate of the species "man": for "man" is terrestrial.

The fact that the parts of substances appear to be present in the whole, as in a subject, should not make us apprehensive lest we should have to admit that such parts are not substances: for in explaining the phrase "being present in a subject," we stated that we meant "otherwise than as parts in a whole."

It is the mark of substances and of differentiae that, in all propositions of which they form the predicate, they are predicated univocally. For all such propositions have for their subject either the individual or the species. It is true that, inasmuch as primary substance is not predicable of anything, it can never form the predicate of any proposition. But of secondary substances, the species is predicated of the individual, the genus both of the species and of the individual. Similarly the differentiae are predicated of the species and of the individuals. Moreover, the definition of the species and that of the genus are applicable to the primary substance, and that of the genus to the species. For all that is predicated of the predicate will be predicated also of the subject. Similarly, the definition of the differentiae will be applicable to the species and to the individuals. But it was stated above that the word "univocal" was applied to those things which had both name and definition in common. It is, therefore, established that in every proposition, of which either substance or a differentia forms the predicate, these are predicated univocally.

All substance appears to signify that which is individual. In the case of primary substance this is indisputably true, for the thing is a unit. In the case of secondary substances, when we speak, for instance, of "man" or "animal," our form of speech gives the impression that we are here also indicating that which is individual, but the impression is not strictly true; for a secondary substance is not an individual, but a class with a certain qualification; for it is not one and single as a primary substance is; the words "man," "animal," are predicable of more than one subject.

Yet species and genus do not merely indicates quality, like the term "white"; "white" indicates quality and nothing further, but species and genus determine the quality with reference to a substance: they signify substance qualitatively differentiated. The determinate qualification covers a larger field in the case of the genus than in that of the species: he who uses the word "animal" is herein using a word of wider extension than he who uses the word "man."

Another mark of substance is that it has no contrary. What could be the contrary of any primary substance, such as the individual man or animal? It has none. Nor can the species or the genus have a contrary. Yet this characteristic is not peculiar to substance, but is true of many other things, such as quantity. There is nothing that forms the contrary of "two cubits long" or of "three cubits long," or of "ten," or of any such term. A man may contend that "much" is the contrary of "little," or "great" of "small," but of definite quantitative terms no contrary exists.

Substance, again, does not appear to admit of variation of degree. I do not mean by this that one substance cannot be more or less truly substance than another, for it has already been stated that this is the case; but that no single substance admits of varying degrees within itself. For instance, one particular substance, "man," cannot be more or less man either than himself at some other time or than some other man. One man cannot be more man than another, as that which is white may be more or less white than some other white object, or as that which is beautiful may be more or less beautiful than some other beautiful object. The same quality, moreover, is said to subsist in a thing in varying degrees at different times. A body, being white, is said to be whiter at one time than it was before, or, being warm, is said to be warmer or less warm than at some other time. But substance is not said to be more or less that which it is: a man is not more truly a man at one time than he was before, nor is anything, if it is substance, more or less what it is. Substance, then, does not admit of variation of degree.

The most distinctive mark of substance appears to be that, while remaining numerically one and the same, it is capable of admitting contrary qualities. From among things other than substance, we should find ourselves unable to bring forward any which possessed this mark. Thus, one and the same color cannot be white and black. Nor can the same one action be good and bad: this law holds good with everything that is not substance. But one and the self-same substance, while retaining its identity, is yet capable of admitting contrary qualities. The same individual person is at one time white, at another black, at one time warm, at another cold, at one time good, at another bad. This capacity is found nowhere else, though it might be maintained that a statement or opinion was an exception to the rule. The same statement, it is agreed, can be both true and false. For if the statement "he is sitting" is true, yet, when the person in question has risen, the same statement will be false. The same applies to opinions. For if any one thinks truly that a person is sitting, yet, when the person has risen, this same opinion, if still held, will be false. Yet although this exception may be allowed, there is, nevertheless, a difference in the manner in which the thing takes place. It is by themselves changing that substances admit contrary qualities. It is thus that that which was hot becomes cold, for it has entered into a different state. Similarly that which was white becomes black, and that which was bad good, by a process of change; and in the same way in all other cases it is by changing that substances are capable of admitting contrary qualities. But statements and opinions themselves remain unaltered in all respects: it is by the alteration in the facts of the case that the contrary quality comes to be theirs. The statement "he is sitting" remains unaltered, but it is at one time true, at another false, according to circumstances. What has been said of statements applies also to opinions. Thus, in respect of the manner in which the thing takes place, it is the peculiar mark of substance that it should be capable of admitting contrary qualities; for it is by itself changing that it does so.

If, then, a man should make this exception and contend that statements and opinions are capable of admitting contrary qualities, his contention is unsound. For statements and opinions are said to have this capacity, not because they themselves undergo modification, but because this modification occurs in the case of something else. The truth or falsity of a statement depends on facts, and not on any power on the part of the statement itself of admitting contrary qualities. In short, there is nothing which can alter the nature of statements and opinions. As, then, no change takes place in themselves, these cannot be said to be capable of admitting contrary qualities.

But it is by reason of the modification which takes place within the substance itself that a substance is said to be capable of admitting contrary qualities; for a substance admits within itself either disease or health, whiteness or blackness. It is in this sense that it is said to be capable of admitting contrary qualities.

To sum up, it is a distinctive mark of substance, that, while remaining numerically one and the same, it is capable of admitting contrary qualities, the modification taking place through a change in the substance itself.

Let these remarks suffice on the subject of substance.

2

On Universals

Peter Abelard

*   *   *

Aristotle,[1] defines the universal as "that which is of such a nature as to be predicated of many." Porphyry, on the other hand, goes on to define the singular or individual as "that which is predicated of a single individual."[2]

Authorities then seem to apply "universal" to things as much as they do to words. Aristotle himself does this, declaring by way of preface to his definition of the universal, that "some things are universal, others individual. Now by 'universal' I mean that which is of such a nature as to be predicated of many, whereas 'individual' is not something of this kind."[3] Porphyry, too, having stated that the species is composed of a genus and difference, proceeds to locate it in the nature of things. From this it is clear that things themselves fall under a universal noun.

Nouns, too, are called universals. That is why Aristotle says: "The genus specifies the quality with reference to substance, for it signifies what sort of thing it is."[4]

"It seems then that things as well as words are called universals. . . ."[5]

However, things taken either singly or collectively cannot be called universals, because they are not predicable of many. Consequently it remains

---

to ascribe this form of universality to words alone. Just as grammarians call certain nouns proper and other appellative, so dialecticians call certain simple words particulars, that is, individuals, and others universals. A universal word is one which is able to be predicated of many by reason of its intention, such as the noun "man," which can b e joined with the names of particular men by reason of the nature of the subject on which they are imposed. A particular word, however, is one which is predicable only of a single subject, as *Socrates* when it is taken as the name of but one individual. For if you take it equivocally, you give it the signification not of one word but of many. For according to Priscian, many nouns can obviously be brought together in a single word.[6] When a universal then is described as "that which is predicable of many," *that which* indicates not only the simplicity of the word as a discrete expression, but also the unity of signification lacking in an equivocal term. . . .[7]

Now that we have defined "universal" and "particular" in regard to words, let us investigate in particular the properties of those which are universal. For questions have been raised about universals, since serious doubts existed as to their meaning because there seemed to be no subject to which they referred. Neither did they express the sense of any one thing. This universal terms then appeared to be imposed on nothing, since it is clear that all things subsisting in themselves are individuals and, as has been shown, they do not share in some one thing by virtue of which a universal name could be given to them. Since it is certain then that (a) universals are not imposed on things by reason of their individual differences, for then they would not be common but singular, (b) nor can they designate things which share in some identical entity, for it is not a thing in which they agree, there seems to be nothing from which universals might derive their meaning, particularly since their sense is not restricted to any one thing. . . . Since "man" is imposed on individuals for an identical reason, viz., because each is a rational, mortal animal, the very generality of the designation prevents one from understanding the term of just one man in the way, for example, that one understands by Socrates just one unique person, which is why, for example, that one understands by Socrates just one unique person, which is why it is called a particular. But the common term "man" does not mean just Socrates, or any other man. Neither does it designate a collection, nor does it, as some think, mean just Socrates insofar as he is man. For even if Socrates alone were sitting in this house and because of that the proposition "A man sits in this house" is true, still by the name "man," there is no way of getting to Socrates except insofar as he too is a man. Otherwise, from the proposition itself, "sitting" would be understood to inhere in Socrates, so that from "A man sits in this house," one could infer "Socrates sits in this house." And the same applies to any other individual man. Neither can "A man sits in this house" be understood of a collection, since the proposition can be true if only one man is there. Consequently, there is not a single thing that "man" or any other universal term seems to signify, since there is not a single thing whose sense the term seems to express. Neither does it seem there could be any sense if no subject is thought of. Universals then appear to be totally devoid of meaning.

And yet this is not the case. For universals do signify distinct individuals to the extent of giving names to them, but this significative function does not require that one grasps a sense which arises out of them and which belongs to each of them. "Man," for example, does name individual things, but for the common reason that they are all men. That is why it is called a universal. Also there is a certain sense—common, not proper—that is applicable to those individuals which one conceives to be alike.

But let us look carefully now into some matters we have touched on only briefly, viz., (a) what is the common reason for imposing a universal name on things, (b) what is this intellectual conception of a common likeness, and (c) is a word said to be common because of some common cause by virtue of which all the things it designates are alike, or is it merely because we have a common concept for all of them, or is it for both of these reasons?

Let us consider first the question of the common cause. As we noted earlier, each individual man is a discrete subject since he has as proper to himself not only an essence but also whatever forms [or qualifications] that essence may have. Nevertheless, they agree in this that they are all men. Since there is no man who is not a discrete or distinct individual thing, I do not say they agree "in man," but "in being a man." Now if you consider the matter carefully, man or any other thing is not the same as "to be a man," even as "not to be in a subject" is not a thing, nor is there anything which is "not to undergo contrariety" or "not to be subject to greater or lesser degrees," and still Aristotle says these are points in which all substances agree. Since there is no *thing* in which things could possibly agree, if there is any agreement among certain things, this must not be taken to be some *thing*. Just as Socrates and Plato are alike in being men, so a horse and donkey are alike in not being men. It is for this reason that they are called "nonmen." Different individuals then agree either in being the same or in not being the same, e.g., in being men or white, or in not being men or being white.

Still this agreement among things (which itself is not a thing) must not be regarded as a case of bringing together things which are real on the basis of nothing. In point of fact we do speak of this agreeing with that to the extent of their having the same status, that of man, i.e., the two agree in that they are men. But what we perceive is merely that they are men, and there is not the slightest difference between them, I say, in their being men, even though we may not call this an essence. But "being a man" (which is not a thing) we do call "the status man" and we have also called it "the common cause for imposing on individuals a universal name." For we frequently give the name "cause" to some characteristic that is not itself a thing as when one says "He was beaten because he did not wish to appear in court." His not wishing to appear in court, cited here as a cause is not a [constitutive] essence [of his being beaten].

We can also designate as "the status of man" those things themselves in a man's nature which the one who imposed the word conceives according to a common likeness.

Having shown how universals signify, namely by functioning as names of things, and having presented what the reason for imposing such general names is, let us indicate just what these universal meanings consist of.

To begin with, let us point out the distinguishing features of all intellectual conception or understanding. Though sense perception as well as intellectual conception are both functions of the soul, there is a difference between the two. Bodies and what inhere in them are objects of sensory knowledge, e.g., a tower or its sensory qualities. In the exercise of this function, however, the soul makes use of corporeal instruments. In understanding or conceiving something intellectually, the soul needs no corporeal organ and consequently no bodily subject in which the thought object inheres is required. It is enough that the mind constructs for itself a likeness of these things and the action called intellection is concerned with this [cognitive content]. Hence, if the tower is removed or destroyed, the sense perception that dealt with it perishes, but the intellectual conception of the tower remains in the likeness preserved in the mind. As the act of sense perception is not the sensed thing itself, so the act of the intellect is not itself the form understood or conceived intellectually. Understanding is an activity of the soul by virtue of which it is said to understand, but the form toward which understanding is directed is a kind of image or construct (*res ficta*) which the mind fashions for itself at will, like those imaginary cities seen in dreams or the form of a projected building which the architect conceives after the manner of a blueprint. This construct is not something one can call either substance or accident.

Nevertheless, there are those who simply identify it with the act itself through which it is understood or conceived. Thus they speak of the tower building itself, which I think of when the tower is not there and which I conceive to be lofty, square, and situated in a spacious plain, as being the same as thinking of a tower. But we prefer to call the [conceptual] image as such the likeness of the thing.

There is of course nothing to prevent the act of understanding itself from being called in some sense a "likeness" because it obviously conceives what is, properly speaking, a likeness of the thing. Still, as we have said—and rightly so—the two are not the same. For, I ask: "Does the squareness or loftiness represent the actual form or quality possessed by the act of understanding itself when one thinks of the height and the way the tower is put together?" Surely the actual squareness and height are present only in bodies and from an imagined quality no act of understanding or any other real essence can be constructed. What remains then but that the substance, like the quality of which it is the subject, is also fictive? Perhaps one could also say that a mirror or reflected image is not itself a true "thing," since there often appears on the whitish surface of the mirror a color of contrary quality. . . .[8]

Having treated in general the nature of understanding, let us consider how a universal and a particular conception differ. The conception associated with a universal name is an image that is general and indiscriminate [imago communis et confusa], whereas the image associated with a singular word represents the proper and characteristic form, as it were, of a single thing, i.e., it applies to one and only one person. When I near the word "man," for instance, a certain likeness arises in my mind which is so related to individual men that it is proper to none but common to all. But when I hear "Socrates," a certain form arises in my mind which is the likeness of a particular person. . . . Hence it is correct to say "man" does not rightly signify Socrates or any other man, since by virtue of this name no one in particular is identified; yet it is a name of particular things. "Socrates," on the other hand, must not only name a particular thing, but it must also determine just what thing is its subject. . . . To show what pertains to the nature of all lions, a picture can be constructed which represents nothing that is the peculiar property of only one of them. On the other hand, a picture suited to distinguish any one of them can be drawn by depicting something proper to the one in question for example, by painting it as limping, maimed, or wounded by the spear of Hercules. Just as one can paint one figure that is general and another that is particular, so too can one form one conception of things that is common and another conception that is proper.

There is some question, however, and not without reason, whether or not this [universal] name also signifies this conceptual form to which the understanding is directed. Both authority and reason, however, seem to be unanimous in affirming that it does.

For Priscian, after first showing how universals were applied commonly to individuals, seemed to introduce another meaning they had, namely the common form. He states that "the general and special forms of things which were given intelligibility in the divine mind before being produced in bodies could be used to reveal what the natural genera and species of things are."[9] In this passage he views God after the fashion of an artist who first conceives in his mind a [model or] exemplar form of what he is to fashion and who works according to the likeness of this form, which form is said to be embodied when a real thing is constructed in its likeness.

It may be all right to ascribe such a common conception to God, but not to man. For those works of God like a man, a soul, or a stone represent general or special states of nature, whereas those of a human artisan like a house or a sword do not. For "house" and "sword" do not pertain to nature as the other terms do. They are the names not of a substance but of something accidental and therefore they are neither genera nor ultimate species. Conceptions by abstraction [of the true nature of things] may well be ascribed to the divine mind but may not be ascribed to that of man, because men, who know things only through the medium of their senses, scarcely ever arrive at such an ideal understanding and never conceive the [underlying] natures of things in their purity. But God knew all things he created for what they were and this even before they actually existed. He can discriminate between these individual states as they are in themselves; senses are no hindrance to him who alone has true understanding of things. Of those things which men have not experienced through the senses, they happen to have opinions rather than understanding, as we learn from experience. For having thought of some city before seeing it, we find on arriving there that it is quite different than we had thought.

And so I believe we have only an opinion about those forms like rationality, mortality, paternity, or what is within. Names for what we experience, however, produce understanding to the extent they can do so, for the one who coined the terms intended that they be imposed in accord with the [true] nature or properties of things, even though he himself was unable to do justice in thought to the nature or property of the thing. It is these common concepts, however, which Priscian calls general and special [i.e., generic and specific], that these general names or the names of species bring to the mind. He says that the universals function as proper names with regard to such conceptions, and although these names refer to the essences named only in an indiscriminate fashion, they direct the mind of the hearer immediately to that common conception in the same way that proper names direct attention to the one thing that they signify.

*   *   *

At this point, let us give an answer to the question we promised earlier to settle, namely whether the ability of universal words to refer to things in general is due to the fact that there is in them a common cause for imposing the words on them, or whether it is due to the fact that a common concept of them exists, or whether it is for both of these reasons. Now there seems to be no ground why it should not be for both of these reasons, but if we understand "common cause" as involving something of the nature of the things, then this seems to be the stronger of the two reasons.

Another point we must clarify is the one noted earlier, namely that these universal conceptions are formed by abstraction, and we must show how one can speak of them as isolated, naked, and pure without their being empty. But first about abstraction. Here we must remember that while matter and form are always fused together, the rational power of the mind is such that it can consider matter alone or form alone or both together. The first two are considerations by way of abstraction, since in order to study its precise nature, they abstract one thing from what does not exist alone. The third type of consideration is by way of synthesis. The substance of man, for instance, is a body, an animal, a man; it is invested with no end of forms. But when I turn my attention exclusively to the material essence of a substance, disregarding all its additional forms or qualifications, my understanding takes the form of a concept by abstraction. If I direct my attention, however, to nothing more than the corporeity of this substance, the resulting concept, though it represents a synthesis when compared with the previous concept (that of substance alone), is still formed by abstraction from the forms other than corporeity, such as animation, sensitivity, rationality, or whiteness, none of which I consider.

Such conceptions by abstraction might appear to be false or empty, perhaps, since they look to the thing in a way other than that in which it exists. For since they consider matter or form exclusively, and neither of these subsists separately, they clearly represent a conception of the thing otherwise than the way it is. Consequently, they seem to be vacuous, yet this is not really the case. For it is only when a thing is considered to have some property or nature which it does not actually possess that the conception which represents the thing otherwise than it is, is indeed empty. But this is not what happens in abstraction. For when I consider this man only in his nature as a substance or a body, but not as an animal, a man, or a grammarian, certainly I do not think of anything that is not in that nature, and still I do not attend to all that it has. And when I say that I attend only to what is in it, "only" refers to my attention and not to the way this characteristic exists, for otherwise my conception would be empty. For the thing does not only have this, but I only consider it as having this. And while I do consider it in some sense to be otherwise than it actually is, I do not consider it to be in a state or condition other than that in which it is, as was pointed out earlier. "Otherwise" means merely that the mode of thought is other than the mode of existing. For the thing in question is thought of not as separated, but separately from the other, even though it does not exist separately. Matter is perceived purely, form simply, even though the former does not exist purely nor the latter simply. Purity and simplicity, in a word, are features of our understanding, not of existence; they are characteristic of the way we think, not of the way things exist. Even the senses often function discriminatively where composite objects are concerned. If a statue is half gold, half silver, I can look separately at the gold and silver combined there, studying first the gold, then the silver exclusively, thus viewing piecemeal what is actually joined together, and yet I do not perceive to be divided what is not divided. In much the same way "understanding by way of abstraction" means "considering separately" but not "considering [it] as separated." Otherwise such understanding would be vacuous. . . .[10]

But let us return to our *universal* conceptions, which must always be produced by way of abstraction. For when I hear "man" or "whiteness" or "white," I do not recall in virtue of the name all the natures or properties in those subjects to which the name refers. "Man" gives rise to the conception, indiscriminate, not discrete, of animal, rational and mortal only, but not of the additional accidents as well. Conceptions of individuals also can be formed by abstraction, as happens for example when one speaks of "this substance," "this body," "this animal," "this white," or "this whiteness." For by "this man," though I consider just man's nature, I do so as related to a certain subject, whereas by "man" I regard this nature simply in itself and not in relation to some one man. That is why a universal concept is correctly described as being *isolated, bare,* and *pure*: i.e., "isolated from sense," because it is not a perception of the thing as sensory; "bare," because it is abstracted from some or from all forms; "pure," because it is unadulterated by any reference to any single individual, since there is not just one thing, be it the matter or the form, to which it points, as we explained earlier when we described such a conception as indiscriminate.

Now that we have considered these matters, let us proceed to answer the questions posed by Porphyry about genera and species. This we can easily do now that we have clarified the nature of universals in general. The point of the first question was whether genera and species exist. More precisely, are they signs of something which really exists or of something that merely exists in thought, i.e., are they simply vacuous, devoid of any real reference, as is the case with words like "chimera" or "goat-stag," which fail to produce any coherent meaning? To this one has to reply that as a matter of fact they do serve to name things that actually exist and therefore are not the subjects of purely empty thoughts. But what they name are the selfsame things named by singular names. And still, there is a sense in which they exist as isolated, bare, and pure only in the mind, as we have just explained. . . .

The second question, viz. "Are they corporeal or incorporeal?" can be taken in the same way, that is, "Granting that they are signs of existing things, are these things corporeal or incorporeal?" For surely everything that exists, as Boethius puts it, is either corporeal or incorporeal, regardless of whether these words mean respectively: (1) a bodily or a bodiless substance, (2) something perceptible to the senses like man, wood, and whiteness, or something imperceptible in this way like justice or the soul. (3) "Corporeal" can also have the meaning of something discrete or individual, so that the question boils down to asking whether genera and species signify discrete individuals or not. A thoroughgoing investigator of truth considers not only what can be factually stated but also such possible opinions as might be proposed. Consequently, even though one is quite certain that only individuals are real, in view of the fact that someone might be of the opinion that there are other things that exist, it is justifiable to inquire about them. Now this third meaning of "corporeal" makes better sense of our question, reducing it to an inquiry as to whether it is discrete individuals or not that are signified. On the other hand, since nothing existing is incorporeal, i.e. nonindividual, "incorporeal" would seem to be superfluous in Boethius' statement that everything existing is either corporeal or incorporeal. Here the order of the questions, it seems, suggests nothing that would be of help except perhaps that corporeal and incorporeal, taken in another sense, do represent divisions of whatever exists and that this might also be the case here. The inquirer in this case would seem to be asking, in effect: "Since I see that some existing things are called corporeal and others incorporeal, I would like to know which of these names we should use for what universals signify?" The answer to this would be: "To some extent, 'corporeal' would be appropriate, since the *significata* are in essence discrete individuals. 'Incorporeal' would be a better description, however, of the way a universal term names things, for it does not point to them in an individual and specific fashion but points only in an indiscriminate way, as we have adequately explained above." Hence universal names are described both as corporeal (because of the nature of the things they point to) and as incorporeal (because of the way these things are signified, for although they name discrete individuals, universals do not name them individually or properly).

The third question ("Do they exist apart from or only in sensible things?") arises from the admission that they are incorporeal, since . . . there is a certain sense in which "existing in the sensible" and "not existing in the sensible" represent a division of the incorporeal. Now universals are said to exist in sensible things to the extent that they signify the inner substance of something which is sensible by reason of its external forms. While they signify this same substance actually existing in sensible garb, they point to what is by its nature something distinct from the sensible thing [i.e., as substance it is other than its accidental garb], as we said above in our reinterpretation of Plato. That is why Boethius does not claim that genera and species exist apart from sensible things, but only that they are understood apart from them, to the extent namely that the things conceived generically or specifically are viewed with reference to their nature in a rational fashion rather than in a sensory way, and they could indeed subsist in themselves [i.e., as individual substances] even if stripped of the exterior or [accidental] forms by which they come to the attention of the senses. For we admit that all genera and species exist in things perceptible to the senses. Since our understanding of them has always been described as something apart from the senses, however, they appeared not to be in sensible things in any way. There was every reason, then, to ask whether they could be in sensibles. And to this question, the answer is that some of them are, but only to the extent, as was explained, that they represent the enduring substrate that lies beneath the sensible.

We can take corporeal and incorporeal in this second question as equivalent to sensible and insensible, so that the sequence of questions becomes more orderly. And since our understanding of universals is derived solely from sense perceptions, as has been said, one could appropriately ask whether universals were sensible or insensible. Now the answer is that some of them are sensible (we refer here to the nature of those things classed as sensible) and the same time not sensible (we refer here to the way they are signified). For while it is sensible things that these universals name, they do not designate these things in the way they are perceived by the senses, i.e., as distinct individuals, and when things are designated only in universal terms the senses cannot pick them out. Hence the question arose: "Do universals designate only sensible things, or is there something else they signify?" And the answer to this is that they signify both the sensible things themselves and also that common concept which Priscian ascribes above all to the divine mind.

As for the fourth question we added to the others, our solution is this. We do not want to speak of there being universal *names*[11] when the things they name have perished and they can no longer be predicated of many and are not common names of anything, as would be the case when all the roses were gone. Nevertheless, "rose" would still have meaning for the mind even though it names nothing. Otherwise, "There is no rose" would not be a proposition.[12]

NOTES

1. Aristotle. *De interpretatione*, chap. 7 (17a 38).
2. Cf. Boethius, *In Isagogen Porphyrii commenta*, ed. G. Schepss and S. Brandt, *Corpus Scriptorum Ecclesiasticorum Latinorum*, Vol. 48 (Vienna: Tempsky, 1906), 148.
3. Aristotle, *De interpretatione*, chap. 76 (17a 38)
4. Aristotle, *Categoriae*, chap. 5 (3b 20).
5. *Peter Abaelards philosophische Schriften*, ed. B. Geyer in *Beiträge zur Geschichte der Philosophie des Mittelalters* XXI (Münster: Aschendorff, 1933), pp. 9-10.

6. Priscian, *Institutiones grammaticae*, XVII, in H. Keil, *Grammatici latini*. Vol. 3 (Lipsiae: in aedibus B. G. Teubneri, 1858), 145[22].

7. *Peter Abaelards philosophische Schriften*, p. 16.

8. Ibid., 18-21.

9. Priscian, *Institutiones grammaticae*, p. 135.

10. *Peter Abaelards philosophische Schriften*, pp. 21-26.

11. When Abelard speaks of "there being universal names," he has in mind terms that have actual reference; he distinguishes in a word between signification in the sense of having meaning or sense and denominating, i.e., actually naming or referring to existing things.

12. *Peter Abaelards philosophische Schriften*, pp. 27-30.

3

Of the Signification of Words, and General Terms

John Locke

CHAPTER 2

1. *Words are sensible signs necessary for communication.* Man, though he have great variety of thoughts, and such from which others as well as himself might receive profit and delight; yet they are all within his own breast, invisible and hidden from others, nor can of themselves be made to appear. The comfort and advantage of society not being to be had without communication of thoughts, it was necessary that man should find out some external sensible signs, whereof those invisible ideas, which his thoughts are made up of, might be made known to others. For this purpose nothing was so fit, either for plenty or quickness, as those articulate sounds, which with so much ease and variety he found himself able to make . . . . The use, then, of words, is to be sensible marks of ideas; and the ideas they stand for are their proper and immediate signification.

2. *Words are the sensible signs of his ideas who uses them.* The use men have of these marks being either to record their own thoughts, for the assistance of their own memory; or, as it were, to bring out their ideas, and lay them before the view of others: words, in their primary or immediate signification, stand for nothing but *the ideas in the mind of him that uses*

From *An Essay Concerning Human Understanding,* Book III, Chapters 2 and 3.

them, how imperfectly soever or carelessly those ideas are collected from the things which they are supposed to represent. . . . Words being voluntary signs, they cannot be voluntary signs imposed by him on things he knows not. That would be to make them signs of nothing, sounds without signification. A man cannot make his words the signs either of qualities in things, or of conceptions in the mind of another, whereof he has none in his own . . . .

3. This is so necessary in the use of language, that in this respect the knowing and the ignorant, the learned and the unlearned, use the words they speak (with any meaning) all alike. They, in every man's mouth, stand for the ideas he has, and which he would express by them. A child having taken notice of nothing in the metal he hears called "gold," but the bright shining yellow color, he applies the word "gold" only to his own idea of that color, and nothing else; and therefore calls the same color in a peacock's tail "gold." Another that hath better observed, adds to shining yellow great weight: and then the sound gold, when he uses it, stands for a complex idea of a shining yellow and very weighty substance. Another adds to those qualities fusibility: and then the word gold signifies to him a body, bright, yellow, fusible, and very heavy. Another adds malleability. Each of these uses equally the word gold, when they have occasion to express the idea which they have applied it to: but it is evident that each can apply it only to his own idea; nor can he make it stand as sign of such a complex idea as he has not.

4. *Words often secretly referred.* But though words, as they are used by men, can properly and immediately signify nothing but the ideas that are in the mind of the speaker; yet they in their thoughts give them a secret reference to two other things.

First, to the ideas in other men's minds. First, They suppose their words to be marks of the ideas in the minds also of other men, with whom they communicate: for else they should talk in vain, and could not be understood, if the sounds they applied to one idea were such as by the hearer were applied to another, which is to speak two languages . . . .

5. *Secondly, to the reality of things.* Secondly, Because men would not be thought to talk barely of their own imagination, but of things as really they are; therefore they often suppose the *words to stand also for the reality of things* . . . .

6. *Words by use readily excite ideas.* Concerning words, also, it is further to be considered: First, that they being immediately the signs of men's ideas, and by that means the instruments whereby men communicate their conceptions, and express to one another those thoughts and imaginations they have within their own breasts; there comes, by constant use, to be such a connection between certain sounds and the ideas they stand for, that the names

heard, almost as readily excite certain ideas as if the objects themselves, which are apt to produce them, did actually affect the senses. Which is manifestly so in all obvious sensible qualities, and in all substances that frequently and familiarly occur to us.

7. *Words often used without signification.* Secondly, That though the proper and immediate signification of words are ideas in the mind of the speaker, yet, because by familiar use from our cradles, we come to learn certain articulate sounds very perfectly, and have them readily on our tongues, and always at hand in our memories, but yet are not always careful to examine or settle their significations perfectly; it often happens that men, even when they would apply themselves to an attentive consideration, do set their thoughts more on words than things. . . .

8. *Their signification perfectly arbitrary.* Words, by long and familiar use, as has been said, come to excite in men certain ideas so constantly and readily, that they are apt to suppose a natural connection between them. But that they signify only men's peculiar ideas, and that by a perfect arbitrary imposition, is evident, in that they often fail to excite in others (even that use the same language) the same ideas we take them to be signs of: and every man has so inviolable a liberty to make words stand for what ideas he pleases, that no one hath the power to make others have the same ideas in their minds that he has, when they use the same words that he does . . . . But whatever be the consequence of any man's using of words differently, either from their general meaning, or the particular sense of the person to whom he addresses them; this is certain, their signification, in his use of them, is limited to his ideas, and they can be signs of nothing else.

CHAPTER 3

1. *The greatest part of words general.* All things that exist being particulars, it may perhaps be thought reasonable that words, which ought to be conformed to things, should be so too,—I mean in their signification: but yet we find quite the contrary. The far greatest part of words that make all languages are general terms: which has not been the effect of neglect or change, but of reason and necessity.

2. *For every particular thing to have a name is impossible.* First, It is impossible that every particular thing should hve a distinct peculiar name. For, the signification and use of words depending on that connection which the mind makes between its ideas and the sounds it uses as signs of them, it is necessary, in the application of names to things, that the mind should

have distinct ideas of the things, and retain also the particular name that belongs to every one, with its peculiar appropriation to that idea. But it is beyond the power of human capacity to frame and retain distinct ideas of all the particular things we meet with: every bird and beast men saw; every tree and plant that affected the senses, could not find a place in the most capacious understanding . . . .

3. *And useless.* Secondly, If it were possible, it would yet be useless; because it would not serve to the chief end of language. Men could in vain heap up names of particular things that would not serve them to communicate their thoughts. Men learn names, and use them in talk with others, only that they may be understood: which is then only done when, by use or consent the sound I make by the organs of speech, excites in another man's mind who hears it, the idea I apply it to in mine, when I speak it. This cannot be done by names applied to particular things; whereof I alone having the ideas in my mind, the names of them could not be significant or intelligible to another, who was not acquainted with all those very particular things which had fallen under my notice.

4. Thirdly, But yet, granting this is also feasible, (which I think is not,) yet a distinct name for every particular thing would not be of any great use for the improvement of knowledge: which, though founded in particular things, enlarges itself by general views: to which things reduced into sorts, under general names, are properly subservient . . . .

6. *How general words are made.* The next thing to be considered is,— How general words come to be made. For, since all things that exist are only particulars, how come we by general terms; or where find we those general natures they are supposed to stand for? Words become general by being made the signs of general ideas: and ideas become general, by separating from them the circumstances of time and place, and any other ideas that may determine them to this or that particular existence. By this way of abstraction they are made capable of representing more individuals than one; each of which having in it a conformity to that abstract idea, is (as we call it) of that sort.

7. But, to deduce this a little more distinctly, it will not perhaps be amiss to trace our notions and names from their beginning, and observe by what degrees we proceed, and by what steps we enlarge our ideas from our first infancy. There is nothing more evident, than that the ideas of the persons children converse with (to instance in them alone) are, like the persons themselves, only particular. The ideas of the nurse and the mother are well framed in their minds; and, like pictures of them there, represent only those individuals. The names they first gave to them are confined to those individuals; and the names of "nurse" and "mamma," the child uses, determine

themselves to those persons. Afterwards, when time and a larger acquaintance
have made them observe that there are a great many other things in the
world, that in some common agreements of shape, and several other qualities,
resemble their father and mother, and those persons they have been used
to, they frame an idea, which they find those many particulars do partake
in; and to that they give, with others, the name "man," for example. And
thus they come to have a general name, and a general idea. Wherein they
make nothing new; but only leave out of the complex idea they had of Peter
and James, Mary and Jane, that which is peculiar to each, and retain only
what is common to them all . . . .

9. *General natures are nothing but abstract ideas* . . . . And he that thinks
general natures or notions are anything else but such abstract and partial
ideas of more complex ones, taken at first from particular existences, will,
I fear, be at a loss where to find them. For let any one reflect, and then
tell me, wherein does his idea of "man" differ from that of "Peter" and "Paul,"
or his idea of "horse" from that of "Bucephalus," but in the leaving out something that is peculiar to each individual, and retaining so much of those particular complex ideas in several particular existences as they are found to agree
in? Of the complex ideas signified by the names "man" and "horse," leaving
out but those particulars wherein they differ, and retaining only those wherein they agree, and of those making a new distinct complex idea, and giving
the name animal to it, one has a more general term, that comprehends with
man, several other creatures. Leave out of the idea of "animal" sense and
spontaneous motion, and the remaining complex idea, made up of the remaining simple ones of body, life, and nourishment, becomes a more general
one, under the more comprehensive term, *vivens* . . . .

11. *General and universal are creatures of the understanding.* To return
to general words: it is plain, by what has been said, that general and universal
belong not to the real existence of things; but are the inventions and creatures of the understanding, made by it for its own use, and concern only
signs, whether words or ideas. Words are general, as has been said, when
used for signs of general ideas, and so are applicable indifferently to many
particular things; and ideas are general when they are set up as the representatives of many particular things: but universality belongs not to things
themselves, which are all of them particular in their existence, even those
words and ideas which in their signification are general. When therefore we
quit particulars, the generals that rest are only creatures of our own making;
their general nature being nothing but the capacity they are put into, by the
understanding, of signifying or representing many particulars. For the signification they have is nothing but a relation that, by the mind of man, is added
to them.

12. *Abstract ideas are the essences of the Genera and Species.* The next thing therefore to be considered is, what kind of signification it is that general words have. For, as it is evident that they do not signify barely one particular thing; for then they would not be general terms, but proper names, so, on the other side, it is as evident they do not signify a plurality; for "man" and "men" would then signify the same; and the distinction of numbers (as the grammarians call them) would be superfluous and useless. That then which general words signify is a sort of things; and each of them does that, by being a sign of an abstract idea in the mind; to which idea, as things existing are found to agree, so they come to be ranked under that name, or, which is all one, be of that sort. Whereby it is evident that the essences of the sorts, or, (if the Latin word pleases better) *species* of things, are nothing else but these abstract ideas. For the having the essence of any species, being that which makes anything to be of that species; and the conformity to the idea to which the name is annexed being that which gives a right to that name; the having the essence, and the having that conformity, must needs be the same thing: since to be of any species, and to have a right to the name of that species, is all one. As, for example, to be a man, or of the species man and to have right to the name "man," is the same thing. Again, to be a man, or of the species man, and have the essence of a man, is the same thing. Now, since nothing can be a man or have a right to the name "man," but what has a conformity to the abstract idea the name "man" stands for; nor anything be a man, or have a right to the species man, but what has the essence of that species; it follows, that the abstract idea for which the name stands, and the essence of the species, is one and the same. From whence it is easy to observe, that the essences of the sorts of things, and, consequently, the sorting of things, is the workmanship of the understanding that abstracts and makes those general ideas.

4

First Principles of Human Knowledge

George Berkeley

INTRODUCTION

1. Philosophy being nothing else but the study of wisdom and truth, it may with reason be expected that those who have spent most time and pains in it should enjoy a greater calm and serenity of mind, a greater clearness and evidence of knowledge, and be less disturbed with doubts and difficulties than other men. Yet so it is, we see the illiterate bulk of mankind that walk the high road of plain common sense, and are governed by the dictates of nature, for the most part easy and undisturbed. To them nothing that is familiar appears unaccountable or difficult to comprehend. They complain not of any want of evidence in their senses, and are out of all danger of becoming skeptics. But no sooner do we depart from sense and instinct to follow the light of a superior principle, to reason, meditate, and reflect on the nature of things, but a thousand scruples spring up in our minds concerning those things which before we seemed fully to comprehend. Prejudices and errors of sense do from all parts discover themselves to our view; and, endeavoring to correct these by reason, we are insensibly drawn into uncouth paradoxes, difficulties, and inconsistencies, which multiply and grow upon us as we advance in speculation, till at length, having wandered through many intricate mazes, we find ourselves just where we were, or, which is worse, sit down in a forlorn skepticism.

"Of Language" from *A Treatise Concerning the Principles of Human Knowledge,* Introduction, 1710, edited by Colin Murry Turbayne.

2. The cause of this is thought to be the obscurity of things, or the natural weakness and imperfection of our understandings. It is said the faculties we have are few and those designed by nature for the support and comfort of life, and not to penetrate into the inward essence and constitution of things. Besides, the mind of man being finite, when it treats of things which partake of infinity it is not to be wondered at if it run into absurdities and contradictions, out of which it is impossible it should ever extricate itself, it being of the nature of infinite not to be comprehended by that which is finite.

3. But, perhaps, we may be too partial to ourselves in placing the fault originally in our faculties and not rather in the wrong use we make of them. It is a hard thing to suppose that right deductions from true principles should ever end in consequences which cannot be maintained or made consistent. . . . Upon the whole, I am inclined to think that the far greater part, if not all, of those difficulties which have hitherto amused philosophers and blocked up the way to knowledge, are entirely owing to ourselves—that we have first raised a dust and then complain we cannot see.

4. My purpose therefore is to try if I can discover what those principles are which have introduced all that doubtfulness and uncertainty, those absurdities and contradictions, into the several sects of philosophy—insomuch that the wisest men have thought our ignorance incurable, conceiving it to arise from the natural dullness and limitation of our faculties. And surely it is a work well deserving our pains to make a strict inquiry concerning the first principles of human knowledge, to sift and examine them on all sides, especially since there may be some grounds to suspect that those lets and difficulties which stay and embarrass the mind in its search after truth do not spring from any darkness and intricacy in the objects or natural defect in the understanding so much as from false principles which have been insisted on, and might have been avoided . . . .

6. In order to prepare the mind of the reader for the easier conceiving of what follows, it is proper to premise somewhat, by way of introduction, concerning the nature and abuse of language. But the unraveling of this matter leads me in some measure to anticipate my design by taking notice of what seems to have had a chief part in rendering speculation intricate and perplexed and to have occasioned innumerable errors and difficulties in almost all parts of knowledge. And that is the opinion that the mind has a power of framing *abstract ideas* or notions of things. He who is not a perfect stranger to the writings and disputes of philosophers must needs acknowledge that no small part of them are spent about abstract ideas. These are in a more especial manner thought to be the object of those sciences which go by the name of logic and metaphysics, and of all that which passes under

the notion of the most abstracted and sublime learning, in all which one shall scarce find any question handled in such a manner as does not suppose their existence in the mind, and that it is well acquainted with them.

7. It is agreed on all hands that the qualities or modes of things do never really exist each of them apart by itself and separated from all others, but are mixed, as it were, and blended together, several in the same object. But we are told the mind, being able to consider each quality singly, or abstracted from those other qualities with which it is united, does by that means frame to itself abstract ideas. For example, there is perceived by sight an object extended, colored, and moved: this mixed or compound idea the mind, resolving into its simple, constituent parts and viewing each by itself, exclusive of the rest, does frame the abstract ideas of extension, color, and motion. Not that it is possible for color or motion to exist without extension, but only that the mind can frame to itself by *abstraction* the idea of color exclusive of extension, and of motion exclusive of both color and extension.

8. Again, the mind having observed that in the particular extensions perceived by sense there is something common and alike in all, and some other things peculiar, as this or that figure or magnitude, which distinguish them one from another, it considers apart or singles out by itself that which is common, making thereof a most abstract idea of extension, which is neither line, surface, nor solid, nor has any figure or magnitude, but is an idea entirely prescinded from all these. So likewise the mind, by leaving out of the particular colors perceived by sense that which distinguishes them one from another, and retaining that only which is common to all, makes an idea of color in abstract, which is neither red, nor blue, nor white, nor any other determinate color. And, in like manner, by considering motion abstractedly not only from the body moved, but likewise from the figure it describes, and all particular directions and velocities, the abstract idea of motion is framed, which equally corresponds to all particular motions whatsoever that may be perceived by sense.

9. And as the mind frames to itself abstract ideas of qualities or modes, so does it, by the same precision or mental separation, attain abstract ideas of the more compounded beings which include several coexistent qualities. For example, the mind, having observed that Peter, James, and John resemble each other in certain common agreements of shape and other qualities, leaves out of the complex or compounded idea it has of Peter, James, and any other particular man that which is peculiar to each, retaining only what is common to all, and so makes an abstract idea wherein all the particulars equally partake—abstracting entirely from and cutting off all those circumstances and differences which might determine it to any particular existence. And after this manner it is said we come by the abstract idea of *man* or,

if you please, humanity, or human nature; wherein it is true there is included color, because there is no man but has some color, but then it can be neither white, nor black, nor any particular color, because there is no one particular color wherein all men partake. So likewise there is included stature, but then it is neither tall stature, nor low stature, nor yet middle stature, but something abstracted from all these. And so of the rest. Moreover, there being a great variety of other creatures that partake in some parts, but not all, of the complex idea of man, the mind, leaving out those parts which are peculiar to men, and retaining those only which are common to all the living creatures, frames the idea of *animal,* which abstracts not only from all particular men, but also all birds, beasts, fishes, and insects. The constituent parts of the abstract idea of animal are body, life, sense, and spontaneous motion. By "body" is meant body without any particular shape or figure, there being no one shape or figure common to all animals, without covering, either of hair, or feathers, or scales, etc., nor yet naked: hair, feathers, scales, and nakedness being the distinguishing properties of particular animals, and for that reason left out of the *abstract idea.* Upon the same account the spontaneous motion must be neither walking, nor flying, nor creeping; it is nevertheless a motion, but what that motion is it is not easy to conceive.

10. Whether others have this wonderful faculty of abstracting their ideas, they best can tell; for myself I find indeed I have a faculty of imagining, or representing to myself, the ideas of those particular things I have perceived, and of variously compounding and dividing them. I can imagine a man with two heads, or the upper parts of a man joined to the body of a horse. I can consider the hand, the eye, the nose, each by itself abstracted or separated from the rest of the body. But then whatever hand or eye I imagine, it must have some particular shape and color. Likewise the idea of man that I frame to myself must be either of a white, or a black, or a tawny, a straight, or a crooked, a tall, or a low, or a middle-sized man. I cannot by any effort of thought conceive the abstract idea above described. And it is equally impossible for me to form the abstract idea of motion distinct from the body moving, and which is neither swift nor slow, curvilinear nor rectilinear; and the like may be said of all other abstract general ideas whatsoever. To be plain, I own myself able to abstract in one sense, as when I consider some particular parts or qualities separated from others, with which, though they are united in some object, yet it is possible they may really exist without them. But I deny that I can abstract one from another, or conceive separately, those qualities which it is impossible should exist so separated; or that I can frame a general notion by abstracting from particulars in the manner aforesaid—which two last are the two proper acceptations of "abstraction." And there are grounds to think most men will acknowledge themselves to

be in my case. The generality of men which are simple and illiterate never pretend to abstract notions. It is said they are difficult and not to be attained without pains and study; we may therefore reasonably conclude that, if such there be, they are confined only to the learned.

11. I proceed to examine what can be alleged in defense of the doctrine of abstraction, and try if I can discover what it is that inclines the men of speculation to embrace an opinion so remote from common sense as that seems to be. There has been a late, deservedly esteemed philosopher who, no doubt, has given it very much countenance by seeming to think the having abstract general ideas is what puts the widest difference in point of understanding betwixt man and beast.—

> The having of general ideas (he says) is that which puts a perfect distinction betwixt man and brutes, and is an excellency which the faculties of brutes do by no means attain unto. For, it is evident we observe no footsteps in them of making use of general signs for universal ideas; from which we have reason to imagine that they have not the faculty of abstracting, or making general ideas, since they have no use of words or any other general signs.

And a little after:

> Therefore, I think, we may suppose that it is in this that the species of brutes are discriminated from men, and it is that proper difference wherein they are wholly separated, and which at last widens to so wide a distance. For, if they have any ideas at all, and are not bare machines (as some would have them), we cannot deny them to have some reason. It seems as evident to me that they do, some of them, in certain instances reason as that they have sense; but it is only in particular ideas, just as they receive them from their senses. They are the best of them tied up within those narrow bounds, and have not (as I think) the faculty to enlarge them by any kind of abstraction.—*Essay on Human Understanding,* Bk. II, chap. 11, sec. 10f.

I readily agree with this learned author that the faculties of brutes can by no means attain to abstraction. But then if this be made the distinguishing property of that sort of animals, I fear a great many of those that pass for men must be reckoned into their number. The reason that is here assigned why we have no grounds to think brutes have abstract general ideas is that we observe in them no use of words or any other general signs; which is built on this supposition—that the making use of words implies the having general ideas. From which it follows that men who use language are able to abstract or generalize their ideas. That this is the sense and arguing of the author will further appear by his answering the question he in another place puts: "Since all things that exist are only particulars, how come we by general terms?" His answer is: "Words become general by being made the signs of general ideas."—(*Essay on Human Understanding,* Bk. III, chap. 3, sec. 6.) But it seems that a word becomes general by being made the sign, not of an abstract general idea, but of several particular ideas, any one of which it indifferently suggests to the mind. For example, when it is said, "the change of motion is proportional to the impressed force," or that, "whatever has extension is divisible," these propositions are to be understood of motion and extension in general; and nevertheless it will not follow that they suggest to my thoughts an idea of motion without a body moved, or any determinate direction and velocity, or that I must conceive an abstract general idea of extension which is neither line, surface, nor solid, neither great nor small, black, white, nor red, nor of any other determinate color. It is only implied that whatever motion I consider, whether it be swift or slow, perpendicular, horizontal, or oblique, or in whatever object, the axiom concerning it holds equally true. As does the other of every particular extension, it matters not whether line, surface, or solid, whether of this or that magnitude or figure.

12. By observing how ideas become general we may the better judge how words are made so. And here it is to be noted that I do not deny absolutely there are general ideas, but only that there are any *abstract* general ideas; for, in the passages above quoted, wherein there is mention of general ideas, it is always supposed that they are formed by abstraction, after the manner set forth in sections 8 and 9. Now, if we will annex a meaning to our words and speak only of what we can conceive, I believe we shall acknowledge that an idea which, considered in itself, is particular, becomes general by being made to represent or stand for all other particular ideas of the same sort. To make this plain by an example, suppose a geometrician is demonstrating the method of cutting a line in two equal parts. He draws, for instance, a black line of an inch in length: this, which in itself is a particular line, is nevertheless with regard to its signification general, since, as it is there used, it represents all particular lines whatsoever; for that which is demonstrated of it is demonstrated of all lines or, in other words, of a line in general. And, as that *particular* line becomes general by being made a sign, so the *name* "line," which taken absolutely is particular, by being a sign is made general. And as the former owes its generality not to its being the sign of an abstract or general line, but of all particular right lines that may possibly exist, so the latter must be thought to derive its generality from the same cause, namely, the various particular lines which it indifferently denotes.

13. To give the reader a yet clearer view of the nature of abstract ideas, and the uses they are thought necessary to, I shall add one more passage out of the *Essay on Human Understanding,* which is as follows:

Abstract ideas are not so obvious or easy to children or the yet unexercised mind as particular ones. If they seem so to grown men it is only because by constant and familiar use they are made so. For, when we nicely reflect upon them, we shall find that general ideas are fictions and contrivances of the mind, that carry difficulty with them, and do not so easily offer themselves as we are apt to imagine. For example, does it not require some pains and skill to form the general idea of a triangle (which is yet none of the most abstract, comprehensive, and difficult); for it must be neither oblique nor rectangle, neither equilateral, equicrural, nor scalenon, but *all and none* of these at once? In effect, it is something imperfect that cannot exist, an idea wherein some parts of several different and *inconsistent* ideas are put together. It is true the mind in this imperfect state has need of such ideas and makes all the haste to them it can, for the convenience of communication and enlargement of knowledge to both which it is naturally very much inclined. But yet one has reason to suspect such ideas are marks of our imperfection. At least this is enough to show that the most abstract and general ideas are not those that the mind is first and most easily acquainted with, nor such as its earliest knowledge is conservant about.— Bk. IV, chap. 7, sec. 9.

If any man has the faculty of framing in his mind such an idea of a triangle as is here described, it is in vain to pretend to dispute him out of it, nor would I go about it. All I desire is that the reader would fully and certainly inform himself whether he has such an idea or no. And this, methinks, can be no hard task for anyone to perform. What more easy than for anyone to look a little into his own thoughts, and there try whether he has, or can attain to have, an idea that shall correspond with the description that is here given of the general idea of a triangle, which is "neither oblique nor rectangle, equilateral, equicrural nor scalenon, but all and none of these at once"?

14. Much is here said of the difficulty that abstract ideas carry with them, and the pains and skill requisite to the forming them. And it is on all hands agreed that there is need of great toil and labor of the mind to emancipate our thoughts from particular objects and raise them to those sublime speculations that are conversant about abstract ideas. From all which the natural consequence should seem to be, that so difficult a thing as the forming abstract ideas was not necessary for *communication,* which is so easy and familiar to all sorts of men. But, we are told, if they seem obvious and easy to grown men, "it is only because by constant and familiar use they are made so." Now, I would fain know at what time it is men are employed in sur-

mounting that difficulty and furnishing themselves with those necessary helps for discourse. It cannot be when they are grown up, for then it seems they are not conscious of any such painstaking; it remains, therefore, to be the business of their childhood. And surely the great and multiplied labor of framing abstract notions will be found a hard task for that tender age. Is it not a hard thing to imagine that a couple of children cannot prate together of their sugar plums and rattles and the rest of their little trinkets till they have first tacked together numberless inconsistencies and so framed in their minds abstract general ideas and annexed them to every common name they make use of?

15. Nor do I think them a whit more needful for the *enlargement of knowledge* than for *communication*. It is, I know, a point much insisted on, that all knowledge and demonstration are about universal notions, to which I fully agree; but then it does not appear to me that those notions are formed by abstraction in the manner premised—*universality*, so far as I can comprehend, not consisting in the absolute, positive nature or conception of any thing, but in the relation it bears to the particulars signified or represented by it; by virtue whereof it is that things, names, or notions, being in their own nature *particular*, are rendered *universal*. Thus, when I demonstrate any proposition concerning triangles, it is to be supposed that I have in view the universal idea of a triangle, which ought not to be understood as if I could frame an idea of a triangle which was neither equilateral, nor scalenon, nor equicrural, but only that the particular triangle I consider, whether of this or that sort it matters not, does equally stand for and represent all rectilinear triangles whatsoever, and is in that sense *universal*. All which seems very plain and not to include any difficulty in it.

*   *   *

18. I come now to consider the *source* of this prevailing notion [the doctrine of abstract ideas], and that seems to me to be language. And surely nothing of less extent than reason itself could have been the source of an opinion so universally received. The truth of this appears, as from other reasons, so also from the plain confession of the ablest patrons of abstract ideas, who acknowledges that they are made in order to naming; from which it is a clear consequence that if there had been no such thing as speech or universal signs there never had been any thought of abstraction. See Bk. III, chap. 6, sec. 39, and elsewhere of the *Essay on Human Understanding*. Let us examine the manner wherein words have contributed to the origin of that mistake: First then, it is thought that every name has, or ought to have, one only precise and settled signification, which inclines men to think there

are certain abstract, determinate ideas which constitute the true and only immediate signification of each general name; and that it is by the mediation of these abstract ideas that a general name comes to signify any particular thing. Whereas, in truth, there is no such thing as one precise and definite signification annexed to any general name, they all signify indifferently a great number of particular ideas. All which does evidently follow from what has been already said, and will clearly appear to anyone by a little reflection. To this it will be objected that every name that has a definition is thereby restrained to one certain signification. For example, a "triangle" is defined to be "a plane surface comprehended by three right lines," by which that name is limited to denote one certain idea and no other. To which I answer that in the definition it is not said whether the surface be great or small, black or white, nor whether the sides are long or short, equal or unequal, nor with what angles they are inclined to each other; in all which there may be great variety, and consequently there is no one settled idea which limits the signification of the word "triangle." It is one thing for to keep a name constantly to the same definition, and another to make it stand everywhere for the same idea; the one is necessary, the other useless and impracticable.

19. But, to give a further account how words came to produce the doctrine of abstract ideas, it must be observed that it is a received opinion that language has no other end but the communicating ideas, and that every significant name stands for an idea. This being so, and it being withal certain that names which yet are not thought altogether insignificant do not always mark out particular conceivable ideas, it is straightway concluded that they stand for abstract notions. That there are many names in use amongst speculative men which do not always suggest to others determinate, particular ideas is what nobody will deny. And a little attention will discover that it is not necessary (even in the strictest reasonings) that significant names which stand for ideas should, every time they are used, excite in the understanding the ideas they are made to stand for—in reading and discoursing, names being for the most part used as letters are in algebra, in which, though a particular quantity be marked by each letter, yet to proceed right it is not requisite that in every step each letter suggest to your thoughts that particular quantity it was appointed to stand for.

20. Besides, the communicating of ideas marked by words is not the chief and only end of language, as is commonly supposed. There are other ends, as the raising of some passion, the exciting to or deterring from an action, the putting the mind in some particular disposition—to which the former is in many cases barely subservient, and sometimes entirely omitted, when these can be obtained without it, as I think does not unfrequently happen in the familiar use of language. I entreat the reader to reflect with himself

and see if it does not often happen, either in hearing or reading a discourse, that the passions of fear, love, hatred, admiration, disdain, and the like, arise immediately in his mind upon the perception of certain words, without any ideas coming between. At first, indeed, the words might have occasioned ideas that were fit to produce those emotions; but, if I mistake not, it will be found that, when language is once grown familiar, the hearing of the sounds or sight of the characters is oft immediately attended with those passions which at first were wont to be produced by the intervention of ideas that are now quite omitted. May we not, for example, be affected with the promise of a *good thing,* though we have not an idea of what it is? Or is not the being threatened with danger sufficient to excite a dread, though we think not of any particular evil likely to befall us, nor yet frame to ourselves an idea of danger in abstract? If anyone shall join ever so little reflection of his own to what has been said, I believe that it will evidently appear to him that general names are often used in the propriety of language without the speaker's designing them for marks of ideas in his own, which he would have them raise in the mind of the hearer. Even proper names themselves do not seem always spoken with a design to bring into our view the ideas of those individuals that are supposed to be marked by them. For example, when a Schoolman tells me, "Aristotle has said it," all I conceive he means by it is to dispose me to embrace his opinion with the deference and submission which custom has annexed to that name. And this effect may be so instantly produced in the minds of those who are accustomed to resign their judgment to the authority of that philosopher, as it is impossible any idea either of his person, writings, or reputation should go before. Innumerable examples of this kind may be given, but why should I insist on those things which everyone's experience will, I doubt not, plentifully suggest unto him?

21. We have, I think, shown the impossibility of abstract ideas. We have considered what has been said for them by their ablest patrons, and endeavored to show they are of no use for those ends to which they are thought necessary. And lastly, we have traced them to the source from whence they flow, which appears to be language. It cannot be denied that words are of excellent use, in that by their means all that stock of knowledge which has been purchased by the joint labors of inquisitive men in all ages and nations may be drawn into the view and made the possession of one single person. But at the same time it must be owned that most parts of knowledge have been strangely perplexed and darkened by the abuse of words, and general ways of speech wherein they are delivered. Since therefore words are so apt to impose on the understanding, whatever ideas I consider, I shall endeavor to take them bare and naked into my view, keeping out of my thoughts so far as I am able those names which long and constant use has

so strictly united with them; from which I may expect to derive the following advantages:

22. *First,* I shall be sure to get clear of all controversies purely verbal—the springing up of which weeds in almost all the sciences has been a main hindrance to the growth of true and sound knowledge. *Secondly,* this seems to be a sure way to extricate myself out of that fine and subtle net of *abstract ideas* which has so miserably perplexed and entangled the minds of men; and that with this peculiar circumstance, that by how much the finer and more curious was the wit of any man, by so much the deeper was he likely to be ensnared and faster held therein. *Thirdly,* so long as I confine my thoughts to my own ideas divested of words, I do not see how I can easily be mistaken. The objects I consider I clearly and adequately know. I cannot be deceived in thinking I have an idea which I have not. It is not possible for me to imagine that any of my own ideas are alike or unlike that are not truly so. To discern the agreements or disagreements there are between my ideas, to see what ideas are included in any compound idea and what not, there is nothing more requisite than an attentive perception of what passes in my own understanding.

23. But the attainment of all these advantages does presuppose an entire deliverance from the deception of words, which I dare hardly promise myself —so difficult a thing it is to dissolve a union so early begun and confirmed by so long a habit as that betwixt words and ideas. Which difficulty seems to have been very much increased by the doctrine of *abstraction.* For so long as men thought abstract ideas were annexed to their words, it does not seem strange that they should use words for ideas—it being found an impracticable thing to lay aside the word and retain the *abstract* idea in the mind, which in itself was perfectly inconceivable. This seems to me the principal cause why those men who have so emphatically recommended to others the laying aside all use of words in their meditations, and contemplating their bare ideas, have yet failed to perform it themselves. Of late many have been very sensible of the absurd opinions and insignificant disputes which grow out of the abuse of words. And, in order to remedy these evils, they advise well that we attend to the ideas signified and draw off our attention from the words which signify them. But, how good soever this advice may be they have given others, it is plain they could not have a due regard to it themselves so long as they thought the only immediate use of words was to signify ideas, and that the immediate signification of every general name was a determinate abstract idea.

24. But, these being known to be mistakes, a man may with greater ease prevent his being imposed on by words. He that knows he has no other

than *particular* ideas will not puzzle himself in vain to find out and conceive the *abstract* idea annexed to any name. And he that knows names do not always stand for ideas will spare himself the labor of looking for ideas where there are none to be had. It were, therefore, to be wished that everyone would use his utmost endeavors to obtain a clear view of the ideas he would consider, separating from them all that dress and encumbrance of words which so much contribute to blind the judgment and divide the attention. In vain do we extend our view into the heavens and pry into the entrails of the earth, in vain do we consult the writings of learned men and trace the dark footsteps of antiquity—we need only draw the curtain of words, to behold the fairest tree of knowledge, whose fruit is excellent and within the reach of our hand.

25. Unless we take care to clear the first principles of knowledge from the embarrassment and delusion of words, we may make infinite reasonings upon them to no purpose; we may draw consequences from consequences, and be never the wiser. The further we go, we shall only lose ourselves the more irrecoverably, and be the deeper entangled in difficulties and mistakes. Whoever, therefore, designs to read the following sheets, I entreat him to make my words the occasion of his own thinking and endeavor to attain the same train of thoughts in reading that I had in writing them. By this means it will be easy for him to discover the truth or falsity of what I say. He will be out of all danger of being deceived by my words, and I do not see how he can be led into an error by considering his own naked, undisguised ideas.

5

Universals

D. F. Pears

"Do universals exist?" This question was debated so long and vehemently because it was mistaken for a factual question about some airy realm of being. But why was this mistake made? One diagnosis is that general words were tacitly assimilated to proper names,[1] and that, when this practice is exposed, it becomes harmless but pointless.[2] But this is a description of what happened rather than an explanation; it gives something more like a symptom than a cause. Could so many philosophers have been so silly in such a simple way? Even moderate skepticism on this point would lead to an attempt to supplement this suggestion. This article is such an attempt.

"Univerals exist" has a deceptive logic. Realists offer it as the conclusion of many arguments; but unlike the premises of these arguments, it cannot be understood as a verifiable statement of fact. On the other hand, if it is taken merely as an esoteric way of stating those premises over again, the vehemence of the controversy becomes inexplicable. Faced with this difficulty of interpretation, some modern philosophers suggest that it is no good puzzling about its literal meaning, just as it is no good puzzling about the literal meaning of dreams. For traditional philosophy provided a small set of possible conclusions to arguments about the generality of thought and language, and tradition was strong. If a tribe educated its children to dream according to a tradition which restricted their manifest dream contents within

From *Philosophical Quarterly* 1 (1951). Reprinted by permission of the publisher.

narrow limits, it would be difficult to discover their much more varied latent dream contents.[3] Similarly, although realists are argumentative, it is difficult to answer the question why they maintain that universals exist. Any answer must be based on a selection from among the many reasons which they themselves proffer; and a good selection will be diagnostic; it will successfully explain the doctrine. There is no sharp boundary here between descriptions of the premises of philosophical arguments and diagnoses of their conclusions: because success in explaining, which is the criterion of a diagnosis, is a matter of degree, and because the reasons which philosophers themselves give for their doctrines sometimes completely explain why they held them. Quine's remark, that realists find a universal for every property which can be existentially generalized,[4] is an extremely brief description. The thesis of Berkeley and Mill was more than this: it was a diagnosis, but an inadequate one. I shall try to provide a less inadequate diagnosis.

"Because universals exist" is the answer to at least two general questions: "Why are things what they are?"[5] and "Why are we able to name things as we do?" Though Plato and Aristotle sometimes distinguished these two questions, it was characteristic of Greek thought to confuse them. Yet they can be clearly distinguished, the first requiring a dynamic answer from scientists, and the second a static answer from logicians. Now philosophy has often staked premature claims in the territory of science by giving quick comprehensive answers to questions which really required laborious detailed answers. And clearly this is what happened to the first of the two questions. When detailed causal answers were provided to it, the comprehensive answer "Because universals exist" was no longer acceptable or necessary.[6] But what would detailed answers to the second question be like? Presumably they would be explanations of the meanings of words. But philosophers are easily led to neglect such detailed progressive answers to the second question, and to seek instead a comprehensive and ultimate explanation of naming. For, though comprehensive answers to the first question are clearly futile, there are no obvious penalties attached to answering the second question in a comprehensive way. Yet, I shall argue—and this will be my first thesis—that any comprehensive explanation of naming is necessarily circular: and that philosophers think that, in spite of this disadvantage, such explanations have some point largely because they wrongly assimilate naming to natural processes. Yet surely naming cannot be utterly artificial? My second thesis will be that the desire to understand naming leads to a hunt for a completely satisfactory analogy: but that all other processes either already contain the very feature of naming which was puzzling, or else are too natural or too artificial to be really analogous; and that it was the inevitable oscillation between these three points which prolonged the controversy about universals.

It is unnecessary to produce evidence that philosophers who proposed the existence of universals thought that they were explaining the unity of classes and hence the possibility of naming. What is debatable is whether this was an important motive, and this can be decided only in the sequel. My first thesis, which I must now try to establish, is that realism is necessarily a circular explanation of naming. Now the answer to the question "Why are we able to name things as we do?" is "The reason varies." For it is always possible with more or less ingenuity, depending on the degree of atomicity of the name, to give a detailed informative reason; and that this reason will vary with the name. But ultimately there must be some exit from the maze of words, and, wherever this exit is made, it will be impossible to give an informative reason except by pointing. For the only other way of giving an informative reason is to give a new word, and this would prevent the exit from the maze of words from being made at this place.[7] Still at the place where the exit is made it is always possible to give a detailed reason like "We are able to call things red because they are red," which is too obviously circular even to look informative. Or alternatively it is possible to say "We are able to call things ϕ because they are ϕ," and this is a general reason which is almost as obviously circular and uninformative. What philosophers who propose the existence of universals do is to propose a general reason which looks informative because it shifts to another level, but unfortunately is not. It merely marks time: but marking time can look very like marching if only the movements of the performers are watched, and not the ground which they profess to be covering. Yet this ground could not be covered. For the reason could not be informative even if it were detailed; since there could be a noncircular answer to the question "What universal?" only if the exit from the maze of words were at some different point, which would merely put off the moment of embarrassment from which in the end neither speech nor thought can be saved. Thus realism fails to escape the limitations of all explanations of naming; that they can be informative only if they are not general but detailed, and then only if they are not given at the point where an exit is made from the maze of words.

Uninformative answers have their point. They are silencing. What is wrong with realism is not this, but that it masquerades as an answer which advances knowledge one step further. The analytic machine acquires a momentum which carries it beyond the point where it ought to stop. And there is an inveterate philosophical habit which strengthens the tendency to go beyond this point, or rather to think that one has gone beyond it. "A thing is called by a certain name because it instantiates a certain universal" is obviously circular when particularized, but it looks imposing when it is left in this general form. And it looks imposing in this general form largely because of the inveterate philosophical habit of treating the shadows cast by words and sentences as if they were separately identifiable. Universals, like facts and propositions, are such shadows; and too often philosophers by appealing to them in general terms have produced in their readers a feeling of satisfaction which ought to have been produced only by specifying them.[8] But universals are specifiable only by reference to words. Similarly facts may be brute and propositions may be definite, but what exactly it is about them which is brute or definite can be specified only by references to the sentences which were the unacknowledged starting-points. In all these cases it is tacit re-duplication which makes philosophers think that they can enjoy the benefits of specifying without actually specifying. Yet the explanation of naming is incomplete until a particular universal is specified, and, when it is specified, the explanation immediately fails through circularity. Naming is hazardous,[9] and any attempt to make it foolproof by basing it on an independent foundation must fail in this way. It is impossible to cross the gap between language and things without really crossing it.[10]

Since the failure of realism to perform this feat is inevitable, its rivals fail too. Nominalism, conceptualism and imagism,[11] in so far as they are rivals of realism, are attempts to provide a unity which will explain naming. Nominalism says that a name is merely connected with a multitude of things, sometimes adding that these things are similar. Conceptualism says that the name is not directly connected with the things but only via a concept, thus changing the nodal point. Imagism says that the nodal point is an image. And realism says that there is really no nodal point, since a name, though it appears to be connected with a multitude of things is all the time connected with only one thing, a universal. This is an oversimplification of what these theories say about the One and the Many; but it is enough for my next purpose, which is to show that these rivals of realism cannot produce a noncircular explanation of naming at those points where an exit is made from the maze of words.

The two psychological theories say that one word can apply to many things only because of the mediation of a concept or of an image. Locke's abstract general idea is "the workmanship of the understanding, but has its foundation in the similitudes of things."[12] And Berkeley replaces it by an idea which "considered in itself is particular but becomes general by being made to represent or stand for all other particular ideas of the same sort."[13] But what similitudes, and what representation? In the end both Locke's concept and Berkeley's image are completely identifiable only by their use.[14] Of course we can partly identify images by describing their features: and in this way we may even almost completely identify them, since certain images most naturally stand for certain things. And the same could be said of concepts, if they were not merely philosophers' reifications of mental processes. But this will not completely identify either of them, since thought may not follow the most natural course; nor is it always clear which is the most natural course. It is not so much that thinking is speaking as that thinking is like speaking in the only way that matters: it uses one thing as a symbol to stand for many things. And the only tool which could not be used differently is the use. Even something which had its use written on it could be used differently.[15] And, if the psychological tool, whether concept or image, can be completely identified only by the things on which it is used, it cannot explain naming without circularity. For, unless we point, the use can be specified only by backward reference to the name. Nor is this circularity surprising. For psychological tools have no advantage over words: they are like them in being symbols, and unlike them only in being shadowy symbols.

The type of nominalism which says that a name is applied to a number of things which are similar immediately falls into the same circularity. For "similar" is an incomplete predicate, anything being similar to anything in some way, perhaps a negative way.[16] And in the end the kind of similarity which is meant can be specified only by a backward reference to the name. Equally the type of nominalism which merely says that a name is applied to a class of things cannot say which class without a backward reference to the name. Here the circularity is so obvious and there is so little to cushion the shock of the realization that naming is naming that this type of nominalism seems hardly tenable. For, however strongly nominalists react against realism, they can never quite escape its influence: once somebody had said that universals exist it could never be quite the same again. Surely, one wants to protest, there must be some way of giving the class besides reference to the name? Well there is, of course, enumeration. But this answer seems to fail to allow for the possibility of ever using the name correctly in any synthetic sentence. For, if the class is given by enumeration, surely every use of the name must be either incorrect or analytic? Since, if to call a thing "ϕ" is to include it in the class of things called "ϕ," then surely it is incorrect to call it "ϕ" or else the class cannot be given without reference to it? It is the example of realism which encourages these protests. But it is a bad example. Such neatness is not to be had. For, first of all, these classes cannot be given by enumeration of all their members, since, except for words belonging to dead languages, they are never complete. Nor is it true even that each member must either contribute or not contribute towards giving a class; since a name may be applied to the same thing twice, once analytically and once synthetically, and even a single use of a name may be synthetic for the speaker and analytic for the hearer. In fact the disjunction "Analytic or Synthetic" cannot be applied simply to the addition of a member to a class without further caveats. But this in itself is not enough to remove the difficulty; it only makes it reappear in a new form. For if the addition of a member to a class can be synthetic for the speaker and analytic for a subsequent lexicographer, then to what class was the member added? Surely we now have two classes on our hands instead of one? An analogy will help us to deal with this new form of the difficulty. Naming is like electing the sort of member who makes a difference to a club. Strictly we cannot say without qualification to what club he was elected, since it was one club before he was elected and another club after he was elected. The club building might be pointed out, and of course there is no parallel move in the case of naming, although realism pretends that there is. But, even if there were no building or anything else of that kind, the puzzle about the two clubs would not be very perplexing. Similarly, when we reject the simple application of the dichotomy "Analytic or Synthetic" the resulting puzzle about two classes is not very perplexing. All that is necessary is to point out that a class is incompletely given by a changing quorum. This may be untidy, but why not? There is something radically wrong with a request to be given a class which is not satisfied either with a reference to the name or with progressive enumeration. It is a request to be given something without being given it; as if somewhere, if only philosophers searched long enough, there could be found something which possessed all the advantages of a word and none of its disadvantages, an epistemological vehicle which carried all its destinations.

I now turn to my second thesis, that nothing is sufficiently like naming without being too like naming. Defenders of realism, like defenders of the other theories of naming, might object that the criticism contained in my first thesis is obvious, superficial and directed against a man of straw. For realism does not offer a noncircular detailed explanation of naming—how could it?—but simply gives a personal characterization of the sort of unity which makes naming possible. But notice how very like a dream realism is. Taken literally it seems to be of little importance. But, if it is taken as the expression of a doctrine which, if *per impossibile* it were true, would give it great importance, the suggestion is immediately repudiated. Yet it does express such a doctrine, even if its exponents intermittently deny that it does; and it is to the devious expression of this doctrine that it owes most of its attractiveness. Its manifest content is little more than a harmless caprice, but its latent content is a serious error.

But has realism no point when it is taken simply as a general characterization of the sort of unity which makes naming impossible? One might answer that it has no point, and that it succeeds in appearing to have some point only by the device of inventing a new comprehensive term: and that this device is considered effective only in philosophy, since outside philosophy it is too obviously like making an impressive gesture in the direction of the interesting object, opening one's mouth and saying absolutely nothing. But such a denial would be tantamount to a denial that any general characterization of the sort of unity which makes naming possible could have a point. And surely such a denial would be wrong, since something can be done towards explaining the general possibility of naming by finding analogous processes? For instance, what makes naming possible is one thing which is in many things as an ingredient.[17] But does this analogy throw much light on naming? Any feature of logical mixing which is at all interesting seems to distinguish it from all other sorts of mixing. The values of an unrestricted variable are strange receptacles. What prevents contrary ingredients from being put in together, or an implicant from appearing without its implicate, is never the causal consequences. And anyway the whole notion of mixing ingredients which were not there before the mixing is peculiar. Could there be a logical conjuring trick?

Here defenders of realism might object that a new misunderstanding had replaced the old one. For, if realism is to be understood, not only must a general characterization of naming be allowed, but also the verification principle must not be applied too crudely. And anyway, if mixing is not a good analogy, this only means that some better analogy must be sought. This objection might lead to a tolerant examination of other analogies.[18] But fortunately it also opens up a short cut to the heart of the matter, which I shall soon take. Now it would be taking too short a cut to repeat the platitude that naming is *sui generis*. For it is natural to seek an analogy even if the search can never be completely successful. And anyway Butler's truism applies to everything. What is needed in order to explain the peculiar persistence of the debate about universals is something slightly longer, a demonstration that no analogy can be sufficiently close to satisfy philosophers without being too close.

It is most natural to seek a visible process as an analogy to naming, particularly for the Greeks who began this controversy.[19] Now previously I insisted that it is impossible in the end to give a detailed noncircular description of what makes it possible to name anything. Here, however, it would be unfair to object that, if naming in general is compared to a visible process, still that process itself must be named. For this sort of circularity is the inevitable result of the philosopher's predicament. However, it is dangerous to begin speaking at all where so little can be said. For it is fatally easy to think that one has separate access to what makes a name applicable just because one has separate access to whatever stands for this in the analogy. But, waiving this, let us now take the short cut and ask what sort of visible process could be analogous to naming. Let us try a rough analogy and say that one word is connected with many objects in the same way that the estuary of a river is connected with its many sources. But this analogy fails because this connection just happens naturally. We might then try to mend the analogy by saying that water follows the easiest course. But this could be called choice only anthropomorphically, in an extended and weak sense of "choice." In order to introduce choice in a restricted, strong sense, it is necessary to alter the analogy and say that people by directing the streams choose which sources shall feed the river. But, if the first process was too natural to be like naming, the second is too artificial, since, for the analogy to work, the sources ought to have something in common besides the fact that the river is fed from them. And it is difficult to find an analogy which is neither too natural nor too artificial. The characteristic of naming which is difficult to match is that the objects have something in common besides being called by one name, but nothing in common which counts except that in virtue of which they are called by one name. And this characteristic can be matched only by allowing that something makes it convenient but not absolutely necessary for people to canalize streams into the river in the way they do, and that whatever it is which makes this choice convenient is the only thing common to the sources which counts. But this compromise between the two extremes introduces into the analogy the very feature which it was intended to explain. For just how something works in influencing usage was what was to be explained. Nor is there a fourth alternative. So after all even general analogical characterizations of naming do fall into a circularity which is closely related to the type of circularity which my first thesis exposed. Neither in detail nor in general is it possible to step outside language.

This short way with analogies looks too superficial. For suppose that it is granted that one of the things that metaphysicians do is to seek the unattainable: that they hunt for definitions which would in no way involve their definienda,[20] and for analogies which would in no way involve what they were intended to explain. Yet even so metaphysics is a natural and inevitable pursuit, since the easiest way to discover how far one can go is to try to go one stage farther. And anyway there is a difference between complete failure and partial success; since, so long as analogies do not reach the point of self-frustration they get better and better as they approach it. These two qualifications are just but they only serve to strengthen my thesis that it was oscillation between the three points which prolonged the controversy about universals. For unless the possible analogies are mapped out in this simple way, it seems always conceivable that some altogether better analogy might lurk in an unexplored corner.

And what more are the rival theories of naming doing than seeking a completely satisfactory analogy? It is only jargon which makes them appear to be doing something more. The type of nominalism which suggests that things which are called by one name have only their name in common represents the extreme of artificiality.[21] It suggests that there are never any ways of telling even approximately whether a word is used in one sense or two senses. At the other extreme stands the type of realism which suggests that there is always one method of getting a precise answer to this question. In between are all the other theories of naming, which allow that it is neither impossible for the lexicographer to succeed in answering this question nor impossible for him to fail. None of these middle theories is really wrong, since of course we do bestow common names on certain chosen groups of things which exhibit certain similarities (why else should we do it?) or instantiate certain universals (why else were they invented?). But on the other hand none of them goes deep enough to satisfy the true metaphysician who is in all of us; since though they take us to the bottom of naming, we were in a simpler way already there, and they do not succeed in showing us how naming is founded on something else which lies even deeper. Hence each of these middle theories (except imagism, which says something empirical which seems to be false) develops its own thesis with embarrassing success up to a point, and can discredit its rivals only by accusing them of not going beyond that point. But, since naming cannot be explained by anything which really goes beyond a reasoned choice of usage, this is an unfair accusation. And its unfairness is concealed from those who make it only because each tacitly and wrongly assumes that his own theory alone does go beyond this point. Thus moderate nominalists maintain that similarity is a better explanation of the unity of a class than the presence of a universal. (But why should people not *just* recognize the presence of universals?) And moderate realists retort that this admits the existence of at least one universal, similarity. (But why should the presence of a universal explain the recognition of similarity if it cannot explain the recognition of anything else? Why should people not *just* recognize similarity?) Really these are not two arguments but two bare assertions of superiority. They are maneuvers which are carried out in a way which suggests that they are difficult and that they must be advances: but both these suggestions are false. Yet these theories do seem to be striving towards something. And they are. Their goal is the unattainable completely satisfactory explanation of naming. And, as so often happens in metaphysics, progress is measured by distance from the starting-point and not by proximity to the goal whose unattainability each uses against its rivals without allowing it to deter itself.

Thus, theories of naming, which seem to flout the verification principle without therefore saying nothing, can be interpreted as disguised analogies. And, though there is a common limit beyond whch they cannot go, the success with which they stealthily approach this limit, camouflaged in the technical terms of epistemology, varies. But if this almost mechanical oscillation is avoided what else can be said about naming? Certainly as the first part of this article showed, detailed answers to the question why we name things as we do will in the end be circular. Only the trick of giving a general answer as if it were a detailed one cloaks their failure. If a word is explained ostensively, then however difficult this process may be it really is explained ostensively. It is no good trying to combine the concreteness of ostensive definition with the clarity of verbal definition. Verbal definitions have such an easy task just because ostensive definitions have such a difficult task. Surveyors find it easier to fix the positions of points which they can visit than to fix the positions of points which they cannot visit. Similarly it is easy to fix the relative positions of words: but the points in things to which words are related are in the end inaccessible to logicians.

Then what else can be said about naming? How *does* the lexicographer tell when a word is used in two senses rather than in one sense? Surely there must be something in common to all well constructed series of things? Yes, just that they *are* well constructed. For this question already contains the equivalent of any possible comprehensive answer which could be given to it. And, though in one way it is hard to see what detailed answers could be given to it, in another way it is only too easy to see. For we never reach a point where an exit *must* be made from the maze of words. Admittedly, if a verbal explanation is given at one point, it is only successful if at some other point a connection with things is already understood; and at some points it is more natural not to offer more words. But at no point is an exit obligatory. So, if detailed reasons why we call a thing what we do are required, it is easy to give them; but never ultimately or in the end, since here *ex vi termini* it is impossible to give them. But philosophers tend to ignore this kind of detailed answer and press on. But where to? Perhaps to experimental psychology, in order to discover how changes in the sense organs in training and in interests alter the ways in which people group things. But this sort of investigation only gives the varying tests of the good construction of a series, and not its essence. But what could its essence be? When general analogical characterizations of naming have been mentioned, and detailed reasons why we call particular things by particular names, and the psychological background of all this, what is left? The desire to go on explaining naming is to some extent the result of the way these three fields have been confused, and to some extent the result of a natural feeling that in such a vast territory there might be something which lies outside these three fields. But above all it is the result of the Protean metaphysical urge to transcend language.

NOTES

1. Cf. J. S. Mill, *Examination of Sir William Hamilton's Philosophy* (5th ed., London, 1878) chap. xvii, p. 381, and Berkeley, *Principles of Human Knowledge*, Introduction § 18.

2. Cf. M. Lazerowitz, "The Existence of Universals," *Mind* (1946): 1 ff.

3. Cf. Freud, *The Interpretation of Dreams*, tr. A. A. Brill (London, 1913), p. 166.

4. Cf. "Designation and Existence" in Feigl and Sellars, *Readings in Philosophical Analysis* (New York, 1949), p. 48.

5. Aristotle criticized Plato's theory largely as an inadequate answer to this question.

6. Socrates in the *Phaedo* (100d) says that it is the only acceptable answer to the first question. But the advance of science has undermined this thesis more thoroughly than the advance of logic has undermined the thesis that it is an acceptable answer to the second question.

7. Cf. the view sketched by Socrates in the *Theaetetus* 201e-202c, and Antisthenes' view given by Aristotle in *Met.* H, 1043 b 23-32; also L. Wittgenstein, *Tractatus* 5; M. Schlick, *Grundzüge der Naturphilosophie* (Vienna, 1948), p. 21; and A. J. Ayer, *Thinking and Meaning* (London, 1947), p. 28.

8. This same trick is played by those who say that laws of nature exhibit connections between universals. This gives the impression that we could independently know the eternal framework in which temporal things move and change, rather as we independently know how a piston must move by looking at a cylinder: cf. what Köhler says about Aristotle's astronomy and Descartes's neurology (*Gestalt Psychology*, London, 1930, pp. 82-86).

9. Cf. Bradley, *Appearance and Reality*, p. 22 and p. 533; and C. S. Peirce, *Collected Papers* (vol. I, para. 145): "Direct experience is neither certain nor uncertain, because it affirms nothing—it just is."

10. Cf. Stuart Hampshire, "Skepticism and Meaning," *Philosophy* (July 1950): 245.

11. Cf. H. H. Price, *Thinking and Representation* (British Academy Lecture, 1946).

12. Locke, *Essay concerning Human Understanding*, Bk. III, Chap. III, § xiii.

13. Berkeley, *Principles of Human Knowledge*, Introduction, § 12.

14. This is due to Wittgenstein: cf. e.g., *Tractatus*, 3.326, "In order to recognize the symbol in the sign we must consider the significant use."

15. W. T. Stace in "Russell's Neutral Monism" in *The Philosophy of Bertrand Russell*, pp. 381-83, complains that neither Berkeley's precise image nor Russell's vague image (in *An Inquiry into Meaning and Truth*) succeeds in explaining the generality of thought. But no description of any item of mental furniture which included only its monetary properties and not its habitual use could possibly explain the generality of thought.

16. Hence the point of many riddles. Cf. Stuart Hampshire, "Skepticism and Meaning," *Philosophy* (July 1950): 238. Also Plato, *Protagoras* 331 d. The Platonic theory avoids the "similarity" difficulty, but not of course the general difficulty of which this is only one form. Speusippus, who abandoned the Platonic theory, seems to have held that, since every species is like every other species in some way, it is impossible to define one species without defining every other species. Cf. Aristotle, *Post. An.* 97 a 6-112. Cf. H. Cherniss, *Aristotle's criticism of Plato and the Academy* (I. 60), quoted by W. D. Ross in his note on this passage. J. Stenzel, in Pauly-Wissowa Real-Encyclopädie, *s.v.* Speusippus, pp. 1650 and 1655, brings out the affinity be-

tween Speusippus' view and Post-Kantian Idealism. Cf. Brand Blanshard on individuals (not species). "One never gets what is fully particular until one has specified its relations of every kind with everything else in the universe," *The Nature of Thought* (London, 1939), vol. I, p. 639. Curiously enough, N. R. Campbell arrives independently at a similar conclusion about species, when he is discussing the definition of such substances as silver, mercury, or lead (*Physics, The Elements*, Cambridge, 1920, p. 50). All attempts to explain the unity of a species by similarity—whether by similarity of the individuals to one another, or by similarities and differences between the species and other species—suffer from the same incompleteness.

17. Cf. A. N. Whitehead, *Science and the Modern World* (Cambridge, 1928), pp. 197 ff. For a criticism of this analogy, cf. Bentham, *Works*, vol. VIII, p. 335.

18. Metaphors must not be dismissed just because they are metaphors, as, e.g., "copying" and "participation" are by Aristotle, *Met.* 991 a 20.

19. Cf. J. Stenzel, *Plato's Method of Dialectic* (Oxford, 1940), p. 37.

20. Cf. J. Wisdom, "Metaphysics and Verification," *Mind* (1938): 465 ff.

21. There are traces of such an extreme form of nominalism in Hobbes. Cf. *Leviathan*, Pt. I, chap. IV, p. 13 (Everyman edition).

6

Universals and Family Resemblances

Renford Bambrough

. . . If I ask you what these three books have in common, or what those four chairs have in common, you will look to see if the books are all on the same subject or by the same author or published by the same firm; to see if the chairs are all Chippendale or all three-legged or all marked "Not to be removed from this room." It will never occur to you to say that the books have in common that they are books or the chairs that they are chairs. And if you find after close inspection that the chairs or the books do not have in common any of the features I have mentioned, and if you cannot see any other specific feature that they have in common, you will say that as far as you can see they have nothing in common. You will perhaps add that you suppose from the form of my question that I must know of some- thing that they have in common. I may then tell you that all the books once belonged to John Locke or that all the chairs came from Ten Rillington Place. But it would be a poor sort of joke for me to say that the chairs were all chairs or that the books were all books.

If I ask you what *all* chairs have in common, or what *all* books have in common, you may again try to find a feature like those you would look for in the case of *these three* books or *those four* chairs; and you may again think that it is a poor sort of joke for me to say that what all books have in common is that they are books and that what all chairs have in common

From *Proceedings of the Aristotelian Society* 60 (1960–61). Copyright The Artistotelian Society 1960–61. Reprinted by courtesy of the editor.

is that they are chairs. And yet this time it is not a joke but an important philosophical truth.

Because the normal case where we ask "What have all *these* chairs, books or games in common?" is one in which we are not concerned with their all being chairs, books or games, we are liable to overlook the extreme peculiarity of the *philosophical* question that is asked with the words "What do *all* chairs, *all* books, *all* games have in common?" For of course games *do* have something in common. They *must* have something in common, and yet when we look for what they have in common we cannot find it. When we try to say what they have in common we always fail. And this is not because what we are looking for lies deeply hidden, but because it is too obvious to be seen; not because what we are trying to say is too subtle and complicated to be said, but because it is too easy and too simple to be worth saying: and so we say something more dramatic, but something false, instead. The simple truth is that what games have in common is that they are games. The nominalist is obscurely aware of this, and by rejecting the realist's talk of transcendent, immanent or subsistent forms or universals he shows his awareness. But by his own insistence that games have nothing in common except that they are called games he shows the obscurity of his awareness. The realist too is obscurely aware of it. By his talk of transcendent, immanent or subsistent forms or universals he shows the obscurity of his awareness. But by his hostility to the nominalist's insistence that games have nothing in common except that they are called games he shows his awareness.

All this can be more fully explained by the application of what I will call "Ramsey's Maxim." F. P. Ramsey, after mapping the course of an inconclusive dispute between Russell and W. E. Johnson, writes as follows:

> Evidently, however, none of these arguments are really decisive, and the position is extremely unsatisfactory to anyone with real curiosity about such a fundamental question. In such cases it is a heuristic maxim that the truth lies not in one of the two disputed views but in some third possibility which has not yet been thought of, which we can only discover by rejecting something assumed as obvious by both the disputants. (*The Foundations of Mathematics*, pp. 115–116.)

It is assumed as obvious by both the nominalist and the realist that there can be no objective justification for the application of a general term to its instances unless its instances have something in common over and above their having in common that they *are* its instances. The nominalist rightly holds that there is no such additional common element, and he therefore wrongly concludes that there is no objective justification for the application of any general term. The realist rightly holds that there is an objective justification for the application of general terms, and he therefore wrongly concludes that there *must* be some additional common element.

Wittgenstein denied the assumption that is common to nominalism and realism, and that is why I say that he solved the problem of universals. For if we deny the mistaken premiss that is common to the realist's argument and the nominalist's argument then we can deny the realist's mistaken conclusion and deny the nominalist's mistaken conclusion; and that is another way of saying that we can affirm the true premiss of the nominalist's argument and can also affirm the true premiss of the realist's argument.

The nominalist says that games have nothing in common except that they are called games.

The realist says that games must have something in common, and he means by this that they must have something in common other than they are games.

Wittgenstein says that games have nothing in common except that they are games.

Wittgenstein thus denies at one and the same time the nominalist's claim that games have nothing in common except that they are called games and the realist's claim that games have something in common other than that they are games. He asserts at one and the same time the realist's claim that there is an objective justification for the application of the word "game" to games and the nominalist's claim that there is no element that is common to all games. And he is able to do all this because he denies the joint claim of the nominalist and the realist that there cannot be an objective justification for the application of the word "game" to games unless there is an element that is common to all games (*univeralia in rebus*) or a common relation that all games bear to something that is not a game (*universalia ante res*).

Wittgenstein is easily confused with the nominalist because he denies what the realist asserts: that games have something in common other than that they are games.

When we see that Wittgenstein is not a nominalist we may easily confuse him with the realist because he denies what the nominalist asserts: that games have nothing in common except that they are called games.

But we can now see that Wittgenstein is neither a realist nor a nominalist: he asserts the simple truth that they both deny and he also asserts the two simple truths of which each of them asserts one and denies the other.

I will now try to put some flesh on to these bare bones.

The value and the limitations of the nominalist's claim that things which are called by the same name have nothing in common except that they are called by the same name can be seen if we look at a case where a set of objects literally and undeniably have nothing in common except that they are called by the same name. If I choose to give the name "alpha" to each of a number of miscellaneous objects (the star Sirius, my fountain-pen, the Parthenon, the color red, the number five, and the letter Z) then I may well succeed in choosing the objects so *arbitrarily* that I shall succeed in preventing them from having any feature in common, other than that I call them by the name "alpha." But this imaginary case, to which the nominalist likens the use of all general words, has only to be described to be sharply contrasted with the typical case in which I apply a general word, say "chair," to a number of the instances to which it applies. In the first place, the *arbitrariness* of my selection of alphas is not paralleled in the case in which I apply the word "chair" successively to the chair in which I am now sitting, the Speaker's Chair in the House of Commons, the chair used at Bisley for carrying the winner of the Queen's Prize, and one of the deck chairs on the beach at Brighton. In giving a list of chairs I cannot just mention anything that happens to come into my head, while this is exactly what I do in giving my list of alphas. The second point is that the class of alphas is a *closed* class. Once I have given my list I have referred to every single alpha in the universe, actual and possible. Although I *might* have included or excluded any actual or possible object whatsoever when I was drawing up my list, once I have in fact made my arbitrary choice, no further application can be given to the word "alpha" according to the use that I have prescribed. For if I later add an object that I excluded from my list, or remove an object that I included in it, then I am making a different use of the word "alpha." With the word "chair" the position is quite different. There are an infinite number of actual and possible chairs. I cannot aspire to complete the enumeration of all chairs, as I can arbitrarily and at any point complete the enumeration of all alphas, and the word "chair," unlike the word "alpha," can be applied to an infinite number of instances without suffering any change of use.

These two points lead to a third and decisive point. I cannot teach the use of the word "alpha" except by specifically attaching it to each of the objects in my arbitrarily chosen list. No observer can conclude anything from watching me attach the label to this, that, or the other object, or to any number of objects however large, about the nature of the object or objects, if any, to which I shall later attach it. The use of the word "alpha" cannot be learned or taught as the use of a general word can be learned or taught. In teaching the use of a general word we may and must refer to characteristics of the objects to which it applies, and of the objects to which it does not apply, and indicate which of these characteristics count for the application of the word and which count against it. A pupil does not have to consult us on every separate occasion on which he encounters a new object, and if he did consult us every time we should have to say that he was not *learning* the use of the word. The reference that we make to a finite number of objects to which the word applies, and to a finite number of objects to which the word does not apply, is capable of equipping the pupil with a capacity for correctly applying or withholding the word to or from an infinite number of objects to which we have made no reference.

All this remains true in the case where it is not I alone, but a large number of people, or all of us, who use the word "alpha" in the way that I suggest. Even if everybody always called a particular set of objects by the same name, that would be insufficient to ensure that the name was a general name, and the claim to the name to be a general name would be defeated by just that necessity for reference to the arbitrary choices of the users of the name that the nominalist mistakenly claims to find in the case of a genuinely general name. For the nominalist is right in thinking that if we always had to make such a reference then there would be no general names as they are understood by the realist.

The nominalist is also right in the stress that he puts on the role of human interests and human purposes in determining our choice of principles of classification. How this insistence on the role of human purposes may be reconciled with the realist's proper insistence on the objectivity of the similarities and dissimilarities on which any genuine classification is based can be seen by considering an imaginary tribe of South Sea Islanders.

Let us suppose that trees are of great importance in the life and work of the South Sea Islanders, and that they have a rich and highly developed language in which they speak of the trees with which their island is thickly clad. But they do not have names for the species and genera of trees as they are recognized by our botanists. As we walk around the island with some of its inhabitants we can easily pick out orange trees, date palms and cedars. Our hosts are puzzled that we should call by the same name trees which appear to them to have nothing in common. They in turn surprise us by giving the same name to each of the trees in what is from our point of view a very mixed plantation. They point out to us what they called a mixed plantation, and we see that it is in our terms a clump of trees of the same species. Each party comes to recognize that its own classifications are as puzzling to the other as the other's are puzzling to itself.

This looks like the sort of situation that gives aid and comfort to the nominalist in his battle against the realist. But if we look as it more closely we see that it cannot help him. We know already that our own classification is based on similarities and differences between the trees, similarities and differences which we can point out to the islanders in an attempt to teach them our language. Of course we may fail, but if we do it will not be because we *must* fail.

Now *either* (*a*) The islanders have means of teaching us their classifications, by pointing out similarities and differences which we had not noticed, or in which we had not been interested, in which case *both* classifications are genuine, and no rivalry between them, of a kind that can help the nominalist, could ever arise;

or (*b*) Their classification is arbitrary in the sense in which my use of the word "alpha" was arbitrary, in which case it is not a genuine classification.

It may be that the islanders classify trees as "boat-building trees," "house-building trees," etc., and that they are more concerned with the height, thickness, and maturity of the trees than they are with the distinctions of species that interest us.

In a particular case of *prima facie* conflict of classifications, we may not in fact be able to discover whether what appears to be a rival classification really *is* a classification. But we can be sure that *if* it is a classification *then* it is backed by objective similarities and differences, and that if it is *not* backed by objective similarities and differences then it is merely an arbitrary system of names. In no case will it appear that we must choose between rival systems of genuine classification of a set of objects in such a sense that one of them is to be recognized as *the* classification for all purposes.

There is no limit to the number of possible classifications of objects. (The nominalist is right about this.)[1]

There is no classification of any set of objects which is not objectively based on genuine similarities and differences. (The realist is right about this.)

The nominalist is so impressed by the infinite diversity of possible classifications that he is blinded by their objectivity.

The realist is so impressed by the objectivity of all genuine classifications that he underestimates their diversity.

Of course we may if we like say that there is one complete system of classification which marks all the similarities and all the differences. (This is the realist's summing up of what we can learn by giving critical attention to the realist and the nominalist in turn.)

Or we may say that there are only similarities and differences, from which we may choose according to our purposes and interests. (This is the nominalist's summing up.)

In talking of genuine or objective similarities and differences we must not forget that we are concerned with similarities and differences between *possible* cases as well as between actual cases, and indeed that we are concerned with the actual cases only because they are themselves a selection of the possible cases.

Because the nominalist and the realist are both right and both wrong, each is driven into the other's arms when he tries to be both consistent and faithful to our language, knowledge and experience. The nominalist talks of resemblances until he is pressed into a corner where he must acknowledge that resemblance is unintelligible except as resemblance *in a respect*, and to specify the respect in which objects resemble one another is to indicate a *quality* or *property*. The realist talks of properties and qualities until, when properties and qualities have been explained in terms of other properties and other qualities, he can at last do nothing but point to the *resemblances* between the objects that are said to be characterized by such and such a property or quality.

The question "Are resemblances ultimate or are properties ultimate?" is a perverse question if it is meant as one to which there must be a simple, *single* answer. They are both ultimate, or neither is ultimate. The craving for a single answer is the logically unsatisfiable craving for something that will be the ultimate terminus of explanation and will yet itself be explained.

NOTE

1. Here one may think of Wittgenstein's remark that "Every application of every word is arbitrary," which emphasizes that we can always find *some* distinction between any pair of objects, however closely similar they may be. What might be called the principle of the diversity of discernibles guarantees that we can never be *forced* to apply the same word to two different things.

Empiricism, Semantics, and Ontology[1]
Rudolf Carnap

THE PROBLEM OF ABSTRACT ENTITIES

Empiricists are in general rather suspicious with respect to any kind of abstract entities like properties, classes, relations, numbers, propositions, etc. They usually feel much more in sympathy with nominalists than with realists (in the medieval sense). As far as possible they try to avoid any reference to abstract entities and to restrict themselves to what is sometimes called a nominalistic language, i.e., one not containing such references. However, within certain scientific contexts it seems hardly possible to avoid them. In the case of mathematics, some empiricists try to find a way out by treating the whole of mathematics as a mere calculus, a formal system for which no interpretation is given or can be given. Accordingly, the mathematician is said to speak not about numbers, functions, and infinite classes, but merely about meaningless symbols and formulas manipulated according to given formal rules. In physics it is more difficult to shun the suspected entities, because the language of physics serves for the communication of reports and predictions and hence cannot be taken as a mere calculus. A physicist who is suspicious of abstract entities may perhaps try to declare a certain part of the language of physics as uninterpreted and uninterpretable, that part which re-

From *Meaning and Necessity,* 2nd. ed. (Chicago: University of Chicago Press, 1956), pp. 228–42. Copyright © 1956 by the University of Chicago Press. Reprinted by permission of the publisher.

fers to real numbers as space-time coordinates or as values of physical magnitudes, to functions, limits, etc. More probably he will just speak about all these things like anybody else but with an uneasy conscience, like a man who in his everyday life does with qualms many things which are not in accord with the high moral principles he professes on Sundays. Recently the problem of abstract entities has arisen again in connection with semantics, the theory of meaning and truth. Some semanticists say that certain expressions designate certain entities, and among these designated entities they include not only concrete material things but also abstract entities e.g., properties as designated by predicates and propositions as designated by sentences.[2] Others object strongly to this procedure as violating the basic principles of empiricism and leading back to a metaphysical ontology of the Platonic kind.

It is the purpose of this article to clarify this controversial issue. The nature and implications of the acceptance of a language referring to abstract entities will first be discussed in general; it will be shown that using such a language does not imply embracing a Platonic ontology but is perfectly compatible with empiricism and strictly scientific thinking. Then the special question of the role of abstract entities in semantics will be discussed. It is hoped that the clarification of the issue will be useful to those who would like to accept abstract entities in their work in mathematics, physics, semantics, or any other field; it may help them to overcome nominalistic scruples.

LINGUISTIC FRAMEWORKS

Are there properties, classes, numbers, propositions? In order to understand more clearly the nature of these and related problems, it is above all necessary to recognize a fundamental distinction between two kinds of questions concerning the existence or reality of entities. If someone wishes to speak in his language about a new kind of entities, he has to introduce a system of new ways of speaking, subject to new rules; we shall call this procedure the construction of a linguistic *framework* for the new entities in question. And now we must distinguish two kinds of questions of existence: first, questions of the existence of certain entities of the new kind *within the framework;* we call them *internal questions;* and second, questions concerning the existence or reality *of the system of entities as a whole,* called *external questions.* Internal questions and possible answers to them are formulated with the help of the new forms of expressions. The answers may be found either by purely logical methods or by empirical methods, depending upon whether the framework is a logical or a factual one. An external question is of a problematic character which is in need of closer examination.

The world of things. Let us consider as an example the simplest kind of entities dealt with in the everyday language: the spatio-temporally ordered system of observable things and events. Once we have accepted the thing language with its framework for things, we can raise and answer internal questions; e.g., "Is there a white piece of paper on my desk?" "Did King Arthur actually live?" "Are unicorns and centaurs real or merely imaginary?" and the like. These questions are to be answered by empirical investigations. Results of observations are evaluated according to certain rules as confirming or disconfirming evidence for possible answers. (This evaluation is usually carried out, of course, as a matter of habit rather than a deliberate, rational procedure. But it is possible, in a rational reconstruction, to lay down explicit rules for the evaluation. This is one of the main tasks of a pure, as distinguished from a psychological, epistemology.) The concept of reality occurring in these internal questions is an empirical, scientific, nonmetaphysical concept. To recognize something as a real thing or event means to succeed in incorporating it into the system of things at a particular space-time position so that it fits together with the other things recognized as real, according to the rules of the framework.

From these questions we must distinguish the external question of the reality of the thing world itself. In contrast to the former questions, this question is raised neither by the man in the street nor by scientists, but only by philosophers. Realists give an affirmative answer, subjective idealists a negative one, and the controversy goes on for centuries without ever being solved. And it cannot be solved because it is framed in a wrong way. To be real in the scientific sense means to be an element of the system; hence this concept cannot be meaningfully applied to the system itself. Those who raise the question of the reality of the thing world itself have perhaps in mind not a theoretical question as their formulation seems to suggest, but rather a practical question, a matter of a practical decision concerning the structure of our language. We have to make the choice whether or not to accept and use the forms of expression in the framework in question.

In the case of this particular example, there is usually no deliberate choice because we all have accepted the thing language early in our lives as a matter of course. Nevertheless, we may regard it as a matter of decision in this sense: we are free to choose to continue using the thing language or not; in the latter case we could restrict ourselves to a language of sense-data and other "phenomenal" entities, or construct an alternative to the customary thing language with another structure, or, finally, we could refrain from speaking. If someone decides to accept the thing language, there is no objection against saying that he has accepted the world of things. But this must not be interpreted as if it meant his acceptance of a *belief* in the reality of the thing world; there is no such belief or assertion or assumption, because it is not a theoretical question. To accept the thing world means nothing more than

to accept a certain form of language, in other words, to accept rules for forming statements and for testing, accepting, or rejecting them. The acceptance
of the thing language leads, on the basis of observations made, also to the
acceptance belief, and assertion of certain statements. But the thesis of the
reality of the thing world cannot be among these statements, because it cannot be formulated in the thing language, or it seems, in any other theoretical
language.

The decision of accepting the thing language, although itself not of a
cognitive nature, will nevertheless usually be influenced by theoretical knowledge, just like any other deliberate decision concerning the acceptance of
linguistic or other rules. The purposes for which the language is intended
to be used, for instance, the purpose of communicating factual knowledge,
will determine which factors are relevant for the decision. The efficiency,
fruitfulness, and simplicity of the use of the thing language may be among
the decisive factors. And the questions concerning these qualities are indeed
of a theoretical nature. But these questions cannot be identified with the question of realism. They are not yes-no questions but questions of degree. The
thing language in the customary form works indeed with a high degree of
efficiency for most purposes of everyday life. This is a matter of fact, based
upon the content of our experiences. However, it would be wrong to describe
this situation by saying: "The fact of the efficiency of the thing language is
confirming evidence for the reality of the thing world"; we should rather say
instead: "This fact makes it advisable to accept the thing language."

The system of numbers. As an example of a system which is of a logical
rather than a factual nature let us take the system of natural numbers. The
framework for this system is constructed by introducing into the language
new expressions with suitable rules: (1) numerals like "five" and sentence forms
like "there are five books on the table"; (2) the general term "number" for
the new entities, and sentence forms like "five is a number"; (3) expressions
for properties of numbers (e.g., "odd," "prime"), relations (e.g., "greater than"),
and functions (e.g., "plus"), and sentence forms like "two plus three is five";
(4) numerical variables ("m," "n," etc.) and quantifiers for universal sentences
("for every n, . . ." and existential sentences "there is an n such that . . .")
with the customary deductive rules.

Here again there are internal questions, e.g., "Is there a prime number
greater than a hundred?" Here, however, the answers are found, not by empirical investigation based on observations, but by logical analysis based on
the rules for the new expressions. Therefore the answers are here analytic,
i.e., logically true.

What is now the nature of the philosophical question concerning the
existence or reality of numbers? To begin with, there is the internal question
which, together with the affirmative answer, can be formulated in the new

terms, say by "There are numbers" or, more explicitly, "There is an n such that n is a number." This statement follows from the analytic statement "five is a number" and is therefore itself analytic. Moreover, it is rather trivial (in contradistinction to a statement like "there is a prime number greater than a million," which is likewise analytic but far from trivial), because it does not say more than that the new system is not empty; but this is immediately seen from the rule which states that words like "five" are substitutable for the new variables. Therefore nobody who meant the question "Are there numbers?" in the internal sense would either assert or even seriously consider a negative answer. This makes it plausible to assume that those philosophers who treat the question of the existence of numbers as a serious philosophical problem and offer lengthy arguments on either side, do not have in mind the internal question. And, indeed, if we were to ask them: "Do you mean the question as to whether the framework of numbers, *if* we were to accept it, would be found to be empty or not?" they would probably reply: "Not at all; we mean a question *prior* to the acceptance of the new framework." They might try to explain what they mean by saying that it is a question of the ontological status of numbers; the question whether or not numbers have a certain metaphysical characteristic called reality (but a kind of ideal reality, different from the material reality of the thing world) or subsistence or status of "independent entities." Unfortunately, these philosophers have so far not given a formulation of their question in terms of the common scientific language. Therefore our judgment must be that they have not succeeded in giving to the external question and to the possible answers any cognitive content. Unless and until they supply a clear cognitive interpretation, we are justified in our suspicion that their question is a pseudo-question, that is, one disguised in the form of a theoretical question while in fact it is nontheoretical; in the present case it is the practical problem whether or not to incorporate into the language the new linguistic forms which constitute the framework of numbers.

The system of propositions. New variables, "p," "q," etc., are introduced with a rule to the effect that any (declarative) sentence may be substituted for a variable of this kind; this includes, in addition to the sentences of the original thing language, also all general sentences with variables of any kind which may have been introduced into the language. Further, the general term "proposition" is introduced. "P is a proposition" may be defined by "p or not p" (or by any other sentence form yielding only analytic sentences). Therefore, every sentence of the form ". . . is a proposition" (where any sentence may stand in the place of the dots) is analytic. This holds, for example, for the sentence:

(a) "Chicago is large is a proposition."

(We disregard here the fact that the rules of English grammar require not a sentence but a that-clause as the subject of another sentence; accordingly, instead of (*a*) we should have to say "That Chicago is large is a proposition.") Predicates may be admitted whose argument expressions are sentences; these predicates may be either extensional (e.g., the customary truthfunctional connectives) or not (e.g., modal predicates like "possible," "necessary," etc.). With the help of the new variables, general sentences may be formed, e.g.,

(*b*) "For every *p*, either *p* or not-*p*."
(*c*) "There is a *p* such that *p* is not necessary and not-*p* is not necessary."
(*d*) "There is a *p* such that *p* is a proposition."

[Sentences] (*c*) and (*d*) are internal assertions of existence. The statement "There are propositions" may be meant in the sense of (*d*); in this case it is analytic [since it follows from (*a*)] and even trivial. If, however, the statement is meant in an external sense, then it is noncognitive.

It is important to notice that the system of rules for the linguistic expressions of the propositional framework (of which only a few rules have here been briefly indicated) is sufficient for the introduction of the framework. Any further explanations as to the nature of the propositions (i.e., the elements of the system indicated, the values of the variables "*p*," "*q*," etc.) are theoretically unnecessary because, if correct, they follow from the rules. For example, are propositions mental events (as in Russell's theory)? A look at the rules shows us that they are not, because otherwise existential statements would be of the form: "If the mental state of the person in question fulfills such and such conditions, then there is a *p* such that . . . ." The fact that no references to mental conditions occur in existential statements (like (*c*), (*d*), etc.) shows that propositions are not mental entities. Further, a statement of the existence of linguistic entities (e.g., expressions, classes of expressions, etc.) must contain a reference to a language. The fact that no such reference occurs in the existential statements here, shows that propositions are not linguistic entities. The fact that in these statements no reference to a subject (an observer or knower) occurs (nothing like: "There is a *p* which is necessary for Mr. *X*"), shows that the propositions (and their properties, like necessity, etc.) are not subjective. Although characterizations of these or similar kinds are, strictly speaking, unnecessary, they may nevertheless be practically useful. If they are given, they should be understood, not as ingredient parts of the system, but merely as marginal notes with the purpose of supplying to the reader helpful hints or convenient pictorial associations which may make his learning of the use of the expressions easier than the bare system of the rules would do. Such a characterization is analogous to an extra-systematic explanation which a physicist sometimes gives to the beginner. He might, for example, tell him to imagine the atoms of a gas as small balls rushing around with great speed, or the electromagnetic field and its oscillations as quasi-elastic tensions and vibrations in an ether. In fact, however, all that can accurately be said about atoms or the field is implicitly contained in the physical laws of the theories in question.[3]

The system of thing properties. The thing language contains words like "red," "hard," "stone," "house," etc., which are used for describing what things are like. Now we may introduce new variables, say "*f*," "*g*," etc., for which those words are substitutable and furthermore the general term "property." New rules are laid down which admit sentences like "Red is a property," "Red is a color," "These two pieces of paper have at least one color in common" (i.e., "There is an *f* such that *f* is a color, and . . ."). The last sentence is an internal assertion. It is of an empirical, factual nature. However, the external statement, the philosophical statement of the reality of properties— a special case of the thesis of the reality of universals—is devoid of cognitive content.

The systems of integers and rational numbers. Into a language containing the framework of natural numbers we may introduce first the (positive and negative) integers as relations among natural numbers and then the rational numbers as relations among integers. This involves introducing new types of variables, expressions substitutable for them, and the general terms "integer" and "rational number."

The system of real numbers. On the basis of the rational numbers, the real numbers may be introduced as classes of a special kind (segments) of rational numbers (according to the method developed by Dedekind and Frege). Here again a new type of variables is introduced, expressions substitutable for them (e.g., " $\sqrt{2}$ "), and the general term "real number."

The spatio-temporal coordinate system for physics. The new entities are the space-time points. Each is an ordered quadruple of four real numbers, called its coordinates, consisting of three spatial and one temporal coordinate. The physical state of a spatio-temporal point or region is described either with the help of qualitative predicates (e.g., "hot") or by ascribing numbers as values of a physical magnitude (e.g., mass, temperature, and the like). The step from the system of things (which does not contain space-time points but only extended objects with spatial and temporal relations between them) to the physical coordinate system is again a matter of decision. Our choice of certain features, although itself not theoretical, is suggested by theoretical knowledge, either logical or factual. For example, the choice of real numbers rather than rational numbers or integers as coordinates is not much influenced by the facts of experience but mainly due to considerations of mathematical simplicity. The restriction to rational coordinates would not be in conflict with any experimental knowledge we have, because the result of any measurement is a rational number. However, it would prevent the use of ordinary geometry (which says, e.g., that the diagonal of a square with the side 1 has the irrational value $\sqrt{2}$) and thus lead to great complications. On the other hand, the decision to use three rather than two or four spatial coordinates is strongly suggested, but still not forced upon us, by the result of common observations. If certain events allegedly observed in spiritualistic séances, eg., a ball moving out of a sealed box, were confirmed beyond any reasonable doubt, it might seem advisable to use four spatial coordinates. Internal questions are here, in general, empirical questions to be answered by empirical investigations. On the other hand, the external questions of the reality of physical space and physical time are pseudo-questions. A question like "Are there (really) space-time points?" is ambiguous. It may be meant as an internal question; there the affirmative answer is, of course, analytic and trivial. Or it may be meant in the external sense: "Shall we introduce such and such forms into our language?"; in this case it is not a theoretical but a practical question, a matter of decision rather than assertion, and hence the proposed formulation would be misleading. Or finally, it may be meant in the following sense: "Are our experiences such that the use of the linguistic forms in question will be expedient and fruitful?" This is a theoretical question of a factual, empirical nature. But it concerns a matter of degree; therefore a formulation in the form "real or not?" would be inadequate.

WHAT DOES ACCEPTANCE OF A KIND OF ENTITIES MEAN?

Let us now summarize the essential characteristics of situations involving the introduction of a new kind of entities, characteristics which are common to the various examples outlined above.

The acceptance of a new kind of entities is represented in the language by the introduction of a framework of new forms of expressions to be used according to a new set of rules. There may be new names for particular entities of the kind in question; but some such names may already occur in the language before the introduction of the new framework. (Thus, for example, the thing language contains certainly words of the type of "blue" and "house" before the framework of properties is introduced; and it may contain words like "ten" in sentences of the form "I have ten fingers" before the framework of numbers is introduced.) The latter fact shows that the occurrence of constants of the type in question—regarded as names of entities of the new kind after the new framework is introduced—is not a sure sign of the acceptance of the new kind of entities. Therefore the introduction of such constants is not to be regarded as an essential step in the introduction of the framework.

The two essential steps are rather the following. First, the introduction of a general term, a predicate of higher level, for the new kind of entities, permitting us to say of any particular entity that it belongs to this kind (e.g., "Red is a *property*," "Five is a *number*"). Second, the introduction of variables of the new type. The new entities are values of these variables: the constants (and the closed compound expressions, if any) are substitutable for the variables.[4] With the help of the variables, general sentences concerning the new entities can be formulated.

After the new forms are introduced into the language, it is possible to formulate with their help internal questions and possible answers to them. A question of this kind may be either empirical or logical; accordingly a true answer is either factually true or analytic.

From the internal questions we must clearly distinguish external questions, i.e., philosophical questions concerning the existence or reality of the total system of the new entities. Many philosophers regard a question of this kind as an ontological question which must be raised and answered *before* the introduction of the new language forms. The latter introduction, they believe, is legitimate only if it can be justified by an ontological insight supplying an affirmative answer to the question of reality. In contrast to this view, we take the position that the introduction of the new ways of speaking does not need any theoretical justification because it does not imply an assertion of reality. We may still speak (and have done so) of "the acceptance of the new entities" since this form of speech is customary; but one must keep in mind that this phrase does not mean for us anything more than acceptance of the new framework, i.e., of the new linguistic forms. Above all, it must not be interpreted as referring to an assumption, belief, or assertion of "the reality of the entities." There is no such assertion. An alleged statement of the reality of the system of entities is a pseudo-statement without cognitive content. To be sure, we have to face at this point an important question; but it is a practical, not a theoretical question; it is the question of whether or not to accept the new linguistic forms. The acceptance cannot be judged as being either true or false because it is not an assertion. It can only be judged as being more or less expedient, fruitful, conducive to the aim for which the language is intended. Judgments of this kind supply the motivation for the decision of accepting or rejecting the kind of entities.[5]

Thus it is clear that the acceptance of a linguistic framework must not be regarded as implying a metaphysical doctrine concerning the reality of the entities in question. It seems to me due to a neglect of this important distinction that some contemporary nominalists label the admission of variables of abstract types as "Platonism."[6] This is, to say the least, an extremely misleading terminology. It leads to the absurd consequence, that the position of everybody who accepts the language of physics with its real number variables (as a language of communication, not merely as a calculus) would be called Platonistic, even if he is a strict empiricist who rejects Platonic metaphysics.

A brief historical remark may here be inserted. The noncognitive character of the questions which we have called here external questions was recognized and emphasized already by the Vienna Circle under the leadership of Moritz Schlick, the group from which the movement of logical empiricism originated. Influenced by ideas of Ludwig Wittgenstein, the Circle rejected both the thesis of the reality of the external world and the thesis of its irreality as pseudo-statements;[7] the same was the case for both the thesis of the reality of universals (abstract entities, in our present terminology) and the nominalistic thesis that they are not real and that their alleged names are not names of anything but merely *flatus vocis*. (It is obvious that the apparent negation of a pseudo-statement must also be a pseudo-statement.) It is therefore not correct to classify the members of the Vienna Circle as nominalists, as is sometimes done. However, if we look at the basic anti-metaphysical and pro-scientific attitude of most nominalists (and the same holds for many materialists and realists in the modern sense), disregarding their occasional pseudo-theoretical formulations, then it is, of course, true to say that the Vienna Circle was much closer to those philosophers than to their opponents.

ABSTRACT ENTITIES IN SEMANTICS

The problem of the legitimacy and the status of abstract entities has recently again led to controversial discussions in connection with semantics. In a semantical meaning analysis certain expressions in a language are often said to designate (or name or denote or signify or refer to) certain extra-linguistic entities.[8] As long as physical things or events (e.g., Chicago or Caesar's death) are taken as designata (entities designated), no serious doubts arise. But strong objections have been raised, especially by some empiricists, against abstract entities as designata, e.g., against semantical statements of the following kind:

(1) "The word 'red' designates a property of things";
(2) "The word 'color' designates a property of properties of things";
(3) "The word 'five' designates a number";
(4) "The word 'odd' designates a property of numbers";
(5) "The sentence 'Chicago is large' designates a proposition."

Those who criticize these statements do not, of course, reject the use of the expressions in question, like "red" or "five"; nor would they deny that these expressions are meaningful. But to be meaningful, they would say, is not the same as having a meaning in the sense of an entity designated. They reject the belief, which they regard as implicitly presupposed by those semantical statements, that to each expression of the types in question (adjectives like "red," numerals like "five," etc.) there is a particular real entity to which the expression stands in the relation of designation. This belief is rejected as incompatible with the basic principles of empiricism or of scientific thinking. Derogatory labels like "Platonic realism," "hypostatization," or " 'Fido'-Fido principle" are attached to it. The latter is the name given by Gilbert Ryle to the criticized belief, which, in his view, arises by a naïve inference of analogy: just as there is an entity well known to me, viz. my dog Fido, which is designated by the name "Fido," thus there must be for every meaningful expression a particular entity to which it stands in the relation of designation or naming, i.e., the relation exemplified by "Fido"-Fido. The belief criticized is thus a case of hypostatization, i.e., of treating as names expressions which are not names. While "Fido" is a name, expressions like "red," "five," etc., are said not to be names, not to designate anything.

Our previous discussion concerning the acceptance of frameworks enables us now to clarify the situation with respect to abstract entities as designata. Let us take as an example the statement:

(a) " 'Five' designates a number."

The formulation of this statement presupposes that our language L contains the forms of expressions which we have called the framework of numbers, in particular, numerical variables and the general term "number." If L contains these forms, the following is an analytic statement in L:

(b) "Five is a number."

Further, to make the statement (a) possible, L must contain an expression like "designates" or "is a name of" for the semantical relation of designation. If suitable rules for this term are laid down, the following is likewise analytic:

(c) " 'Five' designates five."

(Generally speaking, any expression of the form " '. . .' designates . . . " is an analytic statement provided the term ". . ." is a constant in an accepted framework. If the latter condition is not fulfilled, the expression is not a statement.) Since (a) follows from (c) and (b), (a) is likewise analytic.

Thus it is clear that *if* someone accepts the framework of numbers, then he must acknowledge (c) and (b) and hence (a) as true statements. Generally speaking, if someone accepts a framework for a certain kind of entities, then he is bound to admit the entities as possible designata. Thus the question of the admissibility of entities of a certain type or of abstract entities in general as designata is reduced to the question of the acceptability of the linguistic framework for those entities. Both the nominalistic critics, who refuse the status of designators or names to expressions like "red," "five," etc., because they deny the existence of abstract entities, and the skeptics, who express doubts concerning the existence and demand evidence for it, treat the question of existence as a theoretical question. They do, of course, not mean the internal question; the affirmative answer to *this* question is analytic and trivial and too obvious for doubt or denial, as we have seen. Their doubts refer rather to the system of entities itself; hence they mean the external question. They believe that only after making sure that there really is a system of entities or the kind in question are we justified in accepting the framework by incorporating the linguistic forms into our language. However, we have seen that the external question is not a theoretical question but rather the practical question whether or not to accept those linguistic forms. This acceptance is not in need of a theoretical justification (except with respect to expediency and fruitfulness), because it does not imply a belief or assertion. Ryle says that the "Fido"-Fido principle is "a grotesque theory." Grotesque or not, Ryle is wrong in calling it a theory. It is rather the practical decision to accept certain frameworks. Maybe Ryle is historically right with respect to those whom he mentions as previous representatives of the principle, viz. John Stuart Mill. Frege, and Russell. If these philosophers regarded the acceptance of a system of entities as a theory, an assertion, they were victims of the same old, metaphysical confusion. But it is certainly wrong to regard *my* semantical method as involving a belief in the reality of abstract entities, since I reject a thesis of this kind as a metaphysical pseudo-statement.

The critics of the use of abstract entities in semantics overlook the fundamental difference between the acceptance of a system of entities and an internal assertion, e.g., an assertion that there are elephants or electrons or prime numbers greater than a million. Whoever makes an internal assertion is certainly obliged to justify it by providing evidence, empirical evidence in the case of electrons, logical proof in the case of the prime numbers. The demand for a theoretical justification, correct in the case of internal assertions, is sometimes wrongly applied to the acceptance of a system of entities. Thus, for example, Ernest Nagel asks for "evidence relevant for affirming with warrant that there are such entities as infinitesimals or propositions." He characterizes the evidence required in these cases—in distinction to the empirical evidence in the case of electrons—as "in the broad sense logical and dialectical." Beyond this no hint is given as to what might be regarded as relevant evidence. Some nominalists regard the acceptance of abstract entities as a kind of superstition or myth, populating the world with fictitious or at least dubious entities, analogous to the belief in centaurs or demons. This shows again the confusion mentioned, because a superstition or myth is a false (or dubious) internal statement.

Let us take as example the natural numbers as cardinal numbers, i.e., in contexts like "Here are three books." The linguistic forms of the framework of numbers, including variables and the general term "number," are generally used in our common language of communication; and it is easy to formulate explicit rules for their use. Thus the logical characteristics of this framework are sufficiently clear (while many internal questions, i.e., arithmetical questions, are, of course, still open). In spite of this, the controversy concerning the external question of the ontological reality of the system of numbers continues. Suppose that one philosopher says: "I believe that there are numbers as real entities. This gives me the right to use the linguistic forms of the numerical framework and to make semantical statements about numbers as designata of numerals." His nominalistic opponent replies: "You are wrong: there are no numbers. The numerals may still be used as meaningful expressions. But they are not names, there are no entities designated by them. Therefore the word "number" and numerical variables must not be used (unless a way were found to introduce them as merely abbreviating devices, a way of translating them into the nominalistic thing language)." I cannot think of any possible evidence that would be regarded as relevant by both philosophers, and therefore, if actually found, would decide the controversy or at least make one of the opposite theses more probable than the other. (To construe the numbers as classes or properties of the second level, according to the Frege-Russell method, does, of course, not solve the controversy, because the first philosopher would affirm and the second deny the existence of the system of classes or properties of the second level.) Therefore I feel compelled to regard the external question as a pseudo-question, until both parties to the controversy offer a common interpretation of the question as a cognitive question; this would involve an indication of possible evidence regarded as relevant by both sides.

There is a particular kind of misinterpretation of the acceptance of abstract entities in various fields of science and in semantics, that needs to be cleared up. Certain early British empiricists (e.g., Berkeley and Hume) denied the existence of abstract entities on the ground that immediate experience presents us only with particulars, not with universals, e.g., with this red patch, but not with Redness or Color-in-General; with this scalene triangle, but not with Scalene Triangularity or Triangularity-in-General. Only entities belonging to a type of which examples were to be found within immediate experience could be accepted as ultimate constituents of reality. Thus, according to this way of thinking, the existence of abstract entities could be asserted only if one could show either that some abstract entities fall within the given, or that abstract entities can be defined in terms of the types of entities which are given. Since these empiricists found no abstract entities within the realm of sense-data, they either denied their existence, or else made a futile attempt to define universals in terms of particulars. Some contemporary philosophers, especially English philosophers following Bertrand Russell think in basically similar terms. They emphasize a distinction between the data (that which is immediately given in consciousness, e.g., sense-data, immediately past experiences, etc.) and the constructs based on the data. Existence or reality is ascribed only to the data; the constructs are not real entities; the corresponding linguistic expressions are merely ways of speech not actually designating anything (reminiscent of the nominalists' *flatus vocis*). We shall not criticize here this general conception. (As far as it is a principle of accepting certain entities and not accepting others, leaving aside any ontological, phenomenalistic and nominalistic pseudo-statements, there cannot be any theoretical objection to it.) But if this conception leads to the view that other philosophers or scientists who accept abstract entities thereby assert or imply their occurrence as immediate data, then such a view must be rejected as a misinterpretation. References to space-time points, the electro-magnetic field, or electrons in physics, to real or complex numbers and their functions in mathematics, to the excitatory potential or unconscious complexes in psychology, to an inflationary trend in economics, and the like, do not imply the assertion that entities of these kinds occur as immediate data. And the same holds for references to abstract entities as designata in semantics. Some of the criticisms by English philosophers against such references give the impression that, probably due to the misinterpretation just indicated, they accuse the semanticist not so much of bad metaphysics (as some nominalists would do) but of bad psychology. The fact that they regard a semantical method involving abstract entities not merely as doubtful and perhaps wrong, but as manifestly absurd, preposterous and grotesque, and that they show a deep horror and indignation against this method, is perhaps to be explained by a misinterpretation of the kind described. In fact, of course, the semanticist does not in the least assert or imply that the abstract entities to which he refers can be experienced as immediately given either by sensation or by a kind of rational intuition. An assertion of this kind would indeed be very dubious psychology. The psychological question as to which kinds of entities do and which do not occur as immediate data is entirely irrelevant for semantics, just as it is for physics, mathematics, economics, etc., with respect to the examples mentioned above.[9]

CONCLUSION

For those who want to develop or use semantical methods, the decisive question is not the alleged ontological question of the existence of abstract entities but rather the question whether the use of abstract linguistic forms or, in technical terms, the use of variables beyond those for things (or phenomenal data), is expedient and fruitful for the purposes for which semantical analyses are made, viz. the analysis, interpretation, clarification, or construction of languages of communication, especially languages of science. This question is here neither decided nor even discussed. It is not a question simply of yes or no, but a matter of degree. Among those philosophers who have carried out semantical analyses and thought about suitable tools for this work, beginning with Plato and Aristotle and, in a more technical way on the basis of modern logic, with C. S. Peirce and Frege, a great majority accepted abstract entities. This does, of course, not prove the case. After all, semantics in the technical sense is still in the initial phases of its development, and we must be prepared for possible fundamental changes in methods. Let us therefore admit that the nominalistic critics may possibly be right. But if so, they will have to offer better arguments than they have so far. Appeal to ontological insight will not carry much weight. The critics will have to show that it is possible to construct a semantical method which avoids all references to abstract entities and achieves by simpler means essentially the same results as the other methods.

The acceptance or rejection of abstract linguistic forms, just as the acceptance or rejection of any other linguistic forms in any branch of science, will finally be decided by their efficiency as instruments, the ratio of the results achieved to the amount and complexity of the efforts required. To decree dogmatic prohibitions of certain linguistic forms instead of testing them by their success or failure in practical use, is worse than futile; it is positively harmful because it may obstruct scientific progress. The history of science shows examples of such prohibitions based on prejudices deriving from religious, mythological, metaphysical, or other irrational sources, which slowed up the developments for shorter or longer periods of time. Let us learn from the lessons of history. Let us grant to those who work in any special field of investigation the freedom to use any form of expression which seems useful to them; the work in the field will sooner or later lead to the elimination of those forms which have no useful function. *Let us be cautious in making assertions and critical in examining them, but tolerant in permitting linguistic forms.*

NOTES

1. I have made here some minor changes in the formulations to the effect that the term "framework" is now used only for the system of linguistic exressions, and not for the system of the entities in question.

2. The terms "sentence" and "statement" are here used synonymously for declarative (indicative, propositional) sentences.

3. In my book *Meaning and Necessity* (Chicago, 1947) I have developed a semantical method which takes propositions as entities designated by sentences (more specifically, as intensions of sentences). In order to facilitate the understanding of the systematic development, I added some informal, extra-systematic explanations concerning the nature of propositions. I said that the term "proposition" "is used neither for a linguistic expression nor for a subjective, mental occurrence, but rather for something objective that may or may not be exemplified in nature . . . . We apply the term 'proposition' to any entities of a certain logical type, namely, those that may be expressed by (declarative) sentences in a language" (p. 27). After some more detailed discussions concerning the relation between propositions and facts, and the nature of false propositions, I added: "It has been the purpose of the preceding remarks to facilitate the understanding of our conception of propositions. If, however, a reader should find these explanations more puzzling than clarifying, or even unacceptable, he may disregard them" (p. 31) (that is, disregard these extra-systematic explanations, not the whole theory of the propositions as intensions of sentences, as one reviewer understood). In spite of this warning, it seems that some of those readers who were puzzled by the explanations, did not disregard them but thought that by raising objections against them they could refute the theory. This is analogous to the procedure of some laymen who by (correctly) criticizing the ether picture or other visualizations of physical theories, thought they had refuted those theories. Perhaps the discussions in the present paper will help in clarifying the role of the system of linguistic rules for the introduction of a framework for entities on the one hand, and that of extra-systematic explanations concerning the nature of the entities on the other.

4. W. V. Quine was the first to recognize the importance of the introduction of variables as indicating the acceptance of entities. "The ontology to which one's use of language commits him comprises simply the objects that he treats as falling . . . within the range of values of his variables ["Notes on Existence and Necessity," *Journal of Philosophy* 40 (1943): 118; compared also his "Designation and Existence," *Journal of Philosophy* 36 (1939), and "On Universals," *Journal of Symbolic Logic* 12 (1947).]

5. For a closely related point of view on these questions see the detailed discussions in Herbert Feigl, "Existential Hypotheses," *Philosophy of Science* 17 (1950): 35–62.

6. Paul Bernays, "Sur le platonisme dans les mathématiques" *L'Enseignement math.*, 34 (1935: 52–69. W. V. Quine, see previous footnote and a recent paper, "On What There Is." Quine does not acknowledge the distinction which I emphasize above, because according to his general conception there are no sharp boundary lines between

logical and factual truth, between questions of meaning and questions of fact, between the acceptance of a language structure and the acceptance of an assertion formulated in the language. This conception, which seems to deviate considerably from customary ways of thinking, will be explained in his article ["Semantics and Abstract Objects," *Proceedings of the American Academy of Arts and Sciences* 80 (1951)]. When Quine in the article ["On What There Is"] classifies my logicistic conception of mathematics (derived from Frege and Russell) as "platonic realism" (p. 224), this is meant (according to a personal communication from him) not as ascribing to me agreement with Plato's metaphysical doctrine of universals, but merely as referring to the fact that I accept a language of mathematics containing variables of higher levels. With respect to the basic attitude to take in choosing a language form (an "ontology" in Quine's terminology, which seems to me misleading), there appears now to be agreement between us: "the obvious counsel is tolerance and an experimental spirit" ["On What There is," p. 227.]

7. See Carnap, *Scheinprobleme in der Philosophie; das Fremdpsychische und der Realismusstreit*, Berlin, 1928. Moritz Schlick, *Positivismus und Realismus,* reprinted in *Gesammelte Aufsätze*, Wien, 1938.

8. See *Introduction to Semantics* (1943); *Meaning and Necessity* (Chicago, 1947). The distinction I have drawn in the latter book between the method of the name-relation and the method of intention and extension is not essential for our present discussion. The term "designation" is used in the present article in a neutral way; it may be understood as referring to the name-relation or to the intention-relation or to the extension-relation or to any similar relations used in other semantic methods.

9. Wilfrid Sellars ("Acquaintance and Description Again," in *Journal of Philosophy,* 46 [1949]: 496–504; see pp. 502ff.) analyzes clearly the roots of the mistake "of taking the designation relation of semantic theory to be a reconstruction of *being present to an experience.*"

Select Bibliography

BOOKS AND COLLECTIONS

Aaron, R. I. *The Theory of Universals* (2nd ed., Oxford and New York, 1967).

Allan, D. J. *The Philosophy of Aristotle* (Oxford and New York, 1952).

Anscombe, G. E. M. and Geach, P. T. *Three Philosophers* (Oxford and New York, 1961).

Aristotle. *De Interpretatione*, translated by J. L. Ackrill (Oxford and New York, 1963).

Bambrough, R. ed. *New Essays on Plato and Aristotle* (London and New York, 1965).

Bochenski, J. M.; Church, A.; and Goodman, N. *The Problem of Universals* (Notre Dame, Ind., 1956).

Butchkarov, P. K. *Resemblance and Identity* (Bloomington, Ind., 1966).

Cohen, L. J. *The Diversity of Meaning* (London, 1962).

Crombie, I. M. *An Examination of Plato's Doctrines*, Vol. 2 (London and New York, 1963).

Frege, G. *Philosophical Writings*, translated and edited by P. T. Geach and M. Black (Oxford, 1952).

Geache, P. T. *Mental Acts* (London and New York, 1957).

———. *Reference and Generality* (Cornell, N.Y., 1962).

Goodman, N. *The Structure of Appearance* (Cambridge, Mass., 1951).

Holloway, J. *Language and Intelligence* (London, 1955).

Hume, D. "Introduction," *Treatise of Human Nature*, edited by A. D. Lindsay (London and New York, 1960).

Joske, W. D. *Material Objects* (London and New York, 1967).

Kovesi, J. *Moral Notions* (London and New York, 1967), chapters 1, 2, and 3.

Kung, G. *Ontology and the Logistic Analysis of Language* (Dordrecht, Holland, and New York, 1967).

Locke, J. *An Essay Concerning Human Understanding*, 2 vols., edited by J. W. Yolton (London, 1961). Abridged editions by A. S. Pringle Pattison (London and New York, 1924) and A. D. Woozley (London and New York, 1964).

Loux, M. J. ed. *Universals and Particulars* (New York, 1970).

Luschei, E. C. *The Logical Systems of Lesniewski* (Amsterdam and New York, 1962).

Passmore, J. *Philosophical Reasoning* (London and New York, 1961).

Plato. *Parmenides*, translated with commentary by F. M. Cornford in *Plato and Parmenides* (London, 1939).

———. *Phaedo*, translated by H. Tredennick in *The Last Days of Socrates* (Baltimore, Md., 1954).

Price, H. H. *Thinking and Experience* (London and New York, 1953).

Quine, W. V. *Word and Object* (Cambridge, Mass., 1960).

———. *Ontological Relativity and Other Essays* (New York, 1969).

Robinson, R. *Plato's Earlier Dialectic* (Oxford and New York, 1950).

Russell, B. *The Problems of Philosophy* (London and New York, 1912).

———. *The Analysis of Matter* (London and New York, 1927).

———. *Inquiry into Meaning and Truth* (London and Baltimore, 1956).

———. *Introduction to Mathematical Philosophy* (London and New York, 1930).

Searle, J. R. *Speech Acts* (Cambridge, England; and New York, 1969).

Shwayder, D. S. *The Modes of Referring and the Problem of Universals* (Berkeley, Calif., 1961).

Stout, G. F. *The Nature of Universals and Propositions* (London, 1921).

Strawson, P. F. *Individuals* (London and New York, 1959).

Wittgenstein, L. *The Blue and Brown Books* (Oxford and New York, 1958).

———. *Philosophical Investigations*, 2nd ed., translated by G. E. M. Anscombe (Oxford and New York, 1963).

Woolhouse, R. S. *Locke's Philosophy of Science and Knowledge* (Oxford and New York, 1971).

Woozley, A. D. *Theory of Knowledge* (London and New York, 1949).

Zabech, F. *Universals* (The Hague, 1966).

ARTICLES

Aaron, R. I. "Locke's Theory of Universals," *Proceedings of the Aristotelian Society* 33 (1932–33).

Aaron, R. I. "Two Senses of 'Universal,' " *Mind* 48 (1939).

———. "Hume's Theory of Universals," *Proceedings of the Aristotelian Society* 42 (1941–42).

Acton, H. B. "The Theory of Concrete Universals," I, *Mind* 45, no. 9 (1936); II, *Mind* 46 (1937).

Aldrich, V. C. "Colors as Universals," *Philosophical Review* 41 (1952).

Allaire, E. B. "Existence, Independence, and Universals," *Philosophical Review* 69 (1960).

Alston, W. P. "Ontological Commitments," *Philosophical Studies* (Minnesota) 9 (1958).

Ayer, A. J. "Universals and Particulars," *Proceedings of the Aristotelian Society* 34 (1933–34).

Ayer, A. J. "On What There Is," *Aristotelian Society Supplementary* volume (1951).

Bacon, J. "Ontological Commitment and Free Logic," *Monist* 53 (1970).

Baylis, C. A. "Meanings and Their Exemplifications," *Journal of Philosophy* 47 (1930).

———. "Universals, Communicable Knowledge, and Metaphysics," *Journal of Philosophy* 48 (1953). Also in M. J. Loux, ed., *Universals and Particulars* (New York, 1970).

———. "Logical Subjects and Physical Objects," *Philosophy and Phenomenological Research* 17 (1957).

Bennett, J. "Substance, Reality and Primary Qualities," *American Philosophical Quarterly* 2 (1965).

Bergmann, G. "Particularity and the New Nominalism," *Methodos* 6 (1954).

———. "Strawson's Ontology," *Journal of Philosophy* 58 (1961).

Bemays, P. "On Platonism in Mathematics," in Benacerraf and Putnam, eds., *Philosophy of Mathematics* (Englewood Cliffs, N.J., 1964).

Black, M. "The Elusiveness of Sets," *Review of Metaphysics* 24 (1971).

Bochenski, I. M., "The Problem of Universals," in Bochenski, Church, and Goodman, *The Problem of Universals* (Notre Dame, Ind., 1956).

Braithwaite, R. B. "Universals and the 'Method of Analysis,' " *Aristotelian Society Supplementary* 6 (1926).

Brandt, R. B. "The Languages of Realism and Nominalism," *Philosophy and Phenomenological Research* 17 (1957).

Brody, B. A. "Natural Kinds and Essences," *Journal of Philosophy* 64 (1967).

Butchkarov, P. K. "Concrete Entities and Concrete Relations," *Review of Metaphysics* 10 (1957).

Campbell, K. "Family Resemblance Predicates," *American Philosophical Quarterly* 2 (1965).

Carmichael, P. "Derivation of Universals," *Philosophy and Phenomenological Research* 8 (1948).

Carnap, R. "Empiricism, Semantics, and Ontology," *Review Internationale de Philosophie* 11 (1950). Also reprinted in *Meaning and Necessity*, 2nd ed. (Chicago, 1956).

———. "The Methodological Character of Theoretical Concepts," *Minnesota Studies in the Philosophy of Science* 1 (Minneapolis, 1956).

Chomsky, N., and Scheffler, I. "What Is Said to Be," *Proceedings of the Aristotelian Society* 59 (1958–59).

Church, A. "Propositions and Sentences," in *The Problem of Universals* (Notre Dame, Ind., 1956).

———. "Ontological Commitment," *Journal of Philosophy* 55 (1963).

Cooper, N. "Ontological Commitment," *Monist* 50 (1966).

Cornman, J. W. "Language and Ontology," *Australasian Journal of Psychology and Philosophy* 41 (1963).

Darrant, M. "Feature Universals and Sortal Universals," *Analysis* 139 (1970).

Dawes-Hicks, G. "Are the Characteristics of Particular Things Universal or Particular?" *Aristotelian Society Supplementary* 3 (1923).

Donagan, A. "Universals and Metaphysical Realism," *Monist* 47, no. 2 (1963). Also in M. J. Loux, ed., *Universals and Particulars.*

Ducasse, C. J. "Some Critical Comments on a Nominalistic Analysis of Resemblance," *Philosophical Review* 49 (1940).

Dummett, M. "Nominalism," *Philosophical Review* 65 (1940).

———. "Truth," *Proceedings of the Aristotelian Society* 59 (1950).

Duncan-Jones, A. E. "Universals and Particulars," *Proceedings of the Aristotelian Society* 34 (1933–34).

Emmett, E. R. "Philosophy of Resemblances," *Philosophy* 39 (1954).

Ewing, A. C. "The Problem of Universals," *Philosophical Quarterly* 21, no. 84 (1971).

Frege, G. "Concept and Object," translated in *Philosophical Writings*, edited by P. T. Geach and M. Black (Oxford, 1952).

Furlong, E. J.; Mace, C. A.; and O'Connor, D. J. "Abstract Ideas and Images," *Aristotelian Society Supplementary* 27 (1953).

Gasking, D. "Clusters," *Australasian Journal of Psychology and Philosophy* 38 (1960).

Geach, P. T. "On What There Is," *Aristotelian Society Supplementary* volume (1951).

———. "What Actually Exists," *Aristotelian Society Supplementary* 42 (1968).

Ginascol, F. H. "The Question of Universals and Problems of Faith and Reason," *Philosophical Quarterly* 9 (1959).

Goddard, L. "Predicates, Relations and Categories," *Australasian Journal of Psychology and Philosophy* 44 (1966).

Goodman, N. "A World of Individuals," in *The Problem of Universals* (Notre Dame, Ind., 1956).

———. "On Relations that Generate," *Philosophical Studies* 9 (1958). Also in Benacerraf and Putnam, eds., *Philosophy of Mathematics* (Englewood Cliffs, N.J., 1964).

Goodman, N., and Quine, W. V. "Steps towards a Constructive Nominalism," *Journal of Symbolic Logic* 12 (1947).

Haack, R. J. "Natural and Arbitrary Classes," *Australasian Journal of Philosophy* 47 (1969).

Hacking, L. "A Language without Particulars," *Mind* 77 (1968).

Hartshorne, C. "Are There Absolutely Specific Universals?" *Journal of Philosophy* 68, no. 3 (1971).

Hintikka, J. "Existential Presuppositions and Existential Commitments," *Journal of Philosophy* 56 (1959).

Jones, J. R. "Are the Qualities of Particular Things Universal or Particular?" *Philosophical Review* 58 (1949).

———. "What Do We Mean by an 'Instance'?" *Analysis* XI (1950).

———. "Characters and Resemblance," *Philosophical Review* 60 (1951).

Joseph, H. W. "Universals and the 'Method of Analysis,' " *Aristotelian Society Supplementary* 6 (1926).

Kearns, J. T. "Sameness and Similarity," discussion with B. Blanshard, *Philosophy and Phenomenological Research* 29 (1969).

Khatchadourian, H. "Common Names and 'Family Resemblances,' " *Philosophy and Phenomenological Research* 18 (1958).

Khatchadourian, H. "Natural Objects and Common Names," *Methodos* 13 (1961).

Klemke, E. A. "Universals and Particulars in a Phenomenalist Ontology," *Philosopny of Science* 27 (1960).

Knight, H. "A Note on the Problem of Universals,' " *Analysis* 1 (1933).

Knight, T. A. "Questions and Universals," *Philosophy and Phenomenological Research* 27 (1966).

Korner, S. "On Determinables and Resemblances," *Aristotelian Society Supplementary* 33 (1959).

Kultgen, J. H. "Universals, Particular, and Change," *Review of Metaphysics* 9 (1956).

Lazerowitz, M. "The Existence of Universals," *Mind* 15 (1946).

Leonard, H. S. "Essences, Attributes and Predicates," *Proceedings and Addresses of the American Philosophical Association* 37 (1964).

Lloyd, A. C. "On Arguments for Real Universals," *Analysis* 11 (1951).

Lomansky, L. "Nominalism, Replication and Nelson Goodman," *Analysis* 29 (1968–69).

Long, P. "Are Predicates and Relational Expressions Incomplete?" *Philosophical Review* 78 (1969).

Loux, M. J. " 'The Problem of Universals,' " in M. J. Loux, ed., *Universals and Particulars* (New York, 1970).

Manser, A. R. "Games and Family Resemblances," *Philosophy* (1967).

Margolis, J. "Some Ontological Policies," *Monist* 53 (1970).

McCloskey, H. J. "The Philosophy of Linguistic Analysis and the Problem of Universals," *Philosophy and Phenomenological Research* 24 (1964).

Mei, T. L. "Chinese Grammar and the Linguistic Movement in Philosophy," *Review of Metaphysics* 14, No. 3 (1961).

———. "Subject and Predicate: A Grammatical Preliminary," *Philosophical Review* 00 (1961).

Moore, G. E. "Are the Characteristics of Particular Things Universal or Particular?" *Aristotelian Society Supplementary* 3 (1923).

Moravscik, J. "Strawson on Ontological Priority," in R. J. Butler, ed., *Analytical Philosophy* (Oxford and New York, 1965).

Ockham, William of. "The Problem of Universals," translated by P. Boehner from *Ockham: Philosophical Writings* (Saint Bonaventure, N.Y., 1957).

O'Connor, D. J. "On Resemblance," *Proceedings of the Aristotelian Society* 46 (1945–46).

———. "Stout's Theory of Universals," *Australasian Journal for Psychology and Philosophy* 27 (1949).

———. "Names and Universals," *Proceedings of the Aristotelian Society* 53 (1952–53).

O'Shaughnessy, R. J. "On Having Something in Common," *Mind* 79, no. 315 (1970).

Pap, A. "Nominalism, Empiricism, and Universals," I, *Philosophical Quarterly* 9 (1959); II, *Philosophical Quarterly* 10 (1960).

Parsons, C. "Ontology and Mathematics," *Philosophical Review* 80 (1971).

Parsons, T. "Ontological Commitment," *Journal of Philosophy* 64 (1967).

Parsons, T. "Criticism of 'Are Predicates and Relational Expressions Incomplete?' " *Philosophical Review* 79 (1970).

Peats, D. F. "Universals," *Philosophical Quarterly* 1 (1951).

———. "A Critical Study of P. F. Strawson's *Individuals*," I, II, *Philosophical Quarterly* 11 (1961).

Phillips, E. D. "On Instances," *Analysis* 1 (1934).

Pompa, L. "Family Resemblances," *Philosophical Quarterly* 17 (1967).

Prior, A. N. "Determinables, Determinates, and Determinates," I, II, *Mind* 58 (1949).

Quine, W. V. "On Universals," *Journal of Symbolic Logic* 12 (1947).

———. "On Carnap's Views on Ontology," *Philosophical Studies* 2 (1951).

———. "Ontology and Ideology," *Philosophical Studies* 2 (1951).

———. "A Logistical Approach to the Ontological Problem," in W. V. Quine, *The Ways of Paradox* (New York, 1966).

———. "Russell's Ontological Development," *Journal of Philosophy* 63 (1966).

Quinton, A. "Properties and Classes," *Proceedings of the Aristotelian Society* 58 (1957-58).

Ramsey, F. P. "Universals and the 'Method of Analyses,' " *Aristotelian Society Supplementary* 6 (1926).

———. "Universals," in F. P. Ramsey, *Foundations of Mathematics* (New York, 1931).

Rankin, K. W. "The Duplicity of Plato's Third Man," *Mind* 77 (1969).

———. "Is the Third Man Argument an Inconsistent Trial?" *Philosophical Quarterly* 20, No. 81 (1970).

Raphael, D. D. "Universals, Resemblance, and Identity," *Proceedings of the Aristotelian Society* 55 (1954-55).

Roma, E., and Thomas, S. B. "Nominalism and the Distinguishable Is Separable Principle," *Philosophy and Phenomenological Research* 28 (1968).

Russell, B. "On the Relations of Universals and Particulars," *Proceedings of the Aristotelian Society* 12 (1911-12).

Ryle, G. "Systematically Misleading Expressions," *Proceedings of the Aristotelian Society* 32 (1931-32).

Sachs, D. "Does Aristotle Have a Doctrine of Secondary Substances?" *Mind* 18 (1948).

Scheffler, I., and Chomsky, N. "What Is Said to Be," *Proceedings of the Aristotelian Society* 59 (1958-59).

Searle, J. R. "On Determinables and Resemblance," *Aristotelian Society Supplementary* volume (1959).

Sellars, W. "Logical Subjects and Physical Objects," *Philosophy and Phenomenological Research* 17 (1957).

———. "Grammar and Existence: A Preface to Ontology," *Mind* 69 (1960).

———. "Abstract Entities," *Review of Metaphysics* 16 (1963).

Simon, M. A. "When Is a Resemblance a Family Resemblance?" *Mind* 78 (1969).

Sinisi, V. F. "Nominalism and Common Names," *Philosophical Review* 71 (1962).

Smith, N. K. "The Nature of Universals," I, II, III, *Mind* 36 (1927).

Sommers, F. "Types and Ontology," *Philosophical Review* 72 (1963). Also in P. F. Strawson, ed., *Philosophical Logic* (Oxford and New York, 1967).

Stoothoff, R. H. "What Actually Exists," *Aristotelian Society Supplementary* 42 (1968).

Stout, G. F. "Things, Predicates, and Relations," *Australasian Journal of Psychology and Philosophy* 18 (1940).

———. "Are the Characteristics of Particular Things Universal or Particular?" *Aristotelian Society Supplementary* 42 (1968).

Strawson, P. F. "Particular and General," *Proceedings of the Aristotelian Society* 64 (1953–54).

———. "Singular Terms and Predication," *Journal of Philosophy* 58 (1961).

———. "The Asymmetry of Subjects and Predicates," in *Language, Belief and Metaphysics* (Vol. I of *Contemporary Philosophic Thought*, edited by H. E. Kiefer and M. K. Munitz [New York, 1970], and P. F. Strawson, *Logico-Linguistic Papers* (London, 1971).

Stroll, A. "Meaning, Referring and the Problem of Universals," *Inquiry* 4 (1961).

Taylor, C. C. W. "Forms as Causes in the *Phaedo*," *Mind* 78 (1969).

Teichmann, J. "Universals and Common Properties," *Analysis* 29 (1968–69).

Thomas, W. J. "Platonism and the Skolem Paradox," *Analysis* 28 (1967–68).

Thompson, M. H. "Abstract Entities," *Philosophical Review* 69 (1960).

———. "Abstract Entities and Universals," *Mind* 74 (1965).

Toms, E. "Non-Existence and Universals," *Philosophical Quarterly* 6 (1956).

Urmson, J. O. "Recognition," *Proceedings of the Aristotelian Society* 56 (1955–56).

Vision, G. "Searle on the Nature of the Universals," *Analysis*, New Series, No. 137 (1970).

Wallace, J. R. "Sortal Predicates and Quantification," *Journal of Philosophy* 62 (1965).

Welker, D. D. "Linguistic Nominalism," *Mind* 79, no. 316 (1970).

Wolterstorff, N. "Are Properties Meanings?" *Journal of Philosophy* 57 (1960).

———. "On the Nature of Universals" in M. J. Loux, ed., *Universals and Particulars* (New York, 1970).

Woodger, J. H. "Science without Properties," *British Journal for the Philosophy of Science* 2 (1952).

Woozley, A. D. "Universals," *Encyclopedia of Philosophy* 8, pp. 194–206.

Part Two

The Question of Causation

Introduction

The concept of causation is fundamental since everything in the universe presupposes it, including human thinking. All happenings are examples of causation, and all being is a manifestation of causation. 'Cause' is inextricably linked to 'change'. A sizable amount of ancient Greek philosophical thought was directed toward understanding the nature of change. This came about in the most humble of ways. How, for example, is the change in the color of the leaves in autumn to be explained? Clearly, causation is of great concern to the scientist. Yet, the concept of causation is metaphysical in nature. It was the Greeks who originated the idea that causation entailed efficacy, or the power to create change. However, the nature of this power is illusive. Hence, analyses of causation are attempts to arrive at a better understanding of the nature of efficacy.

It has been argued, for example, that the difference between cases of causation and those of superstition is that of necessary connection. If under normal circumstances a person ingests a pint of arsenic, he will necessarily die. On the contrary, there is no necessary connection between a black cat crossing one's path and subsequent bad luck. At the outset, this looks promising. However, as David Hume observed, there is no element of necessary connection involved in instances of causation for there is no contradiction in imagining that under normal circumstances death would not follow the ingestion of arsenic. According to him, we formulate the idea of necessary connection as a result of constant conjunction, and causation is nothing more than that. But as Thomas Reid observed, if constant conjunction was the sole criterion of causation, then day would be the cause of night and night the cause of day.

In an effort to preserve the element of necessity in causal sequence, it

has been observed that whereas there is no necessary logical connection between a cause and an effect, there is a relationship of physical necessity. This
relationship is embodied in laws of nature: e.g., it is a law of nature that
under normal circumstances if a person ingests a pint of arsenic, he will necessarily die. Once again, this explanation looks promising. However, laws of
nature are general. All instances of causation are specific. The import of the
clause "under normal circumstances" is to bridge the gap between the generality of the law and specific instances in which it is said to apply. Without
the assumption of normal circumstances there could be untold exceptions
to the law, thus rendering it uninformative and useless. Now comes the
devastating blow to the view that causal sequences are manifestations of laws
of nature. What are the criteria that properly determine normal circumstances?
The answer to that question is inconclusive.

There still remains the conviction that there is an essential difference between the arsenic and black cat scenarios stated above. Recent attempts to
determine the difference centers on the notion of causal necessity. The arsenic
example is a case of causal necessity whereas the case of the black cat is
not. Causal necessity is embodied in the statement,

(1) If agent A ingests a pint of arsenic under conditions X, Y, and Z,
he will die.

Note that (1) makes no reference to any law of nature. It is a claim stating
the necessary consequences if certain antecedent conditions obtain. This approach appears to possess potential. However, one should scrupulously avoid
the ever-tempting (a) epistemological and (b) teleological snares. (a) When
a demand is made to know for certain just exactly what conditions must
obtain to guarantee a given result, then an epistemological problem arises.
For all scientific and practical purposes it is possible to determine those
antecedent conditions and to know what they are. However, from a strictly
philosophical point of view, such a determination may not be possible. Such
potential impossibility involves the same problem that arose concerning normal circumstances. (b) It is quite tempting to ask *why* arsenic kills and black
cats do not. If causation turns out to be a matter of physical necessity, then
any concern for why X caused Y either (1) collapses into a question asking
for either a relevant law of nature or the antecedent conditions that necessarily guarantee the result, or (2) a reason, divine or otherwise, as to the
prescribed order and therefore predictability of the occurrences of the universe. The former is of epistemological concern. The latter is teleological in
nature and is inappropriate because it is misplaced. Mortals will never know
the (teleological) whys of the universe—its ultimate purpose and goal. The
answers to these why questions are best left to the theologian.

8

Of the Idea of Necessary Connection

David Hume

PART I

. . . There are no ideas which occur in metaphysics more obscure and uncertain than those of "power," "force," "energy," or "necessary connection," of which it is every moment necessary for us to treat in all our disquisitions. We shall, therefore, endeavor in this section to fix, if possible, the precise meaning of these terms and thereby remove some part of that obscurity which is so much complained of in this species of philosophy. . . .

When we look about us toward external objects and consider the operation of causes, we are never able, in a single instance, to discover any power or necessary connection, any quality which binds the effect to the cause and renders the one an infallible consequence of the other. We only find that the one does actually in fact follow the other. The impulse of one billiard ball is attended with motion in the second. This is the whole that appears to the *outward* senses. The mind feels no sentiment or *inward* impression from this succession of objects; consequenty, there is not, in any single particular instance of cause and effect, anything which can suggest the idea of power or necessary connection.

From the first appearance of an object we never can conjecture what effect will result from it. But were the power or energy of any cause discoverable by the mind, we could foresee the effect, even without experience, and

---

From *An Inquiry Concerning Human Understanding* Section VII, Parts I and II.

might, at first, pronounce with certainty concerning it by the mere dint of thought and reasoning. . . .

Since, therefore, external objects as they appear to the senses give us no idea of power or necessary connection by their operation in particular instances, let us see whether this idea be derived from reflection on the operations of our own minds and be copied from any internal impression. It may be said that we are every moment conscious of internal power while we feel that, by the simple command of our will, we can move the organs of our body or direct the faculties of our mind. An act of volition produces motion in our limbs or raises a new idea in our imagination. This influence of the will we know by consciousness. Hence we acquire the idea of power or energy, and are certain that we ourselves and all other intelligent beings are possessed of power. This idea, then, is an idea of reflection since it arises from reflecting on the operations of our own mind and on the command which is exercised by will both over the organs of the body and the faculties of the soul.

We shall proceed to examine this pretension and, first, with regard to the influence of volition over the organs of the body. This influence, we may observe, is a fact which, like all other natural events, can be known only by experience, and can never be foreseen from any apparent energy or power in the cause which connects it with the effect and renders the one an infallible consequence of the other. The motion of our body follows upon the command of our will. Of this we are every moment conscious. But the means by which this is effected, the energy by which the will performs so extraordinary an operation—of this we are so far from being immediately conscious that it must forever escape our most diligent inquiry. . . .

Shall we then assert that we are conscious of a power or energy in our own minds when, by an act or command of our will, we raise up a new idea, fix the mind to the contemplation of it, turn it on all sides, and at last dismiss it for some other idea when we think that we have surveyed it with sufficient accuracy? I believe the same arguments will prove that even this command of the will gives us no real idea of force or energy.

First, it must be followed that when we know a power, we know that very circumstance in the cause by which it is enabled to produce the effect, for these are supposed to be synonymous. We must therefore, know both the cause and effect and the relation between them. But do we pretend to be acquainted with the nature of the human soul and the nature of an idea, or the aptitude of the one to produce the other? This is a real creation, a production of something out of nothing, which implies a power so great that it may seem, at first sight, beyond the reach of any being less than infinite. At least it must be owned that such a power is not felt, nor known, nor even conceivable by the mind. We only feel the event, namely, the existence of an idea consequent to a command of the will; but the manner in which this operation is performed, the power by which it is produced, is entirely beyond our comprehension.

Secondly, the command of the mind over itself is limited, as well as its command over the body; and these limits are not known by reason or any acquaintance with the nature of cause and effect, but only by experience and observation, as in all other natural events and in the operation of external objects. Our authority over our sentiments and passions is much weaker than that over our ideas; and even the latter authority is circumscribed within very narrow boundaries. Will anyone pretend to assign the ultimate reason of these boundaries, or show why the power is deficient in one case, not in another?

Thirdly, this self-command is very different at different times. A man in health possesses more of it than one languishing with sickness. We are more master of our thoughts in the morning than in the evening; fasting, than after a full meal. Can we give any reason for these variations except experience? Where then is the power of which we pretend to be conscious? Is there not here, either in a spiritual or material substance, or both, some secret mechanism or structure of parts upon which the effect depends, and which, being entirely unknown to us, renders the power or energy of the will equally unknown and incomprehensible? . . .

PART II

But to hasten to a conclusion of this argument, which is already drawn out to too great a length: We have sought in vain for an idea of power or necessary connection in all the sources from which we would suppose it to be derived. It appears that in single instances of the operation of bodies we never can, by our utmost scrutiny, discover anything but one event following another, without being able to comprehend any force or power by which the cause operates or any connection between it and its supposed effect. The same difficulty occurs in contemplating the operations of mind on body, where we observe the motion of the latter to follow upon the volition of the former, but are not able to observe or conceive the tie which binds together the motion and volition, or the energy, by which the mind produces this effect. The authority of the will over its own faculties and ideas is not a whit more comprehensible, so that, upon the whole, there appears not, throughout all nature, any one instance of connection which is conceivable by us. All events seem entirely loose and separate. One event follows another, but we never can observe any tie between them. They seem *conjoined,* but never *connected.* But as we can have no idea of anything which never appeared to our outward sense or inward sentiment, the necessary conclusion *seems* to be that we have no idea of connection or power at all, and that these words are absolutely without any meaning when employed either in philosophical reasonings or common life.

But there still remains one method of avoiding this conclusion, and one source which we have not yet examined. When any natural object or event is presented, it is impossible for us, by any sagacity or penetration, to discover, or even conjecture, without experience, what event will result from it, or to carry our foresight beyond that object which is immediately present to the memory and senses. Even after one instance or experiment where we have observed a particular event to follow upon another, we are not entitled to form a general rule or foretell what will happen in like cases, it being justly esteemed an unpardonable temerity to judge of the whole course of nature from one single experiment, however accurate or certain. But when one particular species of events has always, in all instances, been conjoined with another, we make no longer any scruple of foretelling one upon the appearance of the other, and of employing that reasoning which can alone assure us of any matter of fact or existence. We then call the one object "cause," the other "effect." We suppose that there is some connection between them, some power in the one by which it infallibly produces the other and operates with the greatest certainty and strongest necessity.

It appears, then, that this idea of a necessary connection among events arises from a number of similar instances which occur, of the constant conjunction of these events; nor can that idea ever be suggested by any one of these instances surveyed in all possible lights and positions. But there is nothing in a number of instances, different from every single instance, which is supposed to be exactly similar, except only that after a repetition of similar instances the mind is carried by habit, upon the appearance of one event, to expect its usual attendant and to believe that it will exist. This connection, therefore, which we *feel* in the mind, this customary transition of the imagination from one object to its usual attendant, is the sentiment or impression from which we form the idea of power or necessary connection. Nothing further is in the case. Contemplate the subjects on all sides, you will never find any other origin of that idea. This is the sole difference between one instance, from which we can never receive the idea of connection, and a number of similar instances by which it is suggested. The first time a man saw the communication of motion by impulse, as by the shock of two billiard balls, he could not pronounce that the one event was *connected*, but only that it was *conjoined* with the other. After he has observed several instances of this nature, he then pronounces them to be *connected*. What alteration has happened to give rise to this new idea of *connection*? Nothing but that he now *feels* these events to be *connected* in his imagination, and can readily foretell the existence of one from the appearance of the other. When we say, therefore, that one object is connected with another, we mean only that they have acquired a connection in our thought and gave rise to this inference by which they become proofs of each other's existence —a conclusion which is somewhat extraordinary, but which seems founded on sufficient evidence. Nor will its evidence be weakened by any general diffidence of the understanding or skeptical suspicion concerning every conclusion which is new and extraordinary. No conclusion can be more agreeable to skepticism than such as make discoveries concerning the weakness and narrow limits of human reason and capacity.

And what stronger instance can be produced of the surprising ignorance and weakness of the understanding than the present? For surely, if there be any relation among objects which it imports us to know perfectly, it is that of cause and effect. On this are founded all our reasonings concerning matter of fact or existence. By means of it alone we attain any assurance concerning objects which are removed from the present testimony of our memory and senses. The only immediate utility of all sciences is to teach us how to control and regulate future events by their causes. Our thoughts and inquiries are, therefore, every moment employed about this relation; yet so imperfect are the ideas which we form concerning it that it is impossible to give any just definition of cause, except what is drawn from something extraneous and foreign to it. Similar objects are always conjoined with similar. Of this we have experience. Suitably to this experience, therefore, we may define a cause to be *an object followed by another, and where all the objects, similar to the first, are followed by objects similar to the second.* Or, in other words, *where, if the first object had not been, the second never had existed.* The appearance of a cause always conveys the mind, by a customary transition, to the idea of the effect. Of this also we have experience. We may, therefore, suitably to this experience, form another definition of cause and call it *an object followed by another, and whose appearance always conveys the thought to that other.* But though both these definitions be drawn from circumstances foreign to the cause, we cannot remedy this inconvenience or attain any more perfect definition which may point out that circumstance in the cause which gives it a connection with its effect. We have no idea of this connection, nor even any distinct notion what it is we desire to know when we endeavor at a conception of it. We say, for instance, that the vibration of this string is the cause of this particular sound. But what do we mean by that affirmation? We either mean *that this vibration is followed by this sound, and that all similar vibrations have been followed by similar sounds;* or, *that this vibration is followed by this sound, and that, upon the appearance of one, the mind anticipates the senses and forms immediately an idea of the other.* We may consider the relation of cause and effect in either of these two lights; but beyond these we have no idea of it.[1]

To recapitulate, therefore, the reasonings of this section: Every idea is copied from some proceeding impression or sentiment; and where we cannot find any impression, we may be certain that there is no idea. In all single instances of the operation of bodies or minds there is nothing that produces any impression, nor consequently can suggest any idea, of power or necessary connection. But when many uniform instances appear, and the same object is always followed by the same event, we then begin to entertain the notion of cause and connection. We then *feel* a new sentiment or impression, to wit, a customary connection in the thought or imagination between one object and its usual attendant; and this sentiment is the original of that idea which we seek for. For as this idea arises from a number of similar instances, and not from any single instance, it must arise from that circumstance in which the number of instances differ from every individual instance. But this customary connection or transition of the imagination is the only circumstance in which they differ. In every other particular they are alike. The first instance which we saw of motion, communicated by the shock of two billiard balls (to return to this obvious illustration), is exactly similar to any instance that may at present occur to us, except only that we could not at first *infer* one event from the other, which we are enabled to do at present, after so long a course of uniform experience. I know not whether the reader will readily apprehend this reasoning. I am afraid that, should I multiply words about it or throw it into a greater variety of lights, it would only become more obscure and intricate. In all abstract reasonings there is one point of view which, if we can happily hit, we shall go further toward illustrating the subject than by all the eloquence and copious expression in the world. This point of view we should endeavor to reach, and reserve the flowers of rhetoric for subjects which are more adapted to them.

NOTE

1. According to these explications and defintions, the idea of *power* is relative as much as that of *cause*; and both have a reference to an effect, or some other event constantly conjoined with the former. When we consider the *unknown* circumstance of an object by which the degree or quantity of its effect is fixed and determined, we call that its power. And accordingly, it is allowed by all philosophers that the effect is the measure of the power. But if they had any idea of power as it is in itself, why could they not measure it in itself? The dispute, whether the force of a body in motion be as its velocity, or the square of its velocity; this dispute,

I say, need not be decided by comparing its effects in equal or unequal times, but by a direct mensuration and comparison.

As to the frequent use of the words "force," "power," "energy," etc., which everywhere occur in common conversation as well as in philosophy, that is no proof that we are acquainted, in any instance, with the connecting principle between cause and effect, or can account ultimately for the production of one thing by another. These words, as commonly used, have very loose meanings annexed to them, and their ideas are very uncertain and confused. No animal can put external bodies in motion without the sentiment of a *nisus* or endeavor; and every animal has a sentiment or feeling from the stroke or blow of an external object that is in motion. These sensations, which are merely animal, and from which we can *a priori* draw no inference, we are apt to transfer to inanimate objects, and to suppose that they have some such feelings whenever they transfer or receive motion. With regard to energies, which are exerted without our annexing to the many ideas of communicated motion, we consider only the constant experienced conjunction of the events; and as we *feel* a customary connection between the ideas, we transfer that feeling to the objects, as nothing is more usual than to apply to external bodies every internal sensation which they occasion.

9

Of the Law of Universal Causation

John Stuart Mill

1. THE UNIVERSAL LAW OF SUCCESSIVE PHENOMENA IS THE LAW OF CAUSATION

The phenomena of nature exist in two distinct relations to one another: that of simultaneity, and that of succession. Every phenomenon is related, in a uniform manner, to some phenomena that co-exist with it and to some that have preceded and will follow it.

Of the uniformities which exist among synchronous phenomena, the most important, on every account, are the laws of number; and next to them those of space, or, in other words, of extension and figure. The laws of number are common to synchronous and successive phenomena. That two and two make four is equally true whether the second two follow the first two or accompany them. It is as true of days and years as of feet and inches. The laws of extension and figure (in other words, the theorems of geometry, from its lowest to its highest branches) are, on the contrary, laws of simultaneous phenomena only. The various parts of space and of the objects which are said to fill space co-exist; and the unvarying laws which are the subject of the science of geometry are an expression of the mode of their co-existence.

This is a class of laws, or, in other words, of uniformities, for the comprehension and proof of which it is not necessary to suppose any lapse of time, any variety of facts or events succeeding one another. The propositions

From *Philosophy of Scientific Method*, Book III, Chapter V.

of geometry are independent of the succession of events. All things which possess extension, or, in other words, which fill space, are subject to geometrical laws. Possessing extension, they possess figure; possessing figure, they must possess some figure in particular and have all the properties which geometry assigns to that figure. If one body be a sphere and another a cylinder of equal height and diameter, the one will be exactly two thirds of the other, let nature and quality of the material be what it will. Again, each body and each point of a body must occupy some place or position among other bodies, and the position of two bodies relatively to each other, of whatever nature the bodies be, may be unerringly inferred from the position of each of them relatively to any third body.

In the laws of number, then, and in those of space, we recognize in the most unqualified manner the rigorous universality of which we are in quest. Those laws have been in all ages the type of certainty, the standard of comparison for all inferior degrees of evidence. Their invariability is so perfect that it renders us unable even to conceive any exception to them; and philosophers have been led, though (as I have endeavored to show) erroneously, to consider their evidence as lying not in experience but in the original constitution of the intellect. If, therefore, from the laws of space and number we were able to deduce uniformities of any other description, this would be conclusive evidence to us that those other uniformities possessed the same rigorous certainty. But this we cannot do. From laws of space and number alone, nothing can be deduced but laws of space and number.

Of all truths relating to phenomena, the most valuable to us are those which relate to the order of their succession. On a knowledge of these is founded every reasonable anticipation of future facts and whatever power we possess of influencing those facts to our advantage. Even the laws of geometry are chiefly of practical importance to us as being a portion of the premises from which the order of the succession of phenomena may be inferred. Inasmuch as the motion of bodies, the action of forces, and the propagation of influences of all sorts take place in certain lines and over definite spaces, the properties of those lines and spaces are an important part of the laws to which those phenomena are themselves subject. Again, motions, forces, or other influences, and times are numerable quantities, and the properties of number are applicable to them as to all other things. But though the laws of number and space are important elements in the ascertainment of uniformities of succession, they can do nothing toward it when taken by themselves. They can only be made instrumental to that purpose when we combine with them additional premises, expressive of uniformities of succession already known. By taking, for instance, as premises these propositions: that bodies acted upon by an instantaneous force move with uniform velocity in straight lines; that bodies acted upon by a continuous force move with accelerated velocity in straight lines; and that bodies acted upon by two forces in different directions move in the diagonal of a parallelogram, whose sides represent the direction and quantity of those forces, we may, by combining these truths with propositions relating to the properties of straight lines and of parallelograms (as that a triangle is half a parallelogram of the same base and altitude, deduce another important uniformity of succession, viz., that a body moving round a center of force describes areas proportional to the times. But unless there had been laws of succession in our premises, there could have been no truths of succession in our conclusions. A similar remark might be extended to every other class of phenomena really peculiar, and, had it been attended to, would have prevented many chimerical attempts at demonstrations of the indemonstrable and explanations which do not explain.

It is not, therefore, enough for us that the laws of space, which are only laws of simultaneous phenomena, and the laws of number, which though true of successive phenomena do not relate to their succession, possess the rigorous certainty and universality of which we are in search. We must endeavor to find some law of succession which has those same attributes and is therefore fit to be made the foundation of processes for discovering and of a test for verifying all other uniformities of succession. This fundamental law must resemble the truths of geometry in their most remarkable peculiarity, that of never being, in any instance whatever, defeated or suspended by any change of circumstances.

Now among all those uniformities in the succession of phenomena which common observation is sufficient to bring to light, there are very few which have any, even apparent, pretension to this rigorous indefeasibility; and, of those few, one only has been found capable of completely sustaining it. In that one, however, we recognize a law which is universal also in another sense: it is co-extensive with the entire field of successive phenomena, all instances whatever of succession being examples of it. This law is the law of causation. The truth that every fact which has a beginning has a cause is co-extensive with human experience.

This generalization may appear to some minds not to amount to much, since, after all, it asserts only this: "It is a law, that every event depends on some law"; "It is a law, that there is a law for everything." We must not, however, conclude that the generality of the principle is merely verbal; it will be found on inspection to be no vague or unmeaning assertion, but a most important and really fundamental truth.

2. THAT IS, THE LAW THAT EVERY CONSEQUENT HAS AN INVARIABLE ANTECEDENT

The notion of cause being the root of the whole theory of induction, it is indispensable that this idea should, at the very outset of our inquiry, be, with the utmost practicable degree of precision, fixed and determined . . . .

I premise, then, that, when in the course of this inquiry I speak of the cause of any phenomenon, I do not mean a cause which is not itself a phenomenon; I make no rsearch into the ultimate or ontological cause of anything. To adopt a distinction familiar in the writings of the Scotch metaphysicians and especially of Reid, the causes with which I concern myself are not *efficient* but *physical* causes. They are causes in that sense alone in which one physical fact is said to be the cause of another. Of the efficient causes of phenomena, or whether any such causes exist at all, I am not called upon to give an opinion. The notion of causation is deemed, by the schools of metaphysics most in vogue at the present moment, to imply a mysterious and most powerful tie, such as cannot, or at least does not, exist between any physical fact and that other physical fact on which it is invariably consequent and which is popularly termed its cause; and thence is deduced the supposed necessity of ascending higher, into the essences and inherent constitution of things, to find the true cause, the cause which is not only followed by, but actually produces, the effect. No such necessity exists for the purposes of the present inquiry, nor will any such doctrine be found in the following pages. The only notion of a cause which the theory of induction requires is such a notion as can be gained from experience. The law of causation, the recognition of which is the main pillar of inductive science, is but the familiar truth that invariability of succession is found by observation to obtain between every fact in nature and some other fact which has preceded it, independently of all considerations respecting the ultimate mode of production of phenomena and of every other question regarding the nature of "things in themselves."

* * *

3. THE CAUSE OF A PHENOMENON IS THE ASSEMBLAGE OF ITS CONDITIONS

It is seldom, if ever, between a consequent and a single antecedent, that this invariable sequence subsists. It is usually between a consequent and the sum of several antecedents; the concurrence of all of them being requisite to produce, that is, to be certain of being followed by, the consequent. In such cases it is very common to single out one only of the antecedents under the denomination of cause, calling the others merely conditions. Thus, if a person eats of a particular dish and dies in consequence, that is, would not have died if he had not eaten of it, people would be apt to say that eating of that dish was the cause of his death. There needs not, however, be any invariable connection between eating of the dish and death; but there certainly is, among the circumstances which took place, some combination or other on which death is invariably consequent, as, for instance, the act of eating of the dish, combined with a particular bodily constitution, a particular state of present health, and perhaps even a certain state of the atmosphere; the whole of which circumstances perhaps constituted in this particular case the *conditions* of the phenomenon, or, in other words, the set of antecedents which determined it and but for which it would not have happened. The real cause is the whole of these antecedents, and we have, philosophically speaking, no right to give the name of cause to one of them, exclusively of the others. What, in the case we have supposed, disguises the incorrectness of the expression is this: that the various conditions, except the single one of eating the food, were not *events* (that is, instantaneous changes or successions of instantaneous changes) but *states,* possessing more or less of permanency, and might, therefore, have preceded the effect by an indefinite length of duration for want of the event which was requisite to complete the required concurrence of conditions, while as soon as that event, eating the food, occurs, no other cause is waited for, but the effect begins immediately to take place; and hence the appearance is presented of a more immediate and close connection between the effect and that one antecedent than between the effect and the remaining conditions. But though we may think proper to give the name of cause to that one condition the fulfillment of which completes the tale and brings about the effect without further delay, this condition has really no closer relation to the effect than any of the other conditions has. All the conditions were equally indispensable to the production of the consequent, and the statement of the cause is incomplete unless in some shape or other we introduce them all. A man takes mercury, goes out-of-doors, and catches cold. We say, perhaps, that the cause of his taking cold was exposure to the air. It is clear, however, that his having taken mercury may have been a necessary condition of his catching cold; and though it might consist with usage to say that the cause of his attack was exposure to the air, to be accurate we ought to say that the cause was exposure to the air while under the effect of mercury.

If we do not, when aiming at accuracy, enumerate all the conditions, it is only because some of them will in most cases be understood without being expressed, or because for the purpose in view they may without detriment be overlooked. For example, when we say the cause of a man's death was that his foot slipped in climbing a ladder, we omit as a thing unnecessary to be stated the circumstance of his weight, though quite as indispensable a condition of the effect which took place. When we say that the assent of the crown to a bill makes it law, we mean that the assent, being never given until all the other conditions are fulfilled, makes up the sum of the conditions, though no one now regards it as the principal one. When the decision of a legislative assembly has been determined by the casting vote of the chairman, we sometimes say that this one person was the cause of all the effects which resulted from the enactment. Yet we do not really suppose that his single vote contributed more to the result than that of any other person who voted in the affirmative; but, for the purpose we have in view, which is to insist on his individual responsibility, the part which any other person had in the transaction is not material.

*   *   *

Thus we see that each and every condition of the phenomenon may be taken in its turn and, with equal propriety in common parlance, but with equal impropriety in scientific discourse, may be spoken of as if it were the entire cause. And, in practice, that particular condition is usually styled the cause whose share in the matter is superficially the most conspicuous, or whose requisiteness to the production of the effect we happen to be insisting on at the moment . . . .

There is, no doubt, a tendency (which our first example, that of death from taking a particular food, sufficiently illustrates) to associate the idea of causation with the proximate antecedent *event,* rather than with any of the antecedent *states,* or permanent facts, which may happen also to be conditions of the phenomenon, the reason being that the event not only exists, but begins to exist immediately previous, while the other conditions may have preexisted for an indefinite time . . . . But even this peculiarity of being in closer proximity to the effect than any other of its conditions is, as we have already seen, far from being necessary to the common notion of a cause, with which notion, on the contrary, any one of the conditions, either positive or negative, is found, on occasion, completely to accord.

The cause, then, philosophically speaking, is the sum total of the conditions, positive and negative taken together, the whole of the contingencies of every description, which being realized, the consequent invariably follows . . . .

4. THE CAUSE IS NOT THE INVARIABLE ANTECEDENT, BUT THE UNCONDITIONAL INVARIABLE ANTECEDENT

It now remains to advert to a distinction which is of first-rate importance both for clearing up the notion of cause and for obviating a very specious objection often made against the view which we have taken of the subject.

When we define the cause of anything (in the only sense in which the present inquiry has any concern with causes) to be "the antecedent which it invariably follows," we do not use this phrase as exactly synonymous with "the antecedent which it invariably *has* followed in our past experience." Such a mode of conceiving causation would be liable to the objection very plausibly urged by Dr. Reid, namely, that according to this doctrine night must be the cause of day and day the cause of night, since these phenomena have invariably succeeded one another from the beginning of the world. But it is necessary to our using the word cause that we should believe not only that the antecedent always *has* been followed by the consequent, but that, as long as the present constitution of things[1] endures, it always *will* be so. And this would not be true of day and night. We do not believe that night will be followed by day under all imaginable circumstances, but only that it will be so *provided* the sun rises above the horizon. If the sun ceased to rise, which, for aught we know, may be perfectly compatible with the general laws of matter, night would be, or might be, eternal. On the other hand, if the sun is above the horizon, his light not extinct, and no opaque body between us and him, we believe firmly that, unless a change takes place in the properties of matter, this combination of antecedents will be followed by the consequent, day; that, if the combination of antecedents could be indefinitely prolonged, it would be always day; and that, if the same combination had always existed, it would always have been day, quite independently of night as a previous condition. Therefore is it that we do not call night the cause, nor even a condition, of day. The existence of the sun (or some such luminous body) and there being no opaque medium in a straight line[2] between that body and the part of the earth where we are situated are the sole conditions, and the union of these, without the addition of any superfluous circumstance, constitutes the cause. This is what writers mean when they say that the notion of cause involves the idea of necessity. If there be any meaning which confessedly belongs to the term necessity, it is *unconditionalness*. That which is necessary, that which *must* be, means that which will be whatever supposition we may make in regard to all other things. The succession of day and night evidently is not necessary in this sense. It is conditional on the occurrence of other antecedents. That which will be followed by a given consequent when, and only when, some third circumstance also exists is not the cause, even though no case should ever have occurred in which the phenomenon took place without it.

Invariable sequence, therefore, is not synonymous with causation, unless the sequence, besides being invariable, is unconditional. There are sequences, as uniform in past experience as any others whatever, which yet we do not regard as cases of causation, but as conjunctions in some sort accidental. Such, to an accurate thinker, is that of day and night. The one might have existed for any length of time, and the other not have followed the sooner for its existence; it follows only if certain other antecedents exist, and, where those antecedents existed, it would follow in any case. No one, probably, ever called night the cause of day; mankind must so soon have arrived at the very obvious generalization that the state of general illumination which we call day would follow from the presence of a sufficiently luminous body, whether darkness had preceded or not.

We may define, therefore, the cause of a phenomenon to be the antecedent, or the concurrence of antecedents, on which it is invariably and *unconditionally* consequent. Or if we adopt the convenient modification of the meaning of the word cause which confines it to the assemblage of positive conditions without the negative, then instead of "unconditionally," we must say, "subject to no other than negative conditions."

To some it may appear that, the sequence between night and day being invariable in our experience, we have as much ground in this case as experience can give in any case for recognizing the two phenomena as cause and effect, and that to say that more is necessary—to require a belief that the succession is unconditional, or, in other words, that it would be invariable under all changes of circumstances—is to acknowledge in causation an element of belief not derived from experience. The answer to this is that it is experience itself which teaches us that one uniformity of sequence is conditional and another unconditional. When we judge that the succession of night and day is a derivative sequence, depending on something else, we proceed on grounds of experience. It is the evidence of experience which convinces us that day could equally exist without being followed by night and that night could equally exist without being followed by day. To say that these beliefs are "not generated by our mere observation of sequence"[3] is to forget that twice in every twenty-four hours, when the sky is clear, we have an *experimentum crucis* that the cause of day is the sun. We have an experimental knowledge of the sun which justifies us on experimental grounds in concluding that if the sun were always above the horizon there would be day though there had been no night, and that if the sun were always below the horizon there would be night though there had been no day. We thus know from experience that the succession of night and day is not unconditional. Let me add that the antecedent which is only conditionally invariable is not the invariable antecedent. Though a fact may, in experience, have always been followed by another fact, yet if the remainder of our experience teaches us that it might not always be so followed, or if the experience itself is such as leaves room for a possibility that the known cases may not correctly represent all possible cases, the hitherto invariable antecedent is not accounted the cause; but why? Because we are not sure that it *is* the invariable antecedent.

*   *   *

5. IDEA OF A PERMANENT CAUSE, OR ORIGINAL NATURAL AGENT

It continually happens that several different phenomena, which are not in the slightest degree dependent or conditional on one another, are found all to depend, as the phrase is, on one and the same agent; in other words, one and the same phenomenon is seen to be followed by several sorts of effects quite heterogeneous, but which go on simultaneously one with another, provided, of course, that all other conditions requisite for each of them also exist. Thus, the sun produces the celestial motions, it produces daylight, and it produces heat. The earth causes the fall of heavy bodies, and it also, in its capacity of a great magnet, causes the phenomena of the magnetic needle. A crystal of galena causes the sensations of hardness, of weight, of cubical form, of gray color, and many others between which we can trace no interdependence. The purpose to which the phraseology of properties and powers is specially adapted is the expression of this sort of case. When the same phenomenon is followed (either subject or not to the presence of other conditions) by effects of different and dissimilar orders, it is usual to say that each different sort of effect is produced by a different property of the cause. Thus we distinguish the attractive or gravitative property of the earth and its magnetic property; the gravitative, luminiferous, and calorific properties of the sun; the color, shape, weight, and hardness of a crystal. These are mere phrases which explain nothing and add nothing to our knowledge of the subject, but, considered as abstract names denoting the connection between the different effects produced and the object which produces them, they are a very powerful instrument of abridgment and of that acceleration of the process of thought which abridgment accomplishes.

This class of considerations leads to a conception which we shall find to be of great importance, that of a permanent cause, or original natural agent. There exist in nature a number of permanent causes which have subsisted ever since the human race has been in existence and for an indefinite and probably an enormous length of time previous. The sun, the earth, and planets, with their various constituents, air, water, and other distinguishable substances, whether simple or compound, of which nature is made up, are such permanent causes. These have existed, and the effects or consequences which they were fitted to produce have taken place (as often as the other conditions of the production met) from the very beginning of our experience. But we can give no account of the origin of the permanent causes themselves. Why these particular natural agents existed originally and no others, or why they are commingled in such and such proportions, and distributed in such and such a manner throughout space is a question we cannot answer. More than this: we can discover nothing regular in the distribution itself; we can reduce it to no uniformity, to no law. There are no means by which, from the distribution of these causes or agents in one part of space, we could conjecture whether a similar distribution prevails in another. The coexistence, therefore, of primeval causes ranks, to us, among merely casual concurrences, and all those sequences or coexistences among the effects of several such causes, which, though invariable while those causes coexist would, if the coexistence terminated, terminate along with it, we do not class as cases of causation or laws of nature; we can only calculate on finding these sequences or coexistences where we know by direct evidence that the natural agents on the properties of which they ultimately depend are distributed in the requisite manner. These permanent causes are not always objects; they are sometimes events, that is to say, periodical cycles of events, that being the only mode in which events can possess the property of permanence. Not only, for instance, is the earth itself a permanent cause, or primitive natural agent, but the earth's rotation is so too; it is a cause which has produced, from the earliest period (by the aid of other necessary conditions), the succession of day and night, the ebb and flow of the sea, and many other effects, while, as we can assign no cause (except conjecturally) for the rotation itself, it is entitled to be ranked as a primeval cause. It is, however, only the *origin* of the rotation which is mysterious to us; once begun, its continuance is accounted for by the first law of motion (that of the permanence of rectilinear motion once impressed) combined with the gravitation of the parts of the earth toward one another.

All phenomena without exception which begin to exist, that is, all except the primeval causes, are effects either immediate or remote of those primitive facts or of some combination of them. There is no thing produced, no event happening, in the known universe which is not connected by a uniformity, or invariable sequence, with some one or more of the phenomena which preceded it; insomuch that it will happen again as often as those phenomena occur again, and as no other phenomenon having the character of a counteracting cause shall coexist. These antecedent phenomena, again, were connected in a similar manner with some that preceded them; and so on, until we reach, as the ultimate step attainable by us, either the properties of some one primeval cause or the conjunction of several. The whole of the phenomena of nature were therefore the necessary, or, in other words, the unconditional, consequences of some former collocation of the permanent causes.

The state of the whole universe at any instant we believe to be the consequence of its state at the previous instant; insomuch that one who knew all the agents which exist at the present moment, their collocation in space, and all their properties, in other words, the laws of their agency, could predict the whole subsequent history of the universe, at least unless some new volition of a power capable of controlling the universe should supervene . . . .

NOTES

1. I mean by this expression the ultimate laws of nature (whatever they may be) as distinguished from the derivative laws and from the collocations. The diurnal revolution of the earth (for example) is not a part of the constitution of things, because nothing can be so called which might possibly be terminated or altered by natural causes.

2. I use the words "straight line" for brevity and simplicity. In reality the line in question is not exactly straight, for, from the effect of refraction, we actually see the sun for a short interval during which the opaque mass of the earth is interposed in a direct line between the sun and our eyes, thus realizing, though but to a limited extent, the coveted desideratum of seeing round a corner.

3. *Second Burnett Prize Essay,* by Principal Tulloch, p. 25.

10

On the Notion of Cause

Bertrand Russell

In the following paper I wish, first, to maintain that the word "cause" is so inextricably bound up with misleading associations as to make its complete extrusion from the philosophical vocabulary desirable; secondly, to inquire what principle, if any, is employed in science in place of the supposed "law of causality" which philosophers imagine to be employed; thirdly, to exhibit certain confusions, especially in regard to teleology and determinism, which appear to me to be connected with erroneous notions as to causality.

All philosophers, of every school, imagine that causation is one of the fundamental axioms or postulates of science, yet, oddly enough, in advanced sciences such as gravitational astronomy, the word "cause" never occurs. Dr. James Ward, in his *Naturalism and Agnosticism,* makes this a ground of complaint against physics: the business of those who wish to ascertain the ultimate truth about the world, he apparently thinks, should be the discovery of causes, yet physics never even seeks them. To me it seems that philosophy ought not to assume such legislative functions, and that the reason why physics has ceased to look for causes is that, in fact, there are no such things. The law of causality, I believe, like much that passes muster among philosophers, is a relic of a bygone age, surviving, like the monarchy, only because it is erroneously supposed to do no harm.

From *Mysticism and Logic and Other Essays* (New York: Barnes and Noble; London: Allen & Unwin 1949). Reprinted by permission of Barnes and Noble, and Harper Collins publishers.

In order to find out what philosophers commonly understand by "cause," I consulted Baldwin's *Dictionary,* and was rewarded beyond my expectations, for I found the following three mutually incompatible definitions:—

CAUSALITY. (I) The necessary connection of events in the time-series . . . .

CAUSE (notion of). Whatever may be included in the thought or perception of a process as taking place in consequence of another process . . . .

CAUSE AND EFFECT. (I) Cause and effect . . . are correlative terms denoting any two distinguishable things, phases, or aspects of reality, which are so related to each other that whenever the first ceases to exist the second comes into existence immediately after, and whenever the second comes into existence the first has ceased to exist immediately before.

Let us consider these three definitions in turn. The first, obviously, is unintelligible without a definition of "necessary." Under this head, Baldwin's *Dictionary* gives the following:—

NECESSARY. That is necessary which not only is true, but would be true under all circumstances. Something more than brute compulsion is, therefore, involved in the conception; there is a general law under which the thing takes place.

The notion of cause is so intimately connected with that of necessity that it will be no digression to linger over the above definition, with a view to discovering, if possible, *some* meaning of which it is capable; for, as it stands, it is very far from having any definite signification.

The first point to notice is that, if any meaning is to be given to the phrase "would be true under all circumstances," the subject of it must be a propositional function, not a proposition.[1] A proposition is simply true or false, and that ends the matter: there can be no question of "circumstances." "Charles I's head was cut off" is just as true in summer as in winter, on Sundays as on Mondays. Thus when it is worth saying that something "would be true under all circumstances," the something in question must be a propositional function, i.e., an expression containing a variable, and becoming a proposition when a value is assigned to the variable; the varying "circumstances" alluded to are then the different values of which the variable is capable. Thus if "necessary" means "what is true under all circumstances," then "if x is a man, x is mortal" is necessary, because it is true for any possible value of x. Thus we should be led to the following definition:—

NECESSARY is a predicate of a propositional function, meaning that it is true for all possible values of its argument or arguments.

Unfortunately, however, the definition in Baldwin's *Dictionary* says that what is necessary is not only "true under all circumstances" but is also "true." Now these two are incompatible. Only propositions can be "true," and only propositional functions can be "true under all circumstances." Hence the definition as it stands is nonsense. What is meant seems to be this: "A proposition is necessary when it is a value of a propositional function which is true under all circumstances, i.e., for all values of its argument or arguments." But if we adopt this definition, the same proposition will be necessary or contingent according as we choose one or other of its terms as the argument to our propositional function. For example, "If Socrates is a man, Socrates is mortal," is necessary if Socrates is chosen as argument, but not if *man or mortal* is chosen. Again, "If Socrates is a man, Plato is mortal," will be necessary if either Socrates or *man* is chosen as argument, but not if Plato or *mortal* is chosen. However, this difficulty can be overcome by specifying the constituent which is to be regarded as argument, and we thus arrive at the following definition:

"A proposition is *necessary* with respect to a given constituent if it remains true when that constituent is altered in any way compatible with the proposition remaining significant."

We may now apply this definition to the definition of causality quoted above. It is obvious that the argument must be the time at which the earlier event occurs. Thus an instance of causality will be such as: "If the event e_1 occurs at the time t_1, it will be followed by the event e_2" This proposition is intended to be necessary with respect to t_1, i.e., to remain true however t_1 may be varied. Causality, as a universal law, will then be the following: "Given any event e_1, there is an event e_2 such that, whenever e_1 occurs, e_2 occurs later." But before this can be considered precise, we must specify how much later e_2 is to occur. Thus the principle becomes:—

"Given any event e_1, there is an event e_2 and a time-interval τ such that, whenever e_1 occurs, e_2 follows after an interval τ."

I am not concerned as yet to consider whether this law is true or false. For the present, I am merely concerned to discover what the law of causality is supposed to be. I pass, therefore, to the other definitions quoted above.

The second definition need not detain us long, for two reasons. First, because it is psychological: not the "thought or perception" of a process, but the process itself, must be what concerns us in considering causality. Secondly, because it is circular: in speaking of a process as "taking place in consequence of" another process, it introduces the very notion of cause which was to be defined.

The third definition is by far the most precise; indeed as regards clearness it leaves nothing to be desired. But a great difficulty is caused by the temporal contiguity of cause and effect which the definition asserts. No two instants are contiguous, since the time-series is compact; hence either the cause or the effect or both must, if the definition is correct, endure for a finite time; indeed, by the wording of the definition it is plain that both are assumed to endure for a finite time. But then we are faced with a dilemma: if the cause is a process involving change within itself, we shall require (if causality is universal) causal relations between its earlier and later parts; moreover, it would seem that only the later parts can be relevant to the effect, since the earlier parts are not contiguous to the effect, and therefore (by the definition) cannot influence the effect. Thus we shall be led to diminish the duration of the cause without limit, and however much we may diminish it, there will still remain an earlier part which might be altered without altering the effect, so that the true cause, as defined, will not have been reached, for it will be observed that the definition excludes plurality of causes. If, on the other hand, the cause is purely static, involving no change within itself, then, in the first place, no such cause is to be found in nature, and in the second place, it seems strange—too strange to be accepted, in spite of bare logical possibility—that the cause, after existing placidly for some time, should suddenly explode into the effect, when it might just as well have done so at any earlier time, or have gone on unchanged without producing its effect. This dilemma, therefore, is fatal to the view that cause and effect can be contiguous in time; if there are causes and effects, they must be separated by a finite time-interval τ, as was assumed in the above interpretation of the first definition.

What is essentially the same statement of the law of causality as the one elicited above from the first of Baldwin's definitions is given by other philosophers. Thus John Stuart Mill says:—

> The Law of Causation, the recognition of which is the main pillar of inductive science, is but the familiar truth, that invariability of succession is found by observation to obtain between every fact in nature and some other fact which has preceded it.[2]

And Bergson, who has rightly perceived that the law as stated by philosophers is worthless, nevertheless continues to suppose that it is used in science. Thus he says:—

> Now, it is argued, this law [the law of causality] means that every phenomenon is determined by its conditions, or, in other words, that the same causes produce the same effects.[3]

And again:—

> We perceive physical phenomena, and these phenomena obey laws. This means: (1) That phenomena *a, b, c, d,* previously perceived, can occur again in the same shape; (2) that a certain phenomenon P, which appeared after the conditions *a, b, c, d,* and after these conditions only, will not fail to recur as soon as the same conditions are again present."[4]

A great part of Bergson's attack on science rests on the assumption that it employs this principle. In fact, it employs no such principle, but philosophers —even Bergson—are too apt to take their views on science from each other, not from science. As to what the principle is, there is a fair consensus among philosophers of different schools. There are, however, a number of difficulties which at once arise. I omit the question of plurality of causes for the present, since other graver questions have to be considered. Two of these, which are forced on our attention by the above statement of the law, are the following:—

(1) What is meant by an "event"?

(2) How long may the time interval be between cause and effect?

(1) An "event," in the statement of the law, is obviously intended to be something that is likely to recur since otherwise the law becomes trivial. It follows that an "event" is not a particular, but some universal of which there may be many instances. It follows also that an "event" must be something short of the whole state of the universe, since it is highly improbable that this will recur. What is meant by an "event" is something like striking a match, or dropping a penny into the slot of an automatic machine. If such an event is to recur, it must not be defined too narrowly: we must not state with what degree of force the match is to be struck, nor what is to be the temperature of the penny. For if such considerations were relevant, our "event" would occur at most once, and the law would cease to give information. An "event," then, is a universal defined sufficiently widely to admit of many particular occurrences in time being instances of it.

(2) The next question concerns the time interval. Philosophers, no doubt, think of cause and effect as contiguous in time, but this, for reasons already given, is impossible. Hence, since there are no infinitesimal time intervals, there must be some finite lapse of time τ between cause and effect. This, however, at once raises insuperable difficulties. However short we make the interval τ, something may happen during this interval which prevents the expected result. I put my penny in the slot, but before I can draw out my ticket there is an earthquake which upsets the machine and my calculations.

In order to be sure of the expected effect, we must know that there is nothing in the environment to interfere with it. But this means that the supposed cause is not, by itself, adequate to insure the effect. And as soon as we include the environment, the probability of repetition is diminished, until at last, when the whole environment is included, the probability of repetition becomes almost *nil*.

In spite of these difficulties, it must, of course, be admitted that many fairly dependable regularities of sequence occur in daily life. It is these regularities that have suggested the supposed law of causality; where they are found to fail, it is thought that a better formulation could have been found which would have never failed. I am far from denying that there may be such sequences which in fact never do fail. It may be that there will never be an exception to the rule that when a stone of more than a certain mass, moving with more than a certain velocity, comes in contact with a pane of glass of less than a certain thickness, the glass breaks. I also do not deny that the observation of such regularities, even when they are not without exceptions, is useful in the infancy of a science: the observation that unsupported bodies in air usually fall was a stage on the way to the law of gravitation. What I deny is that science assumes the existence of invariable uniformities of sequence of this kind, or that it aims at discovering them. All such uniformities, as we saw, depend upon a certain vagueness in the definition of the "events." That bodies fall is a vague qualitative statement; science wishes to know how fast they fall. This depends upon the shape of the bodies and the density of the air. It is true that there is more nearly uniformity when they fall in a vacuum; so far as Galileo could observe, the uniformity is then complete. But later it appeared that even there the latitude made a difference, and the altitude. Theoretically, the position of the sun and moon must make a difference. In short, every advance in a science takes us farther away from the crude uniformities which are first observed, into greater differentiation of antecedent and consequent, and into a continually wider circle of antecedents recognized as relevant.

The principle "same cause, same effect," which philosophers imagine to be vital to science, is therefore utterly otiose. As soon as the antecedents have been given sufficiently fully to enable the consequent to be calculated with some exactitude, the antecedents have become so complicated that it is very unlikely they will ever recur. Hence, if this were the principle involved, science would remain utterly sterile.

*   *   *

I return now to the question, What law or laws can be found to take the place of the supposed law of causality?

First, without passing beyond such uniformities of sequence as are contemplated by the traditional law, we may admit that, if any such sequence has been observed in a great many cases, and has never been found to fail, there is an inductive probability that it will be found to hold in future cases. If stones have hitherto been found to break windows, it is probably that they will continue to do so. This, of course, assumes the inductive principle, of which the truth may reasonably be questioned; but as this principle is not our present concern, I shall in this discussion treat it as indubitable. We may then say, in the case of any such frequently observed sequence, that the earlier event is the *cause* and the later event the *effect*.

Several considerations, however, make such special sequences very different from the traditional relation of cause and effect. In the first place, the sequence, in any hitherto unobserved instance, is no more than probable, whereas the relation of cause and effect was supposed to be necessary. I do not mean by this merely that we are not sure of having discovered a true case of cause and effect; I mean that, even when we have a case of cause and effect in our present sense, all that is meant is that on grounds of observation, it is probable that when one occurs the other will also occur. Thus in our present sense, A may be the cause of B even if there actually are cases where B does not follow A. Striking a match will be the cause of its igniting, in spite of the fact that some matches are damp and fail to ignite.

In the second place, it will not be assumed that *every* event has some antecedent which is its cause in this sense; we shall only believe in causal sequences where we find them, without any presumption that they always are to be found.

In the third place, *any* case of sufficiently frequent sequence will be causal in our present sense; for example, we shall not refuse to say that night is the cause of day. Our repugnance to saying this arises from the ease with which we can imagine the sequence to fail, but owing to the fact that cause and effect must be separated by a finite interval of time, *any* such sequence *might* fail through the interposition of other circumstances in the interval. Mill, discussing this instance of night and day, says:—

> It is necessary to our using the word cause, that we should believe not only that the antecedent always *has* been followed by the consequent, but that as long as the present constitution of things endures, it always *will* be so.[5]

In this sense, we shall have to give up the hope of finding causal laws such as Mill contemplated; any causal sequence which we have observed may at any moment be falsified without a falsification of any laws of the kind that the more advanced sciences aim at establishing.

In the fourth place, such laws of probable sequence, though useful in daily life and in the infancy of a science, tend to be displaced by quite different laws as soon as a science is successful. The law of gravitation will illustrate what occurs in any advanced science. In the motions of mutually gravitating bodies, there is nothing that can be called a cause, and nothing that can be called an effect; there is merely a formula. Certain differential equations can be found, which hold at every instant for every particle of the system, and which, given the configuration and velocities at one instant, or the configurations at two instants, render the configuration at any other earlier or later instant theoretically calculable. That is to say, the configuration at any instant is a function of that instant and the configurations at two given instants. This statement holds throughout physics, and not only in the special case of gravitation. But there is nothing that could be properly called "cause" and nothing that could be properly called "effect" in such a system.

No doubt the reason why the old "law of causality" has so long continued to pervade the books of philosophers is simply that the idea of a function is unfamiliar to most of them, and therefore they seek an unduly simplified statement. There is no question of repetitions of the "same" cause producing the "same" effect; it is not in any sameness of causes and effects that the constancy of scientific law consists, but in sameness of relations. And even "sameness of relations" is too simple a phrase; "sameness of differential equations" is the only correct phrase. It is impossible to state this accurately in nonmathematical language; the nearest approach would be as follows: "There is a constant relation between the state of the universe at any instant and the rate of change in the rate at which any part of the universe is changing at that instant, and this relation is many-one, i.e., such that the rate of change in the rate of change is determinate when the state of the universe is given." If the "law of causality" is to be something actually discoverable in the practice of science, the above proposition has a better right to the name than any "law of causality" to be found in the books of philosophers.

In regard to the above principle, several observations must be made—

(1) No one can pretend that the above principle is *a priori* or self-evident or a "necessity of thought." Nor is it, in any sense, a premiss of science: it is an empirical generalization from a number of laws which are themselves empirical generalizations.

(2) The law makes no difference between past and future: the future "determines" the past in exactly the same sense in which the past "determines" the future. The word "determine," here, has a purely logical significance: a certain number of variables "determine" another variable *if* that other variable is a function of them.

(3) The law will not be empirically verifiable unless the course of events within some sufficiently small volume will be approximately the same in any two states of the universe which only differ in regard to what is at a considerable distance from the small volume in question. For example, motions of planets in the solar system must be approximately the same however the fixed stars may be distributed, provided that all the fixed stars are very much farther from the sun than the planets are. If gravitation varied directly as the distance, so that the most remote stars made the most difference to the motions of the planets, the world might be just as regular and just as much subject to mathematical laws as it is at present, but we could never discover the fact.

(4) Although the old "law of causality" is not assumed by science, something which we may call the "uniformity of nature" is assumed, or rather is accepted on inductive grounds. The uniformity of nature does not assert the trivial principle "same cause, same effect," but the principle of the permanence of laws. That is to say, when a law exhibiting, e.g., an acceleration as a function of the configuration has been found to hold throughout the observable past, it is expected that it will continue to hold in the future, or that, if it does not itself hold, there is some other law, agreeing with the supposed law as regards the past, which will hold for the future. The ground of this principle is simply the inductive ground that it has been found to be true in very many instances; hence the principle cannot be considered certain, but only probable to a degree which cannot be accurately estimated.

The uniformity of nature, in the above sense, although it is assumed in the practice of science, must not, in its generality, be regarded as a kind of major premise, without which all scientific reasoning would be in error. The assumption that *all* laws of nature are permanent has, of course, less probability than the assumption that this or that particular law is permanent; and the assumption that a particular law is permanent for all time has less probability than the assumption that it will be valid up to such and such a date. Science, in any given case, will assume what the case requires, but no more. In constructing the *Nautical Almanac* for 1915 it will assume that the law of gravitation will remain true up to the end of that year; but it will make no assumption as to 1916 until it comes to the next volume of the almanac. This procedure is, of course, dictated by the fact that the uniformity of nature is not known *a priori,* but is an empirical generalization, like "all men are mortal." In all such cases, it is better to argue immediately from the given particular instances to the new instance, than to argue by way of a major premise; the conclusion is only probable in either case, but acquires a higher probability by the former method than by the latter.

In all science we have to distinguish two sorts of laws: first, those that are empirically verifiable but probably only approximate; secondly, those that are not verifiable, but may be exact. The law of gravitation, for example, in its applications to the solar system, is only empirically verifiable when it is assumed that matter outside the solar system may be ignored for such purposes; we believe this to be only approximately true, but we cannot empirically verify the law of universal gravitation which we believe to be exact. This point is very important in connection with what we may call "relatively isolated systems." These may be defined as follows:—

A system relatively isolated during a given period is one which, within some assignable margin of error, will behave in the same way throughout that period, however the rest of the universe may be constituted.

A system may be called "practically isolated" during a given period if, although there *might* be states of the rest of the universe which would produce more than the assigned margin of error, there is reason to believe that such states do not in fact occur.

Strictly speaking, we ought to specify the respect in which the system is relatively isolated. For example, the earth is relatively isolated as regards falling bodies, but not as regards tides; it is *practically* isolated as regards economic phenomena, although, if Jevons's sun-spot theory of commercial crises had been true, it would not have been even practically isolated in this respect.

It will be observed that we cannot prove in advance that a system is isolated. This will be inferred from the observed fact that approximate uniformities can be stated for this system alone. If the complete laws for the whole universe were known, the isolation of a system could be deduced from them; assuming, for example, the law of universal gravitation, the practical isolation of the solar system in this respect can be deduced by the help of the fact that there is very little matter in its neighborhood. But it should be observed that isolated systems are only important as providing a possibility of *discovering* scientific laws; they have no theoretical importance in the finished structure of a science.

The case where one event A is said to "cause" another event B, which philosophers take as fundamental, is really only the most simplified instance of a practically isolated system. It may happen that, as a result of general scientific laws, whenever A occurs throughout a certain period, it is followed by B; in that case, A and B form a system which is practically isolated throughout that period. It is, however, to be regarded as a piece of good fortune if this occurs; it will always be due to special circumstances, and would not have been true if the rest of the universe had been different though subject to the same laws.

The essential function which causality has been supposed to perform is the possibility of inferring the future from the past, or, more generally, events at any time from events at certain assigned times. Any system in which such inference is possible may be called a "deterministic" system. We may define a deterministic system as follows:—

A system is said to be "deterministic" when, given certain data, $e_1, e_2, \ldots,$ e_n, at times $t_1, t_2, \ldots, t_n$ respectively, concerning this system, if E_t is the state of the system at any time t, there is a functinal relation of the form

$$E_t = f(e_1, t_1, e_2, t_2, \ldots, e_n, t_n, t). \tag{A}$$

The system will be "deterministic throughout a given period" if t, in the above formula, may be any time within that period, though outside that period the formula may be no longer true. If the universe, as a whole, is such a system, determinism is true of the universe; if not, not. A system which is part of a deterministic system I shall call "determined"; one which is not part of any such system I shall call "capricious."

The events $e_1, e_2, \ldots, e_n$ I shall call "determinants" of the system. It is to be observed that a system which has one set of determinants will in general have many. In the case of the motions of the planets, for example, the configurations of the solar system at any two given times will be determinants.

* * *

If formulas of any degree of complexity, however great, are admitted, it would seem that any system, whose state at a given moment is a function of certain measurable quantities, *must* be a deterministic system. Let us consider, in illustration, a single material particle, whose coordinates at time t are x_t, y_t, z_t. Then, however the particle moves, there must be, theoretically, functions f_1, f_2, f_3, such that

$$x_t = f_1(t), \qquad y, = f_2(t), \qquad z_t = f_3(t).$$

It follows that, theoretically, the whole state of the material universe at time t must be capable of being exhibited as a function of t. Hence our universe will be deterministic in the sense defined above. But if this be true, no information is conveyed about the universe in stating that it is deterministic. It is true that the formulas involved may be of strictly infinite complexity, and therefore not practically capable of being written down or apprehended. But except from the point of view of our knowledge, this might seem to be a detail: in itself, if the above considerations are sound, the material universe *must* be deterministic, *must* be subject to laws.

This, however, is plainly not what was intended. The difference between this view and the view intended may be seen as follows. Given some formula which fits the facts hitherto—say the law of gravitation—there will be an infinite number of other formulas, not empirically distinguishable from it in the past, but diverging from it more and more in the future. Hence, even assuming that there are persistent laws, we shall have no reason for assuming that the law of the inverse square will hold in future; it may be some other hitherto indistinguishable law that will hold. We cannot say that *every* law which has held hitherto must hold in the future, because past facts which obey one law will also obey others, hitherto indistinguishable but diverging in future. Hence there must, at every moment, be laws hitherto unbroken which are now broken for the first time. What science does, in fact, is to select the *simplest* formula that will fit the facts. But this, quite obviously, is merely a methodological precept, not a law of Nature. If the simplest formula ceases, after a time, to be applicable, the simplest formula that remains applicable is selected, and science has no sense that an axiom has been falsified. We are thus left with the brute fact that, in many departments of science, quite simple laws have hitherto been found to hold. This fact cannot be regarded as having any *a priori* ground, nor can it be used to support inductively the opinion that the same laws will continue; for at every moment laws hitherto true are being falsified, though in the advanced sciences these laws are less simple than those that have remained true. Moreover it would be fallacious to argue inductively from the state of the advanced sciences to the future state of the others, for it may well be that the advanced sciences are advanced simply because, hitherto, their subject matter has obeyed simple and easily ascertainable laws, while the subject matter of other sciences has not done so.

The difficulty we have been considering seems to be met partly, if not, wholly, by the principle that the *time* must not enter explicitly into our formulas. All mechanical laws exhibit acceleration as a function of configuration, not of configuration and time jointly; and this principle of the irrelevance of the time may be extended to all scientific laws. In fact we might interpret the "uniformity of nature" as meaning just this, that no scientific law involves the time as an argument, unless, of course, it is given in an integrated form, in which case *lapse* of time, though not absolute time, may appear in our formulas. Whether this consideration suffices to overcome our difficulty completely, I do not know; but in any case it does much to diminish it.

It will serve to illustrate what has been said if we apply it to the question of free will.

(1) Determinism in regard to the will is the doctrine that our volitions belong to some deterministic system, i.e., are "determined" in the sense defined above. Whether this doctrine is true or false, is a mere question of fact; no *a priori* considerations (if our previous discussions have been correct) can

exist on either side. On the one hand, there is no *a priori* category of causality, but merely certain observed uniformities. As a matter of fact, there are observed uniformities in regard to volitions; thus there is some empirical evidence that volitions are determined. But it would be very rash to maintain that the evidence is overwhelming, and it is quite possible that some volitions, as well as some other things, are not determined, except in the sense in which we found that everything must be determined.

(2) But, on the other hand, the subjective sense of freedom, sometimes alleged against determinism, has no bearing on the question whatever. The view that it has a bearing rests upon the belief that causes compel their effects, or that nature enforces obedience to its laws as governments do. These are mere anthropomorphic superstitions, due to assimilation of causes with volitions and of natural laws with human edicts. We feel that our will is not compelled, but that only means that it is not other than we choose it to be. It is one of the demerits of the traditional theory of causality that it has created an artificial opposition between determinism and the freedom of which we are introspectively conscious.

(3) Besides the general question whether volitions are determined, there is the further question whether they are *mechanically* determined, i.e., whether they are part of what was above defined as a mechanical system. This is the question whether they form part of a system with purely material determinants, i.e., whether there are laws which, given certain material data, make all volitions functions of those data. Here again, there is empirical evidence up to a point, but it is not conclusive in regard to all volitions. It is important to observe, however that even if volitions are part of a mechanical system, this by no means implies any supremacy of matter over mind. It may well be that the same system which is susceptible of material determinants is also susceptible of mental determinants; thus a mechanical system may be determined by sets of volitions, as well as by sets of material facts. It would seem, therefore, that the reasons which make people dislike the view that volitions are mechanically determined are fallacious.

(4) The notion of *necessity,* which is often associated with determinism, is a confused notion not legitimately deducible from determinism. Three meanings are commonly confounded when necessity is spoken of:—

(α) An *action* is necessary when it will be performed however much the agent may wish to do otherwise. Determinism does not imply that actions are necessary in this sense.

(β) A *propositional function* is necessary when all its values are true. This sense is not relevant to our present discussion.

(γ) A *proposition* is necessary with respect to a given constituent when it is the value, with that constituent as argument, of a necessary propositional function, in other words, when it remains true however that constituent may be varied. In this sense, in a deterministic system, the connection of a volition with its determinants is necessary, if the time at which the determinants occur be taken as the constituent to be varied, the time interval between the determinants and the volition being kept constant. But this sense of necessity is purely logical, and has no emotional importance.

We may now sum up our discussion of causality. We found first that the law of causality, as usually stated by philosophers, is false, and is not employed in science. We then considered the nature of scientific laws, and found that, instead of stating that one event A is always followed by another event B, they stated functional relations between certain events at certain times, which we called determinants, and other events at earlier or later times or at the same time. We were unable to find any *a priori* category involved: the existence of scientific laws appeared as a purely empirical fact, not necessarily universal, except in a trivial and scientifically useless form. We found that a system with one set of determinants may very likely have other sets of a quite different kind, that, for example, a mechanically determined system may also be teleologically or volitionally determined. Finally we considered the problem of free will: here we found that the reasons for supposing volitions to be determined are strong but not conclusive, and we decided that even if volitions are mechanically determined, that is no reason for denying freedom in the sense revealed by introspection, or for supposing that mechanical events are not determined by volitions. The problem of free will *versus* determinism is therefore, if we were right, mainly illusory, but in part not yet capable of being decisively solved.

NOTES

1. A propositional function is an expression containing a variable, or undetermined constituent, and becoming a proposition as soon as a definite value is assigned to the variable. Examples are: "A is A," "x is a number." The variable is called the *argument* of the function.
2. *Logic,* Bk. III, Chap. V, § 2.
3. *Time and Free Will,* p. 199.
4. Ibid., p. 202.
5. *Logic,* Bk. III, Chap. V, § 6.

11

On the Nature and the Observability of the Causal Relation

C. J. Ducasse

The aim of this paper is to set forth two related theses. The first is that the correct definition of the causal relation is to be framed in terms of one single case of sequence, and that constancy of conjunction is therefore no part of it, but merely, under certain conditions, a corollary of the presence of the causal relation. The second thesis is that the causal relation, when correctly defined, is as directly observable as many other facts, and that the alleged mysteriousness of the causal tie is therefore a myth due only to a mistaken notion of what a tie is.

MEANING OF "A CORRECT DEFINITION"

The problem of giving a "correct" definition of the causal relation is that of making analytically explicit the meaning which the term "cause" has in actual concrete phrases that our language intuition acknowledges as proper and typical cases of its use. For obviously it is one thing to "know what cause means" in the cheap sense of being able to understand intuitively such an assertion as that the Santa Barbara earthquake caused the collapse of

From *Journal of Philosophy* 23, no. 3 (February 4, 1926):57–68. Copyright © 1926 The Journal of Philosophy, Inc. Reprinted by permission.

numberless chimneys; and it is another and a much more difficult and rarer thing to "know what cause means" in the sense of being able to give a correct definition of it. To say that a definition of it is correct means that the definition can be substituted for the word "cause" in any such assertion as the above, in which the word occurs, *without in the least changing the meaning which the assertion is felt to have.* Any ventured definition of such a philosophical term as cause is thus capable of being correct or incorrect in strictly the same sense as that in which a scientific hypothesis is so, viz., either it fits the facts or it does not. The only difference is that in the case of scientific hypotheses the facts are perceptual objects and their relations, while in the case of philosophical hypotheses the facts are the intuited meanings of actual phrases in which the word to be defined occurs. The great inductive method of hypothesis-deduction-verification is thus no less that of philosophy than that of science.

TWO PRELIMINARY REMARKS

Before attempting to formulate a definition of the term "cause," attention must briefly be called to two essential preliminary points.[1]

1. The first is that nothing can, in strict propriety, ever be spoken of as a cause or an effect, except an *event*. And by an event is to be understood either a change or an absence of change (whether qualitative or relational) of an object.[2] On the other hand, objects themselves (in the sense of substances, e.g., gold; or things, e.g., a tree) never can properly be spoken of as causes or effects,[3] but only as agents or patients, as components or compounds, as parts or wholes. These relations, although closely allied to the causal relation, are nevertheless distinct from it, and cannot be discussed here.

2. The second point to be borne in mind is that when the term "causal connection" is used, any one of four distinct objective relations may actually be meant, namely, objectively sufficient to, necessary to, necessitated by, contingent upon. And to these four relations correspond respectively the four functional terms, cause, conditions, effect, resultant. So that, more explicitly, if a given particular event is regarded as having been *sufficient to* the occurrence of another, it is said to have been its *cause*; if regarded as having been *necessary to* the occurrence of another, it is said to have been a *condition of* it; if regarded as having been *necessitated by* the occurrence of another, it is said to have been its *effect*; and if regarded as having been *contingent upon* the occurrence of another, it is said to have been a *resultant* of that other. Much confusion has resulted in discussions of causality from the failure to keep these four relations at all times clearly distinguished, Mill, in-

deed, pushing perversity to the point of convincing himself and some of his readers that there was no sound basis for a distinction between cause and condition. But it is, on the contrary, essential to remember that to be sufficient is one thing, to be necessary another thing, and to be *both* sufficient and necessary (which is what Mill's definition would make cause mean) yet a third thing.

Of the four relations, cause, condition, effect, resultant, which a given particular event may have to another with which it is connected, we still have space here to discuss only the first, namely, cause. And we shall, moreover, confine ourselves to cases—much the more frequent—where the events contemplated are changes, rather than absences of change.

DEFINITION OF CAUSE

Taking it as an admitted fact of the language that if the occurrence of a particular change sufficed to the occurrence of a given other it is then said to have caused the other, the all-important question now arises how such sufficing is to be defined. I suggest that the correct definition of it, framed in terms of a hypothetical situation, is as follows:

Considering two changes, C and K (which may be either of the same or of different objects), the change C is said to have been sufficient to, i.e., to have caused, the change K, if:

1. The change C occurred during a time and through a space terminating at the instant I at the surface S.[4]

2. The change K occurred during a time and through a space beginning at the instant I at the surface S.

3. No change other than C occurred during the time and through the space of C, and no change other than K during the time and through the space of K.

More roughly, but in briefer and more easily intuited terms, we may say that *the cause of the particular change K was such particular change C as alone occurred in the immediate environment of K immediately before.*

SOME BEARINGS ON THE DEFINITION

A number of important points may be noted in connection with the above definition of cause.

1. The first is that it presents the causal relation as involving not two terms only, but essentially three terms, namely, (a) the environment of an object, (b) some changes in that environment, (c) the resulting change in the object. As soon as it is clearly realized that the expression "the cause of an event" thus has any meaning at all only in terms of some definite environment, either concretely given or abstractly specified, Mill's contention that the distinction between cause and conditions is arbitrary and capricious is seen to be absurd. To take up the environment into the "cause," as Mill's definition of cause[5] tries to do, is impossible because the cause consists of a change in that environment. No event can be spoken of as the cause of anything, except relatively to certain conditions; and vice versa, as regards conditions.

2. The second remark for which the definition of cause above gives occasion concerns the immediate spatial and temporal contiguity of cause and effect. The alleged impossibility of such immediate contiguity is the chief ground upon which Russell has advocated the extrusion of the term "cause" from the philosophical vocabulary.[6] The difficulties raised by him, however, are easily disposed of if two things are kept in mind. The first is that the terms "a time" and "a place" are ambiguous. It is essential to distinguish clearly "a time" in the sense of an instant, i.e., a *cut* of the time series, from "a time" in the sense of a *segment* of the time series, limited by two cuts. And similarly with regard to the space order, the cuts of it (viz., point, lines, or surfaces according as one-, two-, or three-dimensional space is considered) are to be carefully distinguished from the *parts* of space, which have such cuts as limits. The second thing to bear in mind is that an event (whether a change or an "unchange")[7] cannot be said to occur *at* a time (cut), but only *during* a time (segment); nor *at* a point (or other cut of space), but only *through* a space (between cuts). Thus, a change is essentially a process which has extent both in time and in space, and is therefore divisible; any division yielding segments of the process that are themselves extended in time and space and therefore further divisible, *ad infinitum*.[8] The immediate contiguity of cause and effect in space and time, specified in our definition, then means only that one identical space-time *cut* marks both the end of the cause process and the beginning of the effect process; the one extending up to, and the other from, that cut; the cut itself, however (by the very nature of a cut as distinguished from a segment), having no space-time dimension at all.[9] With cause and effect and their space-time relation[10] so conceived, there is no possibility that, as Russell contended, some other event should creep in between the cause and the effect and thwart the production of the effect. Nor are we compelled, as he also contended, to trim down indefinitely the beginning part of the cause (and, *mutatis mutan-*

dis, the end part of the effect) on the ground that the early part of the cause is not necessary to the effect so long as the end part of the cause occurs. For, once more, the cause means something which was sufficient, and not as the objection assumes, something which was both sufficient and necessary, to the effect. Thus the space-limit of the cause process at the outer end is as elastic as we please, and varies with the space-time scope of the particular description of the cause that we give in each concrete case. And the same is true of the outer end of the effect process.[11]

3. The third observation to be made on the definition of cause proposed is that it defines the cause of a particular event in terms of but a single occurrence of it, and thus in no way involves the supposition that it, or one like it, ever has occurred before or ever will again. The supposition of recurrence is thus wholly irrelevant to the meaning of cause; that supposition is relevant only to the meaning of law. And recurrence becomes related at all to causation only when a law is considered which happens to be a generalization of facts themselves individually causal to begin with. A general proposition concerning such facts is, indeed, a causal law, but it is not causal because general. It is general, i.e., a law, only because it is about a classs of resembling facts; and it is causal only because each of them already happens to be a causal fact individually and in its own right (instead of, as Hume would have it, by right of its co-membership with others in a class of pairs of successive events). The causal relation is essentially a relation between concrete individual events; and it is only so far as these events exhibit likeness to others, and can therefore be grouped with them into kinds, that it is possible to pass from individuial causal facts to causal laws. On the other hand, in the case of laws obtained, not by experimentation and generalization of the result of it by abstraction, but in a purely statistical manner (the only manner directly relevant to Hume's notion of cause), it is only quite accidentally that the terms of such "constant conjunctions" as these laws describe stand one to the other as cause and effect. Much more frequently they are not such and are not regarded as such; and uniformity of success thus constitutes not at all the meaning of the cause-effect relation, but at the most only evidence of the existence of some causal connection, perhaps very remote and indirect, *and yet to be discovered*, between the terms of the succession. A causal connection explains the regularity of the succession, but is not constituted by such regularity, which is but a corollary of the causal connection whenever the cause or the chain of causes happens to occur again. Hume himself, indeed, on the very page of the *Enquiry* where he gives his definition of cause (in terms of regularity of succession), says that the definition is "drawn from circumstances foreign to the cause"; "from something extraneous and foreign to it." And it was to avoid having to say, as Hume's defini-

tion would require, that day was the cause of night and night the cause of day, that Mill added, in his own definition, the requirement of "unconditionality" to that of invariability of sequence—without perceiving, however, that as soon as "unconditionality" was introduced, invariability becomes superfluous. For if the effect "unconditionally" follows from the cause, i.e., is *necessitated by* the cause, then, obviously, as often as the cause recurs the effect *must* recur also. But this so-called unconditionality of an effect upon a cause, i.e., the necessitation of the effect by the cause, was the very thing which Mill had declared was not revealed by mere observed regularity of sequence. It must then be ascertained by the experimental "method of difference," i.e., by the analytical observation of an individual case. But Mill never sees that this amounts to *defining* cause in terms of single difference in one experiment. Hume refers to single difference as a "Rule" by which to judge of causes and effects,[12] and Mill, borrowing the blunder, throughout persists in regarding single difference as a "method" for the roundabout ascertainment of something other than itself, viz., of invariable sequence; instead of, and properly, regarding it as the very definition of cause. This is perhaps in part explicable by the fact that Mill never clearly perceived the difference between experimentation and generalization[13] by abstraction; he never was adequately conscious that it is one thing to introduce a single difference, i.e., make a single change, in a given concrete set of circumstances, and note what happens; and a very different thing to compare two such experiments, one of which yielded a certain effect and the other failed to, and note what single difference there was between the single antecedent changes introduced in the two cases into the (same) set of circumstances.

4. As a last remark upon the definition of cause in terms of a single case given above, it may be noted that it is the only one which is faithful to the manner in which the word "cause" is actually used by every person whose English has not been contaminated by Hume. As Russell himself notes, we cannot without "intolerable circumlocution"[14] avoid speaking of one particular event as causing another particular event. And, I ask, why seek to avoid it, when just that is so plainly what we do mean? When any philosophically pure-minded person sees a brick strike a window and the window break, he judges that the impact of the brick was the cause of the breaking, *because* he believes the impact to have been the only change which took place then in the immediate environment of the window. He may, indeed, have been mistaken, and acknowledge that he was mistaken, in believing that impact to have been the only change in the environment. But if so he will nevertheless maintain that *if* it had been the only change, it would have been the cause. That is, he will stand by the definition of cause, and admit merely that what he perceived was not a true case of what he meant and still means by cause.

THE OBSERVABILITY OF THE CAUSAL RELATION

This now brings us to the second of the two theses mentioned at the beginning of this paper, namely, that concerning the observability of the causal relation. Hume's view that no connection between a cause and its effect is objectively observable would be correct only under the assumption that a "connection" is an entity of the same sort as the terms themselves between which it holds, that is, for Hume and his followers, a sense impression. For it is true that neither a color, nor an odor, nor a sound, nor a taste, nor any other sense impression, "connecting" the cause and the effect, is observable between them. Indeed, we must even add that if a sense impression were present between those said to constitute the cause and the effect, it would, from its very nature as a sense impression, be quite incapable of doing any connecting and would itself but constitute one more of the entities to be connected. This is true in particular of the feeling of expectation which Hume would have us believe is what the words "necessary connection" ultimately denote.

But there is fortunately no need for us to attempt to persuade ourselves that whenever people during the past centuries have talked of objective connection they thus have not really meant it at all. For the fact is that causal connection is not a sensation at all, but a relation. The nature of that relation has already been minutely described above. It is, as we have seen, a relation which has individual concrete events for its terms; and, as analyzed by us, its presence among such events is to be observed every day. We observe it whenever we perceive that a certain change is the *only* one to have taken place immediately before, in the immediate environment of another.

But at this point it becomes necessary for us to consider two apparently weighty objections, which can be urged against the observability of what we have defined as constituting the causal relation. One of them is that we are never theoretically certain that we have observed as much as the definition demands; and the other is that, on the other hand, we are often certain that the cause is less than the definition would permit us so to call. Each of these difficulties in turn must be carefully examined.

1. The first of them, more explicitly stated, is this: We never can be certain that the change which we have observed in any given case was, as the definition requires, the *only* change that occurred then and there, and therefore it is always possible that a part of the cause has escaped us. In considering this objection, it is, of course, well to bear in mind that our definition specifies contiguity in space as well as in time of the cause to the effect, and in addition permits us to set the *outer* space-time limit of the environment to be observed as near to the effect as we find convenient; so that

the definition relieves us of the sometimes alleged obligation to observe the antecedent change of the entire universe. But even confining our observation to as externally limited a region of the contiguous space-time as we please, the possibility still always remains that we have not in a given case observed the whole of the change in that environment.

This predicament, it must frankly be admitted, is inescapable. But we must state also, and with all possible emphasis, that it is not peculiar to the definition of causation proposed.[15] Nor, indeed, is it, in its essence, peculiar even to definitions of cause. Rather it is a predicament involved *in every attempt to observe a universal negative*. Thus, even such an assertion as that "this man is Mr. So-and-so" is theoretically always precarious in exactly the same manner, for there is no theoretically absolute guarantee that the man before us is not someone else, who merely happens to be exactly like Mr. So-and-so in the particular respects to which our observation has turned.[16] The predicament mentioned, thus, does not constitute the least evidence against the correctness of our definition of cause, for the very same difficulty would arise no matter what other definition were proposed.

All that we are then called upon to do in connection with that predicament is, first, to call attention to its existence and nature, and sagely class it as a fact illustrating the platitude that life is a precarious business in many ways; and, second, to state explicitly the proviso subject to which cases of causation as defined are observable. This proviso is obviously that *the change which we observed in the antecedently contiguous space-time was really the only change which occcurred in it*. That is not something which we know to be true, but only something which we hope is true, and which for *practical* purposes we must suppose true; i.e., it is a *postulate*—the first of those underlying the present theory of causation. There is, however, no doubt that when, as in the laboratory, we have a high degree of control over the environment, and good opportunity to observe what occurs in it at a given moment, we do make the assumption just stated.

2. The second of the difficulties which we have to examine is of a logical rather than of a practical nature. It arises from the fact that in the face of the definition of cause given, we cannot without a contradiction refuse to take into the cause *any part* of the total change observed in the contiguous space-time environment of the effect; while, on the contrary, we very frequently in fact seem to use the word "cause" as to do just that. Thus, at the instant a brick strikes a window pane, the pane is struck, perhaps by the air waves due to the song of a canary nearby. Yet we usually would say that the cause of the breakage was the impact of the brick, and that the impact of the air waves, although it was part of the prior total change in the contiguous space-time, was no part of the cause. This being the way

in which the word "cause" actually is used, how, then, can a definition which forbids us to call the cause anything less than *the whole* of the prior change in the contiguous space-time be regarded as a correct analysis of the meaning which the term "cause" actually possesses?

The contradiction, however, is only apparent, and depends upon a confusion between two different questions, due in turn to a certain ambiguity in the expression "the cause of an event." The first of the two questions is, *what did cause, i.e., what did then and there suffice to, the occurrence of that concrete individual event?* The second question, on the other hand, is really a double question, for it assumes the answer to the first as already possessed, and goes on to ask, *which part of what did suffice would be left if we subtracted from what did suffice such portions of it as were unnecessary to such an effect?* This is a perfectly significant question, for to say "sufficient to" is one thing; and to say "no more than sufficient to" is another thing: a hundred-pound rock may well have been that which sufficed to the crushing of a worm, but it cannot be said to have been no more than what would have sufficed, since the tenth part of it would also have been enough. The second and double question, moreover, is usually that which we mean to ask when we inquire concerning the cause of an event; but, as will appear directly, it is not, like the first, really an inquiry after the cause of one individual concrete event strictly as such. It is, on the contrary, an inquiry concerning *what is common to it and to the causes of certain other events of the same kind.* This much of a generalization, indeed, is indissolubly involved in the mere assigning of *a name* to the cause and to the effect perceived; although *it is not involved in the merely perceiving them.* This is an extremely important point, which constitutes the very key to the whole matter. That this is so will become fully evident if the significance of the second of the two questions above is more explicitly analyzed.

If we inquire what exactly is required to define the meaning of that (double) question, we find at least *two* hypothetical cases are needed. For to say that in a given case a certain change *sufficed* to the occurrence of a given event, means, as we have seen, that no other change than it did occur in the prior contiguous space-time; and to say that a certain portion of that change was *unnecessary* means that in a case where that portion of the change did *not* occur—*which case therefore cannot be the very identical case, but only a case that is otherwise similar*—an(other) event of the same sort as the effect considered nevertheless did result. But now the fact that at least two hypothetical cases are thus necessary to define the meaning of our second question above implies that that question is wholly meaningless with regard to one single concrete event. It is a question not, like the first, concerning the cause of one single concrete event, but concerning what was, or would be, *common to the causes* of at least two such.

The apparent contradiction which we faced is therefore now disposed of, for if, by "the cause of an event," we really mean the cause of one individual concrete event, and not merely of some case of a sort of event, then we must include in our answer *the whole* of the antecedent change in the contiguous space-time. And if, on the other hand, our answer leaves out any part of that change (as it often does), then the only question to which it can be a correct answer is one as to *what was common to the individual causes* of two or more individual events of a given sort. Thus, if we say that the impact of a brick was the cause of the breaking of the window, and that the song of the canary had no part in it, then the words "the breaking of the window" do not refer to an individual event considered in its full concreteness, but only to a *case-of-a-kind*, uniquely placed and dated indeed, but not qualitatively specified otherwise than by the characters that define its kind, viz., "breaking of window." And it is solely owing to this that we can truly say that the song of the canary had nothing to do with it, for that means, then, nothing to do with what occurred *in so far as what occurred is viewed merely as a case of breakage of a window.* As already explained, to say that the song of the canary was unnecessary is not to say that it was not part of what did then and there suffice; it *is* to say only that in *another* case, otherwise similar, where the song did not occur, an effect of the *same sort*, viz., breaking, nevertheless did occur.

The whole of our answer to the objection we have been discussing may, after all this detail, be summarized by saying that the expression "the cause of the breaking of this window" has two senses, one strict, and the other elliptical. In the strict sense, it means "the full concrete individual event which caused all the concrete detail of this breaking of the window." In the elliptical (and indeed more practically interesting) sense, it means "that which the cause of this breaking of this window has in common with the individual causes of certain other individual events of the same sort."

THE GENERALIZATIONS OF OBSERVED CAUSAL FACTS

It is, of course, to be acknowledged that, as the parenthesis in the last sentence suggests, we are interested in causes and effects primarily for practical purposes, and that for such purposes causal knowledge is of direct value only so far as it has been generalized. This means that the interest of strictly concrete individual facts of causation to us is chiefly the indirect one of constituting raw material for generalization. And this explains why we so naturally and so persistently confuse the question, what did cause one given concrete event, with the very different question, in what respects does that cause resemble the causes of certain other events of the same sort previously observed in similar environments. For it is from the answer to this second question that we learn what in such environments is the most we must do to cause the occurrence of another event of the given sort. And evidently just that is the very practically valuable information that we desire ultimately to obtain. But although it is true that, as practical beings, we are not directly interested in concrete individual facts of causation, it is not true that there are no such facts; nor, as we have seen, is it true that generality or recurrence is any part of the meaning of cause.

To round out the outline of the theory of the causal relation which this paper sets forth, there remains only to state the two postulates which condition, respectively, the validity of the descriptions by names which we formulate to fit sets of individual causal facts, and the validity of the applications we make of such generalizing descriptions to new cases.

The postulate which conditions the correctness of any answer we venture to give to the problem of description, viz., the problem in what respects the case of a given concrete event resembles the causes of certain others of the same sort previously observed in similar environments,[17] is that *the respects of resemblance which we include in our answer* (through the name by which we describe the cause) *are really the only ones that there were.* This postulate, which may be called that of the *descriptibility* of our causal observations, is then the second postulate of our theory. The first, which it will be recalled was that no change that was not observed occurred in the prior contiguous space-time environment, may be called that of the *observability* of causal facts. And the third postulate, which we may term that of the *applicability* of our descriptions of our observations of causal facts to new cases, is that *the new case (or cases) differs from those on the basis of which the description was formulated not otherwise nor more widely than they differed among themselves.*

NOTES

1. In a monograph on causation by the writer, these two points are argued at some length. See *Causation and the Types of Necessity* (University of Washington Press, 1924), pp. 52 ff.

2. More technically, an event can be defined as either a change or an absence of change in the relation of an object to either an intensive or an extensive standard of reference, during a specified time interval.

3. Cf. Schopenhauer, *The Fourfold Root of the Principle of Sufficient Reason*, trans. Hillebrand, pp. 38 ff.; and Wundt, *Logik*, 3rd ed., i.586.

4. The limit of a change of a solid is obviously a surface, not a point.

5. "The cause . . . is the sum total of the conditions, positive and negative taken together . . . which being realized, the consequent invariably follows" (*Systems of Logic*, bk. III, ch. v, No. 3). This definition is obviously in flagrant contradiction with Mill's characterization of the cause as the single difference in the circumstances, in the canon of the "Method of Difference."

6. "On the Notion of Cause," *Proceedings of the Aristotelian Society* 13 (1912–13).

7. The apt term "unchange" is borrowed from Dr. Charles Mercier's book, *Causation and Belief*.

8. A stage might, however, conceivably be reached, at which the parts obtained by the division of a change, would, *in terms of the particular test of changing used at the previous stages of division*, be themselves not changes, but unchanges (though, of course, nonetheless extended in time and space and therefore divisible). That is, the assertion that something changes, or, equally, does not change, remains ambiguous so long as some definite test of such change has not been specified as standard. Thus the assertion might be true in terms of one test and false in terms of another. Cf. "A Liberalistic View of Truth," by the writer, in the *Philosophical Review* for November 1925.

9. In practice, no space-time dimension of a relevant order of magnitude. Clock ticks and graduation lines as used are never perfectly dimensionless.

10. This view of the space-time relation of cause and effect, I was gratified to find, is also that set forth by Mr. Johnson in vol. III of his *Logic* (p. 74), which appeared at virtually the same time as the monograph on causation referred to above.

11. It is interesting to note that the analysis of the space-time relation of cause and effect given above reveals an essential connection between the two notions of Change and of Causation. For, taking any given change process, by specifying a space-time cut of it, one splits it into a cause and an effect; and, on the other hand, taking any given cause and its effect, by abstracting from the particular space-time cut in terms of which as common limit the cause process is distinguished from the effect process, one obtains a process describable as one change. This calls to mind Kant's very inadequately argued contention in the Second Analogy, that (objective) change involves the category of causation.

12. *Treatise*, bk. I, part III, No. 15.

13. This has been noted by Jevons, *Pure Logic and Other Minor Works*, p. 251.

14. *Scientific Method in Philosophy*, p. 220.

15. The corresponding difficulty with the Humean definition of cause as regular sequence is that experience never can guarantee that exceptions to the regularity of the sequence have not escaped our observation; or, more generally, that the sample of the character of the sequence, which we have observed, is a "fair sample."

16. This difficulty becomes particularly acute when the opportunity for observation is limited, as, e.g., in establishing one's identity over the telephone; or, again, in the endeavor of psychical researchers to check up on the alleged identity of the "controls" of their mediums.

17. Mill correctly states that "It is inherent in a description to be the statement of a resemblance, or resemblances," *Logic*, p. 452.

12

On the So-Called Idea of Causation

R. G. Collingwood

The argument of this paper may be summarized as follows. Causal propositions (propositions of the type "*x* causes *y*") are ambiguous. Such a proposition may have any one of three meanings (possibly more; but three is enough for this paper). The ambiguity, however, is of a rather odd kind. Sense I, which is historically the original sense, is presupposed by the others, and remains strictly speaking the one and only "proper" sense. When we assert propositions containing the word cause in senses II and III, we are "saying" one thing and "meaning" another; we are describing certain things as if they were things of a kind which we do not actually believe them to be. This always has an element of danger in it: the danger of inadvertently beginning to "mean" what one has only intended to "say," i.e., of thinking that things are what we describe them as if they were. This danger is much worse when our "metaphors" get "mixed." This is what has happened with the so-called "idea of causation" from the time of Kant onwards. It is a confusion of certain characteristics belonging to sense II with certain others belonging to sense III. Nothing can be done, therefore, towards clearing up our minds about causation, by merely analyzing the idea as it stands and detailing the various elements it contains; for these elements are mutually contradictory. We must carry the process further, by segregating the elements under different heads, and distinguishing these as different "senses" of the word. But even this is

From *Proceedings of the Aristotelian Society* 38 (1938). Copyright The Aristotelian Society 1938. Reprinted by courtesy of the editor.

not enough. A further step in the process is needed: namely a critical discussion of each "sense" taken singly. When this is done it will be found that the best way of avoiding confusion will be to restrict our use of the word cause to occasions on which it is used in its "proper" sense, No. I; that on the occasions on which we use it in sense II we should be wise to use instead the terminology of means and ends; and that when we use it in sense III we should do better to speak of "laws" and their "instances."

I

In the first sense of the word cause, that which is caused is the free and deliberate act of a conscious and responsible agent, and "causing" him to do it means affording him a motive for doing it. For "causing," we may substitute "making," "inducing," "persuading," "urging," "forcing," "compelling," according to differences in the kind of motive in question.

This is at the present time a current and familiar sense of the word (together with its cognates, correlatives, and equivalents) in English, and of the corresponding words in other modern languages; also of *causa* in ancient Latin and αἴτιον in ancient Greek. A headline in a newspaper in 1936 ran "Mr. Baldwin's speech causes adjournment of House." This did not mean that Mr. Baldwin's speech compelled the Speaker to adjourn the House whether or not that event conformed with his own ideas and intentions; it meant that on hearing Mr. Baldwin's speech the Speaker freely made up his mind to adjourn. In the same sense we say that a solicitor's letter causes a man to pay a debt, or that bad weather causes him to return from an expedition. . . .

A cause in this sense consists of two elements, a *causa quod* or efficient cause and a *causa ut* or final cause. The *causa quod* is a situation, or state of things existing; the *causa ut* is a purpose, or state of things to be brought about. Neither of these could be a cause if the other were absent. A man who tells his stockbroker to sell a certain holding may be caused to act thus by a rumor about the financial position of that company; but this rumor would not cause him to sell out unless he wanted to avoid being involved in the affairs of an unsound business. And *per contra*, a man's wish to avoid falling over a precipice would not cause him to stop walking in a certain direction if he knew there was no precipice in that direction.

The *causa quod* is not a situation or state of things as such, it is a situation or state of things known or believed by the agent in question to exist. If a prospective litigant briefs a certain barrister because of his exceptional ability, the cause of his doing so is not this ability simply as such, it is this ability as something known to the litigant or believed in by him.

The *causa ut* is not a desire or wish as such, it is an intention. A man is "caused" to act in a certain way not by wanting to act in that way (for it is possible to want so to act without so acting) but by meaning to act in that way. There may be causes where mere desire leads to action without the intermediate phase of intention; but such action is not deliberate.

Causes of this kind may come into operation through the act of a second conscious and responsible agent, insofar as he (1) informs or persuades the first that a certain state of things exists, as when a man's solicitor informs or persuades him of a certain barrister's exceptional ability; or (2) exhorts or otherwise persuades the first to form a certain intention. This second agent is said to "cause" the first to do a certain act or to "make him do it."

The act so caused, however, is still an act; it could not be done (and therefore could not be caused) unless the agent did it of his own free will. If A causes B to do an act β, β is B's act and not A's; B is a free agent in doing it, and is responsible for it. If β is a murder, which A persuaded B to commit by pointing out certain facts or urging certain expediencies, B is the murderer. There is no contradiction between the proposition that the act β was caused by A, and the proposition that B was a free agent in respect of β, and is thus responsible for it. On the contrary, the first proposition implies the second.

Nevertheless, in this case A is said to "share the responsibility" for the act β. This does not imply that a responsibility is a divisible thing, which would be absurd; an absurdity into which people do no doubt fall, e.g., when they speak of collective guarantees. It means that whereas B is responsible for the act β, A is responsible for his own act, α, viz., the act of pointing out certain facts to B or urging upon him certain expediencies, whereby he induces him to commit the act β. When a child, accused of a misdeed, rounds on his accuser saying, "you made me do it," he is not excusing himself, he is implicating his accuser as an accessory. This is what Adam was doing when he said "the woman whom thou gavest me, she gave me of the tree and I did eat."

A man is said to act "on his own responsibility" or "on his sole responsibility" when (1) his knowledge or belief about the situation is not dependent on information or persuasion from anyone else, and (2) his intentions or purposes are similarly independent. In this case (the case in which a man is ordinarily said to exhibit "initiative") his action is not uncaused. It still has both a *causa quod* and a *causa ut*. But because he has done for himself, unaided, the double work of envisaging the situation and forming the intention, which in the alternative case another man (who is therefore said to cause his own action) has done for him, he can now be said to *cause* his own action as well as to *do* it. If he invariably acted in that way, the total complex of his activities could be called self-causing (*causa sui*); an expression which simply refers to an absence of persuasion or inducement on the part of another, and has been unintelligently denounced as nonsensical only because people will not ask themselves what they mean by the word cause.

II

In sense II, no less than in sense I, the word cause expresses an idea relative to human action; but the action in this case is an action intended to control, not other human beings, but things in "nature," or "physical" things. In this sense, the "cause" of an event in nature is the handle, so to speak, by which we can manipulate it. If we want to produce or to prevent such a thing, and cannot produce or prevent it immediately (as we can produce or prevent certain movements of our own bodies), we set about looking for its "cause." The question "What is the cause of an event *y*?" means in this case "How can we produce or prevent *y* at will?"

This sense of the word may be defined as follows. *A cause is an event or state of things which it is in our power to produce or prevent, and by producing or preventing which we can produce or prevent that whose cause it is said to be.* When I speak of "producing" something, I refer to such occasions as when, e.g., one turns a switch and thus produces the states of things described by the proposition "The switch is now at the ON position." By preventing something I mean producing something incompatible with it, e.g., turning the switch to the OFF position.

This is an extremely common sense in modern everyday usage. The cause of a bruise is the kick which a man received on his ankle; the cause of malaria is the bite of a mosquito; the cause of a boat's sinking is her being overloaded; the cause of books going moldy is their being kept in a damp room; the cause of a person's sweating is that he has taken aspirin; the cause of a furnace going out in the night is that the draught door was insufficiently open; the cause of seedlings dying is that nobody watered them; and so forth.

The search for causes in sense II is "natural science," in that sense of the phrase in which natural science is what Aristotle calls a "practical science," valued not for its truth pure and simple but for its utility, for the "power over nature" which it gives us: Baconian science, where "knowledge is power" and where "nature is conquered by obeying her." The field of a "practical science" is the contingent, or in Aristotle's terminology "what admits of being otherwise." The switch, for example, is on, but it admits of being off; i.e., I find by experiment that I am able to turn it to the OFF position. To discover that things are contingent is to discover that we can produce and prevent them.

A conspicuous example of practical natural science is medicine. A great deal of time and money is now being spent on "cancer research," whose purpose is "to discover the cause of cancer." If we knew the cause of it, we should be able to prevent or cure it; that is the aim of all this work. But why should it be assumed that knowing the cause of cancer would enable us to produce or prevent it? Suppose someone claimed to have discovered the cause of cancer, but added that his discovery though genuine would not in practice be of any use because the cause he had discovered was not a thing that could be produced or prevented at will. Such a person would be universally ridiculed and despised. No one would admit that he had done what he claimed to do. It would be pointed out that he did not know what the word cause (in the context of medicine, be it understood) meant. For in such a context a proposition of the form "*x* causes *y*" implies the proposition "*x* is something that can be produced or prevented at will" as part of the definition of "cause." . . .

A "cause" in sense II never means something which is able by itself to produce the "effect." When in this sense we say that *x* causes *y*, we are never talking about *x* by itself. We are always talking about *x* in combination with other things which we do not specify; these being called *conditiones sine quibus non*. For example, damp will not cause books to go moldy unless there are mold spores about.

The relation between the cause and these "conditions," as I shall call them, has often been misunderstood, for example by Mill. Mill defines the cause of an event as its invariable antecedent (a definition applicable to sense III, not to sense II). If so, the event should follow given the cause and nothing else. If certain conditions are necessary, over and above the cause, in order that the event should follow (which is true of sense II not of sense III), then surely the *true* cause is not what we have just called the cause but this *plus* the said conditions. Mill concludes that the true cause is the sum of a set of conditions, and that what people ordinarily call the cause is one of these, arbitrarily selected and, by a mere misuse of language, dignified with a name that properly belongs only to the whole set.

Closer inspection would have shown Mill that this "selection" is by no means arbitrary. It is made according to a definite principle. If my car "conks out" on a hill and I wonder what the cause is, I shall not consider my problem solved by a passer-by who tells me that the top of a hill is further away from the earth's center than its bottom, and that consequently more power is needed to take a car uphill than to take her along the level. All this is quite true; what the passer-by has described is one of the conditions which, together, form the "true cause" of my car's stopping; and as he has "arbitrarily selected" one of these and called it the cause, he has done just what Mill says we always do. But now suppose an A.A. man comes along, opens the bonnet, holds up a loose high-tension lead, and says "Look here, sir, you're running on three cylinders." My problem is now solved. I know the cause of the stoppage. It is *the* cause, just because it has not been "arbitrarily selected"; it has been correctly identified as the thing that I can put right, after which the car will go properly. If had I been a person who could flatten out hills by stamping on them, the passer-by would have been right to call my attention to the hill as the cause of the stoppage; not because the hill is a hill, but because I can flatten it out.

The cause is not "arbitrarily selected," it is identified according to a principle which is in fact the definition of the term cause in sense II. It is not, properly speaking, "selected" at all; for selection implies that the person selecting has before him a finite number of things from among which he takes his choice. But this does not happen. In the first place, the conditions of any given event are quite possibly infinite in number, so that no one *could* thus marshal them for selection even if he tried. In the second place, no one ever tries to enumerate them completely. Why should he? If I find that I can get a result by certain means, I may be pretty sure that I should not be getting it unless a great many conditions were fulfilled; but so long as I get it I do not mind what these conditions are. If owing to a change in one of them I fail to get it, I still do not want to know what they *all* are; I only want to know what the one is that has changed.

From this a principle follows which I shall call "the relativity of causes." Suppose that the conditions of an event y include three things, α β γ; and suppose that there are three persons, A, B, C, of whom A is able to produce or prevent α and only α; B is able to produce or prevent β and only β; and C is able to produce or prevent γ and only γ. Then if each of them asks "What was the cause of y?" each will have to give a different answer. For A, α is the cause; for B, β; and for C, γ. The principle may be started by saying that *for any given person, the cause of a given thing is that one of its conditions which he is able to produce or prevent*. For example, a car skids while cornering at a certain point, turns turtle, and bursts into flame. From the car-driver's point of view, the cause of the accident was cornering too fast, and the lesson is that one must drive more carefully. From the county surveyor's point of view, the cause was a defective road surface, and the lesson is that one must make skid-proof roads. From the motor manufacturer's point of view, the cause was defective design, and the lesson is that one must place the center of gravity lower.

If one of these three parties "threw the blame" for the accident on one of the others, if for example the surveyor said "It is the business of drivers to prevent accidents of that sort; it isn't mine," we all know that nothing would be done, by him at any rate, towards preventing them; that is to say, his "knowledge" of their cause would be a "knowledge" that did not result in power. But since a cause in this sense of the word is by definition something whose knowledge *is* power, this means that his so-called knowledge is not knowledge at all. The proposition in which he states it is in fact a nonsense proposition: "The cause of *y* from my point of view, i.e., that one of its conditions which I am able to produce or prevent, is something which somebody else is able to produce or prevent, but I am not." Hence the futility of blaming other people in respect of events in which we and they are together involved. Everyone knows that such blame is futile; but without such analysis of the idea of cause as I am here giving, it is not easy to see why it should be.

A further corollary of the same principle is that, for a person who is not able to produce or prevent any of its conditions, a given event has no cause at all, and any statement he makes about it will be a nonsense statement. Thus, the managing director of a large insurance company once told me that his wide experience of motor accidents had convinced him that the cause of all accidents was people driving too fast. This of course was a nonsense statement; but one could expect nothing better from a man whose practical concern with these affairs was limited to their after-effects. In sense II of the word cause, only a person who is practically concerned with a certain kind of event can form an opinion about its cause. For a mere spectator there are no causes. When Hume tried to show how the mere act of spectation could in time generate the idea of a cause, where "cause" meant the cause of empirical science, he was trying to explain how something happens which in fact does not happen.

If sciences are constructed consisting of causal propositions in sense II of the word cause, they will of course be in essence codifications of the various ways in which the people who construct them can bend nature to their purposes, and of the means by which in each case this can be done. Their constitutional propositions will be (*a*) experimental (*b*) general.

(*a*) In calling them experimental I mean that their assertion will depend on "experiment." No amount of "observation" will serve to establish such a proposition; for any such proposition is a declaration of our ability to produce or prevent a certain state of things by the use of certain means, and no one knows what he can do, or how he can do it, until he tries. Nevertheless, he may by "observing" and "thinking" form the opinion that he can *probably* do a given thing that resembles one he has done in the past.

(*b*) Because the proposition "*x* causes *y*" is a constituent part of a practical science, it is essentially something that can be "applied" to cases arising in practice; that is to say, the terms *x* and *y* are not individuals but universals, and the proposition itself, rightly understood, reads "Any instance of *x* is a thing whose production or prevention is means respectively of producing or preventing some instance of *y*." It would be nonsense, in this sense of the word cause, to inquire about the cause of any individual thing as such. It is a peculiarity of sense II, that every causal proposition is a "general proposition" or "propositional function." In sense I, every causal proposition is an "individual proposition," which cannot be read in the above form. In sense III, causal propositions might equally well be either individual or general.

If the above analysis of the cause-effect relation (in sense II) into a means-end relation is correct, why do people describe this means-end relation in cause-effect terminology? People do not choose words at random, they choose them because they think them appropriate. If they apply cause-effect terminology to things whose relation is really that of means and end, the reason must be that they want to apply to those things some idea which is conveyed by the cause-effect terminology and not by the means-end terminology. What is this idea? The answer, I think, is not doubtful. The cause-effect terminology conveys an idea not only of one thing's leading to another, but of one thing's forcing another to happen or exist; an idea of power or compulsion or constraint.

From what impression, as Hume pertinently asks, is this idea derived? I answer, from impressions received in our social life, in the practical relations of man to man; specifically, from the impression of "compelling" or "causing" some other man to do something when, by argument or command or threat or the like, we place him in a situation in which he can only carry out his intentions by doing that thing; and conversely, from the impression of being compelled or caused to do something.

Why, then, did people think it appropriate to apply this idea, thus derived, to the case of actions in which we achieve our ends by means, not of other human beings, but of things in nature? In order to answer this question we must remember that sense II of the word cause is especially a Greek sense, and in modern times especially associated with the revival of Greek ideas in the earlier Renaissance thinkers; and that both the Greeks and the earlier Renaissance thinkers held quite seriously an animistic theory of nature. They thought of what we call the material or physical world as a living organism or complex of living organisms, each with its own sensations and desires and intentions and thoughts. In Plato's *Timaeus*, and in the Renaissance Platonists whose part in the formation of modern science was so decisive, the constant use of language with animistic implications is neither an accident nor a metaphor; these expressions are meant to be taken literally and to imply what they seem to imply, namely, that the way in which men use what we nowadays call inorganic nature as means to our ends is not in principle different from the way in which we use other men. We use other men by assuming them to be free agents with wills of their own, and influencing them in such a way that they shall decide to do what is in conformity with our plans. This is "causing" them so to act, in the first and original sense of the word. If "inorganic nature" is alive in much the same way as human beings, we must use it according to the same principles; and therefore we can apply to this use of it the same word "cause" in the same sense, viz., as implying—

(1) That there are certain ways in which natural things behave if left to themselves;

(2) That man, being more powerful than they, is able to thwart their inclination to behave in these ways, and by the exercise of his superior magic to make them behave, not as they like, but as he likes.

And if anybody is so truthful as to admit that, in our experimental science, we do constantly use language which taken literally implies all this, but argues that it is "mere metaphor" and never meant to be taken literally, I reply: then express yourself literally; and you will find that all this language about causation disappears, and that you are left with a vocabulary in which all that is said is that we find certain means useful to certain ends.

III

Sense III of the word cause represents an attempt to apply it not to "practical science" but to "theoretical science." I shall first explain the characteristics which would belong to this sense if the attempt were successful, and then consider certain difficulties which in the long run prove fatal to it.

(1) In the contingent world to which sense II belongs, a cause is contingent (*a*) in its existence, as depending for its existence on human volition (*b*) in its operation, as depending for the production of its effect on *conditiones sine quibus non*. In the necessary world to which sense III belongs, a cause is necessary (*a*) in its existence, as existing whether or not human beings want it to exist (*b*) in its operation, as producing its effect no matter what else exists or does not exist. There are no *conditiones sine quibus non*. The cause leads to its effect by itself, or "unconditionally"; in other words the relation between cause and effect is a one-one relation. There can be no relativity of causes, and no diversity of effects due to fulfillment or nonfulfillment of conditions.

I propose to distinguish the one-many and many-one[1] character of the cause-effect relation in sense II from its one-one character in sense III by calling these senses *loose* and *tight* respectively. A loose cause requires some third thing extraneous both to itself and to its effect to bind the two together; a tight cause is one whose connection with its effect is independent of such adventitious aids.

In order to illustrate the implications of sense III, I will refer to the contradiction between the traditional denial of *actio in distans* (which, I suppose, would hold as against action across a lapse of time, no less than across a distance in space) and the assumption, commonly made nowadays, that a cause precedes its effect in time. I shall argue that *action in distans* is perfectly intelligible in sense II, but nonsense in sense III.

If I set fire to the end of a time-fuse, and five minutes later the charge at its other end explodes, there is a "causal" connection between the first and second events, and a time interval of five minutes between them. But this interval is occupied by the burning of the fuse at a determinate rate of feet per minute; and this process is a *conditio sine qua non* of the causal efficacy ascribed to the first event. That is to say, the connection between the lighting of the fuse and the detonation of the charge is "causal" in the loose sense, not the tight one. If in the proposition "*x* causes the explosion" we wish to use the word cause in the tight sense, *x* must include any such *conditio sine qua non*. That is, it must include the burning of the whole fuse; not its burning until "just before" that process reaches the detonator, for then there would still be an interval to be bridged, but its burning until the detonator is reached. Only then is the cause in sense III complete; and when it is complete it produces its effect, not afterwards (however soon afterwards) but then. Cause in sense III is simultaneous with effect.

Similarly, it is coincident with its effect in space. The cause of the explosion is where the explosion is. For suppose *x* causes *y*, and suppose that *x* is in a position p_1 and *y* in a position p_2, the distance from p_1 to p_2 being δ. If "cause" is used in sense II, δ may be any distance, so long as it is bridged by a series of events which are *conditiones sine quibus non* of *x* causing *y*. But if "cause" is used in sense III, δ must = zero. For if it did not, p_2 would be any position on the surface of a sphere whose center was p_1 and whose radius would be δ; so the relation between p_1 and p_2 would be a one-many relation. But the relation between *x* and *y*, where *x* causes *y* in sense III, is a one-one relation. Therefore where δ does not = 0, *x* cannot cause *y* in sense III.

The denial of *actio in distans*, spatial or temporal, where the "agent" is a cause in sense III, is therefore logically involved in the definition of sense III.

(2) The main difficulty about sense III is to explain what is meant by saying that a cause "produces" or "necessitates" its effect. When similar language is used of senses I and II we know what it means: in sense I it means that *x* affords somebody a motive for doing *y*, in sense II that *x* is somebody's means of bringing *y* about. But what (since it cannot mean either of these) does it mean in sense III?

There are two well-known answers to this question, which may be called the rationalist and empiricist answers respectively.

(i) The rationalist answer runs: "necessitation means implication." A cause, on this view, is a "ground" and its relation to its effect is the relation of ground to consequent, a logical relation. When someone says that x necessitates y he means on this view that x implies y, and is claiming the same kind of insight into y which one has (for example) into the length of one side of a triangle given the lengths of the other two sides and the included angle. Whatever view one takes as to the nature of implication, one must admit that in such a case the length of the third side can be ascertained without measuring it and even without seeing it, e.g., when it lies on the other side of a hill. The implication theory, therefore, implies that "if the cause is given the effect follows," not only in the sense that if the cause exists the effect actually follows, but that if the cause is thought the effect follows logically. That is to say, anyone who wishes to discover the effect of a given thing x can discover the answer by simply thinking out the logical implications of x. Nothing in the nature of observation or experiment is needed.

This is in itself a tenable position in the sense that, if anyone wants to construct a system of science in which the search for causes means a search for grounds, there is nothing to prevent him from trying. This was in fact what Descartes tried to do. His projected "universal science" was to be a system of grounds and consequents. And if, as is sometimes said, modern physics represents a return in some degree to the Cartesian project, it would seem that the attempt is being made once more. But the rationalist theory of causation, however valuable it may be as the manifesto of a particular scientific enterprise, cannot be regarded as an "analysis" of the causal propositions asserted by existing science. If it were accepted, these propositions would have to be abandoned as untrue. For no one thinks that they can be established by sheer "thinking," that is, by finding the so-called effects to be logically implied in the so-called causes; it is just because this is impossible that the questions what causes a given effect, and what effect a given cause produces, have to be answered by observation and experiment. Hence the result of establishing a science of the Cartesian type would be, not an analysis of propositions of the type "x causes y" into propositions of the type "x implies y," but the disuse of causal propositions in that kind of science and the use of implicational propositions instead; while in the sciences of observation and experiment causal propositions not analyzable into implicational propositions would still be used; the meaning of "necessity" in these causal propositions being still doubtful.

This situation would not be really illuminated by alleging that the sciences in which causal propositions occur are "backward" or "immature sciences." Such a statement would imply that the idea of causation is a half-baked idea which when properly thought out will turn into the different idea of implication. This I take to be the Hegelian theory of the dialectic of concepts, and if anyone wishes to maintain it I do not want to prevent him; but I must observe that it does not excuse him from answering the question what the half-baked idea is "*an sich*," that is, before its expected transformation has happened.

(ii) I turn to the empiricist answer: "necessitation means observed uniformity of conjunction." Like the former answer, this one cannot be taken literally; for no one, I think, will pretend that the proposition "*x* necessitates *y*" means *merely* "all the observed *x*'s have been observed to be conjoined with *y*'s," and does not also imply "*x*'s observed in the future will also be conjoined with *y*'s." In fact the question (so urgent for, e.g., Hume and Mill) how we proceed from the mere experience of conjunction to the assertion of causal connection resolves itself into the question how we pass from the first of these two propositions to the second; so that the proposition "all the observed *x*'s have been observed to be conjoined with *y*'s" is not what we mean by saying "*x* necessitates *y*," but is only the empirical evidence on the strength of which we assert the very different proposition "*x* necessitates *y*." Thus, if anyone says "necessitation means observed uniformity of conjunction, it must be supposed either that he is talking without thinking; or that he is carelessly expressing what, expressed more accurately, would run:—"necessitation is something we assert on the strength of observed uniformity of conjunction," without telling us what he thinks necessitation to be; or, thirdly, that he is expressing still more carelessly what should run:—"in order to assert a necessitation we must pass from the first of the above propositions to the second; now I cannot see how this is possible; therefore we ought never to assert necessitations, but on the occasions when we do assert them we ought to be asserting something quite different, namely, observed conjunction."

(iii) A third answer to our question has been given by Mr. Russell, in a paper[2] of very great importance, to which I shall have to refer again; but I want here and now to express my great admiration for it and my great indebtedness to it. He says "*necessary* is a predicate of a propositional function meaning that it is true for all possible values of its argument or arguments." This I will call the "functional" answer. Insofar as it amounts to saying that causation in sense III implies a one-one relation between cause and effect, I entirely agree. But I find myself, very reluctantly, unable to accept all of what I take Mr. Russell to mean.

(α) How, on the functional theory, could anyone ever know a causal proposition to be true, or even know that the facts in his possession tended to justify a belief in it? Only, I submit, if there is a relation of implication between *x* and *y*. For "all *possible* values" of *x* may be an infinite number; and, even if they are not, it may not be practicable to examine them individually. If *a, b, c*, are the sides of any triangle, we know that $a + b - c$ will always be a positive quantity, because that is implied in the definition of a triangle. Thus the functional theory presupposes the rationalistic or implicational theory, which I have already given reason for rejecting.

(β) I do not know whether Mr. Russell's statement quoted above was intended to mean "*necessity* is, etc., and never anything else." But if so, I deny it. Necessity has a second meaning, as when on receiving Mr. Hannay's demand for a paper last summer I said "I can't get out of it this time," i.e., "I am necessitated or compelled to read a paper on this occasion." If I say "It is necessary for me to read a paper," the word necessary is not a predicate of a propositional function; it refers to a case of causation in sense I, and means that Mr. Hannay has compelled me so to act. The second sense of necessity, in which it refers to compulsion, is (I shall try to show) the sense which is involved not only in sense I and sense II of the word cause but in sense III also.

(γ) The functional theory would imply that there can be no necessitation and therefore no causation of the individual. Anything that happened only once, like the origin of life on the earth (assuming that all organisms are derived from one original organism and that life exists nowhere else), would be "contingent" not in the sense of being capable of alteration by human interference, but in the sense of being a causeless event in nature. No doubt, it would be impossible on Hume's theory of knowledge, and also on Mill's, to discover the cause of an event *sui generis*; but it seems to be generally agreed nowadays that every event has a cause, even though we cannot discover what its cause is; and if a theory is put forward to the effect that an event *sui generis* has no cause, it may or may not be metaphysically true, but it certainly cannot be a true account of "our idea" of causation; for it contradicts that idea.

(3) Most people think that when we use the word causation in sense III we mean to express by it something different from logical implication, and something more than uniformity of conjunction, whether observed only, or observed in the past and also expected in the future; and that this "something different" and "something more" is in the nature of compulsion. I think that this view is correct.

We have now to ask the same question which we asked when we found the same idea present in sense II; and we shall have to answer it in the same way. From what impression is this idea derived? It seems to be quite clear that it is derived from our experience of occasions on which we have compelled others to act in certain ways by placing them in situations (or calling their attention to the fact that they are in situations) of such a kind that only by so acting can they realize the intentions we know or rightly assume them to entertain: and conversely, occasions in which we have ourselves been thus compelled. Compulsion is an idea derived from our social experience, and applied in what is called a "metaphorical" way not only to our relations with things in nature (sense II of the word cause) but also to the relations which these things have among themselves (sense III). Causal propositions in sense III are descriptions of natural events in anthropomorphic terms.

The reason why we are in the habit of using these anthropomorphic terms is, of course, that they are traditional. Inquiry into the history of the tradition shows that it grew up in connection with the same animistic theory of nature to which I referred in discussing sense II of the word cause, but that in this case the predominant factor was a theology of neo-Platonic inspiration.

If a man can be said to "cause" certain events in nature by adopting certain means to bringing them about, and if God is conceived anthropomorphically as having faculties like those of the human mind but greatly magnified, it will follow that God also will be regarded as bringing about certain things in nature by the adoption of certain means. Now comes a step in the argument which, if we tried to reconstruct it without historical knowledge, we should probably reconstruct quite wrongly. If x is a thing in nature produced by God as a means of producing y, we might fancy x to be a purely passive instrument in God's hand, having no power of its own, but "inert," as Berkeley in the true spirit of post-Galilean physics insists that matter must be. And in that case God alone would possess that compulsive force which is expressed by the word cause; that word would not be given as a name to x, and God would be the "sole cause." Actually, God is for medievel thinkers not the "sole cause" but the "first cause." This does not mean the first term in a series of efficient causes (a barbarous misinterpretation of the phrase), but a cause of a peculiar kind, as distinct from "secondary causes." The *Liber de Causis*, a neo-Platonic Arabic work of the ninth century, whose influence on medieval cosmology was at this point decisive, lays it down that God in creating certain instruments for the realization of certain ends, confers upon these instruments a power in certain ways like his own, though inferior to it. Thus endowed with a kind of minor and derivative godhead, these instruments accordingly acquire the character of causes, and constitute that division of nature which, according to John the Scot, "both is created and creates." Their causality is thus a special kind of causality existing wholly within nature, whereby one thing in nature produces or necessitates another thing in nature. The words "produces" and "necessitates" are here used literally and deliberately to convey a sense of volition and compulsion; for the anthropomorphic account of natural things is taken as literally true; the activity of these secondary causes is a scaled-down version of God's and God's is a scaled-up version of man's.

This was the atmosphere in which our modern conception of nature took shape, and in which the categories appertaining to that conception were worked out. For in the sixteenth and seventeenth centuries, when the animistic conception of nature was replaced among scientists and philosophers by a mechanical one, the word cause was not a novelty; it was a long-established term, and its meaning was rooted in these neo-Platonic notions.

Thus, when we come to Newton, and read the *Scholium* appended to his first eight definitions, we find him using as a matter of course a whole vocabulary which, taken literally, ascribes to "causes" in nature a kind of power which properly belongs to one human being inducing another to act as he wishes him to act. Newton assumes that a cause is something capable of "impressing some force" upon that in which its effect is produced. For example, if what is produced is a movement of a certain body, Newton says that such movement "is neither generated nor altered, but by some force impressed upon the body moved." Here, and throughout his treatment of the subject, it is perfectly clear that for him the idea of causation is the idea of force, compulsion, constraint, exercised by something powerful over another thing which if not under his constraint would behave differently; this hypothetical different behavior being called by contrast "free" behavior. This constraint of one thing in nature by another is simply the secondary causation of medieval cosmology. Taken *au pied de la lettre*, Newton is implying that a billiard-ball struck by another and set in motion would have liked to be left in peace; it is reluctant to move, and this reluctance, which is called inertia, has to be overcome by an effort on the part of the ball that strikes it. This effort costs the striker something, namely, part of its own momentum, which it pays over to the sluggard ball as an inducement to move. I am not suggesting that this reduction of physics to social psychology is the doctrine Newton set out to teach; all I say is that he expounded it, no doubt as a metaphor beneath which the truths of physics are concealed.

It is worthwhile to notice that in Newton there is no law of universal causation. He not only does not assert that every event must have a cause, he explicitly denies it; and this in two ways. (i) In the case of a body moving freely (even though its motion be what he calls "true" motion as distinct from relative motion), there is uncaused motion; for caused means constrained, and free means unconstrained. If a body moves freely from p_1 to p_2 and thence to p_3, the "event" which is its moving from p_2 to p_3 is in no sense caused by the preceding "event" of its moving from p_1 to p_2; for it is not caused at all. Newton's doctrine is that any movement which happens according to the laws of motion is an uncaused event; the laws of motion are in fact the laws of free or causeless motion. (ii) He asserts that there is such a thing as relative motion; but, as he puts it, "relative motion may be generated or altered without any force impressed upon the body." If, therefore, it were possible to show, either that all motion is "free," that is to say, takes place according to laws having the same logical character as the Newtonian laws of motion; or that all motion is "relative"; then on Newton's own principles it would follow that no motion is caused, and the cat would be out of the bag. It would have become plain that there is *no* truth concealed beneath the animistic metaphor; and that "the idea of causation" is simply a relic of animism foisted upon a science to which it is irrelevant.

This, I take it, is what modern physics has done. Developing the Newtonian doctrine in the simplest and most logical way, it has eliminated the notion of cause altogether. In place of that notion, we get a new and highly complex development of the Newtonian "laws of motion." Of the two Newtonian classes of events, (a) those that happen according to law (b) those that happen as the effects of causes, class (a) has expanded to such an extent as to swallow up (b). At the same time, the survival of the term cause in certain sciences other than physics, such as medicine, is not a symptom of their "backwardness," because in them the word cause is not used in the same sense. They are practical sciences, aiming at results, and they accordingly use the word cause in sense II. Doubtless, the use of the word in that sense carries with it a flavor of magic; but this is not disliked by, e.g., the medical profession. A dose of superstition may serve its purpose.

IV

The situation in post-Newtonian philosophy has been very different. Kant, whose gigantic effort at a synthesis of all existing philosophies here over-reached itself, swept into one bag the Baconian tradition, with its insistence on causes in sense II, the Cartesian identification of causes (in sense III) with grounds, the Leibnizian law of sufficient reason, and the Humian conception of the cause as an event prior in time to its effect; and, unhappily neglecting the one thing in Newton which modern physics has found most valuable, namely, the doctrine that what happens according to a law does not need a cause, produced as the result a doctrine which has oppressed mankind ever since: the doctrine that (a) *every event has a cause; (b) the cause of every event is a prior event;* and (c) *this is known to us not from experience but a priori.*

(a) What could be meant by saying that every event has a cause? It would plainly be nonsense if "cause" were used in sense I. In sense II it would mean "there is nothing in nature that man is not able" (or, if we allow for looseness of expression," may not hope to become able") "to produce or prevent at will," which is hardly what Kant intended, though a Bacon might have played with the idea in a rash moment. "Cause" must be used in sense III. But what warrant can there be for Kant's statement? I can only suppose that he was assuming the identity of cause with ground (though he accepted Hume's disproof of that identification) and accordingly thought that (a) was a mere restatement of the Law of Sufficient Reason.

(b) The cause of an event can be a prior event (see III, 1) only when cause is used in sense II. If, in the proposition "*x* causes *y*," "causes" means "logically necessitates," *x* cannot be an event happening before *y*. An event may have implications, but its implications cannot be subsequent events. The birth of a second son logically necessitates the first son's becoming a brother; these two events happen simultaneously; not successively, however close together. Thus the only assumption that can justify Kant's first assertion is an assumption that is incompatible with his second. Assertion (*a*) is in fact a relic of his Leibnizian upbringing, (*b*) is a lesson from his later empiricist teachers. The combination of the two is an unsuccessful attempt at philosophical syncretism, marred by the fact (which Kant has failed to observe) that in the two component propositions the word "cause" is used in different senses. Their combination is therefore, to put it plainly, nonsense; a hybrid concept, deserving the description once given to the mule, as a creature having "neither pride of ancestry nor hope of posterity."

Mill, unlike most of his philosophical critics and disciples, showed a certain understanding of the situation in which science had been left by Newton when he tried to reject sense III and get back to sense II; rejecting the notion of a cause "which is not only followed by, but actually *produces* the effect" in favor of "such a notion of cause as can be gained from experience." Consistently with this, he does away with the one-one relation of cause to effect, and insists on a real plurality of causes—a scandal to his critics, who have commonly assumed that the only possible sense of the word cause is sense III. But when he defines causation as "invariability of succession," he goes back unawares from loose causation to tight causation, for "invariability" implies the impossibility of variation, i.e., the necessity of the conjunction. If he is using it loosely for uniformity in cases hitherto observed, his advocacy of sense II becomes consistent. And in any case, Mill's pages on the subject stand out from those of almost all other writers as exceptionally clear-headed as to the sense in which the word cause is used.

Among more recent writers I will first refer to Mr. Russell, whose brilliant paper "On the Notion of Cause," mentioned above, is worth everything else put together that has been written on the subject during the present century. The neglect of this paper by the crowd of subsequent writers on the same subject is to my mind a very disquieting symptom of the state of English philosophy.

Mr. Russell has shown once for all that the "law of causation" commonly so called is valueless and meaningless, and that in theoretical science propositions about causes either have been or are being replaced by propositions about laws. I am glad to confess my obligations to him and to add that where I differ from him it may be only because I misunderstand him.

Even in Mr. Russell's paper, however, I find a few—a very few—confusions. Speaking of the interval of time which elapses between cause and effect, he says: "however short we make the interval τ, something may happen during this interval which prevents the expected result." Now if "cause" is here used in the tight sense, this proposition is nonsense; for it means "given everything that is required for a certain result, something may be lacking which is so required." Therefore he must be using "cause" in the loose sense. But if so, there is nothing to worry about. If x is the cause, in the loose sense, of y, there are also *conditions sine quibus non*, such as a, b, c. If a is lacking, y is "prevented"; but that does not mean that x is not, *in that sense*, its cause. Hence the consideration "raises insuperable difficulties" only to a person who is slipping unawares from one cause to the other.

Again, when he criticizes the "vulgar prejudice" against *actio in distans*, and says that the maxim "a cause cannot operate except where it is" "rests upon the assumption that causes 'operate', i.e., that they are in some obscure way analogous to volitions," I think he is similarly confused. I agree that such words as "operate" (and, I would add, "necessary," though he does not allow this) imply that causes are in some way analogous to volitions; I would go further and say that this is true of the word "cause" by itself. But what makes *actio in distans* a stumbling-block is not this analogy: it is the one-one relation between cause and effect. I have explained this above. . . .

NOTES

1. One-many, because a cause in sense II leads to its effect not only when the *conditione sine quibus non* are fulfilled. Many-one, because of the relativity of causes.

2. "On the Notion of Cause," *Proceedings of the Aristotelian Society* 1912, and reprinted in the volume *Mysticism and Logic*. [See selection 10 of this volume.]

13

Law Statements and Counterfactual Inference

Roderick M. Chisholm

The problems I have been invited to discuss arise from the fact that there are two types of true synthetic universal statement: statements of the one type, in the context of our general knowledge, seem to warrant counterfactual inference and statements of the other type do not. I shall call statements of the first type "law statements" and statements of the second type "nonlaw statements." Both law and nonlaw statements may be expressed in the general form, "For every x, if x is S, x is P." Law statements, unlike nonlaw statements, seem to warrant inference to statements of the form, "If a, which is not S, *were* S, a would be P" and "For every x, if x *were* S, x would be P." I shall discuss (I) this distinction between law and nonlaw statements and (II) the related problem of interpreting counterfactual statements.[1]

I

Let us consider the following as examples of law statements:

L1. Everyone who drinks from this bottle is poisoned.

L2. All gold is malleable.

From *Analysis* (15 (1955): 97–105. Reprinted by permission of Basil Blackwell Publisher and the author.

And let us consider the following as examples of nonlaw statements:

N1. Everyone who drinks from———bottle wears a necktie.

N2. Every Canadian parent of quintuplets in the first half of the twentieth century is named "Dionne."

Let us suppose that L1 and N1 are concerned with the same bottle (perhaps it is one of short duration and has contained only arsenic). Let us suppose, further, that the blank in N1 is replaced by property terms which happen to characterize the bottle uniquely (perhaps they describe patterns of finger-prints). I shall discuss certain philosophical questions which arise when we make the following "pre-analytic" assumptions. From L1 we can infer

L1.1 If Jones had drunk from this bottle, he would have been poisoned.

and from L2 we can infer

L2.1 If that metal were gold, it would be malleable.

But from N1 we cannot infer

N1.1 If Jones had drunk from———bottle, he would have worn a necktie.

and from N2 we cannot infer

N2.1 If Jones, who is Canadian, had been parent of quintuplets during the first half of the twentieth century, he would have been named "Dionne."

I shall not defend these assumptions beyond noting that, in respects to be dis-cussed, they correspond to assumptions which practically everyone does make.

There are two preliminary points to be made concerning the interpretation of counterfactual statements. (1) We are concerned with those counterfactuals whose antecedents, "if a were S," may be interpreted as meaning the same as "if a had property S." There is, however, another possible interpretation: "if a were S" could be interpreted as meaning the same as "if a were identical with something which in fact does have property S."[2] Given the above assumptions, N2.1 is false according to the first interpretation, which is the interpretation with which we are concerned, but it is true according to the second (for if Jones were identical with one of the Dionnes, he would be named "Dionne"). On the other hand, the statement

N2.2 If Jones, who is Canadian, had been parent of quintuplets during the first half of the twentieth century, there would have been at least two sets of Canadian quintuplets.

is true according to the first interpretation and false according to the second. (2) It should be noted, secondly, that there is a respect—to be discussed at greater length below—in which our counterfactual statements may be thought of as being elliptical. If we assert L1.1, we might, nevertheless, accept the following qualification: "Of course, if Jones had emptied the bottle, cleaned it out, filled it with water, and *then* drunk from it, he might not have been poisoned." And, with respect to L2.1, we might accept this qualification: "If that metal were gold it would be malleable—provided, of course, that what we are supposing to be contrary-to-fact is the statement 'That metal is not gold' and *not* the statement 'All gold is malleable.' "

Can the relevant difference between law and nonlaw statements be described in familiar terminology without reference to counterfactuals, without use of modal terms such as "causal necessity," "necessary condition," "physical possibility," and the like, and without use of metaphysical terms such as "real connections between matters of fact"? I believe no one has shown that the relevant difference *can* be so described. I shall mention three recent discussions.

(1) It has been suggested that the distinction between law statements and nonlaw statements may be made with respect to the universality of the nonlogical terms which appear in the statements. A term may be thought of as being universal, it has been suggested, if its meaning can be conveyed without explicit reference to any particular object; it is then said that law statements, unlike nonlaw statements, contain no nonlogical terms which are not universal.[3] (These points can be formulated more precisely.) This suggestion does not help, however, if applied to what we have been calling "law statements" and "nonlaw statements," for L1 is a law statement containing the *non*universal nonlogical term "this bottle" and N1 (we have supposed) is a nonlaw statement all of whose nonlogical terms *are* universal. It may be that, with respect to ordinary usage, it is incorrect to call L1 a "law statement"; this point does not affect our problem, however, since we are assuming that L1, whether or not it would ordinarily be called a "law statement," does, in the context of our general knowledge, warrant the inference to L1.1

(2) It has been suggested that the two types of statement might be distinguished epistemologically. P. F. Strawson, in his *Introduction to Logical Theory,* suggests that in order to *know,* or to have good evidence or good reason for believing, that a given nonlaw statement is true, it is necessary to know that all of its instances have in fact been observed; but in order to know, or to have good evidence or good reason for believing, that a given law statement is true, it is *not* necessary to know that all of its instances have been examined. (We need not consider the problem of defining "instance" in this use.) "An essential part of our grounds for accepting" a nonlaw statement must be "evidence that there will be no more" instances and "that there never were more than the limited number of which observations have been recorded"

(p. 199). Possibly this suggestion is true, but it leaves us with our problem. For the suggestion itself requires use of a modal term; it refers to what a man *needs* to know, or what it is *essential* that he know, in order to know that a law statement is true. But if we thus allow ourselves the use of modal terms, we could have said at the outset merely that a law statement is true. But if we thus allow ourselves the use of modal terms, we could have said at the outset merely that a law statement describes what is "physically necessary," etc., and that a nonlaw statement does not.

(3) R. B. Braithwaite, in *Scientific Explanation,* suggests that a law statement, as distinguished from a nonlaw statement, is one which "appears as a deduction from higher-level hypotheses which have been established independently of the statement" (p. 303). "To consider whether or not a scientific hypothesis would, if true, be a law of nature is to consider the way in which it could enter into an established scientific deductive system" (ibid.). In other words, the question whether a statement is lawlike may be answered by considering certain logical, or epistemological, relations which the statement bears to certain *other* statements. Our nonlaw statement N2, however, is deducible from the followng two statements: (i) "Newspapers which are generally reliable report that all parents of quintuplets during the first half of the twentieth century are named 'Dionne,' " and (ii) "If newspapers which are generally reliable report that all parents of quintuplets during the first half of the twentieth century are named 'Dionne,' then such parents are named 'Dionne.' "Statements (i) and (ii) may be considered as "higher level" parts of a "hypothetical-deductive system" from which the nonlaw statement N2 can be deduced; indeed (i) and (ii) undoubtedly express the grounds upon which most people accept N2. It is not enough, therefore, to describe a nonlaw statement as a statement which "appears as a deduction from higher level hypotheses which have been established independently." (I suggest, incidentally, that it is only at an advanced stage of inquiry that one regards a synthetic universal statement as being a nonlaw statement.)

II

Even if we allow ourselves the distinction between law statements and nonlaw statements and characterize the distinction philosophically, by reference, say, to physical possibility (e.g., "All *S* is *P*" is a law statement provided it is not physically possible that anything be both *S* and not *P,* etc.), we find that contrary-to-fact conditionals still present certain difficulties of interpretation.[4] Assuming that the distinction between law statement and nonlaw statement is available to us, I shall now make some informal remarks which I hope will throw light upon the ordinary use of these conditionals.

Henry Hiz has suggested that a contrary-to-fact conditional might be interpreted as a metalinguistic statement, telling us something about what can be inferred in a given system of statements. "It says that, if something is accepted in this system to be true, then something else can be accepted in this sytem to be true."[5] This suggestion, I believe, can be applied to the ordinary use of contrary-to-fact conditionals, but it is necessary to make some qualifying remarks concerning the relevant "systems of statements."

Let us consider one way of justifying the assertion of a contrary-to-fact conditional, "If *a* were *S*, *a* would be *P*." The antecedent of the counterfactual is taken, its indicative form, as a *supposition* or *assumption*.[6] One says, in effect, "Let us *suppose* that *a* is *S*," even though one may believe that *a* is not *S*. The indicative form of the consequent of the counterfactual—viz., "*a* is *P*"—is then shown to follow logically from the antecedent taken with certain other statements already accepted. This demonstration is then taken to justify the counterfactual. The point of asserting the counterfactual may be that of *calling attention to, emphasizing,* or *conveying,* one or more of the premises which, taken with the antecedent, logically imply the consequent.

In simple cases, where singular counterfactuals are asserted, we may thus think of the speaker: (i) as having deduced the consequences of a singular supposition, viz., the indicative form of the counterfactual antecedent, taken with a statement he interprets as a law statement; and (ii) as being concerned in part to call attention to, emphasize, or convey, the statement interpreted as a law statement. We can usually tell, from the context of a man's utterance, what the supposition is and what the other statements are with which he is concerned. He may say, "If that were gold, it would be malleable"; it is likely, in this case, that the statement interpreted as a law statement is L2, "All gold is malleable"; it is also likely that this is the statement he is concerned to emphasize.

F. H. Bradley suggested, in his *Principles of Logic,* that when a man asserts a singular counterfactual "the real judgement is concerned with the individual's *qualities,* and asserts no more than a connection of adjectives."[7] Bradley's suggestion, as I interpret it, is that the *whole* point of asserting a singular counterfactual, normally, is to call attention to, emphasize, or convey the statement interpreted as a law statement. It might be misleading, however, to say that the man is *affirming* or *asserting* what he takes to be a law statement, or statement describing a "connection of adjectives," for he has not formulated it explicitly. It would also be misleading to say, as Bradley did (p. 89), that the man is merely *supposing* the law statement to be true, for the law statement is something he *believes,* and not merely supposes, to be true. If he were merely supposing "All gold is malleable," along with "That is gold," then it is likely he would include this supposition in the antecedent of his counterfactual and say "If that were gold and if all gold were malleable, then that would be malleable." Let us say he is *presupposing* the law statement.

We are suggesting, then, that a man in asserting a counterfactual is telling us something about what can be deduced from some "system of statements" when the indicative version of the antecedent is added to this system as a *supposition*. We are referring to the statements of this system (other than the indicative version of the antecedent) as the *presuppositions* of his assertion. And we are suggesting that, normally, at least part of the point of asserting a counterfactual is to *call attention to, emphasize,* or *convey,* one or more of these presuppositions.

The statements a man presupposes when he asserts a counterfactual will, presumably, be statements he accepts or believes. But they will not include the denial of the antecedent of his counterfactual (even if he believes this denial to be true) and they will not include any statements he would treat as nonlaw statements.[8] And normally there will be many other statements he believes to be true which he will deliberately exclude from his presuppositions. The peculiar problem of interpreting ordinary counterfactual statements is that of specifying which, among the statements the asserter believes, he intends to *exclude* from his presuppositions. What statements he will exclude will depend upon what it is he is concerned to call attention to, emphasize, or convey.

Let us suppose a man accepts the following statements, taking the universal statements to be law statements: (1) All gold is malleable; (2) No cast-iron is malleable; (3) Nothing is both gold and cast-iron; (4) Nothing is both malleable and not malleable; (5) That is cast-iron; (6) That is not gold; and (7) That is not malleable. We may contrast three different situations in which he asserts three different counterfactuals having the same antecedents.

First, he asserts, pointing to an object his hearers don't know to be gold and don't know not to be gold, "If that *were* gold, it would be malleable." In this case, he is supposing the denial of (6); he is excluding from his presuppositions (5), (6), and (7); and he is concerned to emphasize (1).

Secondly, he asserts, pointing to an object he and his hearers agree to be cast-iron, "If *that* were gold, then some gold things would not be malleable." He is again supposing the denial of (6); he is excluding (1) and (6), but he is no longer excluding (5) or (7); and he is concerned to emphasize either (5) or (2).

Thirdly, he asserts, "If that were gold, then some things would be both malleable and not malleable." He is again supposing the denial of (6); he is now excluding (3) and no longer excluding (1), (5), (6), or (7); and he is now concerned to emphasize (1), (2), or (5).

Still other possibilites readily suggest themselves.

If, then, we were to ask "What if that were gold?" our question would have a number of possible answers—e.g., the subjunctive forms of the denial of (7), the denial of (1), and the denial of (4). Any one of these three answers might be appropriate, but they would not *all* be appropriate in conjunction. Which answer is the appropriate one will depend upon what we wish to know. If, in asking "What if that were gold?" we wish to know of some law statement describing gold, the denial of (7) is appropriate; if we wish to know what are the properties of the thing in question, the denial of (1) is appropriate; and if we wish to know whether the thing has properties such that a statement saying nothing gold has those properties is a law statement, the denial of (4) is appropriate. The counterfactual question "What if that were gold?" is, therefore, clearly ambiguous. But in each case, the question could be formulated clearly and unambiguously.

Counterfactuals are similar to *probability* statements in that each type of statement is, in certain sense, elliptical. If we ask "What is the probability that this man will survive?" our question is incompletely formulated; and a more explicit formulation would be, "With respect to such-and-such evidence, what is the probability that this man will survive?" Similarly, if we ask "What would American policy in Asia be if Stevenson were President?" our question is incompletely formulated; a more explicit formulation would be, "Supposing that Stevenson were President, and presupposing so-and-so, but not so-and-so, what would be the consequences with respect to American policy in Asia?" But there is an important respect in which counterfactual statements *differ* from such probability statements. If a man wishes to know what is the probability of a certain statement, i.e., if he wishes to know the truth of a categorical probability statement, then, we may say, he should take into consideration *all* the relevant evidence available to him; the premises of his probability inference should omit no relevant statement which he is justified in believing.[9] But this "requirement of total evidence" cannot be assumed to hold in the case of counterfactual inference. If a man asks "What would American policy in Asia be, if Stevenson were President?" and if his question may be interpreted in the way in which it ordinarily would be interpreted, then there are many facts included in his store of knowledge which we would expect him to *overlook,* or *ignore* in answering his question; i.e., there are many facts which we would expect him deliberately to *exclude* from his presuppositions. Normally we would expect him to exclude the fact that Eisenhower's programme is the one which has been followed since 1953; another is the fact that Mr. Dulles is Secretary of State. But there are other facts, which may also be included in the man's store of knowledge, whose status is more questionable. Does he intend to exclude the fact that Congress was Republican; does he intend to exclude those Asiatic events which have occurred as a result of Eisenhower's policies; does he intend to exclude the fact that Stevenson went to Asia in 1953? There is no point in insisting either that he consider or that he exclude these facts. But, if he wishes to be understood, he should tell us which are the facts that he is considering, or presupposing, and which are the ones he is excluding.

Bradley suggested the ambiguity of some counterfactual statements may be attributed to the fact that "the supposition is not made evident" (op. cit., p. 89). In our terminology, it would be more accurate to say that the *presupposition* is not made evident; for the supposition is usually formulated explicitly in the antecedent of the counterfactual statement. (But when a man says, "If that thing, which is not *S,* were *S* . . ., the subordinate indicative clause expresses neither a supposition nor a presupposition.) Ideally it might be desirable to formulate our counterfactuals in somewhat the following way: "Supposing that that is *S,* and presupposing so-and-so, then it follows that that is *P.*" In practice, however, it is often easy to tell, from the context in which a counterfactual is asserted, just what it is that is being presupposed and what it is that is being excluded.[10]

Although I have been using the terms "counterfactual" and "contrary-to-fact" throughout this discussion, it is important to note that, when a man arrives at a conditional statement in the manner we have been discussing, his supposition—and thus also the antecedent of his conditional—need *not* be anything he believes to be false. For example, a man in deliberating will consider the consequences of a supposition, taken along with certain presuppositions, and he will also consider the consequences of its denial, taken along with the same presuppositions. It is misleading to say, therefore, that the conditionals he may then affirm are "counterfactual," or "contrary-to-fact," for he may have no beliefs about the truth or falsity of the respective antecedents and one of these antecedents will in fact be true.[11] A better term might be "suppositional conditional" or, indeed, "hypothetical statement."

NOTES

1. Detailed formulations of this problem are to be found in the following works: W. E. Johnson, *Logic,* Vol. III, chapter I; C. H. Langford, review of W. B. Gallie's "An Interpretation of Causal Laws," *Journal of Symbolic Logic* vi (1941): 67; C. I. Lewis, *An Analysis of Knowledge and Valuation,* Part II; Roderick M. Chisholm, "The Contrary-to-fact Conditional," *Mind* 55 (1946): 289–307 (reprinted in H. Feigl and W. S. Sellars, *Readings in Philosophical Analysis*); Nelson Goodman, "The Problem of Counterfactual Conditionals," *Journal of Philosophy* 44 (1947): 113–28 (reprinted in L. Linsky, *Semantics and the Philosophy of Language*); F. L. Will, "The Contrary-to-fact Conditional," *Mind* 56 (1947): 236–49; and William Kneale, "Natural Laws and Contrary to Fact Conditionals," *Analysis* 10 (1950): 121–25. See further references below and in Erna Schneider, "Recent Discussion of Subjunctive Conditionals," *Review of Metaphysics* vi (1953): 623–47. My paper, referred to above, contains some serious errors.

2. Compare K. R. Popper, "A Note on Natural Laws and so-called 'Contrary-to-fact Conditionals,' " *Mind* 58 (1949): 62–6.

3. Compare C. G. Hempel and Paul Oppenheim, "Studies in the Logic of Explanations," *Philosophy of Science* 15 (1948): 135–75 (reprinted in H. Feigl and M. Brodbeck, *Readings in the Philosophy of Science*). It should be noted that these authors (i) attempt to characterize laws with respect only to formalized languages, (ii) concede that "the problem of an adequate definition of purely qualitative (universal) predicates remains open," and (iii) propose a distinction between "derived" and "fundamental" laws. The latter distinction is similar to a distinction of Braithwaite, discussed below. See also Elizabeth Lane Beardsley, "Non-Accidental and Counter-factual Sentences," *Journal of Philosophy* 46 (1949): 573–91; review of the latter by Roderick M. Chisholm, *Journal of Symbolic Logic* 16 (1951), 63–64.

4. Modal analyses of law statements are suggested by Hans Reichenbach, *Elements of Symbolic Logic,* Ch. VIII, and Arthur Burks, "The Logic of Causal Propositions," *Mind* 60 (1951): 363–82.

5. Henry Hiz, "On the Inferential Sense of Contrary-to-fact Conditionals," *Journal of Philosophy* 48 (1949): 586–87.

6. Compare S. Jaskowski, "On the Rules of Suppositions in Formal Logic," *Studia Logica* 1 (Warsaw, 1934): and A. Meinong, *Über Annahmen,* concerning this use of "assumption."

7. Op. cit., p. 90. Compare D. J. O'Connor, "The Analysis of Conditional Sentences" *Mind* 60 (1951): 360; Robert Brown and John Watling, "Counterfactual Conditionals" *Mind* 61 (1952): 226.

8. Instead of saying his presuppositions include no statement he treats as a law statement, it might be more accurate to say this: if his presuppositions include any statement *N* he would interpret as a nonlaw statement, then *N* and the man's supposition cannot be so formulated that the supposition constitutes a substitution-instance of *N*'s antecedent.

9. Compare Rudolf Carnap, *Logical Foundations of Probability,* pp. 211 ff.

10. "The Contrary-to-fact Conditional" (pp. 303–304; Feigl-Sellars, p. 494). I discuss what I take to be certain conventions of ordinary language pertaining to this point.

11. Compare Alan Ross Anderson, "A Note on Subjunctive and Counterfactual Conditionals" *Analysis* 12 (1951): 35–38; Roderick M. Chisholm, review of David Pears's "Hypotheticals," *Journal of Symbolic Logic* 15 (1950): 215–16.

14

The Metaphysics of Causation

Richard Taylor

The ancient idea of efficient causation . . . is generally considered by contemporary philosophers to be metaphysical and obscure, and quite plainly erroneous. Scientists, too, insofar as they permit themselves to think about causation at all, share this disdain—though it is worth noting that both continue to *speak* quite unguardedly and unabashedly in terms of the very concepts that are involved in this ancient conception, employing quite freely the ideas of making certain things happen, of this or that agent's control over this or that state of affairs, and so on. It has become almost a commonplace in philosophy that we have officially got rid of such esoteric concepts as power and necessitation, reducing causation to such simple and discoverable relationships as invariant succession between states, processes, and events.

I believe, on the contrary, that the older metaphysical idea of an efficient cause is superior to and far closer to the truth of things than the conceptions of causation that are now usually taken for granted. Indeed, I believe that if we did not *already* have precisely the idea of an efficient cause that once played such a significant role in philosophical thought, we would not even *understand* the conceptions of causation with which modern philosophy has tried to supplant it, and that it is therefore quite idle to dream of *reducing* the former to the latter.

It is my aim here to defend this claim. I shall do so by showing that the

---

attempts of modern philosophy to expurgate from causation the ideas . . . of power and necessity, and to reduce causation to constancy of sequence, have failed. Many philosophers are now apparently agreed that causation cannot be described without in one way or another introducing modal concepts, which amounts to re-establishing the necessity which Hume was once thought to have gotten rid of; but hardly anyone, apparently, has noticed that we need also the idea of power or efficacy. If, as I believe, both these ideas are indispensable, then it will be found that the advance of contemporary philosophy over that of our predecessors is much less impressive than we had supposed.

SOME CAUSAL STATEMENTS

Statements like "That window was shattered by a brick," "This fire was started by a cigarette," "A nail punctured that tire," and so on, express, though perhaps not accurately, the idea of cause and effect. The ideas expressed in them can also be expressed by saying, for example, "A brick *caused* that window to break," "A nail *caused* the puncture in that tire," and so on. The idea of causation involved in such examples is, in fact, so obvious that discussion is hardly needed to elicit it.

Two things about our manner of expressing such causal relationships in common speech give us pause. The first is that an object or substance seems often to be referred to as a cause. Thus, our statements above seem to say that a certain *brick,* which is an object, broke a window, that a *cigarette* started a fire, and that a *nail* punctured a tire. The second is that each of these objects seems to be alleged to have *done* something, in the same sense in which men, for example, are often described as *doing* various things. Thus, it does not seem wildly incongruous to say that the brick *flew* through the window, that the cigarette *started* a fire, that the nail *punctured* a tire; all these things can be said in answer to questions concerning what these various objects had *done.*

Such expressions of causation seem, in short, to express something very like the idea of efficient causation we were just considering, for there is at least a perfect grammatical similarity between two such statements as, say, "A man started this fire" and "A cigarette started this fire." It is certainly the consensus of contemporary thinkers, however, that no such idea is expressed, that statements of the kind we are now considering express certain relations between *events, states,* or *processes,* and that for the obscure and possibly esoteric idea of efficient causation by a substance that might at first seem to be involved in them we can substitute perfectly clear ideas of certain relationships between such events, states, or processes.

Thus, the statement "That window was shattered by a brick" expresses the idea that the *striking* of that brick upon the window in a certain way was the cause of the latter's breaking, and both cause and effect here are events. To say simply that the *brick* broke the window is not to say something really false, but rather something incomplete; for unless this is understood as saying that the brick's impact, or some other event in which the brick was conspicuously involved, was the cause of the breaking, the statement is quite unintelligible.

Now this is doubtless true. If the statements we are now considering express the basic idea of causation, then causation is indeed a relationship between events, for each of those statements can be more precisely formulated in those terms. What, then, of such a statement as "That window was shattered by a man," which appears to express a causal relationship between a certain being, that is, an agent, and some effect wrought by him? Is that statement elliptical in a similar way? It does not at first seem so. It might indeed suggest that there was some event in which that agent was conspicuously involved which was the cause of the window's breaking—such as the motion of his hand or, indeed, the motion of a brick which was moved by his hand—but that is not what it *means,* and that does not seem to be the idea of causation that it expresses. It might be true that the motion of his hand, or the motion of a brick which was moved by his hand, caused the window to break, without it being at all true that *he* broke it—in case it was not he, but someone else, who moved his hand, for example. This seems obvious. But how absurd it would be, on the other hand, to say that, while the brick's impact had indeed shattered the window, the brick itself really had nothing to do with it—on the ground that the brick had not moved itself through the window but had instead depended upon some agent to impel it!

The question before us now is simply this: Whether causation, as it is exemplified in the relationship between certain events, processes, or states, is the basic idea of causation, in terms of which, for example, causation of certain things by agents is to be understood; or whether, on the contrary, causation as it is exemplified in the actions of agents is the basic idea of causation, in terms of which, for example, the so-called causal relations between events, processes, or states are to be understood. It was once generally supposed that the latter was the correct view, that events, processes, and states were only "secondary causes," and that a cause in the original and proper sense had to be something, such as a man, having the power to make certain things happen. It is now generally supposed, on the other hand, that the former view is the correct one, and that the causation of events by agents— by men, for example—can be understood only in terms of a causal relationship between certain events, processes, or states. It is in terms of this that men are quite generally thought to cause certain things to happen only in the sense that certain things happening *inside* men—certain events, processes, or states —are the real causes of those happenings.

I want to show that, whatever grave and justified misgivings one might have concerning the older idea of efficient causation, this contemporary conception is in any case totally wrong. I think this will stand if it can be shown, *first,* that no conception of causation can possibly work unless it includes the idea of a certain kind of *necessary connection* between cause and effect, and also the idea of *efficacy* or *power* of a cause to produce its effect— the very two ideas modern philosophy has boasted it has banished from the concept of causation; *second,* that there is in the contemporary analyses of causation no basis whatsoever for affirming the temporal priority of causes to their effects apart from appealing to certain conventions of language which are, however, not a sufficient basis for affirming such priority; and *third,* that even making use of such ideas as necessitation and power, no one can *say* what causation is without involving himself in circularity or redundancy. Everyone, I maintain, *knows* what causation is—simply because, in my opinion, everyone thinks of *himself* as an efficient cause, in the traditional and generally considered archaic sense of that term. Everyone knows what it is to make something happen and to exercise such power as he has over his body and his environment; but no one can *say* what this is, other than to say, simply, that it is causation.

NECESSITY VERSUS INVARIABLE SEQUENCE

Let the letters A, B, C . . . etc., designate events, states of affairs, conditions, or substances which *have existed.* These symbols, in other words, shall designate anything we please that was ever real. This stipulation excludes from our consideration not only things future, but also things that might have existed but in fact did not exist, as well as impossible things, kinds or classes of things as distinguished from things themselves, and so on. Now I want to consider true assertions of the form, "A was the cause of B," wherein I assume that A was in fact, as asserted, the cause of B, and I want to ask just what such a statement asserts.

Let A, for example, be the beheading of Anne Boleyn, and B her subsequent death, and assume that the former was the cause of the latter. What, then, is asserted by that statement? Does it mean that A and B are constantly conjoined, B following upon A? Plainly not, for the event A, like B, occurred only once in the history of the universe. The assertion that A and B are constantly conjoined—that the one never occurs without the other—is therefore true, but not significant. Each is also constantly conjoined with every other event that has occurred only once. Nor do we avoid this obvious difficulty by saying that B must follow immediately upon A, in order to be the effect of A; for there were numberless things that followed immediately upon A. At the moment of Anne's death, for instance, numberless persons were being born here and there, others were dying, and, let us suppose, some bird was producing a novel combination of notes from a certain twig nearby, any of which events we may assume not to have happened before or since. Yet the beheading of that queen had nothing to do with these. Mere constancy of conjunction, then, even with temporal contiguity, does not constitute causation.

THE RESORT TO SIMILARITY

Here there is an enormous temptation to introduce classes or kinds and to say, after the fashion familiar to all students of philosophy, that A was the cause of B, provided A was immediately followed by B, and that things similar to A are in similar circumstances always followed by things similar to B. This, however, only permits one temporarily to avoid speaking of necessary connections by exploiting the vagueness in the notion of similarity. When confronted with counterexamples one can always say that the requisite similarity was lacking, and thus avoid having to say that the necessary connection was lacking. What does "similar" mean in this context? If we construe it to mean *exactly* similar, then the class of things similar to A and the class of things similar to B each has only one member, namely, A and B, and we are back where we started. The only thing exactly similar to the beheading of Anne Boleyn, for instance, is the beheading of Anne Boleyn, and the only thing exactly similar to her death is her death. Other things are only more or less similar to these—similar, that is, in some respects, and dissimilar in others. If, however, we allow the similarity to be one of degree, then the statement that things similar to A are always followed by things similar to B is not true. A stage dramatization of the beheading of Anne Boleyn is similar—perhaps quite similar—to the beheading of Anne Boelyn, but it is not followed by anything similar to her death. Here it is tempting to introduce the idea of relevance and say that things similar to A in all relevant respects are followed by things similar to B in all relevant respects; but this just gives the whole thing away. "Relevant respects," it soon turns out, are nothing but those features of the situation that have some causal connection with each other. Or consider another example: Suppose we have two pairs of matches; the first two are similar to each other in all respects, let us suppose, except that one is red and the other blue. The other two are likewise similar in all respects, except that one is wet and the other dry. Now the *degree* of similarity between the members of each pair is the same. One of the differences, however, is "relevant" to the question of what happens when the matches are rubbed, while the other is not. Whether the match is red or blue is irrelevant, but whether it is wet or dry is not. But all this means, obviously, is that the dryness of a match is causally connected to its igniting, while its color is not.

LAWS

Sometimes difficulties of the kind suggested have been countered by introducing the idea of a *law* into the description of causal connections. For instance, it is sometimes suggested that a given event A was the cause of a given event B, provided there is a law to the effect that whenever A occurs in certain circumstances it is followed by B. This appears, however, to involve the same problems of uniqueness and similarity that we have just considered. There can be no law connecting just two things. It can be no law, for example, that whenever Anne Boleyn is beheaded, *she* dies, or whenever a particular match is rubbed, *it* ignites.

One could, perhaps, overcome these difficulties by embodying in the statement of the law precisely those respects in which things must be similar in order to behave similarly under certain specified conditions, all other similarities and differences being disregarded as irrelevant. For example, there could be a law to the effect that whenever *any* match of such and such precisely stated chemical composition is treated in a certain specified way, under certain specified conditions, then it ignites. A match of that description would, of course, be similar to any other fitting the same description; other similarities and differences between them, however conspicuous, would be considered "irrelevant," that is, not mentioned in the law.

That overcomes the difficulty of specifying how similar two causes must be in order to have similar effects. They must, according to this suggestion, be exactly similar in certain respects only, and can be as dissimilar as one pleases in other respects. But here we find that, by introducing the idea of a law, we have tacitly reintroduced the idea of a necessary connection between cause and effect—precisely the thing we were trying to avoid. A general statement counts as a *law* only if we can use it to infer, not only what does or will happen, but also what *would* happen if something else were to happen, and this we can never do from a statement that is merely a true general statement.

To make this clear, assume that there is a true and perfectly general statement to the effect that any match having a certain set of specified properties ignites when rubbed in a certain specified manner under specified conditions. Now such a statement, though true, need not be a law. Suppose, for example, someone took a quantity of matches—a thousand, say—and gave them a common set of properties which uniquely distinguished them from all other matches that have in fact ever existed and, we can suppose, will in fact ever exist. Suppose, for example, he decorated the sticks in a certain elaborate way such that all the matches were similar with respect to those decorations, and suppose further that, as a matter of fact (but not of necessity) no other match so decorated has ever existed or ever will. Now if all those matches were rubbed in a similar way, it might be true that *every* match (in the history of the universe) having those properties ignites when rubbed. But this, though a true and perfectly general statement asserting how certain precisely described things invariably behave under certain conditions, admitting of not a single exception in the history of the universe, would be no law, simply because there is no necessary connection between a match's having those properties and behaving as it does when rubbed. If, contrary to fact, another match *were* to have those properties, but lacked, say, the property of dryness, it might not ignite. For a true general statement of this kind to count as a law, then, we must be able to use it to infer what would happen if something else, which does not happen, were to happen; for instance, that a certain match which lacks some property would ignite if only it had that property. This, however, expresses some necessary and not merely *de facto* connection between properties and events. There is some connection between a match's being dry and igniting when rubbed. There is not the same connection between its being decorated in a certain way and igniting when rubbed—even though it may be true that every match so decorated does ignite when rubbed. But this only means that the decoration on its stick does not have anything to do—has no necessary connection—with a match's igniting when rubbed, while its being dry does.

THE NATURE VERSUS THE KNOWLEDGE OF CAUSAL CONNECTIONS

Here one is apt to be reminded that we have no way of *knowing* what states, properties, and events are causally connected other than by noting which are invariably conjoined in our experience. If, for example, in terms of the foregoing example, we had no knowledge of matches other than that all the matches known to us did ignite when decorated in the manner assumed and then rubbed, we would have every reason to believe that there was a causal connection between such decorations and the igniting of the matches, it being, in fact, the same kind of inductive reason that we have for supposing a causal connection between the chemical composition of matches and their behavior when rubbed.

Whether this is true or not it has no relevance whatever to the point at issue. We are not inquiring how causal connections are known or inferred. We are asking, rather, what a causal connection is, and this is an entirely different question. We began by *assuming,* as is certainly true, that we sometimes know, by induction or otherwise, that certain events are causally connected—that the beheading of Anne Boleyn caused her death, for example. Our question is not, then, how we *know* this, but what we *mean* in asserting what we thus claim to know. It can be assumed, of one likes, that our knowledge of causal connections arises entirely from induction, from repeatedly observing what does in fact happen when certain other things happen; or it can be assumed, if one likes, that this is false. It is in either case irrelevant to the question at issue, which is a question concerned solely with the nature of the causal connection and not with the knowledge of it.

CAUSES AS NECESSARY AND SUFFICIENT CONDITIONS

In the light of all the foregoing we can now set forth our problem more clearly in the following way.

Every event occurs under innummerable and infinitely complex conditions. Some of these are relevant to the occurrence of the event, others have nothing to do with it. This means that some of the conditions under which a given event occurs are *conditiones sine quibus non,* or conditions such that the event would not have occurred had those conditions been absent, while others are such that their presence or absence makes no difference.

Suppose, for instance, that a given match has ignited, and assume that this was caused by something. Now it would be impossible to set forth all the conditions under which this occurred, for they are numberless. A description of them would be incomplete if it were not a description of the entire universe at that moment. But among those conditions there were, let us suppose, those consisting of (a) the match's being dry, (b) its being rubbed in a certain way, (c) its being of such and such chemical composition, (d) the rubbing surface being of such and such roughness, (e) the presence of dust motes in the air nearby, (f) the sun shining, (g) the presence of an observer named Smith, and so on. Now some of these conditions—namely, (a) through (d), and others as well—had something to do with the match igniting, while others—(e), for instance—had no causal connection with it. This we have learned from experience. Our problem, then, is not to state how we *know* which were the causal conditions of its igniting and which were not. The answer to this is obvious—we know by experience and induction. Our problem is, rather, to state just what relationship those *causal* conditions had to the match's igniting, but which the numberless irrelevant conditions had not;

to state, for example, what connection the match's being rubbed had to its igniting, but which the presence of dust motes had not.

The most natural way of expressing this connection is to say that had the match not been rubbed then it would not have ignited given that all the other conditions were satisfied, whereas, given those other conditions that occurred, including the match's being rubbed as it was, it would still have ignited even had the dust motes been absent. This appears to be exactly what one has in mind in saying that the friction on the match head had something to do with its igniting, while the presence of the dust motes did not—the latter condition was not at all necessary for the igniting of the match, whereas the former was, given only those other conditions which in fact occurred. This, however, is simply a way of saying that the friction was a *necessary condition* of the match's igniting, given the other conditions that occurred but no others, whereas the presence of dust motes was not.

If this is correct then we can simply assert that the cause, A, of an event, B, is that totality of conditions, from among all those, but only those, that occurred, each of which was necessary for the occurrence of B. Now if this set of conditions, A, is thus understood, as it should be, to include *every* condition, out of that totality that occurred, that was necessary for the occurrence of B, then we can say that the set of conditions, A, is also *sufficient* for B, since no other condition was necessary. We can, accordingly, understand the relationship between any set of conditions A, and any set B, expressed in the statement that A was the cause of B, to be simply described in this fashion: That A was the set, from among all those conditions that occurred, each of which was necessary, and the totality of which was sufficient, for the occurrence of B. This appears to be exactly what distinguishes the causal conditions of any event from all those that occurred but which were not causally connected with the event in question.

It is now evident that this reintroduces the concept of necessity which Hume was once so widely believed to have eliminated. For to say of any condition that a certain event would not have occurred if that condition had been absent is exactly equivalent to saying that this condition was necessary for its occurrence, or, that it was such that the event in question would not have occurred without it, given only those other conditions that occurred. There seems, however, as we have seen, to be no other way to distinguish the causal conditions of any given event from those infinitely numerous and complex other conditions under which it occurs. We cannot distinguish them by introducing the concept of a law, unless we understand the law to be, not merely a statement of what does happen, but what must happen; for we can find true statements of what does happen, and happens without exception or invariably, which are not laws. The conjunction of properties and events can be as constant as we please, with no exception whatever, without there being any causal connections between them at all. It is not until we can say what would have happened, had something else happened which did not happen, that we leave the realm of mere constancy of conjunction and find ourselves speaking of a causal connection; and as soon as we speak in this fashion we are speaking of necessary connections.

Now to say of a given event that it would not have occurred without the occurrence of another is the same as saying that the occurrence of the one without the other was causally, though not logically, impossible; or, that in a nonlogical sense, the one without the other could not have occurred. We can accordingly define the concepts of necessity and sufficiency in the following way.

To say of any condition or set of conditions, *x*, that it was *necessary* for the occurrence of some event E, means that within the totality of other conditions that occurred, but only those, the occurrence of E without *x* was impossible, or could not obtain. Similarly, to say of any condition or set of conditions, *x*, that it was *sufficient* for some event E, means that within the totality of other conditions that occurred, but only those, the occurrence of *x* without E was impossible, or could not obtain. The expression "was impossible" in these definitions has, of course, the same sense as "could not have occurred" in the discussion preceding and not the sense of *logical* impossibility. There are, we can grant at once, no logically necessary connections between causes and effects. In terms of our earlier example we can say that Anne Boleyn could not live long after being beheaded, or that it was impossible for her to do so, without maintaining that this was *logically* impossible, which it evidently was not.

The concepts of necessity and sufficiency, as thus defined, are of course the converse of each other, such that if any condition or set of conditions is necessary for another, that other is sufficient for it, and vice versa. The statement that *x* is necessary for E is logically equivalent to saying that E is sufficient for *x*, and similarly, the statement that *x* is sufficient for E is logically equivalent to saying that E is necessary for *x*. This fact enables us now to introduce a very convenient notation, as follows. If we let *x* and E represent any conditions, events, or sets of these, we can symbolize the expression, "*x* is sufficient for E," with an arrow in this way:

$$x \longrightarrow E.$$

Similarly, we can symbolize the expression "*x* is necessary for E" with a reverse arrow, in this way:

$$x \longleftarrow E.$$

Since, moreover, the expression "x is sufficient for E" is exactly equivalent to "E is necessary for x," we can regard as exactly equivalent the following representations of this relationship,

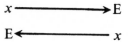

since the first of these means that the occurrence of x without E is impossible, and the second means exactly the same thing. It should be noted, however, that the arrows symbolize no *temporal* relations whatever.

With this clear and convenient way of symbolizing these relationships, we can now represent the conception of causation at which we have tentatively arrived in the following way.

Consider again a particular event that has occurred in just the way it has at a particular time and place, such as the igniting of a particular match, and call this E. Now E, we can be sure, occurred under a numerous set of conditions, which we can represent as $a, b, c, \ldots n$. Let a, for instance, be the condition consisting of the match's being dry, b its being rubbed, c its being of such and such chemical composition, d the rubbing surface being of such and such roughness, e the presence of dust motes in the air, f the sun shining, and so on, *ad infinitum*. Now some of these conditions—namely, $a, b, c,$ and d— were presumably necessary for E, in the sense that E would not have occurred in the absence of any of them, given only the other conditions that occurred, whereas others, such as e and f, had nothing to do with E. If, furthermore, as we can assume for illustration, $a, b, c,$ and d were jointly sufficient for E, the relations thus described can be symbolized as follows:

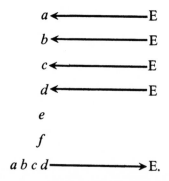

And since $a, b, c,$ and d are each individually necessary for E, it follows that E is sufficient for each of these, and, being sufficient for each of them, it is sufficient for all of them, and we can accordingly symbolize this:

$$a\ b\ c\ d \longleftarrow\!\!\!\!\!\!\!\!\!\!\!\!\!\!\!\text{———————} E.$$

And this permits us to express the causal relation, in this example, with the utmost simplicity as follows,

$$a\ b\ c\ d \overset{\longrightarrow}{\longleftarrow} E.$$

which means, simply, that the cause of E was that finite set of conditions, within the totality, only, of those that actually occurred, that was necessary and sufficient for E.

It is at this point that our metaphysical difficulties really begin, but before turning to those, two points of clarification must be made.

The first point is that this analysis does not exactly express the "ordinary use" of the word "cause," and does not purport to. The reason for this is not that the analysis itself is imprecise, but rather that ordinary usage, in most cases, is. Most persons, for example, are content to call "the cause" of any event some *one* condition that is conspicuous or, more commonly, some *part* of the causal conditions that is novel or within some agent's control. In the illustration we have been using, for example, the friction on the match would normally be regarded as "the cause" of its igniting, without regard to its dryness, its chemical composition, and so on. But the reason for this, quite obviously, is that these other conditions are taken for granted. They are not mentioned, not because they are thought to have nothing to do with the match's igniting, but rather because they are presupposed. Philosophically it makes no difference at all whether we say that given the other conditions necessary for the match's igniting, it was then caused to ignite by being rubbed, or whether we say that its being rubbed was, together with these other necessary conditions, the cause of its igniting. Its being rubbed has neither more nor less to do with its igniting than does, say, its being dry. The only difference is that it was, presumably, dry all the while and, in that state, was rubbed. It might just as well have been rubbed all the while and, in that state, suddenly rendered dry, in which case we could say that it was ignited by suddenly becoming dry.

The second point is that there is a perfectly natural point of view from which perhaps no condition is ever really necessary for the occurrence of any event, nor any set of conditions really sufficient for it, from which one could derive the absurd result that, on the analysis suggested, no events have any causes. We said, for instance, that the match's being rubbed was a necessary condition for its igniting. But, it might at first seem, that is not a necessary condition at all, since there are other ways of igniting matches—touching them to hot surfaces, for instance. Similarly, we said that rubbing the match was, together with certain other conditions, sufficient for its igniting. But this might seem false, since it would be possible to prevent it from igniting, even under these conditions—by applying a fire extinguisher, for instance.

This objection overlooks an essential qualification in the analysis, however. I said that the cause of an event E is that set of conditions that were, *within the totality of those other conditions, only, that in fact occurred,* individually necessary and jointly sufficient for E. If, in terms of our example, that totality of other conditions that actually occurred did not, in fact, include some such condition as the match's being in contact with a hot surface, nor the application of any fire extinguisher, and so on, then within the totality of conditions that *did* occur, its being rubbed *was* necessary for its igniting, and was also, together with certain other conditions that occurred, sufficient for its igniting.

TIME AND EFFICACY

The analysis of the causal relationship, as it now stands, has one strange consequence that is immediately obvious; namely, that it does not enable us to draw any distinction between cause and effect. I have suggested that the cause of an event is that set of conditions, among all those that occur, which is necessary and sufficient for that event, from which it of course follows that if any condition or set of conditions, A, is the cause of another, B, then B is automatically also the cause of A. For concerning any A and B, if A is necessary and sufficient for B, and therefore, on this analysis, the cause of B, then it logically follows that B is necessary and sufficient for A, and therefore the cause of A. This is quite plainly absurd. One cannot possibly say that a match's igniting is any part of the cause of its being rubbed, that a stone's being warm is the cause of the sun's shining upon it, or that a man's feeling intoxicated is the cause of his having alcohol in his blood, despite the fact that the relationships of necessity and sufficiency between cause and effect are the same in both directions.

Earlier metaphysicians took for granted that the difference between cause and effect was one of power or efficacy or, what amounts to the same thing, that the cause of anything was always something active, and its effect some change in something that is passive. Thus, the sun has the power to warm, a stone, but the stone has no power to make the sun shine; it is simply the passive recipient of a change wrought by the sun. Similarly, alcohol in the blood has the power to produce feelings of intoxication, but a man cannot, by having such feelings, produce alcohol in his blood.

Modern philosophers, on the contrary, have almost universally supposed that the difference between cause and effect is not to be found in anything so esoteric as power or efficacy, but is simply a temporal difference, nothing more. The cause of an event, it is now almost universally supposed, is some condition or set of conditions that *precedes* some other, its effect, in time. Thus, if our analysis of the causal relationship is otherwise correct then it should, according to this prevalent view, have some qualification added about time, such as to require that the cause should occur before its effect.

I believe this is one of the profoundest errors in modern philosophy and the source of more misconceptions than almost any other. By this simple expedient of introducing considerations of time, philosophers imagine that they no longer need to talk metaphysically of causal power or efficacy. In fact, of course, philosophers, like everyone else, do still speak freely of power and efficacy—of the power of various substances to corrode, to dissolve, to cause intoxication, to cause death, and so on. But in their philosophies they imagine that such terms express only ideas of *time,* and that they can be omitted from any exact description of causal connections just by the simple device of introducing temporal qualifications.

. . . I intend to show that what I have called an error—namely, that causes *must* precede their effects in time—is an error indeed simply by citing perfectly clear and typical instances of causation in which this is not so.

Before doing this, however, let us consider a related question. Let us suppose that there *is* a temporal interval between a cause and its effect, such that it is true to say that one occurs *before* the other. Now if the relationships between the two are otherwise identical—namely, are simply the relationships of necessity and sufficiency set forth above, or, for that matter, any other nontemporal relationships whatever—the question can be asked, *Why* should it be thought so important to regard only the prior condition or set of conditions as the cause of the subsequent one, and never the subsequent as the cause of the prior? There is, certainly, an absurdity in saying that a man's dying is the cause of his being shot, or that a man's being intoxicated is the cause of his having imbibed alcohol, rather than the other way around; but what *kind* of absurdity is it? Is it merely a verbal error, a wrong choice of vocabulary, or is it a metaphysical absurdity? If one were to point out that a woman cannot bear a child before being impregnated, he would probably not be *merely* calling attention to a point of vocabulary. He would be stating an obvious truth of biology. If, on the other hand, one were to say that one's brother's sons cannot be his nieces, but must be his nephews, he would obviously be making only a point about language, about the use of certain words. Now then, when one says that a cause cannot come after its effect, which kind of point is he making? Is he *merely* calling attention to a matter of vocabulary, or is he saying something metaphysically significant about causes and their effects?

It seems fairly clear that there is something metaphysically absurd, and not merely an inept choice of words, in supposing that efficient causes might work "backward." There is surely some reason why nothing can produce an effect in the past, and the reason cannot just be that if it did, we would not then *call* it a cause.

Consider the following illustration. There is a variety of ways in which one might ensure that a certain man—say, some political rival—is dead on a certain day. One way would be to shoot him through the head the day before. We can assume that this, together with all the other conditions prevailing, is sufficient for his being dead the next day and further, that in case conditions are such that he would not have died had he not been shot, then it is also necessary for his being dead then. But another, equally good way of ensuring that he is dead on that day would be to attend his funeral later on. This would surely be sufficient for his prior death and, in case conditions are such that his being dead is sufficient for someone's attending his funeral, then it is also a necessary condition of his prior death. Suppose, then, that one man shoots him, and another attends his funeral, and that both of these acts are related to that man's death in exactly the same way, except only for the difference in time; that is, that each act is, given only those other conditions that occur, both necessary and sufficient for his being dead on the day in question. Why should one man be blamed more than the other, or held any more responsible for the death? Each man, equally with the other, did something necessary and sufficient for that man's death. Either act guarantees the death as well as the other. The thing to note is that this question is *not* answered by merely observing that one of these acts occurred before the death, and the other after; that is already quite obvious and begs the question. Nor is it answered by noting that we do not, as it happens, *call* the subsequent event the cause. That is obvious and irrelevant; the word "cause" was not even used in the example. We do not hold a man responsible for causing an event unless something he does is a necessary and sufficient *prior* condition of it. That is granted. But merely *stating* that fact does not answer the question, Why not? It cannot be a mere question of *vocabulary* whether, for example, a certain man should be hanged for what he has done and another one not.

Part of the answer to this question, I believe, is that no cause exerts any power over the past, esoteric as that comment may be. The same idea is expressed, more metaphysically, by saying that all past things are actualized, and never at some later time potentially what they are not then actually, whereas a present thing can be actually one thing but potentially another. This would be expressed in terms of our example by saying that a man who shoots another *acts upon* him, or does something to him, or is an agent, whereas the man who is thus killed does not, in dying, act upon his assassin, but is the passive recipient, patient, or sufferer, of the other's causal activity. The man who merely attends the funeral, on the other hand, does not act upon him who is already dead. He is merely the passive observer of what has already been done.

This way of conceiving these relationships seems, moreover, to be the way all men do think of causes and effects, and it explains the enormous absurdity in the supposition that causes might act so as to alter things already past. For anything to be a cause it must act upon something and, as a matter of fact—indeed, of metaphysical necessity—nothing past can be acted upon by anything. The profound error of modern philosophy has been to suppose that, in making that point, one is making only a point about language.

CONTEMPORANEOUS CAUSES AND EFFECTS

If we can now cite clear examples of causal connections wherein those conditions that constitute the cause and those that constitute the effect are entirely contemporaneous, neither occurring before the other, then it will have been proved that the difference between a cause and its effect cannot be a temporal one, but must consist of something else.

In fact such examples are not at all hard to find. Consider, for instance, a locomotive that is pulling a caboose, and to make it simple, suppose this is all it is pulling. Now here the motion of the locomotive is sufficient for the motion of the caboose, the two being connected in such a way that the former cannot move without the latter moving with it. But so also, the motion of the caboose is sufficient for the motion of the locomotive, for given that the two are connected as they are, it would be impossible for the caboose to be moving without the locomotive moving with it. From this it logically follows that, conditions being such as they are—both objects are in motion, there are no other moves present, no obstructions to motion, and so on—the motion of each object is also necessary for the motion of the other. But is there any temporal gap between the motion of one and the motion of the other? Clearly there is not. They move together, and in no sense is the motion of one temporally followed by the motion of the other.

Here it is tempting to say that the locomotive must *start* moving before the caboose can start moving, but this is both irrelevant and false. It is irrelevant, because the effect we are considering is not the caboose's *beginning* to move, but its moving. And it is false because we can suppose the two to be securely connected, such that as soon as either begins to move the other must move, too. Even if we do not make this supposition, and suppose, instead, that the locomotive does begin moving first, and moves some short distance before overcoming the looseness and elasticity of its connection with the caboose, still it is no cause of the motion of the caboose until that looseness is overcome. When that happens, and not until then, the locomotive imparts its motion to the caboose. Cause and effect are, then, perfectly contemporaneous.

Again, consider the relationships between one's hand and a pencil he is holding while writing. We can ignore here the difficult question of what causes the *hand* to move. It is surely true, in any case, that the motion of the pencil is caused by the motion of the hand. This means, first, that conditions are such that the motion of the hand is sufficient for the motion of the pencil. Given precisely *those* conditions, however, the motion of the pencil is sufficient for the motion of the hand; neither can move, under the conditions assumed —that the fingers are grasping the pencil—without the other moving with it. It follows, then, that under these conditions the motion of either is also necessary for the motion of the other. And, manifestly, both motions are contemporaneous; the motion of neither is *followed* by the motion of the other.

Or again, consider a leaf that is being fluttered by the wind. Here it would be quite clearly erroneous to say that the wind currents impinge upon the leaf and then, some time later, the leaf flutters in response. There is no gap in time at all. One might want to say that the leaf, however light, does offer some resistance to the wind, and that the wind must overcome this slight resistance before any fluttering occurs. But then we need only add that the wind is no cause of the leaf's motion until that resistance is overcome. Cause and effect are again, then, contemporaneous.

What, then, distinguishes cause and effect in the foregoing examples? It is not the time of occurrence, for both occur together. It is not any difference in the relations of necessity and sufficiency, for these are identical both ways. But there is one thing which, in all these cases, appears to distinguish the cause from the effect; namely, that the cause acts upon something else to produce some change. The locomotive *pulls* the caboose, but the caboose does not *push* the locomotive; it just follows passively along. The hand pushes the pencil and imparts motion to it, while the pencil is just passively moved. The wind acts upon the leaf to move it; but it is no explanation of the wind's blowing to say that the leaf is moving. In all these cases, to be sure, what has been distinguished as the cause is itself moved by something else—the locomotive by steam in its cylinders, the hand by a man, the wind by things more complex and obscure; but that only calls attention to the fact that causes can themselves be the effects of other causes. . . .

ARE ALL CAUSES CONTEMPORANEOUS WITH THEIR EFFECTS?

In order to show that it can be no part of the analysis of a causal connection that causes precede their effects in time, all that is needed is a *single* clear example of a cause or set of causal conditions which is entirely contemporaneous with its effect, and examples of this, we have just seen, are easy enough to point out. It should, in any case, be obvious just from philosophical considerations, for it is not difficult to imagine beginningless processes producing effects throughout all time past, even though it is doubtful whether any such processes exist. If it were discovered, for example, that the sun had always shone upon the moon, that this state of affairs, had always existed, no one would be led by that alone to doubt that moonlight is caused by the sun, or to suppose that it would be arbitrary, in such a state of affairs, what one called the cause and what the effect.

It has, however, sometimes been argued most acutely that *all* causes are contemporaneous with their effects, that just in the nature of things neither a cause nor its effect *can* occur before or after the other. Thus it is sometimes maintained that a ball, for example, which is moved by the impact of another ball, is not caused to move by anything happening *prior* to such impact, but by the impact itself, and that this is simultaneous with the initial motion of the ball that is thus moved. Again, it can be argued that water is not caused to boil by *first* being heated to a certain point. Rather, it boils as soon as it is heated to that point, and not sometime later, such that cause and effect are again contemporaneous. And we get the same result, it is sometimes claimed, in the case of any causal connection described with sufficient exactness.

Now it is in no way essential, for the point of this [discussion], either to affirm or to deny this. In order to show that a cause *need* not precede its effect in time, which has already been done, it is by no means necessary to show that *no* cause ever precedes its effect. Nor need we address ourselves to the arguments upon which this latter claim rests. They are, in my opinion, impossible to meet, for they involve enormous unresolved problems concerning the continuity of processes and the continuity of time itself. The reason we nevertheless need not address ourselves to them is that, however difficult they may be of refutation, their conclusion—that *all* causes are contemporaneous with their effects—is probably false. For if this were true, then there would be no such thing as a causal chain. Indeed, it would be impossible for any two events whatever to have any causal connection with each other in case there were any lapse of time at all between their occurrences. If some event A, for example, causes B, which in turn causes C, which in turn caused D, then in case every cause is simultaneous with its effect, it follows that when A occurs, then the others, and indeed every event in the universe that is in any way causally connected with A, must occur *at the same time*. This, however, is false. There *are* causal chains, and sometimes temporally separated events are causally related in one way or another. When a stone is dropped into the middle of a pond, for instance, this has at least *some* causal connection with the ripples that appear at the shore some moments later. There are, to be sure, many intervening causal connections, but this common state of affairs would be logically impossible if every cause were simultaneous with its effect—for all the intervening causal connections would then have to occur simultaneously with both the initial disturbance of the water and the subsequent appearance of ripples at the shore, which is absurd.

My conclusions, then, are compatible with the supposition that causes sometimes precede their effects in time. I only deny that they *must* precede them, and hence that this supposition plays any part in the nature or analysis of a causal connection. My conclusions are also compatible with saying that a given set of conditions, which is *antecedently* necessary for, or sufficient for, or both necessary and sufficient for another state of affairs, is the *cause* of that state of affairs. I only deny that its causal relationship to that state of affairs *consists* in that relationship, for a cause, as I have maintained, must *also* be something having the power to produce that state of affairs. My conclusions are *not* compatible with saying that a given set of conditions, which is subsequently necessary for, or sufficient for, or both necessary and sufficient for another state of affairs, is the cause of that state of affairs. This, however, is no consequence of "the way we use words." On the contrary, the reason we use words as we do here, and refuse to call such a set of conditions the cause of something happening earlier on, is that it would be absurd to do so. And the only basis for this, as far as I can see, is that causes have no power over the past—even though they may have precisely the same relationships of necessity and sufficiency with respect to things past as they have with respect to things future.

WHAT IS A CAUSE?

A true interpreted statement of the form "A was the cause of B" means, in light of the foregoing, that both A and B are conditions or sets of conditions that occurred; that each was, given all the other conditions that occurred, but only those, both necessary and sufficient for the occurrence of the other; that B did not precede A in time; *and* that A made B happen by virtue of its power to do so. But this final qualification, *alas!* renders the whole analysis empty. For to say that A made B happen obviously only means that A *caused* B, and to say that it did this by virtue of its power to do so obviously means nothing more than that A produced B by virtue of its efficacy as a *cause*—or, in short, that A caused B. To say of anything, then, that it was the cause of something else, means simply and solely that it *was* the cause of the thing in question, and there is absolutely no other conceptually clearer way of putting the matter except by the introduction of mere synonyms for causation. Positively, what this means is that causation is a philosophical category, that while the concept of causation can perhaps be used to shed light upon other problems or used in the analysis of other relationships, no other concepts can be used to analyze it.

Select Bibliography

BOOKS

Berofsky, B. *Determinism* (Princeton, 1971).

Bunge, M. *Causality* (Cambridge, Mass., 1959).

Ducasse, C. J. *Causation and the Types of Necessity* (Seattle, 1924; Dover paperbacks, 1969).

Goodman, N. *Fact, Fiction and Forecast*, 2nd ed., (Indianapolis, 1965).

Hart, H. L., and Honore, A. M. *Causation and the Law* (Oxford, 1959).

Michotte, A. *The Perception of Causality* (New York, 1963).

Rescher, N. *Hypothetical Reasoning* (Amsterdam, 1964).

Suppes, P. *A Probabilistic Theory of Causality* (Amsterdam, 1970).

von Wright, G. H. *Explanation and Understanding* (Ithaca, N.Y., 1971), 34–82.

ARTICLES

Anderson, J. "The Problem of Causality," *Australasian Journal of Philosophy* 2 (1938): 127–42.

Anscombe, G. E. M. "Causality and Extensionality," *Journal of Philosophy* 66 (1969): 152–59.

———. "Causality and Determinism," An Inaugural Lecture delivered at Cambridge University, and published by the Cambridge University Press (1971).

Ayer, A. J. "Why Cannot Cause Succeed Effect?" in *The Problem of Knowledge* (Harmondsworth, England, 1956).

Black, M. "Why Cannot an Effect Precede Its Cause?" *Analysis* 16 (1955): 49–58.

Blanshard, B. "Necessity in Causation," in *Reason and Analysis* (La Salle, Ill., 1962), 444–71.

Brand, M., and Swain, M. "On the Analysis of Causation," *Synthese* 21 (1970): 222–27.

Bromberger, S. "What Are Effects?" in R. J. Butler ed., *Analytical Philosophy*, 1st series (Oxford, 1966).

Burks, A. W. "The Logic of Causal Propositions," *Mind* 60 (1951): 363–82.

Chisholm, R. M. "The Contrary-to-Fact Conditional," *Mind* 55 (1946): 289–307.

Chisholm, R. M. and Taylor, R. T. "Making Things to Have Happened," *Analysis* 20 (1960): 73–82.

Collins, A. "Explanation and Causality," *Mind* 75 (1965): 482–500.

Davidson, D. "Causal Relations," *Journal of Philosophy* 64, No. 21 (1967): 691–703.

Dray, W. H. "Must Effects Have Causes?" in R. J. Butler ed., *Analytical Philosophy*, 1st series (Oxford, 1966).

Dummett, M. "Bringing About the Past," *Philosophical Review* 73 (1964): 338–59.

Ewing, A. C. "A Defence of Causality," in W. E. Kennick and M. Lazerowitz eds., *Metaphysics* (La Salle, Ill., 1966): 258–75.

Føllesdal, D. "Quantification in Causal Contexts," in R. S. Cohen and M. W. Wartofsky eds., *Boston Studies in the Philosophy of Science* (New York, 1965): 263–74. Reprinted in L. Linsky (ed.), *Reference and Modality* (Oxford, 1971).

———. "A Model Theoretic Approach to Causal Logic," in *Det Kgl Norske Videnskabers Selskabs Skrifter* 2 (1966).

Gale, R. "Why a Cause Cannot Be Later Than Its Effect," *Review of Metaphysics* 19 (1965–66): 209–34.

Gaking, D. "Causation and Recipes," *Mind* 6 (1955): 479–87.

Goodman, N. "The Problem of Counterfactual Conditionals," in *Fact, Fiction and Forecast* (Indianapolis, 1965): 3–27.

Gorovitz, S. "Leaving the Past Alone," *Philosophical Review* 73 (1964): 360–71.

———. "Causal Judgments and Causal Explanations," *Journal of Philosophy* 62 (1965): 695–711.

Hampshire, S. "Subjunctive Conditionals," *Analysis* 9 (1948): 9–14. Reprinted in M. Macdonald, *Philosophy and Analysis* (Oxford, 1954): 204–10

Hanson, N. R. "Causal Chains," *Mind* 64 (1955): 289–311.

Hiz, H. "On the Inferential Sense of Contrary-to-Fact Conditionals," *Journal of Philosophy* 48 (1951): 587–87.

Kim, J. "Causation, Nomic Subsumption, and the Concept of Event," *Journal of Philosophy* 70 (1973): 217–36.

Kneale, W. "Natural Laws and Contrary-to-Fact Conditionals," *Analysis* 10 (1950): 121–25. Reprinted in M. Macdonald, *Philosophy and Analysis* (Oxford, 1954).

Lewis, E. "Causation," *Journal of Philosophy* 70 (1973): 556–67.

Lucas, J. R., "Causation," in R. J. Butler (ed.), *Analytical Philosophy*, 1st series (Oxford, 1966).

Mackie, J. L. "Causes and Conditions," *American Philosophical Quarterly* 2, no. 4 (1965): 245–64.

Mackie, J. L. "Counterfactuals and Causal Laws," in R. J. Butler ed., *Analytical Philosophy*, 1st series (Oxford, 1966).

Madden, E. H. "A Third View of Causality," *Review of Metaphysics* 23 (1969): 67–84.

Mandelbaum, M. "Causal Analysis in History," *Journal of the History of Ideas* 3 (1942).

Marc-Wogau, K. "On Historical Explanation," *Theoria* 28 (1962): 213.

Martin, R. "The Sufficiency Thesis," *Philosophical Studies* 23 (1972): 205–11.

Montague, R. "Logical Necessity, Physical Necessity, Ethics Quantifiers," *Inquiry* 4 (1960): 259–69.

Nagel, E. "The Logical Character of Scientific Laws," in *The Structure of Science* (New York, 1961): 49–78.

Pap, A. "Philosophical Analysis, Translation Schemas, and the Regularity Theory of Causation," *Journal of Philosophy* 49 (1952): 657–66.

Parry, W. T. "Re-examination of the Problem of Counterfactual Conditionals," *Journal of Philosophy* 54 (1957): 85–94.

Rescher, N. "Belief-Contravening Synpositions and the Problem of Contrary-to-Fact Conditionals," *Philosophical Review* 60 (1961): 176–96.

Ruddick, W. "Causal Connection," *Synthese* 18 (1968): 46–67.

Schlick, M. "Causality in Contemporary Physics, I and III," *Philosophical Studies* 12 (1962): 177–93, 281–98.

Scriven, M. "Defects of the Necessary Condition Analysis of Causation," in W. Dray ed., *Philosophical Analysis and History* (New York, 1966): 258–62.

Sellars, W. S. "Conterfactuals," from "Counterfactuals, Dispositions and the Causal Modalities," *Minnesota Studies in the Philosophy of Science*, edited by Feigl, Scriven, and Maxwell (Minneapolis, 1958), vol. 2, 227–48.

Shope, R. K., "Explanations in Terms of 'The Cause,' " *Journal of Philosophy* 64 (1967): 312–30.

Shorter, J. M. "Causality and a Method of Analysis," in R. J. Butler ed., *Analytical Philosophy*, 2nd series (Oxford, 1968).

Simon, H., and Rescher, N. "Cause and Counterfactual," *Philosophical Studies* 33 (1966).

Sosa, E. "Hypothetical Reasoning," *Journal of Philosophy* 64 (1967): 293–305.

Stalnaker, R. "A Theory of Conditionals," in N. Rescher ed., *Studies in Logical Theory* APQ Monograph No. 2 (Oxford, 1968).

Stalnaker, R. C., and Thomason, R. H. "A Semantic Analysis of Conditional Logic," *Theoria* 36 (1970): 23–42.

Stevenson, C. L. "If-Iculties," *Philosophical Studies* 37 (1970): 27–49.

Vendler, Z. "Effects, Results and Consequences," in R. J. Butler ed., *Analytical Philosophy*, 1st series (Oxford, 1966).

———. "Causal Relations," *Journal of Philosophy* 60 (1963).

Walters, R. S. "The Problem of Counterfactual Conditionals," *Australasian Journal of Philosophy* 39 (1961): 30–46.

Warnock, G. J. "Every Event Has a Cause," in A. Flew ed., *Logic and Language* (Oxford, 1951), pp. 107–109.

Watling, J. "The Problem of Contrary-to-Fact Conditionals," *Analysis* 17 (1957): 73–80.

von Wright, G. H. "On Conditionals," in *Logical Studies* (London, 1957), pp. 127–65.

Part Three

The Question of Personal Identity

Introduction

The question of personal identity can be formulated best by asking two related questions: (a) What is it about a person whereby it can be truly said of him that he is the same person at time t_2 that he was at time t_1? and (b) What is the referent of the first person pronoun 'I'? Neither question has an easy answer. In the case of (a) it is far easier to isolate the changes in a person from time to time than to determine some characteristic that remains constant. People constantly change from both a physical as well as a psychological point of view. Nevertheless it does make sense for us to maintain that some particular person is the same person today that he was a month ago or five years ago. But in just what sense?

As formulated, the question of personal identity turns on the nature of the identity relationship over time. If the criteria of this identity are the same as hold true for mathematical formulas, then it is almost for certain that a person is not the same from time to time. It is analogous to a ship. Let us suppose that we were invited to spend an evening aboard our friend's yacht, The Ladybug. A year later we are invited back to the yacht and, upon observing her name, announce to the host, "We see that you still own the same yacht." He replies, "No, she is not the same." Puzzled by our host's comment we are compelled to say, "Funny, it certainly appears to be the same yacht. But then again, we haven't seen her in a year. Did you get a new one?" "No, its not a different yacht," retorts the host. "But you said it's not the same!" "I did. You see," says our host, "since you were last aboard her, I replaced that winch over there and added that porthole. Therefore, technically it is not the *same* yacht as it was last year." Technically, the host is correct but that is not what we normally mean by it being the same yacht.

The yacht's owner was construing identity in what Joseph Butler called the strict and philosophical sense. Butler also maintained that there is a loose and popular sense of identity; this is the everyday sense with which we use the notion of identity and the one being employed when we maintain that a person is the same from time to time. However, the problem with so construing identity in the loose and popular sense is summed up in this question: Just how loose can we be concerning anything other than strict identity and still meaningfully talk about identity at all?

(b) Traditionally the question of personal identity has been approached from the perspective of that to which the first person pronoun 'I' refers. Is it mind or body or a combination of both? Descartes, for example, argues that it is the soul *qua* mind that constitutes personal identity. Such an analysis inevitably introduces the problem concerning the relationship between mind and body—a problem that Descartes introduces but never solves. Note the ambiguity between soul and mind. Obviously, one's mind is in a constant state of change. The soul, however, is presumed to be stable and constitutes the source of identity. The soul, of course, is an unidentifiable entity, unless attached to some ever-changing beast, as that of mind.

Therefore, some philosophers have chosen the body as the principal element constituting personal identity. If taken in the loose and popular sense, such a view carries with it some potential. After all, physical appearance changes constantly, *albeit* gradually, yet we are recognized as the same person, both by ourselves and by others. Once again the problem of criteria raises its ugly head. Just how much change is necessary before we are justified in maintaining that someone is *not* the same person as at time t_1? Surely, many of us know of someone who has been in a dreadful automobile accident and is now rendered physically and mentally handicapped. In the aftermath we say, "He simply is not the same person he was before." Note that the word 'same,' as so used, applies to both his mind and his body.

Because of the difficulty in establishing the mind or the body as the source of identity, it has been tempting to introduce memory as the thread that binds both together thus constituting personal identity. Unfortunately memory is faulty. The breakdown in memory creates two problems: (1) It entails that there is no continuity between memory lapses and, strictly speaking, no (personal) identity. (2) Due to the reality of (1), it follows that if (and that hypothetical is very often satisfied) agent A does remember circumstance X, and if agent B also remembers circumstance X, then A and B are the same person; or if agent A does not remember circumstance X and agent B does remember circumstance X, then agent B is agent A even though in reality B is not A. Memory may be the principle *source* of the belief in the existence of personal identity, as Hume maintained, but clearly memory does not constitute personal identity. Consequently, it appears that we are back where we started, hopefully with some fresh answers to questions (a) and (b).

15

On Thinking Things and the Soul

René Descartes

I AM ESSENTIALLY A THINKING SOUL

The Meditation of yesterday filled my mind with so many doubts that it is no longer in my power to forget them. . . . I shall nevertheless make an effort and follow anew the same path as that on which I yesterday entered, i.e., I shall proceed by setting aside all that in which the least doubt could be supposed to exist, just as if I had discoverd that it was absolutely false; and I shall ever follow in this road until I have met with something which is certain, or at least, if I can do nothing else, until I have learned for certain that there is nothing in the world that is certain. . . .

I suppose, then, that all the things that I see are false; I persuade myself that nothing has ever existed of all that my fallacious memory represents to me. I consider that I possess no senses; I imagine that body, figure, extension, movement, and place are but the fictions of my mind. What, then, can be esteemed as true? Perhaps nothing at all, unless that there is nothing in the world that is certain.

But how can I know there is not something different from those things that I have just considered, of which one cannot have the slightest doubt? Is there not some God, or some other being by whatever name we call it, who puts these reflections into my mind? That is not necessary, for is it not

---

Selected passages from *Meditations II* and *VI, The Principles of the First Philosophy,* and *The Passions of the Soul.*

possible that I am capable of producing them myself? I myself, am I not at least something? But I have already denied that I had senses and body. Yet I hesitate, for what follows from that? Am I so dependent on body and senses that I cannot exist without these? But I was persuaded that there was nothing in all the world, that there was no heaven, no earth, that there were no minds, nor any bodies: was I not then likewise persuaded that I did not exist? Not at all; of a surety I myself did exist since I persuaded myself of something (or merely because I thought of something). But there is some deceiver or other, very powerful and very cunning, who ever employs his ingenuity in deceiving me. Then without doubt I exist also if he deceives me, and let him deceive me as much as he will, he can never cause me to be nothing so long as I think that I am something. So that after having reflected well and carefully examined all things, we must come to the definite conclusion that this proposition: I am, I exist, is necessarily true each time that I pronounce it, or that I mentally conceive it.

But I do not yet know clearly enough what I am, I who am certain that I am; and hence I must be careful to see that I do not imprudently take some other object in place of myself, and thus that I do not go astray in respect of this knowledge that I hold to be the most certain and most evident of all that I have formerly learned. That is why I shall not consider anew what I believed myself to be before I embarked upon these last reflections; and of my former opinions I shall withdraw all that might even in a small degree be invalidated by the reasons which I have just brought forward, in order that there may be nothing at all left beyond what is absolutely certain and indubitable.

What then did I formerly believe myself to be? Undoubtedly I believed myself to be a man. But what is a man? Shall I say a reasonable animal? Certainly not; for then I should have to inquire what an animal is, and what is reasonable; and thus from a single question I should insensibly fall into an infinitude of others more difficult; and I should not wish to waste the little time and leisure remaining to me in trying to unravel subtleties like these.

*   *   *

But what am I, now that I suppose that there is a certain genius which is extremely powerful, and, if I may say so, malicious, who employs all his powers in deceiving me? Can I affirm that I possess the least of all those things which I have just said pertain to the nature of body? I pause to consider, I revolve all these things in my mind, and I find none of which I can say that it pertains to me. I would be tedious to stop to enumerate them. Let us pass to the attributes of soul and see if there is any one which is in me? What of nutrition or walking [the first mentioned]? But if it is so that I have no body it is also true that I can neither walk nor take nourishment. Another attribute is sensation. But one cannot feel without body, and besides I have thought I perceived many things during sleep that I recognized in my waking moments as not having been experienced at all. What of thinking? I find here that thought is an attribute that belongs to me; it alone cannot be separated from me. I am, I exist, that is certain. But how often? Just when I think; for it might possibly be the case if I ceased entirely to think, that I should likewise cease altogether to exist. I do not now admit anything which is not necessarily true: to speak accurately I am not more than a thing which thinks, that is to say a mind or a soul, or an understanding, or a reason, which are terms whose significance was formerly unknown to me. I am, however, a real thing and really exist; but what thing? I have answered: a thing which thinks.

*   *   *

And first of all, because I know that all things which I apprehend clearly and distinctly can be created by God as I apprehend them, it suffices that I am able to apprehend one thing apart from another clearly and distinctly in order to be certain that the one is different from the other, since they may be made to exist in separation at least by the omnipotence of God; and it does not signify by what power this separation is made in order to compel me to judge them to be different: and, therefore, just because I know certainly that I exist, and that meanwhile I do not remark that any other thing necessarily pertains to my nature or essence, excepting that I am a thinking thing, I rightly conclude that my essence consists solely in the fact that I am a thinking thing (or a substance whose whole essence or nature is to think). And although possibly (or rather certainly, as I shall say in a moment) I possess a body with which I am very intimately conjoined, yet because, on the one side, I have a clear and distinct idea of myself inasmuch as I am only a thinking and unextended thing, and as, on the other, I possess a distinct idea of body, inasmuch as it is only an extended and unthinking thing, it is certain that this I (that is to say, my soul by which I am what I am), is entirely and absolutely distinct from my body, and can exist without it.

THOUGHT COMPRISES EVERY SORT OF CONSCIOUSNESS

What thought is

By the word thought I understand all that of which we are conscious as operating in us. And that is why not alone understanding, willing, imagining, but also feeling, are here the same thing as thought. For if I say I see, or I walk, I therefore am, and if by seeing and walking I mean the action of my eyes or my legs, which is the work of my body, my conclusion is not absolutely certain; because it may be that, as often happens in sleep, I think I see or I walk, although I never open my eyes or move from my place, and the same thing perhaps might occur if I had not a body at all. But if I mean only to talk of my sensation, or my consciously seeming to see or to walk, it becomes quite true because my assertion now refers only to my mind, which alone is concerned with my feeling or thinking that I see and I walk.

That conceptions which are perfectly simple and clear of themselves are obscured by the definitions of the Schools, and that they are not to be numbered as amongst those capable of being acquired by study [but are inborn in us]

I do not here explain various other terms of which I have availed myself or will afterwards avail myself, because they seem to me perfectly clear of themselves. And I have often noticed that philosophers err in trying to explain by definitions logically constructed, things which were perfectly simple in themselves; they thereby render them but more obscure. And when I stated that this proposition *I think, therefore I am* is the first and most certain which presents itself to those who philosophize in orderly fashion, I did not for all that deny that we must first of all know *what is knowledge, what is existence, and what is certainty,* and that *in order to think we must be,* and such like; but because these are notions of the simplest possible kind, which of themselves give us no knowledge of anything that exists, I did not think them worthy of being put on record.

How we may know our mind better than our body

But in order to understand how the knowledge which we possess of our mind not only precedes that which we have of our body, but is also more evident, it must be observed that it is very manifest by the natural light which is in our souls, that no qualities or properties pertain to nothing; and that where some are perceived there must necessarily be some thing or substance on which they depend. And the same light shows us that we know a thing or substance so much the better the more properties we observe in it. And we certainly observe many more qualities in our mind than in any other thing, inasmuch as there is nothing that excites us to knowledge of whatever kind, which does not even much more certainly compel us to a consciousness of our thought. To take an example, if I persuade myself that there is an earth because I touch or see it, by that very same fact, and by a yet stronger reason, I should be persuaded that my thought exists; because it may be that I think I touch the earth even though there is possibly no earth existing at all, but it is not possible that I who form this judgment and my mind which judges thus, should be nonexistent; and so in other cases.

The reason why everyone does not comprehend this in the same way

Those who have not studied philosophy in an orderly way have held other opinions on this subject because they never distinguished their mind from their body with enough care. For although they had no difficulty in believing that they themselves existed, and that they had a greater assurance of this than of any other thing, yet because they did not observe that by themselves they ought merely to understand their minds (when metaphysical certainty was in question), and since on the contrary they rather meant that it was their bodies which they saw with their eyes, touched with their hands, and to which they wrongly attributed the power of perception, they did not distinctly comprehend the nature of the mind. . . .

What sensation is, and how it operates

We must know, therefore, that although the mind of man informs the whole body, it yet has its principal seat in the brain, and it is there that it not only understands and imagines, but also perceives; and this by means of the nerves which are extended like filaments from the brain to all the other members, with which they are so connected that we can hardly touch any part of the human body without causing the extremities of some of the nerves spread over it to be moved; and this motion passes to the other extremities of those nerves which are collected in the brain round the seat of the soul. . . . But the movements which are thus excited in the brain by the nerves, affect in diverse ways the soul or mind, which is intimately connected with the brain, according to the diversity of the motions themselves. And the diverse affections of our mind, or thoughts that immediately arise from these notions, are called perceptions of the senses, or, in common language, sensations. . . .

That the soul does not perceive excepting in as far as it is in the brain

It is however easily proved that the soul feels those things that affect the body not in so far as it is in each member of the body, but only in so far as it is in the brain, where the nerves by their movements convey to it the diverse actions of the external objects which touch the parts of the body (in which they are inserted). For, in the first place, there are many maladies which, though they affect the brain alone, yet either disorder or altogether take away from us the use of our senses; just like sleep itself which affects the brain alone, and yet every day takes from us during a great part of our time the faculty of perception, which is afterwards restored to us on awakening. Secondly, from the fact that though the brain be healthy (as well as the members in which the organs of the external senses are to be found), if the paths by which the nerves pass from the external parts to the brain are obstructed, that sensation is lost in these external parts of the body. And finally we sometimes feel pain as though it were in certain of our members, and yet its cause is not in these members where it is felt, but in others through which the nerves pass that extend to the brain from the parts where the pain is felt. And this I could prove by innumerable experiments; here, however, one will suffice. When a girl suffering from a serious affection of the hand was visited by the surgeon, her eyes were usually bandaged lest seeing the dressing should have a bad effect upon her. After some days, as gangrene set in, her arm had to be cut off from the elbow and several linen cloths tied together were substituted in place of the amputated limb, such a way that she was quite ignorant of what had been done; meanwhile, however, she had various pains, sometimes in one of the fingers of the hand which was cut off, and sometimes in another. This could clearly only happen because the nerves which previously had been carried all the way from the brain to the hand, and afterwards terminated in the arm near the elbow, were there affected in the same way as it was their function to be stimulated for the purpose of impressing on the mind residing in the brain the sensation of pain in the hand is not felt by the mind inasmuch as it is in the hand, but as it is in the brain.)

*   *   *

That the heat and movement of the members proceed from the body, the thoughts from the soul

Thus because we have no conception of the body as thinking in any way, we have reason to believe that every kind of thought which exists in us belongs to the soul; and because we do not doubt there being inanimate bodies which can move in as many as or in more diverse modes than can ours, and which have as much heat or more (experience demonstrates this to us in flame, which of itself has much more heat and movement than any of our members), we must believe that all the heat and all the movements which are in us pertain only to body, inasmuch as they do not depend on thought at all.

That it is an error to believe that the soul supplies the movement and heat to the body

By this means we shall avoid a very considerable error into which many have fallen; so much so that I am of opinion that this is the primary cause which has prevented our being able hitherto satisfactorily to explain the passions and the other properties of the soul. It arises from the fact that from observing that all dead bodies are devoid of heat and consequently of movement, it has been thought that it was the absence of soul which caused these movements and this heat to cease; and thus, without any reason, it was thought that our natural heat and all the movements of our body depend on the soul: while in fact we ought on the contrary to believe that the soul quits us on death only because this heat ceases, and the organs which serve to move the body disintegrate.

The difference that exists between a living body and a dead body

In order, then, that we may avoid this error, let us consider that death never comes to pass by reason of the soul, but only because some one of the principal parts of body decays; and we may judge that the body of living man differs from that of a dead man just as does a watch or other automaton (i.e., a machine that moves of itself), when it is wound up and contains in itself the corporeal principle of those movements for which it is designed along with all that is requisite for its action, from the same watch or other machine when it is broken and when the principle of its movement ceases to act.

*   *   *

That the soul is united to all the portions of the body conjointly

But in order to understand all these things more perfectly, we must know that the soul is really joined to the whole body, and that we cannot, properly speaking, say that it exists in any one of its parts to the exclusion of the others, because it is one and in some manner indivisible, owning to the disposition of its organs, which are so related to one another that when any one of them is removed, that renders the whole body defective; and because it is of a nature which has no relation to extension, nor dimensions, nor other properties of the matter of which the body is composed, but only to the whole conglomerate of its organs, as appears from the fact that we could not in any way conceive of the half or the third of a soul, nor of the space it occupies, and because it does not become smaller owning to the cutting off of some portion of the body, but separates itself from it entirely when the union of its assembled organs is dissolved.

That there is a small gland in the brain in which the soul exercises its functions more particularly than in the other parts

It is likewise necessary to know that although the soul is joined to the whole body, there is yet in that a certain part in which it exercises its functions more particularly than in all the others; and it is usually believed that this part is the brain, or possibly the heart; the brain, because it is with it that the organs of sense are connected, and the heart because it is apparently in it that we experience the passions. But, in examining the matter with care, it seems as though I had clearly ascertained that the part of the body in which the soul exercises its functions immediately is in nowise the heart, nor the whole of the brain, but merely the most inward of all its parts, to wit, a certain very small gland which is situated in the middle of its substance and so suspended above the duct whereby the animal spirits in its anterior cavities have communications with those in the posterior, that the slightest movements which take place in it may alter very greatly the course of these spirits; and reciprocally that the smallest changes which occur in the course of the spirits may do much to change the movements of this gland.

How we know that this gland is the main seat of the soul

The reason which persuades me that the soul cannot have any other seat in all the body than this gland wherein to exercise its functions immediately, is that I reflect that the other parts of our brain are all of them double, just as we have two eyes, two hands, two ears, and finally all the organs of our outside senses are double; and inasmuch as we have but one solitary and simple thought of one particular thing at one and the same moment, it must necessarily be the case that there must somewhere be a place where the two images which come to us by the two eyes, where the two other impressions which proceed from a single object by means of the double organs of the other senses, can unite before arriving at the soul, in order that they may not represent to it two objects instead of one. And it is easy to apprehend how these images or other impressions might unite in this gland by the intermissions of the spirits which fill the cavities of the brain: but there is no other place in the body where they can be thus united unless they are so in this gland.

That the seat of the passions is not in the heart

As to the opinion of those who think that the soul receives its passions in the heart, it is not of much consideration, for it is only founded on the fact that the passions cause us to feel some change taking place there; and it is easy to see that this change is not felt in the heart excepting through the medium of a small nerve which descends from the brain towards it, just as pain is felt as in the foot by means of the nerves of the foot, and the stars are perceived as in the heavens by means of their light and of the optic nerves; so that it is not more necessary that our soul should exercise its functions immediately in the heart, in order to feel its passions there, than it is necessary for the soul to be in the heavens in order to see the stars there.

How the soul and the body act on one another

Let us then conceive here that the soul has its principal seat in the little gland which exists in the middle of the brain, from whence it radiates forth through all the remainder of the body by means of the animal spirits, nerves, and even the blood, which, participating in the impressions of the spirits, can carry them by the arteries into all the members. And recollecting what has been said above about the machine of our body, i.e., that the little filaments of our nerves are so distributed in all its parts, that on the occasion of the diverse movements which are there excited by sensible objects, they open in diverse ways the pores of the brain, which causes the animal spirits contained in these cavities to enter in diverse ways into the muscles, by which means they can move the members in all the different ways in which they are capable of being moved; and also that all the other causes which are capable of moving the spirits in diverse ways suffice to conduct them into diverse muscles; let us here add that the small gland which is the main seat of the soul is so suspended between the cavities which contain the spirits that it can be moved by them in as many different ways as there are sensible diversities in the object, but that it may also be moved in diverse ways by the soul, whose nature is such that it receives in itself as many diverse impressions, that is to say, that it possesses as many diverse perceptions as there are diverse movements in this gland. Reciprocally, likewise, the machine of the body is so formed that from the simple fact that this gland is diversely moved by the soul, or by such other cause, whatever it is, it thrusts the spirits which surround it towards the pores of the brain, which conduct them by the nerves into the muscles, by which means it causes them to move the limbs.

Example of the mode in which the impressions of the objects unite in the gland which is in the middle of the brain

Thus, for example, if we see some animal approach us, the light reflected from its body depicts two images of it, one in each of our eyes, and these two images form two others, by means of the optic nerves, in the interior surface of the brain which faces its cavities; then from there, by means of the animal spirits with which its cavities are filled, these images so radiate towards the little gland which is surrounded by these spirits, that the movement which forms each point of one of the images tends towards the same point of the gland towards which tends the movement which forms the point of the other image, which represents the same part of this animal. By this means the two images which are in the brain form but one upon the gland, which, acting immediately upon the soul, causes it to see the form of this animal.

16

The Body, the Soul, and the Person

John Locke

BODY, SOUL, AND CONSCIOUSNESS

I grant that the soul, in a waking man, is never without thought, because it is the condition of being awake. But whether sleeping without dreaming be not an affection of the whole man, mind as well as body, may be worth a waking man's consideration; it being hard to conceive that anything should think and not be conscious of it. If the soul doth think in a sleeping man without being conscious of it, I ask whether, during such thinking, it has any pleasure or pain, or be capable of happiness or misery? I am sure the man is not; no more than the bed or earth he lies on. For to be happy or miserable without being conscious of it, seems to me utterly inconsistent and impossible. Or if it be possible that the *soul* can, whilst the body is sleeping, have its thinking, enjoyments, and concerns, its pleasures or pain, apart, which the *man* is not conscious of nor partakes in,—it is certain that Socrates asleep and Socrates awake are not the same person; but his soul when he sleeps, and Socrates the man, consisting of body and soul, when he is waking, are two persons: since waking Socrates has no knowledge of, or concernment for that happiness or misery of his soul, which it enjoys alone by itself whilst he sleeps, without perceiving anything of it; no more than he has for the happiness or misery of a man in the Indies, whom he knows not. For,

Selected passages from *An Essay Concerning Human Understanding* (Book II, chapters I and XXVII; Book III, chapters VI, and Book IV, chapter IV.

if we take wholly away all consciousness of our actions and sensations, especially of pleasure and pain, and the concernment that accompanies it, it will be hard to know wherein to place personal identity. . . . Let us suppose the soul of Castor, while he is sleeping, retired from his body; which is no impossible supposition for the men I have here to do with, who so liberally allow life, without a thinking soul, to all other animals. These men cannot then judge it impossible, or a contradiction, that the body should live without the soul; nor that the soul should subsist and think, or have perception, even perception of happiness or misery, without the body. Let us then, I say, suppose the soul of Castor separated during his sleep from his body, to think apart. Let us suppose, too, that it chooses for its scene of thinking the body of another man, e.g., Pollux, who is sleeping without a soul. For, if Castor's soul can think, whilst Castor is asleep, what Castor is never conscious of, it is no matter what *place* it chooses to think in. We have here, then, the bodies of two men with only one soul between them, which we will suppose to sleep and wake by turns; and the soul still thinking in the waking man, whereof the sleeping man is never conscious, has never the least perception. I ask, then, whether Castor and Pollux, thus with only one soul between them, which thinks and perceives in one what the other is never conscious of, nor is concerned for, are not two as distinct *persons* as Castor and Hercules, or as Socrates and Plato were? And whether one of them might not be very happy, and the other very miserable? . . .

THE IDENTITY OF THE MAN AND OF THE PERSON

Never finding, nor conceiving it possible, that two things of the same kind should exist in the same place at the same time, we rightly conclude, that, whatever exists anywhere at any time, excludes all of the same kind, and is there itself alone. When therefore we demand whether anything be the *same* or no, it refers always to something that existed such a time in such a place, which it was certain, at that instant, was the same with itself, and no other. From whence it follows, that one thing cannot have two beginnings of existence, nor two things one beginning; it being impossible for two things of the same kind to be or exist in the same instant, in the very same place; or one and the same thing in different places. That, therefore, that had one beginning, is the same thing; and that which had a different beginning in time and place from that, is not the same, but diverse. That which has made the difficulty about this relation has been the little care and attention used in having precise notions of the things to which it is attributed.

*   *   *

We must therefore consider wherein an oak differs from a mass of matter, and that seems to me to be in this, that the one is only the cohesion of particles of matter any how united, the other such a disposition of them as constitutes the parts of an oak; and such an organization of those parts as is fit to receive and distribute nourishment, so as to continue and frame the wood, bark, and leaves, &c., of an oak, in which consists the vegetable life. That being then one plant which has such an organization of parts in one coherent body, partaking of one common life, it continues to be the same plant as long as it partakes of the same life, though that life be communicated to new particles of matter vitally united to the living plant, in a like continued organization, comformable to the sort of plants. For this organization, being at any one instant in any one collection of matter, is in that particular concrete distinguished from all other, and *is* that individual life, which existing constantly from that moment both forwards and backwards, in the same continuity of insensibly succeeding parts united to the living body of the plant, it has that identity which makes the same plant, and all the parts of it, parts of the same plant, during all the time that they exist united in that continued organization, which is fit to convey that common life to all the parts so united.

The case is not so much different in *brutes* but that any one may hence see what makes an animal and continues it the same. . . .

This also shows wherein the identity of the same *man* consists; viz., in nothing but a participation of the same continued life, by constantly fleeting particles of matter, in succession vitally united to the same organized body. He that shall place the identity of man in anything else, but, like that of other animals, in one fitly organized body, taken in any one instant, and from thence continued, under on organization of life, in several successively fleeting particles of matter united to it, will find it hard to make an embryo, one of years, mad and sober, the *same* man, by any supposition, that will not make it possible for Seth, Ismael, Socrates, Pilate, St. Austin, and Caesar Borgia, to be the same man. For if the identity of *soul alone* makes the same *man;* and there be nothing in the nature of matter why the same individual spirit may not be united to different bodies, it will be possible that those men, living in distant ages, and of different tempers, may have been the same man; which way of speaking must be from a very strange use of the word man, applied to an idea out of which body and shape are excluded. And that way of speaking would agree yet worse with the notions of those philosophers who allow of transmigration, and are of opinion that the souls of men may, for their miscarriages, be detruded into the bodies of beasts, as fit habitations, with organs suited to the satisfaction of their brutal inclinations. But yet I think nobody, could he be sure that the *soul* of Heliogabalus were in one of his hogs, would yet say that hog were a *man* or *Heliogabalus.*

*   *   *

An animal is a living organized body; and consequently the same animal, as we have observed, is the same continued *life* communicated to different particles of matter, as they happen successively to be united to that organized living body. And whatever is talked of other definitions, ingenious observation puts it past doubt, that the idea in our minds, of which the sound man in our mouths is the sign, is nothing else but of an animal of such a certain form. Since I think I may be confident, that, whoever should see a creature of his own shape or make, though it had no more reason all its life than a cat or a parrot, would call him still a *man*; or whoever should hear a cat or a parrot discourse, reason, and philosophize, would call or think it nothing but a *cat* or a *parrot*; and say, the one was a dull irrational man, and the other a very intelligent rational parrot. A relation we have in an author of great note, is sufficient to countenance the supposition of a rational parrot. His words are:

> I had a mind to know, from Prince Maurice's own mouth, the account of a common, but much credited story, that I had heard so often from many others, of an old parrot he had in Brazil, during his government there, that spoke, and asked, and answered common questions, like a reasonable creature: so that those of his train there generally concluded it to be witchery or possession; and one of his chaplains, who lived long afterwards in Holland, would never from that time endure a parrot, but said they all had a devil in them. I had heard many particulars of this story, and assevered by people hard to be discredited, which made me ask Prince Maurice what there was of it. He said, with his usual plainness and dryness in talk, there was something true, but a great deal false of what had been reported.

*   *   *

For I presume it is not the idea of a thinking or rational being alone that makes the *idea of a man* in most people's sense: but of a body, so and so shaped, joined to it; and if that be the idea of a man, the same successive body not shifted all at once, must, as well as the same immaterial spirit, go to the making of the same man.

This being premised, to find wherein personal identity consists, we must consider what *person* stands for;—which, I think, is a thinking intelligent being, that has reason and reflection, and can consider itself as itself, the same thinking thing, in different times and places; which it does only by that consciousness which is inseparable from thinking, and, as it seems to me, essential to it: it being impossible for any one to perceive without *perceiving* that he does perceive. When we see, hear, smell, taste, feel, meditate, or will anything, we know that we do so. Thus it is always as to our present sensations and perceptions: and by this every one is to himself that which he calls *self*:— it not being considered, in this case, whether the same self be continued in the same or divers substances. For, since consciousness always accompanies thinking, and it is that which makes every one to be what he calls *self*, thereby distinguishes himself from all other thinking things, in this alone consists personal identity, i.e., the sameness of a rational being: and as far as this consciousness can be extended backwards to any past action or thought, so far reaches the identity of that person; it is the same self now it was then; and it is by the same self with this present one that now reflects on it that that action was done.

*   *   *

But next, as to the . . . question, Whether, if the same thinking substance (supposing immaterial substances only to think) be changed, it can be the same person? I answer, that cannot be resolved but by those who know what kind of substances they are that do think; and whether the consciousness of past actions can be transferred from one thinking substance to another. I grant were the same consciousness the same individual action it could not: but it being a present representation of a past action, why it may not be possible, that that may be represented to the mind to have been which really never was, will remain to be shown. And therefore how far the consciousness of past actions is annexed to any individual agent, so that another cannot possibly have it, will be hard for us to determine, till we know what kind of action it is that cannot be done without a reflex act of perception accompanying it, and how performed by thinking substances, who cannot think without being conscious of it. But that which we call the same consciousness, not being the same individual act, why one intellectual substance may not have represented to it, as done by itself, what *it* never did, and was perhaps done by some other agent—why, I say, such a representation may not possibly be without reality of matter of fact, as well as several representations in dreams are, which yet whilst dreaming we take for true —will be difficult to conclude from the nature of things. And that it never is so, will by us, till we have clearer views of the nature of thinking substances, be best resolved into the goodness of God; who, as far as the happiness or misery of any of his sensible creatures is concerned in it, will not, by a fatal error of theirs, transfer from one to another that consciousness which draws reward or punishment with it. How far this may be an argument against those who would place thinking in a system of fleeting animal spirits, I leave to be considered. But . . . it must be allowed, that, if the same consciousness (which, as has been shown, is quite a different thing from the same numerical figure or motion in body) can be transferred from one thinking substance to another, it will be possible that two thinking substances may make but one person. For the same consciousness being preserved, whether in the same or different substances, the personal identity is preserved.

*   *   *

But though the same immaterial substance or soul does not alone, wherever it be, and in whatsoever state, make the same *man*; yet it is plain, consciousness, as far as ever it can be extended—should it be to ages past—unites existences and actions very remote in time into the same *person*, as well as it does the existences and actions of the immediately preceding moment: so that whatever has the consciousness of present and past actions, is the same person to whom they both belong. Had I the same consciousness that I saw the ark and Noah's flood, as that I saw an overflowing of the Thames last winter, or as that I write now, I could no more doubt that I who write this now, that saw the Thames overflowed last winter, and that viewed the flood at the general deluge, was the same *self*,—place that self in what *substance* you please—than that I who write this am the same *myself* now whilst I write (whether I consist of all the same substance, material or immaterial, or no) that I was yesterday. For as to this point of being the same self, it matters not whether this present self be made up of the same or other substances—I being as much concerned, and as justly accountable for any action that was done a thousand years since, appropriated to me now by this self-consciousness, as I am for what I did the last moment.

Self is that conscious thinking thing,—whatever substance made up of (whether spiritual or material, simple or compounded, it matters not)—which is sensible or conscious of pleasure and pain, capable of happiness or misery, and so is concerned for itself, as far as that consciousness extends Thus every one finds that, whilst comprehended under than consciousness, the little finger is as much a part of himself as what is most so. Upon separation of this little finger, should this consciousness go along with the little finger, and leave the rest of the body, it is evident the little finger would be the person, the same person; and self then would have nothing to do with the rest of the body. As in this case it is the consciousness that goes along with the substance, when one part is separate from another, which makes the same person, and constitutes this inseparable self: so it is in reference to substances remote in time. That with which the consciousness of this present thinking thing *can* join itself, makes the same person, and is one self with it, and with nothing else; and so attributes to itself, and owns all the actions of that thing, as its own, as far as that consciousness reaches, and no further; as every one who reflects will perceive.

In this personal identity is founded all the right and justice of reward and punishment; happiness and misery being that for which every one is concerned for *himself,* and not mattering what becomes of any *substance,* not joined to, or affected with that consciousness. For, as it is evident in the instance I gave but now, if the consciousness went along with the little finger when it was cut off, that would be the same self which was concerned for the whole body yesterday, as making part of itself, whose actions then it cannot but admit as its own now. Though, if the same body should still live, and immediately from the separation of the little finger have its own peculiar consciousness, whereof the little finger knew nothing, it would not at all be concerned for it, as a part of itself, or could own any of its actions, or have any of them imputed to him.

This may show us wherein personal identity consists: not in the identity of substance, but, as I have said, in the identity of consciousness, wherein if Socrates and the present mayor of Queenborough agree, they are the same person: if the same Socrates waking and sleeping do not partake of the same consciouness, Socrates waking and sleeping is not the same person. And to punish Socrates waking for what sleeping Socrates thought, and waking Socrates was never conscious of, would be no more of right than to punish one twin for what his brother-twin did, whereof he knew nothing, because their outsides were so like, that they could not be distinguished; for such twins have been seen.

But yet possibly it will still be objected,—Suppose I wholly lose the memory of some parts of my life, beyond a possibility of retrieving them, so that perhaps I shall never be conscious of them again; yet am I not the same person that did those actions, had those thoughts that I once was conscious of, though I have now forgot them? To which I answer, that we must here take notice what the word *I* is applied to; which, in this case, is the *man* only. And the same man being presumed to be the same person, I is easily here supposed to stand also for the same person. But if it be possible for the same man to have distinct incommunicable consciousness at different times, it is past doubt the same man would at different times make different persons; which, we see, is the sense of mankind in the solemnest declaration of their opinions, human laws not punishing the mad man for the sober man's actions, nor the sober man for what the mad man did,— thereby making them two persons: which is somewhat explained by our way of speaking in English when we say such an one is "not himself," or is "beside himself"; in which phrases it is insinuated, as if those who now, or at least first used them, thought that self was changed; the self-same person was no longer in that man.

*   *   *

But is not a man drunk and sober the same person? Why else is he punished for the fact he commits when drunk, though he be never afterwards conscious of it? Just as much the same person as a man that walks, and does other things in his sleep, is the same person, and is answerable for any mischief he shall do in it. Human laws punish both, with a justice suitable to *their* way of knowledge:—because, in these cases, they cannot distinguish certainly what is real, what counterfeit: and so the ignorance in drunkenness or sleep is not admitted as a plea. For, though punishment be annexed to personality, and personality to consciousness, and the drunkard perhaps be not conscious of what he did, yet human judicatures justly punish him; because the fact is proved against him, but want of consciousness cannot be proved for him. But in the Great Day, wherein the secrets of all hearts shall be laid open, it may be reasonable to think, no one shall be made to answer for what he knows nothing of; but shall receive his doom, his conscience accusing or excusing him.

HOW IMPORTANT IS THE HUMAN SHAPE?

He that annexes the name man to a complex idea, made up of sense and spontaneous motion, joined to a body of such a shape, has thereby one *essence* of the species man; and he that, upon further examination, adds rationality, has another *essence* of the species he calls man; by which means the same individual will be a true man to the one which is not so to the other. I think there is scarce anyone will allow this upright figure, so well known, to be the essential difference of the species man; and yet how far men determine of the sorts of animals rather by their shape than descent, is very visible; since it has been more than once debated, whether several human fetuses should be preserved or received to baptism or no, only because of the difference of their outward configuration from the ordinary make of children, without knowing whether they were not as capable of reason as infants cast in another mold: some whereof, though of an approved shape, are never capable of as much appearance of reason all their lives as is to be found in an ape, or an elephant, and never give any signs of being acted by a rational soul. Whereby it is evident, that the outward figure, which only was found wanting, and not the faculty of reason, which nobody could know would be wanting in its due season, was made essential to the human species. The learned divine and lawyer must, on such occasions, renounce his sacred definition of *animale rationale*, and substitute some other essence of the human species. Monsieur Menage furnishes us with an example worth the taking notice of on this occasion: "When the abbot of Saint Martin," says he, "was born, he had so little of the figure of a man, that it bespake him rather a monster. It was for some time under deliberation, whether he should be baptized or no. However, he was baptized, and declared a man provisionally till time should show what he would prove. Nature had molded him so untowardly, that he was called all his life the Abbot Malotru; i.e., ill-shaped. He was of Caen." (*Menagiana*, 278, 430.) This child, we see, was very near being excluded out of the species of man, barely by his shape. He escaped very narrowly as he was; and it is certain, a figure a little more oddly turned had cast him, and he had been executed, as a thing not to be allowed to pass for a man. And yet there can be no reason given why, if the lineaments of his face had been a little altered; a rational soul could not have been lodged in him; why a visage somewhat longer, or a nose flatter, or a wider mouth, could not have consisted, as well as the rest of his ill figure, with such a soul, such parts, as made him, disfigured as he was, capable to be a dignitary in the church.

Wherein, then, would I gladly know, consist the precise and unmovable boundaries of that species?

OUR VOCABULARY IS NOT A COMPLETE LIST OF POSSIBLE KINDS

We rightly consider, and confine not our thoughts and abstract ideas to names, as if there were, or could be no other *sorts* of things than what known names had already determined, and, as it were, set out, we should think of things with greater freedom and less confusion than perhaps we do. It would possibly be thought a bold paradox, if not a very dangerous falsehood, if I should say that some *changelings*, who have lived forty years together, without any appearance of reason, are something between a man and a beast: which prejudice is founded upon nothing else but a false supposition, that these two names, man and beast, stand for distinct species so set out by real essences, that there can come no other species between them: whereas if we will abstract from those names, and the supposition of such specific essences made by nature, wherein all things of the same denominations did exactly and equally partake; if we would not fancy that there were a certain number of these essences, wherein all things, as in molds, were cast and formed; we should find that the ideas of the shape, motion, and life of a man without reason, is as much a distinct idea, and makes as much a distinct sort of things from man and beast, as the idea of the shape of an ass with reason would be different from either that of man or beast, and be a species of an animal between, or distinct from both.

Here everybody will be ready to ask, if changelings may be supposed something between man and beast, pray what are they? I answer, *change-*

lings; which is as good a word to signify something different from the signification of *man* or *beast*, as the names man and beast are to have significations different one from the other. This, well considered, would resolve this matter, and show my meaning without any more ado.

17

Of Personal Identity

Joseph Butler

Whether we are to live in a future state, as it is the most important question which can possibly be asked, so it is the most intelligible one which can be expressed in language. Yet strange perplexities have been raised about the meaning of that identity or sameness of person, which is implied in the notion of our living now and hereafter, or in any two successive moments. And the solution of these difficulties hath been stranger than the difficulties themselves. For, personal identity has been explained so by some, as to render the inquiry concerning a future life of no consequence at all to us the persons who are making it. And though few men can be misled by such subtleties; yet it may be proper a little to consider them.

Now when it is asked, wherein personal identity consists, the answer should be the same, as if it were asked, wherein consists similitude, or equality; that all attempts to define would but perplex it. Yet there is no difficulty at all in ascertaining the idea. For as, upon two triangles being compared or viewed together, there arises to the mind the idea of similitude; or upon twice two and four, the idea of equality: so likewise, upon comparing the consciousnesses of one's self, or one's own existence, in any two moments, there as immediately arises to the mind the idea of personal identity. And as the two former comparisons not only give us the ideas of similitude and equality; but also show us, that two triangles are alike, and twice two and four are equal: so the latter comparison not only gives us the idea of personal identity, but

From *The Analogy of Religion,* chapter 1.

also shows us the identity of ourselves in those two moments; the present, suppose, and that immediately past; or the present, and that a month, a year, or twenty years past. Or in other words, by reflecting upon that, which is my self now, and that, which was myself twenty years ago, I discern they are not two, but one and the same self.

But though consciousness of what is past does thus ascertain our personal identity to ourselves, yet to say, that it makes personal identity, or is necessary to our being the same persons, is to say, that a person has not existed a single moment, nor done one action, but what he can remember; indeed none but what he reflects upon. And one should really think it self-evident, that consciousness of personal identity presupposes, and therefore cannot constitute, personal identity; any more than knowledge, in any other case, can constitute truth, which it presupposes.

This wonderful mistake may possibly have arisen from hence; that to be endued with consciousness is inseparable from the idea of a person, or intelligent being. For, this might be expressed inaccurately thus, that consciousness makes personality: and from hence it might be concluded to make personal identity. But though present consciousness of what we at present do and feel is necessary to our being the persons we now are; yet present consciousness of past actions or feelings is not necessary to our being the same persons who performed those actions, or had those feelings.

The inquiry, what makes vegetables the same in the common acceptation of the word, does not appear to have any relation to this of personal identity; because, the word *same*, when applied to them and to persons, is not only applied to different subjects, but it is also used in different senses. For when a man swears to the same tree, as having stood fifty years in the same place, he means only the same as to all the purposes of property and uses of common life, and not that the tree has been all that time the same in the strict philosophical sense of the word. For he does not know, whether any one particle of the present tree be the same with any one particle of the tree which stood in the same place fifty years ago. And if they have not one common particle of matter, they cannot be the same tree in the proper philosophic sense of the word *same*: it being evidently a contradiction in terms, to say they are, when no part of their substance, and no one of their properties is the same: no part of their substance, by the supposition: no one of their properties, because it is allowed, that the same property cannot be transferred from one substance to another. And therefore, when we say the identity or sameness of a plant consists in a continuation of the same life, communicated under the same organizaton, to a number of particles of matter, whether the same or not; the word *same*, when applied to life and to organization, cannot possibly be understood to signify, what it signifies in this very sentence, when applied to matter. In a loose and popular sense then, the life and the organization and the plant are justly said to be the same, notwithstanding the perpetual change of the parts. But in a strict and philosophical manner of speech, no man, no being, no mode of being, no anything, can be the same with that, with which it hath indeed nothing the same. Now sameness is used in this latter sense, when applied to persons. The identity of these, therefore, cannot subsist with diversity of substance.

The thing here considered, and demonstratively, as I think, determined, is proposed by Mr. Locke in these words, *Whether it*, i.e., the same self or person, *be the same identical substance?* And he has suggested what is a much better answer to the question, than that which he gives it in form. For he defines Person, *a thinking intelligent being,* etc., and personal identity, *the sameness of a rational being.* The question then is, whether the same rational being is the same substance: which needs no answer, because Being and Substance, in this place, stand for the same idea. The ground of the doubt, whether the same person be the same substance, is said to be this; that the consciousness of our own existence, in youth and in old age, or in any two joint successive moments, is not the *same individual action,* i.e., not the same consciousness, but different successive consciousnesses. Now it is strange that this should have occasioned such perplexities. For it is surely conceivable, that a person may have a capacity of knowing some object or other to be the same now, which it was when he contemplated it former- ly: yet in this case, where, by the supposition, the object is perceived to be the same, the perception of it in any two moments cannot be one and the same perception. And thus though the successive consciousnesses, which we have of our own existence, are not the same, yet are they consciousnesses of one and the same thing or object; of the same person, self, or living agent. The person, of whose existence the consciousness is felt now, and was felt an hour or a year ago, is discerned to be, not two persons, but one and the same person; and therefore is one and the same.

Mr. Locke's observations upon this subject appear hasty: and he seems to profess himself dissatisfied with suppositions, which he has made relating to it. But some of those hasty observations have been carried to a strange length by others, whose notion, when traced and examined to the bottom, amounts, I think, to this: "That personality is not a permanent, but a tran- sient thing: that it lives and dies, begins and ends continually: that no one can any more remain one and the same person two moments together, than two successive moments can be one and the same moment; that our sub- stance is indeed continually changing; but whether this be so or not, is, it seems, nothing to the purpose; since it is not substance, but consciousness alone, which constitutes personality; which consciousness, being successive, cannot be the same in any two moments, nor consequently the personality constituted by it." And from hence it must follow, that it is a fallacy upon ourselves, to charge our present selves with anything we did, or to imagine our present selves interested in anything which befell us yesterday; or that our present self will be interested in what will befall us tomorrow: since our present self is not, in reality, the same with the self of yesterday, but another like self or person coming in its room, and mistaken for it; to which another self will succeed tomorrow. This, I say, must follow: for if the self or person of today, and that of tomorrow, are not the same, but only like persons; the person of today is really no more interested in what will befall the person of tomorrow, than in what will befall any other person. It may be thought, perhaps, that this is not a just representation of the opinion we are speaking of: because those who maintain it allow, that a person is the same as far back as his remembrance reaches. And indeed they do use the *words, identity* and *same person.* Nor will language permit these words to be laid aside; since if they were, there must be I know not what ridiculous periphrasis substituted in the room of them. But they cannot, consistently with themselves, mean, that the person is really the same. For it is self-evident, that the personality cannot be really the same, if, as they expressly assert, that in which it consists is not the same. And as, consistently with themselves, they cannot, so, I think it appears, they do not, mean, that the person is *really* the same, but only that he is so in a fictitious sense: in such a sense only as they assert, for this they do assert, that any number of persons whatever may be the same person. The bare unfolding this notion, and laying it thus naked and open, seems the best confutation of it. However, since great stress is said to be put upon it, I add the following things.

First, This notion is absolutely contradictory to that certain conviction, which necessarily and every moment rises within us, when we turn our thoughts upon ourselves, when we reflect upon what is past, and look forward upon what is to come. All imagination of a daily change of that living agent which each man calls himself, for another, or of any such change throughout our whole present life, is entirely borne down by our natural sense of things. Nor is it possible for a person in his wits to alter his conduct, with regard to his health or affairs, from a suspicion, that, though he should live tomorrow, he should not, however, be the same person he is today. And yet, if it be reasonable to act, with respect to a future life, upon this notion, that personality is transient; it is reasonable to act upon it, with respect to the present.

Here then is a notion equally applicable to religion and to our temporal concerns; and everyone sees and feels the inexpressible absurdity of it in the latter case. If, therefore, any can take up with it in the former, this cannot proceed from the reason of the thing, but must be owing to an inward unfairness, and secret corruption of heart.

Secondly, It is not an idea, or abstract notion, or quality, but a being only, which is capable of life and action, of happiness and misery. Now all beings confessedly continue the same, during the whole time of their exist-ence. Consider then a living being now existing, and which has existed for any time alive: this living being must have done and suffered and enjoyed, what it has done and suffered and enjoyed formerly (this living being, I say, and not another), as really as it does and suffers and enjoys, what it does and suffers and enjoys this instant. All these successive actions, enjoyments, and sufferings, are actions, enjoyments, and sufferings, of the same living be-ing. And they are so, prior to all consideration of its remembering or for-getting: since remembering or forgetting can make no alteration in the truth of past matter of fact. And suppose this being endued with limited powers of knowledge and memory, there is no more difficulty in conceiving it to have a power of knowing itself to be the same living being which it was some time ago, of remembering some of its actions, sufferings, and enjoy-ments, and forgetting others, than in conceiving it to know or remember or forget any thing else.

Thirdly, Every person is conscious, that he is now the same person or self he was as far back as his remembrance reaches: since when anyone re-flects upon a past action of his own, he is just as certain of the person who did that action, namely, himself, the person who now reflects upon it, as he is certain that the action was at all done. Nay, very often a person's assur-ance of an action having been done, of which he is absolutely assured, arises wholly from the consciousness that he himself did it. And this he, person, or self, must either be a substance, or the property of some substance. If he, if person, be a substance; then consciousness that he is the same person is consciousness that he is the same substance. If the person, or he, be the property of a substance, still consciousness that he is the same property is as certain a proof that his substance remains the same, as consciousness that he remains the same substance would be: since the same property cannot be transferred from one substance to another.

But though we are thus certain, that we are the same agents, living beings, or substances, now, which we were as far back as our remembrance reaches; yet it is asked, whether we may not possibly be deceived in it? And this ques-tion may be asked at the end of any demonstration whatever; because it is a question concerning the truth of perception by memory. And he who can doubt, whether perception by memory can in this case be depended upon, may doubt also, whether perception by deduction and reasoning, which also include memory, or indeed whether intuitive perception can. Here then we can go no further. For it is ridiculous to attempt to prove the truth of those perceptions, whose truth we can not otherwise prove, than by other perceptions of exactly the same kind with them, and which there is just the same ground to suspect; or to attempt to prove the truth of our faculties, which can not otherwise be proved, than by the use or means of those very suspected faculties themselves.

18

On Personal Identity

David Hume

I

There are some philosophers, who imagine we are every moment intimately conscious of what we call our SELF; that we feel its existence and its continuance in existence; and are certain, beyond the evidence of a demonstration, both of its perfect identity and simplicity. The strongest sensation, the most violent passion, say they, instead of distracting us from this view, only fix it the more intensely, and make us consider their influence on *self* either by their pain or pleasure. To attempt a farther proof of this were to weaken its evidence; since no proof can be deriv'd from any fact, of which we are so intimately conscious; nor is there any thing, of which we can be certain, if we doubt of this.

Unluckily all these positive assertions are contrary to that very experience, which is pleaded for them, nor have we any idea of *self*, after the manner it is here explain'd. For from what impression cou'd this idea be deriv'd? This question 'tis impossible to answer without a manifest contradiction and absurdity; and yet 'tis a question, which must necessarily be answer'd, if we wou'd have the idea of self pass for clear and intelligible. It must be some one impression, that gives rise to every real idea. But self or person is not any one impression, but that to which our several impressions and ideas are suppos'd to have a reference. If any impression gives rise to the idea of self,

---

From *A Treatise of Human Nature,* Book I, Part IV, Section VI.

that impression must continue invariably the same, thro' the whole course of our lives; since self is suppos'd to exist after that manner. But there is no impression constant and invariable. Pain and pleasure, grief and joy, passions and sensations succeed each other, and never all exist at the same time. It cannot, therefore, be from any of these impressions, or from any other, that the idea of self is deriv'd; and consequently there is no such idea.

But farther, what must become of all our particular perceptions upon this hypothesis? All these are different, and distinguishable, and separable from each other, and may be separately consider'd, and may exist separately, and have no need of any thing to support their existence. After what manner, therefore, do they belong to self; and how are they connected with it? For my part, when I enter most intimately into what I call *myself*, I always stumble on some particular perception or other, of heat or cold, light or shade, love or hatred, pain or pleasure. I never can catch *myself* at any time without a perception, and never can observe any thing but the perception. When my perceptions are remov'd for any time, as by sound sleep; so long am I insensible of *myself*, and may truly be said not to exist. And were all my perceptions remov'd by death, and cou'd I neither think, nor feel, nor see, nor love, nor hate, after the dissolution of my body, I shou'd be entirely annihilated, nor do I conceive what is farther requisite to make me a perfect nonentity. If any one upon serious and unprejudic'd reflexion, thinks he has a different notion of *himself*, I must confess I can reason no longer with him. All I can allow him is, that he may be in the right as well as I, and that we are essentially different in this particular. He may, perhaps, perceive something simple and continu'd, which he calls *himself*; tho' I am certain there is no such principle in me.

But setting aside some metaphysicians of this kind, I may venture to affirm of the rest of mankind, that they are nothing but a bundle or collection of different perceptions, which succeed each other with an inconceivable rapidity, and are in a perpetual flux and movement. Our eyes cannot turn in their sockets without varying our peceptions. Our thought is still more variable than our sight; and all our other senses and faculties contribute to this change; nor is there any single power of the soul, which remains unalterably the same, perhaps for one moment. The mind is a kind of theatre, where several preceptions successively make their appearance; pass, re-pass, glide away, and mingle in an infinite variety of postures and situations. There is properly no *simplicity* in it at one time, nor *identity* in different; whatever natural propension we may have to imagine that simplicity and identity. The comparison of the theatre must not mislead us. They are the successive perceptions only, that constitute the mind; nor have we the same distant notion of the place, where these scenes are represented, nor of the materials, of which it is compos'd.

* * *

We now proceed to explain the nature of *personal identity,* which has become so great a question in philosophy, especially of late years in England, where all the abstruser sciences are study'd with a peculiar ardor and application. And here 'tis evident, the same method of reasoning must be continu'd, which has so successfully explain'd the identity of plants, and animals, and ships, and houses, and of all the compounded and changeable productions either of art or nature. The identity, which we ascribe to the mind of man, is only a fictitious one, and of a like kind with that which we ascribe to vegetables and animal bodies. It cannot, therefore, have a different origin, but must proceed from a like operation of the imagination upon like objects.

But lest this argument shou'd not convince the reader; tho' in my opinion perfectly decisive; let him weigh the following reasoning, which is still closer and more immediate. 'Tis evident, that the identity, which we attribute to the human mind, however perfect we may imagine it to be, is not able to run the several different perceptions into one, and make them lose their characters of distinction and difference, which are essential to them. 'Tis still true, that every distinct perception, which enters into the composition of the mind, is a distinct existence, and is different, and distinguishable, and separable from every other perception, either contemporary or successive. But, as, notwithstanding this distinction and separability, we suppose the whole train of perceptions to be united by identity, a question naturally arises concerning this relation of identity; whether it be something that really binds our several perceptions together, or only associates their ideas in the imagination. That is, in other words, whether in pronouncing concerning the identity of a person, we observe some real bond among his perceptions, or only feel one among the ideas we form of them. This question we might easily decide, if we wou'd recollect what has been already prov'd at large, that the understanding never observes any real connexion among objects, and that even the union of cause and effect, when strictly examin'd, resolves itself into a customary association of ideas. For from thence it evidently follows, that identity is nothing really belonging to these different perceptions, and uniting them together; but is merely a quality, which we attribute to them, because of the union of their ideas in the imagination, when we reflect upon them. Now the only qualities, which can give ideas a union in the imagination, are these three relations above-mention'd. These are the uniting principles in the ideal world, and without them every distinct object is separable by the mind, and may be separately consider'd, and appears not to have any more connexion with any other object, than if disjoin'd by the greatest difference and remoteness. 'Tis, therefore, on some of these three relations of resemblance, contiguity and causation, that identity depends; and as the very essence of these relations consists in their producing an easy transition of ideas; it follows, that our notions of personal identity, proceed entirely from the smooth and uninterrupted progress of the thought along a train of connected ideas, according to the principles above-explain'd.

The only question, therefore, which remains, is, by what relations this uninterrupted progress of our thought is produc'd, when we consider the successive existence of a mind or thinking person. And here 'tis evident we must confine ourselves to resemblance and causation, and must drop contiguity, which has little or no influence in the present case.

To begin with *resemblance;* suppose we cou'd see clearly into the breast of another, and observe that succession of perceptions, which constitutes his mind or thinking principle, and suppose that he always preserves the memory of a considerable part of past perceptions; 'tis evident that nothing cou'd more contribute to the bestowing a relation on this succession amidst all its variations. For what is the memory but a faculty, by which we raise up the images of past perceptions? And as an image necessarily resembles its object, must not the frequent placing of these resembling perceptions in the chain of thought, convey the imagination more easily from one link to another, and make the whole seem like the continuance of one object? In this particular, then, the memory not only discovers the identity, but also contributes to its production, by producing the relation of resemblance among the perceptions. The case is the same whether we consider ourselves or others.

As to *causation;* we may observe, that the true idea of the human mind, is to consider it as a system of different perceptions or different existences, which are link'd together by the relation of cause and effect, and mutually produce, destroy, influence, and modify each other. Our impressions give rise to their correspondent ideas; and these ideas in their turn produce other impressions. One thought chases another, and draws after it a third, by which it is expell'd in its turn. In this respect, I cannot compare the soul more properly to any thing than to a republic or commonwealth, in which the several members are united by the reciprocal ties of government and subordination, and give rise to other persons, who propagate the same republic in the incessant changes of its parts. And as the same individual republic may not only change its members, but also its laws and constitutions; in like manner the same person may vary his character and disposition, as well as his impressions and ideas, without losing his identity. Whatever changes he endures, his several parts are still connected by the relation of causation. And in this view our identity with regard to the passions serves to corroborate that with regard to the imagination, by the making our distant perceptions influence each other, and by giving us a present concern for our past or future pains or pleasures.

As memory alone acquaints us with the continuance and extent of this succession of perceptions, 'tis to be consider'd, upon that account chiefly, as the source of personal identity. Had we no memory, we never shou'd have any notion of causation, nor consequently of that chain of causes and effects, which constitute our self or person. But having once acquir'd this notion of causation from the memory, we can extend the same chain of causes, and consequently the identity of our persons beyond our memory, and can comprehend times, and circumstances, and actions, which we have entirely forgot, but suppose in general to have existed. For how few of our past actions are there, of which we have any memory? Who can tell me, for instance, what were his thoughts and actions on the 1st of January 1715, the 11th of March 1719, and the 3rd of August 1733? Or will he affirm, because he has entirely forgot the incidents of these days, that the present self is not the same person with the self of that time; and by that means overturn all the most establish'd notions of personal identity? In this view, therefore, memory does not so much *produce* as *discover* personal identity, by shewing us the relation of cause and effect among our different perceptions. 'Twill be incumbent on those, who affirm that memory produces entirely our personal identity, to give a reason why we can thus extend our identity beyond our memory . . . .

II

I had entertain'd some hopes, that however deficient our theory of the intellectual world might be, it wou'd be free from those contradictions, and absurdities, which seem to attend every explication, that human reason can give of the material world. But upon a more strict review of the section concerning personal identity, I find myself involv'd in such a labyrinth, that, I must confess, I neither know how to correct my former opinions, nor how to render them consistent. If this be not a good *general* reason for scepticism, 'tis at least a sufficient one (if I were not already abundantly supplied) for me to entertain a diffidence and modesty in all my decisions. I shall propose the arguments on both sides, beginning with those that induc'd me to deny the strict and proper identity and simplicity of a self or thinking being.

When we talk of *self* or *substance,* we must have an idea annex'd to these terms, otherwise they are altogether unintelligible. Every idea is deriv'd from preceding impressions; and we have no impression of self or substance, as something simple and individual. We have, therefore, no idea of them in that sense.

Whatever is distinct, is distinguishable; and whatever is distinguishable, is separable by the thought or imagination. All perceptions are distinct. They are, therefore, distinguishable, and separable, and may be conceiv'd as separately existent, and may exist separately, without any contradiction or absurdity.

*   *   *

So far I seem to be attended with sufficient evidence. But having this loosen'd all our particular perceptions, when I proceed to explain the principle of connexion, which binds them together, and makes us attribute to them a real simplicity and identity; I am sensible, that my account is very defective, and that nothing but the seeming evidence of the precedent reasonings cou'd have induc'd me to receive it. If perceptions are distinct existences, they form a whole only by being connected together. But no connexions among distinct existences are ever discoverable by human understanding. We only *feel* a connexion or determination of the thought, to pass from one object to another. It follows, therefore, that the thought alone finds personal identity, when reflecting on the train of past perceptions, that compose a mind, the ideas of them are felt to be connected together, and naturally introduce each other. However extraordinary this conclusion may seem, it need not surprise us. Most philosophers seem inclin'd to think, that personal identity *arises* from consciousness; and consciousness is nothing but a reflected thought or perception. The present philosophy, therefore, has so far a promising aspect. But all my hopes vanish, when I come to explain the principles, that unite our successive perceptions in our thought or consciousness. I cannot discover any theory, which gives me satisfaction on this head.

In short there are two principles, which I cannot render consistent; nor is it in my power to renounce either of them, viz., *that all our distinct perceptions are distinct existences,* and *that the mind never perceives any real connexion among distinct existences.* Did our perceptions either inhere in something simple and individual, or did the mind perceive some real connexion among them, there wou'd be no difficulty in the case. For my part, I must plead the privilege of a sceptic, and confess, that this difficulty is too hard for my understanding. I pretend not, however, to pronounce it absolutely insuperable. Others, perhaps, or myself, upon more mature reflexions, may discover some hypothesis, that will reconcile those contradictions.

19

Personal Identity and Memory

Sydney Shoemaker

Persons, unlike other things, make statements about their own pasts, and can be said to know these statements to be true. This fact would be of little importance, as far as the problem of personal identity is concerned, if these statements were always grounded in the ways in which people's statements about the past histories of things other than themselves are grounded. But while our statements about our own pasts are sometimes based on diaries, photographs, fingerprints, and the like, normally they are not. Normally they are based on our own memories, and the way in which one's memory provides one with knowledge concerning one's own past is quite unlike the way in which it provides one with knowledge concerning the past history of another person or thing. It is largely for this reason, I believe, that in addition to whatever problems there are about the notion of identity in general there has always been felt to be a special problem about *personal* identity. It is, for example, the way in which one knows one's own past that has led some philosophers to hold that personal identity is the only *real* identity that we have any knowledge of, the identity we ascribe to ships and stones being only, as Thomas Reid expressed it, "something which, for convenience of

From *The Journal of Philosophy* 56 (1959): 868ff. Copyright © 1959 by The Journal of Philosophy, Inc. Reprinted by permission of the publisher and the author. Professor Shoemaker wishes it known that his views on this topic have significantly changed since this artricle was first published.

speech, we call identity."[1] What I wish to do [here] is to consider how the concept of memory and the concept of personal identity are related. In particular, I want to consider the view that memory provides a criterion of personal identity, or, as H. P. Grice expressed it some years ago, that "the self is a logical construction and is to be defined in terms of memory."[2]

1. Clearly the concepts of memory and personal identity are not logically independent. As has often been pointed out, it is a logical truth that, if a person remembers[3] a past event, then he, the very person who remembers, must have been a witness to that event. It is partly this logical truth that has led some philosophers to hold that personal identity can be wholly or partially defined in terms of memory. And this view may seem to be supported by the fact that we sometimes use, as grounds for saying that a person was present when an event occurred, the fact that he apparently remembers the event, i.e., is able to give a correct and detailed account of it and does not appear to have anything other than his own memory on the basis of which he could know of it.

But it does not seem, offhand, that these considerations force us to accept this view. For it might be held that while there is a logical relationship between the concepts of memory and personal identity, this is because the former is definable or analyzable in terms of the latter and not vice versa. The assertion that a person A remembers an event X can plausibly be analyzed as meaning (1) that A now has knowledge of X, (2) that A's knowledge is not grounded inductively or based on the testimony of other persons, and (3) that A witnessed X when it occurred. To know with certainty that A remembers X, it might be held, we would have to know all three of these conditions were satisfied, and we could know that (3) is satisfied only if we had a criterion of personal identity by which we could judge that A, the person who now has knowledge of X, is identical with one of the persons who witnessed X. Obviously our criterion of identity here could not be the fact that A remembers X, for we could know this fact only if we had already established that such an identity holds.

The view just described, I think, must be the view of any philosopher who thinks that the identity of a human body is the sole criterion of personal identity. And this view seems compatible with the fact that sometimes, when we do not have independent grounds for saying that a person witnessed an event, we accept his being able to describe the event as evidence that he was a witness to it. For it might be held that in such cases we are reasoning inductively. We have, it might be said, found out empirically (using bodily identity as our criterion of personal identity) that when someone claims to remember a past event it is generally the case that such an event did occur and that he was a witness to it. On this view it is an inductively established correlation, and not any logical relationship between memory and personal identity, that justifies us in using the memory claims of persons as evidence for identity judgments about them.

2. On the view just described the criteria of personal identity are simply the criteria of bodily identity (i.e., I suppose, spatiotemporal continuity). But it is often argued that bodily identity is not even a necessary condition of personal identity, let alone a sufficient condition, and the same arguments have been alleged to show that memory is a criterion of personal identity. We must now consider some of these arguments.

Considerable attention has been paid, in discussions of personal identity, to so-called "puzzle cases," ostensible cases of what I will call "bodily transfer." It has been argued that if certain imaginable events were to occur, we would be obliged to say, or at least would have good grounds for saying, that someone had changed bodies, i.e., had come to have a body that is numerically different from the body that had been his in the past. Locke, it may be recalled, thought it conceivable that the soul of a prince might "enter and inform" the body of a cobbler, "carrying with it the consciousness of the prince's past life," and said that if this happened the cobbler would become "the same person with the prince, accountable only for the prince's actions."[4] And it is certainly imaginable that a cobbler, living somewhere in the Bronx, might awake some morning and show great surprise at the appearance of his body, that he might claim to find his surroundings, and the persons who claim to know him, totally unfamiliar, that he might exhibit a detailed knowledge of the past life of Prince Philip, reporting the prince's actions as his own, and that he might, in his subsequent behavior, exhibit all of the mannerisms, interests, and personality and character traits that Prince Philip had displayed in the past. Let us imagine this happening immediately after the death of the man now known as Prince Philip.

As our consciousness sometimes ceases to exist, as in sound sleep, our personal identity must cease with it. Mr. Locke allows, that the same thing cannot have two beginnings of existence, so that our identity would be irrecoverably gone every time we ceased to think, if it was but for a moment.

What we say about such cases is clearly relevant to the question whether memory is a criterion of personal identity. If the above case inclines us to say that bodily transfer is possible, this is largely because the cobbler is imagined to be able to describe in detail, thereby giving evidence of being able to remember, the past life of Prince Philip. That this so much inclines us to admit the possibility of bodily transfer, whether or not we do admit it, seems to be grounds for saying that bodily identity is not our sole criterion of personal identity, and that memory, and perhaps also sameness of personality, has a place among our criteria.

Many philosophers have held that personal identity and bodily identity are logically quite distinct. This view is implied by the Cartesian conception of the mind (or soul) as a substance distinct from the body, and it also seems to be implied by the view of Locke, that it is "same consciousness" that "makes" the same person, and by the views, of those philosophers, such as Hume and (at one time) Russell, who have held that the persistence of a person through time consists simply in the occurrence of a series of mental events ("perceptions," "experiences") that are bound together by a nonphysical relationship of "co-personality" (perhaps the relation "being the memory of"). In short, it is implied by any view according to which the identity of a person is essentially the identity of a mind, and according to which a mind (whether regarded as a Cartesian "spiritual substance" or a Humeian "bundle" of mental events) is something logically distinct from a human body. To hold such a view is to admit the possibility of bodily transfer, and it is partly the prevalence of such views that accounts for the attention that philosophers have paid to "puzzle cases" such as the one I have described. But it is hardly plausible to suppose that those who have held such views have come to hold them because they have been persuaded by such cases that bodily transfer is possible. For even if it is admitted that such cases would be cases of bodily transfer, it by no means follows that personal identity and bodily identity are logically independent. It does not follow that bodily transfer could become the rule rather than the exception, and it certainly does not follow that a person could exist without having a body at all. Indeed, the view that bodily transfer is possible is quite compatible with a completely behavioristic view concerning the nature of mind and a completely materialistic conception of the nature of a person. After all, in the case I have imagined it is bodily and behavioral facts (the behavior of the cobbler and the past behavior of Prince Philip) that incline one to say that a bodily transfer has occurred.

So while such cases provide some grounds for thinking that memory is among the criteria of personal identity, we must look further if we wish to account for the plausibility of the view that the criteria of personal identity are "mental" or "psychological," one version of which being the view that memory is, to the exclusion of bodily identity, the sole criterion of personal identity. But we need not look much further; all that we have to do, in fact, is to describe such cases in the first person rather than in the third person. For it is when one considers the way in which one knows, or seems to know, one's *own* identity that it becomes plausible to regard personal identity as something logically independent of bodily identity. One does not have to observe, or (it seems) know anything about, the present state of one's body in order to make past tense statements about oneself on the basis of memory. But such statements imply the persistence of a person through time, and it is natural to regard them as expressing knowledge of one's own identity, knowledge that a "present self" (that to which the word "I" refers) is identical with a "past self" (the person who did such and such in the past). One is inclined to suppose that the real criteria of personal identity must be criteria that one uses in making statements about one's own identity. And since it appears that one can make such statements, and know them to be true, without first knowing the facts that would justify an assertion about the identity of one's body, the conclusion would seem to be that bodily identity cannot be a criterion of personal identity. The real criteria of personal identity, it seems, cannot be bodily or behavioral criteria of any sort, but must be criteria that one can know to be satisfied in one's own case without knowing anything about one's body. For similar reasons one is inclined to reject the view that the notion of memory is definable or analyzable in terms of the notion of personal identity. For when one says that one remembers a past event it is surely not the case that one has first established that one is the same as someone who witnessed the event, and then concluded, on the basis of this fact and others, that one remembers the event. That one remembers an event seems, from one's own point of view, a brute, unanalyzable fact. But if there is a logical relationship between the concepts of memory and personal identity, and if the former is not definable or analyzable in terms of the latter, what seems to follow is that the latter is somehow definable in terms of the former, and that memory provides the criterion of personal identity.

3. Whether or not memory is *a* criterion of personal identity, it is not *the* criterion. As I will argue later, it cannot be the sole criterion that we use in making identity statements about other persons. And while it is true that one does not use bodily identity as a criterion of personal identity when one says on the basis of memory that one did something in the past, this is not because one uses something else as a criterion, but is rather because one uses no criterion at all.

Suppose that I make the statement "I broke the front window yesterday." If this statement is based on a criterion of personal identity it must be the case that I know that someone broke the front window yesterday, and that I have found out, by use of my criterion, that that person was myself. And my statement must be based, at least in part, on what I know about that person as he was at the time at which he broke the window. Let us suppose that my own memory is my only source of knowledge concerning the past event in question, for that is the sort of case that we are interested in. Then my statement must be a conclusion from what I remember about the person who broke the window yesterday, and perhaps from other facts as well (facts about my "present self"), and my criterion of identity must be what justifies me in drawing this conclusion from these facts. Presumably, if I had remembered different facts about that person I would have drawn a different conclusion, namely that he was not myself. It should be noted that, if all of this were so, then, strictly speaking, it would be incorrect for me to say "*I remember* that I broke the front window yesterday." For if my statement

"I broke the front window yesterday" expresses a conclusion *from* what I remember it is not itself a memory statement, i.e., is not simply a description or report of what I actually remember. We must distinguish statements that are "based" on memory simply in the sense of being memory statements from those that are "based" on memory in the sense of being conclusions drawn from remembered facts.[5] If one thinks that one cannot make a first person past tense statement except on the basis of a criterion of identity, one must accept the consequence that no such statement can be a memory statement. In the case at hand, if my statement is grounded on a criterion of identity then what I actually remember cannot be that *I* broke the window yesterday, but must be that someone of such and such a description broke the window, the assertion that it was myself being a conclusion from what I remember about the person.

Now it is a logical truth, as I have already said, that if a person remembers a past event then he, that same person, must have been a witness to the event, i.e., must have been present when it occurred and in a position to know of its occurrence. So if I remember someone breaking the front window yesterday it follows that I was present at the time. And since, if I remember this, I am entitled to say "I remember someone breaking the front window yesterday," I am also entitled to say "I was present yesterday when the front window was broken." But this last statement is a first person past tense state-ment, so let us see whether it can be grounded on any criterion of personal identity. Clearly it cannot be. It is not, as it would have to be if based on a criterion of identity, a conclusion from what I know about someone who existed in the past. What I know about the past, in the case we are considering, is what I remember, but this statement is not a conclusion from *what* I re-member at all; it is a conclusion from the fact *that I remember something,* not from any of the facts that I remember.

But if I can know that I was present when an action was done without using a criterion of identity, why can't I know in this way that I did the action? Is it that I must employ a criterion in order to know *which* of the persons present was myself? In that case, presumably, I would not need to employ my criterion if I remembered that only one person was present, for that person would obviously have to be myself. But the trouble is that he would have to be myself *no matter what* I remembered about him. i.e., even if the remembered facts were such that I would have to conclude, in accord-ance with my criterion, that he was *not* myself. If I had a criterion of identity that I could use in such cases, it seems to me, it would be possible for me to remember someone doing a certain action, discover by the use of my cri-terion that he was not myself, and then find, by consulting my memory of the event, that he was the only person present when the action was done. And clearly this is not possible.

It is sometimes suggested that one is able to identify a remembered "past self" as one's own self by the fact that one is able to remember the private thoughts, feelings, sensations, etc., of that self. There does seem to be a sense in which my own thoughts and feelings are the only ones that I can remember. Certainly they are the only ones that I can remember *having*. But it is a mistake to conclude from this that memory is used as a first person criterion of personal identity. The sentence "I remember having a headache yesterday" does not differ in meaning from the sentence "I remember my having a headache yesterday." But if what I remember when I remember a past headache is *my having* a headache, or that *I* had a headache, my statement "I had a headache" is a memory statement, not a conclusion from what I remember, and cannot be grounded on any criterion of identity. If, however, what I remember is that someone had a headache, or that a headache occurred, it is clear that the remembered facts provide no grounds for the conclusion that *I* had a headache. Nor can we say, as some have said, that the relation "being the memory of" is the relation of "co-personality" between mental events, and that I know that a past sensation was mine because I have established that one of my present mental states is a memory of it and therefore co-personal with it. For, contrary to what Hume and others seem to have supposed, in the sort of case we are considering it makes no sense to speak of comparing one's present memory with a past sensation and finding that the one is the memory of (on Hume's theory, that it resembles) the other. One could make such a comparison only if one knew of the past sensation on some grounds other than one's memory of it, and our concern here is with cases in which one's memory is one's only source of knowledge concerning the past events in question. In such a case, comparing a past sensation with one's memory of it could only be comparing one's memory with itself— and comparing something with itself (if that means anything) is certainly not a way of discovering whether two events are related in a certain way. One can raise the question whether two events are related in a particular way (in *any* given way) only if one knows of the occurrence of both events. And if one knows of one of the events on the basis of memory, one must, in inquiring whether it is related in some way to the other event, be relying on one's memory of it, and clearly cannot be raising any question as to whether one does remember it (or whether one of one's present mental states is a memory of it). Indeed, if one's knowledge of a past sensation is memory knowledge it is misleading to say that one knows that one remembers a particular past sensation. It makes sense to speak of knowing that one remembers a particular event (knowing of an event that one remembers it) only where it would also make sense to speak of knowing of that event that one does not remember it (as is the case if one's knowledge of an event is based on something other than, or in addition to, one's memory). When I say that

I have a headache I am not mentioning some particular headache and reporting, as a fact that I know about it, that it is experienced by me; likewise, when I say that I remember a headache I am not, in most cases, saying of some particular headache that I remember it. Normally I can identify a past sensation only as one that I remember (or, as I should prefer to say, one that I remember having). And when this is so there cannot arise any question concerning the ownership of the sensation, and there is no room for the employment of criteria of ownership or criteria of personal identity.

4. If, as I have argued, one does not use criteria of identity in making statements about one's own past on the basis of memory, the criteria of personal identity must be third person criteria. And if memory were the sole criterion of personal identity it would have to be the sole criterion that we use in making identity statements about persons other than ourselves. It is easily shown, however, that if we did not have some criterion other than memory that we could use in making statements of personal identity we could not use what others remember, or claim to remember, as evidence of any sort (criteriological or otherwise) for identity statements about them.

To begin with, if the word "remember" is to have any meaning it must be possible to establish whether someone is using it correctly. If some of the utterances that persons make are to count as memory claims, and therefore as evidence of what they remember or seem to remember, it must be possible to establish what a person means by the words he utters. But establishing what a person means by a term, or whether he is using it correctly, involves observing his use of it in various circumstances and over a period of time. This, of course, involves being able to know that it was one and the same person who uttered a given word on two different occasions, and to be able to know this one must have a criterion of identity. What could this criterion be if not bodily identity? It could not be any "psychological" criterion (such as memory or sameness of personality), for the use of such criteria (if criteria they are) involves accepting what a person says as indicating what his psychological state is (e.g., that he seems to remember doing a certain thing), and one could not do this if one were trying to establish what he means by, or whether he understands, the expressions he is using. In *some* circumstances, at least, bodily identity must be a criterion of personal identity.

Moreover, memory claims can be mistaken, and there must, accordingly, be such a thing as checking on the truth of a memory claim, i.e., establishing whether a person remembers something without taking his word for it that he does. And this, if he claims to have done a certain thing in the past, would involve establishing whether he, the person who claims this, is the same as someone who did do such an action in the past. In establishing this we could not use memory as our criterion of personal identity, and it is difficult to see what we could use if not bodily identity. And if, in such cases, we could not use bodily identity (or something other than memory) as a criterion of identity, it would not be possible to establish whether someone understands the use of the term "remember," and that term could not so much as have a meaning. It is, I believe, a logical or conceptual truth, not a contingent truth, that memory beliefs, and therefore honest memory claims, are generally true.[6] If someone frequently prefaced past tense statements with the words "I remember that," and these statements generally turned out to be false, this would be grounds for saying that he did not understand the use of these words. We would not think that we had succeeded in teaching a child the use of the word "remember" if he commonly said "I remember doing such and such" when he had not done the thing in question. Again, suppose that we had discovered a new people whose language we did not know, and that someone had proposed a way of translating their language that involved regarding a certain class of statements (or utterances) as memory statements. Clearly, if all or most of those statements turned out to be false if translated as proposed, there could be no reason for accepting that way of translating them as correct, and there would be every reason for rejecting it as mistaken. But if it is a conceptual truth that memory claims are generally true, establishing that someone understands the use of the term "remember" must surely involve establishing whether his memory claims (or what appear to be his memory claims) are true or false. And to be able to do this we must have something other than memory that we can use as a criterion of personal identity.

5. The arguments of the last section may seem to give support to the view that bodily identity is, to the exclusion of memory, the sole criterion of personal identity. But this view seems to me to be mistaken. Bodily identity is certainly *a* criterion of personal identity, and if it were not, I have argued, nothing else could be so much as evidence of personal identity. But I do not think that it can be the sole criterion, and I think that there is an important sense in which memory, though certainly not the sole criterion, is one of the criteria.

Let us consider one consequence of the view that bodily identity is the sole criterion of personal identity. As I said in section 1, if this view were correct it would have to be the case that we are reasoning inductively when we use the fact that someone claims to remember something as grounds for a statement about his past. It would be a contingent fact, one that we have discovered empirically, that most memory claims are true, or that people generally remember what they claim to remember. This would, indeed, be nothing other than the fact that the memory claims that issue from the mouth of a certain body generally correspond to events in the past history of that same body. But I have argued that it is a logical fact, not a contingent fact, that memory claims are generally true. If this is so, inferences of the form "He claims to remember doing X, so he probably did X" are not simply inductive inferences, for they are warranted by a generalization that is logically rather than empirically true.[7]

Now let us return briefly to the case of the cobbler and the prince. If one is inclined to use the memory claims of the cobbler as grounds that he is (has become) the prince, the inference one is inclined to make is not of the form "He claims to remember doing X, so he probably did do X," but is of a more complex sort. Roughly, it is of the form "He claims to remember doing X, Y, and Z under such and such circumstances and at such and such times and places, and X, Y, and Z were done by someone under precisely those circumstances and at those times and places, so there is reason to believe that he is the person who did those actions." But it seems to me that if inferences of the first sort are not inductive, neither are inferences of the second sort. And I think that to say that inferences of the second sort are legitimate (as they certainly are, at least under certain circumstances), and that they are noninductive, is tantamount to saying that memory is a criterion of personal identity.

It should be noted that if such inferences were merely inductive, and if bodily identity were the sole criterion of personal identity, it would be patently absurd to make such an inference in a case in which the body of the person making a memory claim is known not to be identical with the body of the person who did the action that he claims to remember. The absurdity would be that of asserting something to be true, or probably true, on the basis of indirect evidence, when one has direct and conclusive evidence that it is false. But in the imaginary case I have described, the claim that the cobbler is (has become) the prince does not, I think, strike us as having *this* sort of absurdity. I have not attempted to say whether, if the events I have described were to occur, it would be correct to say that the cobbler had become the prince, and I do not know how this question could be settled. But this in itself seems to me significant. The fact that such cases so much as incline us to admit the possibility of bodily transfer, or leave us in doubt as to what to say, seems to me *prima facie* evidence that memory is a criterion of personal identity. It is not as if our doubts were due to ignorance of empirical facts that, if known, would settle the issue. Doubts of that sort are easily removed, for we need only add further details to the description of the case. But if, knowing all of the relevant facts, we are in doubt as to how we should answer a question of identity, this is surely an indication that the case is such that the question is not unambiguously decidable by our criterion of identity. This, in turn, suggests that there is a conflict of criteria. In the case at hand, our doubts are evidence that one criterion of personal identity, namely bodily identity, is in conflict with another, namely memory.

But now I must try to meet an objection. It might be argued that while the inference "He claims to remember doing X, so he probably did X" is not inductive, we are nevertheless reasoning inductively when we take what a person says as evidence for a statement about his past history. For what justifies us in taking the sounds that a person utters as expressing a memory claim? As was argued earlier, if a question arises as to whether a person understands the use of the word "remember," or is using it to mean what we mean by it, the question can be settled only by establishing, independently of what he says, whether the things that he claims (or apparently claims) to remember are things he actually did, endured, or witnessed in the past. If in a number of cases it turns out that the actions that he apparently claims to remember having done are actions that he actually did, this is evidence that he does understand the use of such words as "remember," and that his apparent memory claims are really memory claims and can generally be relied upon. Must it not be much the same sort of considerations, i.e., our having observed certain correlations between the sounds that people utter and what they have done in the past, that justifies our general reliance on people's memory claims, or rather our acceptance of people's utterances as memory claims? If so, it would seem that our use of people's memory claims as evidence for statements about their own pasts, including identity statements about them, is, in the end, inductively based. Though it is a logical fact that memory claims are generally true, what does this come to except the fact that if there did not exist correlations of the sort mentioned none of the utterances of persons would be memory claims? But the existence of such correlations is a contingent fact, and it is on this contingent fact, it might be argued, that inferences of the sort "He claims to remember doing X, so he probably did X" are ultimately based. As for the case of the cobbler and the prince, it might be argued that if what I said in section 4 is correct then the facts that I have imagined would be evidence, not that the cobbler had become the prince, but rather that his utterances were not memory claims at all, and that he did not understand the use of the term "remember."

To take the last point first, suppose that we were in doubt as to whether the cobbler really understood the words that he was using. Could we not satisfy ourselves that he did by observing his subsequent behavior, and by establishing (using bodily identity as our criterion of personal identity) that when he claims to have done an action that occurred *after* the alleged bodily transfer it is generally the case that he did do that action? When we are trying to establish whether a person understands the words he utters we must, I have argued, use bodily identity as a criterion of identity, but it does not follow from this that there cannot, in exceptional cases, be personal identity in the absence of bodily identity.

As for the rest of the objection, it is certainly true that unless there existed certain correlations between the sounds people utter and events in the past histories of those who utter them it would be impossible to have knowledge of the past that is based on the memory claims of other persons. These correlations are those that must exist if any of the utterances that people make are to be memory claims. But it cannot be the case, I believe, that we regard certain of the utterances of other persons as memory claims *because* we have established, inductively, that such correlations hold. To be sure, from the fact that a person utters the sounds that I would utter if making a certain memory claim it does not necessarily follow that he speaks the language that I speak and means by those sounds what I would mean by them. Under exceptional circumstances I might raise a question as to whether what sounds to me like a memory claim is really one, and such a question could be settled empirically, by observing the behavior of the person who made the claim. But except when we have definite grounds for supposing the contrary, we must, I believe, regard other persons as speaking a language, our own if the words sound familiar, without having any general empirical justification for doing so. Let us consider whether it would be possible for me to question whether there is anyone at all (other than myself) who speaks the language that I speak, and then to discover empirically, by observing correlations between the sounds people utter and their present and past behavior, that those around me do speak the language that I speak and that certain of their utterances are memory claims and can generally be relied upon. In carrying on such an investigation I would, of course, have to rely on my own memory. But one's memory can be mistaken. It is essential to the very notion of memory that there be a distinction between remembering something and merely seeming to remember something. And for there to be such a distinction there must be such a thing as checking up on one's own memory and finding that one does, or does not, remember what one seems to remember. As Wittgenstein pointed out,[8] there are and must be circumstances in which we would accept other sorts of evidence concerning the past as more authoritative than our own memories. But an important—I think essential—check on one's own memory is the testimony of other persons. And this sort of check would not be available to me if I could not even regard the utterances of other persons as testimony until I had completed my investigation and established the required set of correlations. Unless there were some persons whose utterances I would be willing to accept as memory claims without having conducted such an investigation I would in effect be admitting no distinction between finding the correlations and merely seeming to have found them.

It is, I should like to say, part of the concept of a person that persons are capable of making memory statements about their own pasts. Since it is a conceptual truth that memory statements are generally true, it is a conceptual truth that persons are capable of knowing their own pasts in a special way, a way that does not involve the use of criteria of personal identity, and it is a conceptual truth (or a logical fact) that the memory claims that a person makes can be used by others as grounds for statements about the past history of that person. This, I think, is the kernel of truth that is embodied in the view that personal identity can be defined in terms of memory.

NOTES

1. Thomas Reid, *Essays on the Intellectual Powers of Man,* ed. by A. D. Woozley (London: Macmillan, 1941), p. 206.

2. H. P. Grice, "Personal Identity," *Mind* (October 1941): 340.

3. I use "remember" in its most common sense, in which "I remember that P" entails "P," and "I remember X occurring" entails "X occurred."

4. John Locke, *An Essay Concerning Human Understanding,* I, ed. by Fraser (Oxford: The Clarendon Press, 1894), p. 457.

5. Roughly speaking, a statement is a memory statement if (supposing it to be an honest assertion) it cannot be false unless the speaker has misremembered. A conclusion from what is remembered, on the other hand, can be false without there being a mistaken memory. E.g., I mistakenly identify the man I saw as John when in fact it was his identical twin.

6. The word "generally" is vague, but I doubt if this can be made much more precise. This statement should perhaps be qualified so as to apply only to memory beliefs concerning the *recent* past.

7. We can, of course, have inductive grounds for believing that one person's memory claims are exceptionally reliable and that another's are exceptionally unreliable.

8. Ludwig Wittgenstein, *Philosophical Investigations* (Oxford: Basil Blackwell, 1953), I, paras. 56 and 265.

20

The Soul

Anthony Quinton

1. THE SOUL AND SPIRITUAL SUBSTANCE

Philosophers in recent times have had very little to say about the soul. The word, perhaps, has uncomfortably ecclesiastical associations, and the idea seems to be bound up with a number of discredited or at any rate generally disregarded theories. In the history of philosophy the soul has been used for two distinct purposes: first, as an explanation of the vitality that distinguishes human beings, and also animals and plants, from the broad mass of material objects, and, secondly, as the seat of consciousness. The first of these, which sees the soul as an ethereal but nonetheless physical entity, a volatile collection of fire-atoms or a stream of animal spirits, on some views dissipated with the dissolution of the body, on others absorbed at death into the cosmic soul, and on others again as capable of independent existence, need not detain us. The second, however, the soul of Plato and Descartes, deserves a closer examination than it now usually receives. For it tends to be identified with the view that in each person there is to be found a spiritual substance which is the subject of his mental states and the bearer of his personal identity. But on its widest interpretation, as the nonphysical aspect of a person, its acceptance need not involve either the existence of a spiritual substance over and above the mental states that make up a person's inner, conscious life or the proposition that this

---

From *The Journal of Philosophy* 59 (1962): 393–409. Copyright 1962 by Journal of Philosophy, Inc. Reprinted by permission of the author and publisher.

spiritual substance is what ultimately determines a person's identity through time. When philosophers dismiss the soul it is usually because they reject one or both of these supposed consequences of belief in it.

It is worth insisting, furthermore, that the existence of a spiritual substance is logically distinct from its being the criterion of personal identity. So the strong, and indeed fatal, arguments against the substance theory of personal identity do not at the same time refute the proposition, self-evident to Berkeley and many others, that there can be no conscious state that is not the state of some subject.

As a criterion of identity spiritual substance has three main weaknesses. First, it is regressive in just the same way as is an account of the identity of a material object through time in terms of its physical components. No general account of the identity of a kind of individual thing can be given which finds that identity in the presence of another individual thing within it. For the question immediately arises, how is the identity through time of the supposed identifier to be established? It, like the thing it is supposed to identify, can present itself at any one time only as it is at that time. However alike its temporally separate phases may be, they still require to be identified as parts of the same, continuing thing. In practice we do identify some wholes through their parts, normally where the parts are more stable and persistent unities than the wholes they compose and where, in consequence, the parts are more readily identifiable, as, for example, when we pick out one person's bundle of laundry from the bundles of others after the labels have been lost. But this can be only a practical expedient, not a theoretical solution.

A second difficulty is to find any observable mental entity that can effectively serve as a criterion in this case. The only plausible candidate is that dim, inchoate background, largely composed of organic sensations, which envelops the mental states occupying the focus of attention. This organic background is a relatively unchanging environment for the more dramatic episodes of conscious life to stand out against. But both the fixity and the peripheral status of this background are only relative. It does change, and it, or its parts, can come or be brought into the focus of attention. Even if its comparatively undisturbed persistence of character suggests it as a criterion, its vagueness makes it even less accessible to public application than the general run of mental criteria and leaves it with little power to distinguish between one person and another. The organic background is, of course, as regressive a criterion as any other part of a person's mental life. Its only virtues are that it is observable and that it does seem to be a universal constituent of the momentary cross sections of a person's experience. In this last respect it is preferable to most distinguishable features of a person's mental life. For, generally speaking, the parts of a complex and enduring thing are not necessary to the identity of that thing. Just as a cathedral is still the same cathedral if a piece has been knocked off it, whatever the piece may be, so a person is the same person if he ceases to have a particular belief or emotion, whatever that belief or emotion may be.

Finally, if it is held that the spiritual substance is nevertheless a permanent and unaltering constituent of a person's conscious life, it follows that it must be unobservable and so useless for purposes of identification. Suppose that from its very first stirrings my consciousness has contained a continuous whistling sound of wholly unvarying character. I should clearly never notice it, for I can only notice what varies independently of my consciousness— the whistles that start and stop at times other than those at which I wake up and fall asleep. It is this fact that ensured from the outset that Hume's search for a self over and above his particular perceptions was bound to fail. The unobservability of spiritual substance, and its consequent inapplicability as a criterion, can also be held to follow directly from taking its status as substance seriously, as an uncharacterized substratum for qualities and relations to inhere in with no recognizable features of its own.

But to admit that spiritual substance cannot possibly be the criterion of a person's identity and that it cannot be identified with any straightforwardly observable part of a person's mental life does not mean that it does not exist. It has seemed self-evident to many philosophers that every mental state must have an owner. To believe this is not to commit oneself to the existence of something utterly unobservable. If it is true, although both subjects and mental states are unobservable in isolation, each can be observed in conjunction with the other. There is a comparison here with the relations and observability of the positions and qualities of material things. One cannot be aware of a color except as present at some place and at some time or of a position except as the place and time where some discernible characteristics are manifested. So it might be argued that one can be aware of a conscious subject only as in some mental state or other and of a mental state only as belonging to some subject or other. Critics of the Berkeleyan principle sometimes suggest that it is no more than a faulty inference from the subject-object structure of the sentences in which mental facts are reported. It would certainly be a mistake to infer that a conscious subject is something entirely distinct from all its states from the linguistic fact that we commonly assign mental states to owners. We say of a chair that it has a back, a seat, arms, and legs, but this should not and does not lead us to conclude that the chair is something over and above the parts that it has, appropriately arranged. A more usual argument for the principle starts from the premise that mental states are acts that cannot be conceived without an agent in the same way as there cannot be a blow without a striker or a journey without a traveler. The premise of this argument has been much criticized by recent philosophers. A feeling of depression or a belief in the trustworthiness of a friend is not a precisely datable occurrence but a more or less persisting dispositional state. Nor is it an instance of agency in the sense of being the intentional execution of a decision. But these mistaken implications do not affect the validity of the argument under consideration. A disposition requires a possessor as much as an act requires an agent, and the blow I get from a swinging door still presupposes the existence of the door even though it did not mean to hit me.

The strength of the argument lies in the fact that we can assert the existence of some mental state, a feeling of anger let us say, only when we are in a position to assert either that we ourselves are angry or that somebody else is. We have given no sense to the words "discovering the existence of a mental state that is not my own or anyone else's." The nearest we come to speaking in this way is when we say, for example, "there is a sadness about the place," when walking about some ruins in a contemplative frame of mind. What we mean in this case is that the place inclines us to feel sad and might well give rise to the same inclination in others. And this capacity for producing sad feelings in myself and others, as a disposition, has its own substance, so to speak: the broken columns and collapsed walls with which it is bound up.

The subject in this rather thin and formal sense is not borne down in the ruin of that concept of spiritual substance in which it is proposed as the determinant of personal identity. It could be argued that it is a loose way of referring to the related series of other mental states or to the body or both with which any given mental state is universally associated by our manner of reporting such states. If it is something distinct from both of these, as it has traditionally been believed to be, it is not properly to be called the soul. It could not exist without any states at all, and even if it could it would be an emotionally useless form of survival of bodily death. Its existence, in fact, is irrelevant to the problem of the soul, which is that of whether a person is essentially mental in character and so distinct from his body, a connected sequence of mental states and not a physical object. It is irrelevant whether the sequence of mental states composing a person on this theory presupposes a distinguishable subject or not.

Spiritual substance cannot be the criterion of personal identity, and it may or may not be presupposed by the existence of conscious mental states. Whether as part or presupposition of our mental life, it should not be identified with the soul when this is conceived as the nonbodily aspect of a person. The well-founded conviction that there is no spiritual substance in the first sense and widespread doubts as to its existence in the second should not be allowed to obscure the issue of whether there is a unitary nonbodily aspect to a person and, if there is, whether it is the fundamental and more important aspect. Locke saw that spiritual substance could not account for personal identity and, although he believed in its existence, speculated whether it might not have been possible for God to endow a material substance with the power of thinking. Yet he clearly believed in the soul as the connected sequence of a person's conscious states, regarded this sequence as what a person essentially was, and held it to be capable of existing independently of the body. I want to consider whether an empirical concept of the soul, which, like Locke's, interprets it as a sequence of mental states logically distinct from the body and is neutral with regard to the problem of the subject, can be constructed.

2. THE EMPIRICAL CONCEPT OF THE SOUL

It will be admitted that among all the facts that involve a person there is a class that can be described as mental in some sense or other. Is it enough to define the soul as the temporally extended totality of mental states and events that belong to a person? It will not be enough to provide a concept of the soul as something logically distinct from the body if the idea of the series of a person's mental states involves some reference to the particular human body that he possesses. In the first place, therefore, a nonbodily criterion of personal identity must be produced. For if the soul were the series of mental states associated with a given body, in the sense of being publicly reported by it and being manifested by its behavior, two temporally separate mental states could belong to the history of the same soul only if they were in fact associated with one and the same human body. This notion of the soul could have no application to mental states that were not associated with bodies. The soul must, then, be a series of mental states that is identified through time in virtue of the properties and relations of these mental states themselves. Both the elements of the complex and the relations that make an identifiable persisting thing out of them must be mental. To establish the possibility of such a mental criterion of identity will be the hardest part of the undertaking.

Locke's criterion of memory has been much criticized, and it is certainly untenable in some of the interpretations it has been given. It will not do to say that two mental states belong to the same soul if and only if whoever has the later one can recollect the earlier one if the possibility of recollection involved is factual and not formal. For people forget things, and the paradox of the gallant officer is generated in which he is revealed as identical with both his childish and his senile selves while these are not identical with each other. However, a more plausible criterion can be offered in terms of continuity of character and memory. Two soul-phases belong to the same soul, on this view, if they are connected by a continuous character and memory path. A soul-phase is a set of contemporaneous mental states belonging to the same momentary consciousness. Two soul-phases are directly continuous if they are temporally juxtaposed, if the character revealed by the constituents of each is closely similar, and if the later contains recollections of some elements of the earlier. Two soul-phases are indirectly continuous and connected by a continuous character and memory path if there is a series of soul-phases all of whose members are directly continuous with their immediate predecessors and successors in the series and if the original soul-phases are the two end points of the series. There is a clear analogy between this criterion and the one by means of which material objects, including human bodies, are identified. Two object-phases belong to the same object if they are connected by a continuous quality and position path. Direct continuity in this case obtains between two temporally juxtaposed object-phases which are closely similar in qualities and are in the same position or in closely neighboring positions. Indirect continuity is once again the ancestral of direct continuity. There is no limit to the amount of difference in position allowed by the criterion to two indirectly continuous object-phases, but in normal discourse a limit is set to the amount of qualitative difference allowed by the requirement that the two phases be of objects of the same kind. Character in the mental case corresponds to quality in the physical and memory to spatial position. The soul, then, can be defined empirically as a series of mental states connected by continuity of character and memory.

Now there is an objection to the idea that memory can be any sort of fundamental criterion of identity which rests on the view that a memory criterion presupposes a bodily criterion. I shall defer the consideration of this issue, however, until two less serious difficulties have been met. These are that the construction suggested requires an exploded Cartesian dualism about the nature of mental states and, arising out of this, that a person's character is not clearly distinguishable from his body. The former, Rylean, objection can be met without difficulty. Even if the most extreme and reductive version of logical behaviorism were correct, even if a person's mental states were simply and solely behavioral dispositions, actual or potential, his character a complex property of these dispositions, and his memory a particular disposition to make first-person statements in the past tense without inference or reliance on testimony, the empirical concept of the soul would still apply to something distinct from any particular human body, though some body or other, not necessarily human perhaps, would be required to manifest the appropriate dispositions in its behavior and speech. In other words, an extreme, reductive, logical behaviorism is perfectly compatible with reincarnation, with the manifestation by one body of the character and memories that were previously manifested by another body that no longer exists. The second objection is that the soul as here defined and the body cannot be clearly distinguished, since the possession of some sorts of character trait requires the possession of an appropriate sort of body. I do not see that there is much empirical foundation for this to start with. It would be odd for a six-year-old girl to display the character of Winston Churchill, odd indeed to the point of outrageousness, but it is not utterly inconceivable. At first, no doubt, the girl's display of dogged endurance, a world-historical comprehensiveness of outlook, and so forth, would strike one as distasteful and pretentious in so young a child. But if she kept it up the impression would wear off. We do not, after all, find the story of Christ disputing with the doctors in the temple literally unintelligible. And a very large number of character traits seem to presume nothing about the age, sex, build, and general physical condition of their host. However, even if this were an empirically well-founded point, it would not be a relevant one. It would merely show that the possession of a given trait of character required the possession of an appropriate *kind* of body, a large one or a male one or an old one, and not the possession of a *particular* body. As things are, characters can survive large and even emotionally disastrous alterations to the physical type of a person's body, and these changes may have the effect of making it hard for others to recognize the continuity of character that there is. But courage, for example, can perfectly well persist even though the bodily conditions for its more obvious manifestations do not.

3. MENTAL AND BODILY CRITERIA OF IDENTITY

In recent philosophy there have been two apparently independent aspects to the view that the mind is logically dependent on the body. On the one hand, there are the doctrines that hold mental states either to be or necessarily to involve bodily states, whether bodily movement and dispositions thereto or neural events and configurations. With these doctrines, I have argued, the empirical concept of the soul can be reconciled. On the other hand, many philosophers have insisted that the basic and indispensable criterion of personal identity is bodily. Even mind-body dualists like Ayer, who have accepted the existence of a categorically clear-cut class of mental events, have sometimes taken this position. In his first treatment of the problem he appears at first to give a mental account of the concept of a person as being a series of experiences. But the relation that connects them in his theory involves an indispensable reference to a particular persisting human body. A person is made up of those total mental states which contain organic sensations belonging to one particular human body, presumably to be identified itself in terms of continuity of qualities and spatial position. Ayer draws the conclusion that properly follows from this and from any other account of personal identity that involves reference to a particular human body, namely that the notion of a person's disembodied existence is a self-contradictory one and, further, that even the association of a personality with different bodies at different times is inconceivable. These conclusions may well seem to constitute a *reductio ad absurdum* of the bodily criterion of personal identity rather than a disproof of the possibility of a person's survival of death. To explore them a little further will help to present the claims of mental as against bodily criteria in a clearer light.

At the outset it must be admitted that the theory of a bodily criterion has a number of virtues. It has, first, the theoretical attraction of simplicity, in that it requires only one mode of treatment for the identification through time of all enduring things, treating human beings as just one variety of concrete objects. Second, it has a practical appeal, in that its application yields uncontentiously correct answers in the very great majority of the actual cases of personal identification with which we are called upon to deal. Finally, it has the merit of realism, for it is, in fact, the procedure of identification that we do most commonly apply. Even where, for lack of relevant evidence, it is inapplicable, as in the case of the Tichborne claimant, it would not be supposed that the result of applying other criteria such as memory would conflict with what the bodily evidence would have shown if it had been forthcoming. Is there anything better to set against these powerful recommendations in favor of a bodily criterion than that it entails that things many people have wanted very deeply to say about the survival of death are inconsistent? A supporter of the bodily criterion might argue that it was so much the worse for them, that their inconsistent assertions arose from attempting to assert and deny at the same time that a person no longer existed.

It does seem strange, all the same, to say that all statements about disembodied or reincarnated persons are self-contradictory. Is it really at all plausible to say this about such familiar things as the simpler type of classical ghost story? It may be argued that there are plenty of stories which are really self-contradictory and yet which can be, in a way, understood and enjoyed, stories about time machines, for example. To try to settle the case we had better consider some concrete instances. Suppose I am walking on the beach with my friend *A*. He walks off a fair distance, treads on a large mine that someone has forgotten to remove, and is physically demolished in front of my eyes. Others, attracted by the noise, draw near and help to collect the scattered remains of *A* for burial. That night, alone in my room, I hear *A's* voice and see a luminous but intangible object, of very much the shape and size of *A,* standing in the corner. The remarks that come from it are in *A's* characteristic style and refer to matters that only *A* could have known about. Suspecting a hallucination, I photograph it and call in witnesses who hear and see what I do. The apparition returns afterwards and tells of where it has been and what it has seen. It would be very peculiar to insist, in these circumstances, that A no longer existed, even though his body no longer exists except as stains on the rocks and in a small box in the mortuary. It is not essential for the argument that the luminous object look like A or that it speak in A's voice. If it were a featureless cylinder and spoke like a talking weighing machine we should simply take longer becoming convinced that it really was A. But if continuity of character and memory were manifested with normal amplitude, we surely should be convinced.

Consider a slightly different case. I know two men B and C. B is a dark, tall, thin, puritanical Scotsman of sardonic temperament with whom I have gone on bird-watching expeditions. C is a fair, short, plump, apolaustic Pole of indestructible enterprise and optimism with whom I have made a number of more urban outings. One day I come into a room where both appear to be, and the dark, tall, thin man suggests that he and I pursue tonight some acquaintances I made with C, though he says it was with him, a couple of nights ago. The short, fair, plump, cheerful-looking man reminds me in a strong Polish accent of a promise I had made to B, though he says it was to him, and which I had forgotten about, to go in search of owls on this very night. At first I suspect a conspiracy, but the thing continues far beyond any sort of joke, for good perhaps, and is accompanied by suitable amazement on their part at each other's appearance, their own reflections in the mirror, and so forth.

Now what would it be reasonable to say in these circumstances: that B and C have changed bodies (the consequences of a mental criterion), that they have switched character and memories (the consequence of a bodily criterion), or neither? It seems to me quite clear that we should not say that B and C had switched characters and memories. And if this is correct, it follows that bodily identity is not a logically complete criterion of personal identity; at best it could be a necessary condition of personal identity. Of the other alternatives, that of refusing to identify either of the psychophysical hybrids before us with B or C may seem the most scrupulous and proper. But the refusal might take a number of different forms. It might be a categorical denial that either of the hybrids is B or C. It might, more sophisticatedly be an assertion that the concept of personal identity had broken down and that there was no correct answer, affirmative or negative, to the question: which of these two is B and which C? It might, uninterestingly, be a state of amazed and inarticulate confusion.

What support is there for the conclusion required by the empirical concept of the soul, that B and C have substituted bodies? First of all, the rather weak evidence of imaginative literature. In F. Anstey's story *Vice Versa* the corpulent and repressive Mr. Bultitude and his athletic and impulsive schoolboy son are the victims of a similar rearrangement. The author shows not the smallest trace of hesitation in calling the thing with the father's character and memories the father and the thing with the father's body the son. (Cf. also Conan Doyle's *Keinplatz Experiment.*) A solider support is to be found by reflecting on the probable attitude after the switch of those who are most concerned with our original pair, *B* and *C,* as persons, those who have the greatest interest in answering the question of their personal identity: their parents, their wives, their children, their closest friends. Would they say that *B* and *C* had ceased to exist, that they had exchanged characters and memories or that they had exchanged bodies? It is surely plain that if the character and memories of *B* and *C* really survived intact in their new bodily surroundings those closely concerned with them would say that the two had exchanged bodies, that the original persons were where the characters and memories were. For why, after all, do we bother to identify people so carefully? What is unique about individual people that is important enough for us to call them by individual proper names? In our general relations with other human beings their bodies are for the most part intrinsically unimportant. We use them as convenient recognition devices enabling us to locate without difficulty the persisting character and memory complexes in which we are interested, which we love or like. It would be upsetting if a complex with which we were emotionally involved came to have a monstrous or repulsive physical appearance, it would be socially embarrassing if it kept shifting from body to body while most such complexes stayed put, and it would be confusing and tiresome if such shifting around were generally widespread, for it would be a laborious business finding out where one's friends and family were. But that our concern and affection would follow the character and memory complex and not its original bodily associate is surely clear. In the case of general shifting about we should be in the position of people trying to find their intimates in the dark. If the shifts were both frequent and spatially radical we should no doubt give up the attempt to identify individual people, the whole character of relations between people would change, and human life would be like an unending sequence of shortish ocean trips. But, as long as the transfers did not involve large movements in space, the character and memory complexes we are concerned with could be kept track of through their audible identification of themselves. And there is no reason to doubt that the victim of such a bodily transfer would regard himself as the person whom he seems to remember himself as being. I conclude, then, that although, as things stand, our concept of a person is not called upon to withstand these strains and, therefore, that in the face of a psychophysical transfer we might at first not know what to say, we should not identify the people in question as those who now have the bodies they used to have and that it would be the natural thing to extend our concept of a person, given the purposes for which it has been constructed, so as to identify anyone present to us now with whoever it was who used to have the same character and memories as he has. In other words the soul, defined as a series of mental states connected by continuity of character and memory, is the essential constituent of personality. The soul, therefore, is not only logically distinct from any particular human body with which it is associated; it is also what a person fundamentally is.

It may be objected to the extension of the concept of personal identity that I have argued for that it rests on an incorrect and even sentimental view of the nature of personal relations. There are, it may be said, personal relationships which are of an exclusively bodily character and which would not survive a change of body but which would perfectly well survive a change of soul. Relations of a rather unmitigatedly sexual type might be instanced and also those where the first party to the relationship has violent racial feelings. It can easily be shown that these objections are without substance. In the first place, even the most tired of entrepreneurs is going to take some note of the character and memories of the companion of his later nights at work. He will want her to be docile and quiet, perhaps, and to remember that he takes two parts of water to one of scotch, and no ice. If she ceases to be plump and red-headed and vigorous he may lose interest in and abandon her, but he would have done so anyway in response to the analogous effects of the aging process. If he has any idea of her as a person at all, it will be as a unique cluster of character traits and recollections. As a body, she is simply an instrument of a particular type, no more and no less interesting to him than a physically identical twin. In the case of a purely sexual relationship no particular human body is required, only one of a more or less precisely demarcated kind. Where concern with the soul is wholly absent there is no interest in individual identity at all, only in identity of type. It may be said that this argument cuts both ways: that parents and children are concerned only that they should have round them children and parents with the same sort of character and memories as the children and parents they were with yesterday. But this is doubly incorrect. First, the memories of individual persons cannot be exactly similar, since even the closest of identical twins must see things from slightly different angles; they cannot be in the same place at the same time. More seriously, if more contingently, individual memories, even of identical twins, are seldom, if ever, closely similar. To put the point crudely, the people I want to be with are the people who remember me and the experiences we have shared, not those who remember someone more or less like me with whom they have shared more or less similar experiences. The relevant complexity of the memories of an individual person is of an altogether different order of magnitude from that of the bodily properties of an entrepreneur's lady friend. The lady friend's bodily type is simply enough defined for it to have a large number of instances. It is barely conceivable that two individual memories should be similar enough to be emotionally adequate substitutes for each other. There is the case of the absolutely identical twins who go everywhere together, side by side, and always have done so. Our tendency here would be to treat the pair as a physically dual single person. There would be no point in distinguishing one from the other. As soon as their ways parted sufficiently for the question of which was which to arise, the condition of different memories required for individuation would be satisfied.

It may be felt that the absolutely identical twins present a certain difficulty for the empirical concept of the soul. For suppose their characters and memories to be totally indistinguishable and their thoughts and feelings to have been precisely the same since the first dawning of consciousness in them. Won't the later phases of one of the twins be as continuous in respect of character and memory with the earlier phases of the other as they are with his own earlier phases? Should we even say that there are two persons there at all? The positional difference of the two bodies provides an answer to the second question. Although they are always excited and gloomy together, the thrills and pangs are manifested in distinct bodies and are conceivable as existing separately. We might ignore the duality of their mental states, but we should be able in principle to assert it. As to the matter of continuity, the environment of the two will be inevitably asymmetrical, each will at various times be nearer something than the other, each will block some things from the other's field of vision or touch; so there will always be some, perhaps trivial, difference in the memories of the two. But even if trivial, the difference will be enough to allow the application in this special case of a criterion that normally relies on radical and serious differences. However alike the character and memories of twin no. 1 on Tuesday and twin no. 2 on Wednesday, they will inevitably be less continuous than those of twin no. 2 on the two days.

4. MEMORY AND BODILY IDENTITY

I must now return to the serious objection to the use of memory as a criterion of personal identity whose consideration was postponed earlier. This has been advanced in an original and interesting article on personal identity recently published by Sydney S. Shoemaker[1]. . . . He argues that memory could not be the sole or fundamental criterion for the identity of other people, because in order to establish what the memories of other people are I have to be able to identify them in a bodily way. I cannot accept sentences offered by other people beginning with the words "I remember" quite uncritically. I must be assured, first, that these utterances really are memory claims, that the speaker understands the meaning of the sentences he is using, and, secondly, that his memory claims are reliable. Mr. Shoemaker contends that it is essential, if either of these requirements is to be satisfied, for me to be able to identify the maker of the apparent memory claims in an independent, bodily way. In order to be sure that his remarks really are intended as memory claims, I have to see that he generally uses the form of words in question in connection with antecedent states of affairs of which he has been a witness. And to do this I must be assured that he is at one time uttering a memory sentence and at another, earlier, time is a witness of the event he purports to describe; in other words I must be able to identify him at different times without taking his apparent memories into account. The point is enforced by the second requirement about the conditions under which I can take his memory claims as trustworthy. To do this I must be able to establish at least that he was physically present at and, thus, in a position to observe the state of affairs he now claims to recollect.

There is a good deal of force in these arguments, but I do not think they are sufficient to prove that the soul is not logically distinct from the particular body with which it happens to be associated at any given time. In the first place, the doubt about the significance of someone's current memory claims is not one that I must positively have laid to rest before taking these claims as evidence of his identity. The doubt could seriously arise only in very special and singular circumstances. If someone now says to me, "I remember the battle of Hastings," I will presume him to be slightly misusing the words, since I have good reasons for thinking that no one now alive was present at that remote event. I shall probably take him to be saying that he remembers that there was such a thing as the battle of Hastings, having learnt of it at school, or that it took place in 1066, that Harold was killed at it, that it was the crucial military factor in the Norman conquest, and so forth. But if, on being questioned, he says that these reinterpretations distort the meaning he intended, that he remembers the battle of Hastings in the same way as he remembers having breakfast this morning, if perhaps a little more dimly, then I cannot reasonably suppose that he doesn't understand the meaning of his remark though I may well think that it is false, whether deliberately or not. Mr. Shoemaker admits that in a case of apparent bodily transfer the significance of a person's memory claims could be established by considering the way in which he used memory sentences after the transfer had taken place. So at best this part of his argument could prove that in order to identify people we need to be able to make at least local applications of the criterion of bodily identity. They must be continuous in a bodily way for a period of time sufficient to enable us to establish that they are using memory sentences correctly. But in view of the somewhat strained and artificial character of the doubt in question, I am inclined to reject even this modest conclusion. At best it is a practical requirement: people must be sufficiently stable in a bodily way for me to be able to accumulate a large enough mass of apparent memory claims that are prima facie there to infer from the coherence of these apparent claims that they really are memory claims and not senseless noises.

The reliability of the memory claims of others is a more substantial issue. For, unlike significance, it is a feature of apparent memory claims that we commonly do have serious reason to doubt. It must be admitted, further, that if I have independent reasons for believing that Jones's body was physically present at an event that Jones now claims to remember, I have a piece of strong evidence in support of the correctness of his claim. It is not, of course, conclusive. Even if he were looking in the direction at the time, he might have been in a condition of day-dreaming inattentiveness. The question is, however: is it in any sense a necessary condition for the correctness of my acceptance of a man's present memory claim that I should be able, in principle, to discover that the very same body from which the claim under examination now emerges was actually present at the event now purportedly remembered? I cannot see that it is. To revert to the example of a radical psychophysical exchange between B and C. Suppose that from B's body memory claims emerge about a lot of what I have hitherto confidently taken to be C's experiences. I may have good reason to believe that C's body was present at the events apparently recalled. If the claims are very numerous and detailed, if they involve the recollection of things I didn't know B had seen although I can now establish that they were really present for C to observe, and if the emission of apparent C memories from B's body and vice versa keeps up for a fair period, it would be unreasonable not to conclude that the memory claims emerging from B's body were in fact correct, that they were the memory claims of C not of B, and that therefore the person with B's body was in fact not now B and C. Here again a measure of local bodily continuity seems required. I shall not say that C inhabits B's body at all unless he seems to do so in a fairly substantial way and over a fair period of time. But as long as the possibility of psychophysical exchange is established by some salient cases in which the requirement of local bodily continuity is satisfied I can reasonably conjecture that such exchange has taken place in other cases where the translocation of memory claims is pretty short-lived. At any rate it is only the necessity of local bodily continuity that is established, not the necessary association of a person with one particular body for the whole duration of either. Bodily continuity with a witness is a test of the reliability of someone's memory claims, and it is an important one, but it is not a logically indispensable one.

5. THE PROBLEM OF DISEMBODIMENT

Nothing that I have said so far has any direct bearing on the question whether the soul can exist in an entirely disembodied state. All I have tried to show is that there is no necessary connection between the soul as a series of mental states linked by character and memory and any particular continuing human body. The question now arises: must the soul be associated with some human body? The apparent intelligibility of my crude ghost story might seem to suggest that not even a body is required, let alone a human one. And the same point appears to be made by the intelligibility of stories in which trees, toadstools, pieces of furniture, and so on are endowed with personal characteristics. But a good deal of caution is needed here. In the first place, even where these personal characteristics are not associated with any sort of body in the physiological sense, they are associated with a body in the epistemological sense; in other words, it is an essential part of the story that the soul in question have physical manifestations. Only in our own case does it seem that strictly disembodied existence is conceivable, in the sense that we can conceive circumstances in which there would be some good reason to claim that a soul existed in a disembodied state. Now how tenuous and nonhuman could these physical manifestations be? To take a fairly mild example, discussed by Professor Malcolm, could we regard a tree as another person? He maintains with great firmness that we could not, on the rather flimsy ground that tress haven't got mouths and, therefore, could not be said to speak or communicate with us or make memory claims. But if a knothole in a tree trunk physically emitted sounds in the form of speech, why should we not call it a mouth? We may presume that ventriloquism, hidden record-players and microphones, dwarfs concealed in the foliage, and so forth have all been ruled out. If the remarks of the tree were coherent and appropriate to its situation and exhibited the type of continuity that the remarks of persons normally do exhibit, why shouldn't we regard the tree as a person? The point is that we might, by a serious conceptual effort, allow this in the case of one tree or even several trees or even a great many nonhuman physical things. But the sense of our attribution of personality to them would be logically parasitic on our attributions of personality to ordinary human bodies. It is from their utterances and behavior that we derive our concept of personality, and this concept would be applicable to nonhuman things only by more or less far-fetched analogy. That trees should be personal presupposes, then, the personality of human beings. The same considerations hold in the extreme case of absolutely minimal embodiment, as when a recurrent and localized voice of a recognizable tone is heard to make publicly audible remarks. The voice might give evidence of qualitative and positional continuity sufficient to treat it as an identifiable body, even if of an excessively diaphanous kind.

The possibility of this procedure, however, is contingent on there being persons in the standard, humanly embodied sense to provide a clear basis for the acquisition of the concept that is being more or less speculatively applied to the voice.

Whatever the logic of the matter, it might be argued, the causal facts of the situation make the whole inquiry into the possibility of a soul's humanly or totally disembodied existence an entirely fantastic one. That people have the memories and characters that they do, that they have memories and characters at all, has as its causally necessary condition the relatively undisturbed persistence of a particular bit of physiological apparatus. One can admit this without concluding that the inquiry is altogether without practical point. For the bit of physiological apparatus in question is not the human body as a whole, but the brain. Certainly lavish changes in the noncerebral parts of the human body often affect the character and perhaps even to some extent the memories of the person whose body it is. But there is no strict relationship here. Now it is sometimes said that the last bit of the body to wear out is the brain, that the brain takes the first and lion's share of the body's nourishment, and that the brains of people who have starved to death are often found in perfectly good structural order. It is already possible to graft bits of one human body on to another, corneas, fingers, and, even, I believe, legs. Might it not be possible to remove the brain from an otherwise worn-out human body and replace it either in a manufactured human body or in a cerebrally untenanted one? In this case we should have a causally conceivable analogue of reincarnation. If this were to become possible and if the resultant creatures appeared in a coherent way to exhibit the character and memories previously associated with the brain that had been fitted into them, we could say that the original person was still in existence even though only a relatively minute part of its original mass and volume was present in the new physical whole. Yet if strict bodily identity is a necessary condition of personal identity, such a description of the outcome would be ruled out as self-contradictory. I conclude, therefore, not only that a logically adequate concept of the soul is constructible but that the construction has some possible utility even in the light of our knowledge of the causal conditions of human life.

NOTE

1. "Personal Identity and Memory," *Journal of Philosophy* 56, no. 22 (October 22, 1959): 868. (See selection 19 of this volume—Ed.)

21

Persons

P. F. Strawson

1

Each of us distinguishes between himself and states of himself on the one hand, and what is not himself or a state of himself on the other. What are the conditions of our making this distinction, and how are they fulfilled? In what way do we make it, and why do we make it in the way we do? It might appear a misnomer to refer to this group of questions as the issue of solipsism. But I have no qualms about appropriating the name: for that which customarily bears it is not, as we shall see, a genuine issue at all.

In the discussion of this topic, the notion of identification of particulars is once more crucial: primarily in the sense of distinguishing one particular from others in thought, or observation; but also in the original speaker-hearer senses.

Let me recall some of the steps which led to this issue of solipsism. I had argued that, in our actual conceptual scheme, material bodies, in a broad sense of the expression, were basic particulars: that is to say, that material bodies could be identified and reidentified without reference to particulars of other types or categories than their own, whereas the identification and reidentification of particulars of other categories rested ultimately on the identification of material bodies. I then inquired whether we could make intelli-

From *Individuals: An Essay in Descriptive Metaphysics* (London: Methuen, 1964), pp. 81–113. Reprinted by permission of the publishers.

gible to ourselves the idea of a conceptual scheme which provided for a system of objective particulars, but in which material bodies were not basic. This led to the construction of a model No-Space world, in which all the sensory items were auditory, but in which it did seem possible to find a place for the idea of a reidentifiable particular, by exploiting certain auditory analogues of the idea of spatial distance. The requirement, however, was for a scheme in which a distinction was made between oneself and what is not oneself. Though it seemed possible that the conditions for this distinction could be fulfilled in such a world, it was not obvious *how* they were to be fulfilled. The introduction of the idea of agency—of a distinction between changes which were deliberately initiated, and those that just occurred—seemed inadequate to compel this crucial distinction; and a final attempt to produce in the auditory world the conditions of a nonsolipsistic consciousness seemed just an attempt to copy indiscriminately the features of our ordinary human experience in the very restricted sensory terms available. So, to try to get clearer about what in general those conditions are, it seemed advisable to inquire how in fact they are fulfilled in ordinary human experience.

But though I want to ask this question in relation to our ordinary human experience, yet there is a certain advantage in keeping before our minds the picture of the purely auditory world, the picture of an experience very much more restricted than that which we in fact have. For it may help to sharpen for us the question we are concerned with; it may help to give us a continuing sense of the strangeness of what we in fact do; and this sense of strangeness we want to keep alive in order to see that we really meet it and remove it, and do not just lose or smother it. It helps in this way. We drew a picture of a purely auditory experience, and elaborated it to a point at which it seemed that the being whose experience it was—if any such being were possible at all—might recognize sound-universals and reidentify sound-particulars and in general form for himself an idea of his audiutory world; but still, it seemed, he would have no place for the idea of himself as the subject of this experience, would make no distinction between a special item in his world, namely himself, and the other items in it. Would it not seem utterly strange to suggest that he might distinguish himself as one item among others in his auditory world, that is, as a sound or sequence of sounds? For how could such a thing—a sound—be also what *had* all those experiences? Yet to have the idea of himself, must he not have the idea of the subject of the experiences, of that which has them? So it might begin to look impossible that he should have the idea of himself—or at any rate the right idea. For to have the idea at all, it seems that it must be an idea of some particular thing of which he has experience, and which is set over against or contrasted with other things of which he has experience, but which are not himself. But if it is just an item *within* his experience of which he has this idea, how can it be the idea of that which *has* all of his experiences? And now we seem to have come upon a form of problem which is completely general, which applies as much to the ordinary as to the auditory world. It must, it seems, be soluble for the ordinary world.

Let us now think of some of the ways in which we ordinarily talk of ourselves, of some of the things which we do ordinarily ascribe to ourselves. They are of many kinds. We ascribe to ourselves *actions* and *intentions* (I am doing, did, shall do this); *sensations* (I am warm, in pain); *thoughts* and *feelings* (I think, wonder, want this, am angry, disappointed, contented); *perceptions* and *memories* (I see this, hear the other, remember that). We ascribe to ourselves, in two senses, position: *location* (I am on the sofa) and *attitude* (I am lying down). And of course we ascribe to ourselves not only temporary conditions, states, situations like these, but also relatively enduring characteristics, including physical characteristics like height, coloring, shape, and weight. That is to say, among the things we ascribe to ourselves are things of a kind that we also ascribe to material bodies to which we should not dream of ascribing others of the things that we ascribe to ourselves. Now there seems nothing needing explanation in the fact that the particular height, coloring, physical position which we ascribe to ourselves should be ascribed to *something or other* for that which one calls one's body is, at least, a body, a material thing. It can be picked out from others, identified by ordinary physical criteria and described in ordinary physical terms. But so long as we keep that for the present indispensable sense of strangeness, it can and must seem to need explanation that one's states of consciousness, one's thoughts and sensations, are ascribed *to the very same thing* to which these physical characteristics, this physical situation, is ascribed. That is, we have not only the question: *Why are one's states of consciousness ascribed to anything at all?* We have also the question: *Why are they ascribed to the very same thing as certain corporeal characteristics, a certain physical situation, etc.?* It is not to be supposed that the answers to these questions will be independent of one another.

2

It might indeed be thought that an answer to both of them could be found in the unique role which each person's body plays in his experience, particularly his perceptual experience. All philosophers who have concerned themselves with these questions have referred to the uniqueness of this role. Descartes was well aware of its uniqueness: "I am *not* lodged in my body like a pilot in a vessel." In what does this uniqueness consist? It consists, of course, in a great many things. Consider merely some of the ways in which the character of a person's *perceptual experience* is dependent on facts about his own body. Let us take his visual experience. The dependence is more complicated and many-sided than may at first be obvious. First, there is that group of empirical facts of which the most familiar is that if the eyelids of that body are closed, the person sees nothing. To this group belong all the facts known to ophthalmic surgeons. Second, there is the fact that what falls within his field of vision at any moment depends in part on the *orientation* of his eyes, i.e., on the direction his head is turned in, and on the *orientation* of his eyeballs in their sockets. And, third, there is the fact that *where he sees from*— or what his possible field of vision at any moment is—depends on where his body, and in particular his head, is located. I divide these facts into three groups because I want to emphasize that the fact that visual experience is, in all three ways, dependent on facts about some body or bodies, does not entail that the body should be the same body in each case. It is a contingent fact that it is the same body. For it is possible to imagine the following case. There is a subject of visual experience, S, and there are three different relevant bodies: A, B, and C. (1) Whether the eyelids of B and C are open or not is causally irrelevant to whether S sees; but S sees only if the eyelides of A are open. And if an operation is performed on the eyes of A, the result affects S's sight, but not if an operation is performed on the eyes of B and C. (2) Where A and B may be, however, is quite irrelevant to where S sees from, i.e., to what his possible field of vision is. This is determined only by where C is. So long as C is in the drawing-room and the curtains are drawn, S can only see what is in the drawing-room. (If one has any difficulty with this idea of "where one sees from," one may think of the way one tells, from looking at a photograph, where the camera was when it was taken. Just so S's perspective on the world is given by the position of C.) But (3) the direction in which the heads and eyeballs of A and C are turned is quite irrelevant to what S sees. Given the station of C, then which of all the views which are possible from this position is the view seen by S, depends on the direction in which the head and eyeballs of B are turned, wherever B may find himself. I have described now a situation in which the visual experience of S is dependent in three different ways on the state or position of each of the bodies, A, B, and C. The dependence in each case will have certain repercussions on the way in which each of those bodies itself can be an object of visual experience to S. Thus S may never see A or B at all: but if S does see A or B, he can never see A with A's eyelids closed and he can never see B's face, though he may sometimes catch a glimpse of B's profile "out of the corner of his eye" (as *we* say), and will perhaps become quite familiar with the view of the back of B's head. Whenever S is "looking in" a mirror, i.e., has a direct frontal view of a mirror, he will see the head of C; but he may get *any* view of the head, i.e., he will not necessarily see the face.

Now, of course, our actual situation is not like this. Of course, in fact, for any subject of visual experience, S, there is just one body on the state and position of which the character of his visual experience is dependent in all three of these ways; and this triple dependence has its own familiar repercussions on the way in which that body itself becomes an object of visual experience for S. We have noted the contingency and the complexity of this independence. If we turn to hearing and smell, the other "distance" senses, the dependence is less complicated, in that orientation is comparatively unimportant. But there is still the double dependence of the character of the experience of both the location and the state of certain organs of one and the same body. Again these could be imagined coming apart. We could, e.g., give an independent definition of the point "from which" a sound is heard as follows: a sound α produced by a given source of sound β is *"heard from"* point P by subject S, if, given that no other changes take place except the movement of β, then α is heard more loudly by S when β is at P than when it is at any other point, and is heard by S with steadily diminishing loudness as β is moved in any direction away from P. Again, then, we might imagine "the point from which" sound is heard by a given hearer being dependent on the location of one body, while whether the hearer heard anything at all depended on the condition of the ears, the eardrums, etc. of another body. Equally obvious is the special position of one body in relation to all those experiences of a given subject which are assigned to the sense of touch. Countless material bodies may be observed by a given subject to be in, or to come into, contact with others; but there is only one body of which it is true that when that body is a party to such a situation of "establishing contact," then the subject normally has those experiences to which he alludes when he speaks of *feeling* some material body or other. The subject *feels* the dagger or the feather only when the dagger enters, or the feather lightly brushes, *this* body.

Such points illustrate some of the ways in which each person's body occupies a special position in relation to that person's perceptual experience. We may summarize such facts by saying that for each person there is one body which occupies a certain *causal* position in relation to that person's perceptual experience, a causal position which in various ways is unique in relation to each of the various kinds of perceptual experience he has; and— as a further consequence—that this body is also unique for him as an *object* of the various kinds of perpetual experience which he has. We also noted that this complex uniqueness of the single body appeared to be a contingent matter, or rather a cluster of contingent matters; for it seems that we can imagine many peculiar combinations of dependence and independence of aspects of our perceptual experience on facts about different bodies.

We reminded ourselves of the special position which a person's body occupies in his experience in the hope that it might help to provide an answer to two questions: viz., (1) Why are one's states of consciousness ascribed to anything at all? and (2) Why are they ascribed to the very same thing as certain corporeal characteristics, a certain physical situation etc.? But now I must say straight away that the facts I have been recalling do not seem to me to provide, by themselves, any answer to our questions at all. Of course, these facts explain something. They provide a good reason why a subject of experience should have a very special regard for just one body, why we should think of it as unique and perhaps more important than any other. They explain—if I may be permitted to put it so—why I feel peculiarly attached to what in fact I call my own body; they even might be said to explain why, granted that I am going to speak of one body as *mine*, I should speak of *this* body as mine. But they do not explain why I should have the concept of *myself* at all, why I should ascribe my thoughts and experiences to *anything*. Moreover, even if we were satisfied with some other explanation of why one's states of consciousness, thoughts, and feelings and perceptions, were ascribed to *something*, and satisfied that the facts in question sufficed to explain why the "possession" of a particular body should be ascribed to the *same* thing (i.e., to explain why a particular body should be spoken of as standing in some special relation—called "being possessed by"—to that thing), yet the facts in question still do not explain why we should, as we do, ascribe certain corporeal characteristics not simply to the body standing in this special relation to the thing to which we ascribe thoughts and feelings, etc., but to the thing itself to which we ascribe those thoughts and feelings. For we say "I am bald" as well as "I am cold," "I am lying on the hearthrug" as well as "I see a spider on the ceilng." Briefly, the facts in question explain why a subject of experience should pick out one body from others, give it, perhaps, an honored name and ascribe to it whatever characteristics it has; but they do not explain why the experience should be ascribed to any subject at all; and they do not explain why, if the experiences are to be ascribed to something, they *and* the corporeal characteristics which might be truly ascribed to the favored body should be ascribed to the same thing. So the facts in question do not explain the use that we make of the word "I," or how any word has the use that word has. They do not explain the concept we have of a person.

3

A possible reaction at this point is to say that the concept we have is wrong or confused, or, if we make it a rule not to say that the concepts we have are confused, that the usage we have, whereby we ascribe, or seem to ascribe, such different kinds of predicate to one and the same thing, is confusing, that it conceals the true nature of the concepts involved, or something of this sort. This reaction can be found in two very important types of view about these matters. The first type of view is Cartesian, the view of Descartes and of others who think like him. Over the attribution of the second type of view I am more hesitant; but there is some evidence that it was held, at one period, by Wittgenstein and possibly also by Schlick. On both of these views, one of the questions we are considering—viz., "Why do we ascribe our states of consciousness to the very same thing as certain corporeal characteristics etc.?"—is a question which does not arise; for, on both views, it is only a linguistic illusion that both kinds of predicate are properly ascribed to one and the same thing, that there is a common owner, or subject, of both types of predicate. On the second of these views, the other question we are considering—viz., "Why do we ascribe our states of consciousness to anything at all?"—is also a question which does not arise; for on this view it is only a linguistic illusion that one ascribes one's states of consciousness to all, that there is any proper subject of these apparent ascriptions, that states of consciousness being to, or are states of, anything.

That Descartes held the first of these views is well enough known.[1] When we speak of a person, we are really referring to one or both of two distinct substances, two substances of different types, each of which has its own appropriate types of states and properties; and none of the properties or states of either can be a property or state of the other. States of consciousness belong to one of these substances and not to the other. I shall say no more about Cartesian view for the moment—what I have to say about it will emerge later on—except to note again that while it escapes one of our questions, it does not escape, but indeed invites, the other: "Why are one's states of consciousness *ascribed* at all, to *any* subject?"

The second of these views I shall call the "no-ownership" or "no-subject" doctrine of the self. Whether or not anyone has explicitly held this view, it is worth reconstructing, or constructing, in outline.[2] For the errors into which it falls are instructive. The "no-ownershp" theorist may be presumed to start his explanation with facts of the sort which illustrate the unique causal position of a certain material body in a person's experience. The theorist maintains that the uniqueness of this body is sufficient to give rise to the idea that one's experiences can be ascribed to some particular, individual thing, can be said to be possessed by, or owned by, that thing. This idea, he thinks, though infelicitously and misleadingly expressed in terms of ownership, would have some validity, would make some sort of sense, so long as we thought of this individual thing, the possessor of the experiences, as the body itself. So long as we thought in this way, then to ascribe a particular state of consciousness to this body, this individual thing, would at least be to say something that might have been false; for the experience in question might have been causally dependent on the state of some other body; in the present admissible, though infelicitous, sense of the word, it might have "belonged" to some other individual thing. But now, the theorist suggests, one becomes confused: one slides from the admissible sense in which one's experiences may be said to belong to, or be possessed by, some particular thing, to a wholly inadmissible and empty sense of these expressions, in which the particular thing is not thought of as a body, but as something else, say an Ego, whose sole function is to provide an owner for experiences. Suppose we call the first type of possession, which is really a certain kind of causal dependence, "having$_1$," and the second type of possession "having$_2$"; and call the individual of the first type "B" and the supposed individual of the second type "E." Then the difference is that while it is genuinely a contingent matter that *all my experiences are had$_1$ by B*, it appears as a necessary truth that *all my experiences are had$_2$ by E*. But the belief in E and the belief in "having$_2$" is an illusion. Only those things whose ownership is logically transferable can be owned at all. So experiences are not owned by anything except in the dubious sense of being causally dependent on the state of a partiuclar body; this is at least a genuine relationship to a thing, in that they might have stood in it to another thing. Since the whole function of E was to own experiences, in a logically nontransferable sense of "own," and since experiences are not owned by anything in this sense, for there is no such sense of "own," E must be eliminated from the picture altogether. It only came in because of a confusion.

I think it must be clear that this account of the matter, though it contains some of the facts, is not coherent. It is not coherent, in that one who holds it is forced to make use of that sense of possession of which he denies the existence, in presenting his case for the denial. When he tries to state the contingent fact, which he thinks gives rise to the illusion of the "ego," he has to state it in some such form as "All *my* experiences are had$_1$ by (i.e., uniquely dependent on the state of) Body B." For any attempt to eliminate the "*my*," or any expression with a similar possessive force, would yield something that was not a contingent fact at all. The proposition that *all* experiences are causally dependent on the state of a single body B, for example, is just false. The theorist means to speak of all the experiences *had by a certain person* being contingently so dependent. And the theorist cannot consistently argue that "all the experiences of person P" *means the same thing* as "all experiences contingently dependent on a certain body B"; for then his proposition would not be contingent, as his theory requires, but analytic. He must mean to be speaking of some class of experiences of the members of which it is in fact contingently true that they are all dependent on body B. The defining characteristic of this class is in fact that they are "*my* experiences" or "the experiences *of* some person," where the idea of possession expressed by "my" and "of" is the one he calls into question.

This internal incoherence is a serious matter when it is a question of denying what *prima facie* is the case: that is, that one does genuinely ascribe one's states of consciousness to something, viz., oneself, and that this kind of ascription is precisely such as the theorist finds unsatisfactory, i.e., in such that it does not seem to make sense to suggest, for example, that the identical pain which was in fact one's own might have been another's. We do not have to seek far in order to understand the place of this logically nontransferable kind of ownership in our general scheme of thought. For if we think, once more, of the requirements of identifying reference in speech to *particular* states of consciousness, or private experiences, we see that such particulars cannot be thus identifyingly referred to except as the states of experiences *of* some identified *person*. States, or experiences, one might say, *owe* their identity as particulars to the identity of the person whose states or experiences they are. From this it follows immediately that if they can be identified as particular states or experiences at all, they must be possessed or ascribable in just that way which the no-ownership theorist ridicules; i.e., in such a way that it is logically impossible that a particular state or experience in fact possessed by someone should have been possessed by anyone else. The requirements of identity rule out logical transferability of ownership. So the theorist could maintain his position only by denying that we could ever refer to particular states or experiences at all; and *this* position is ridiculous.

We may notice, even now, a possible connection between the no-ownership doctrine and the Cartesian position. The latter is, straightforwardly enough, a dualism of two subjects, or two types of subject. The former could, a little paradoxically, be called a dualism too: a dualism of one subject—the body—and one nonsubject. We might surmise that the second dualism, paradoxically so called, arises out of the first dualism, nonparadoxically so called; in other words, that if we try to think of that to which one's states of consciousness are ascribed as something utterly different from that to which certain corporeal characteristics are ascribed, then indeed it becomes difficult to see why states of consciousness should be ascribed to, thought of as belonging to, anything at all. When we think of this possibility, we may also think of another: viz., that both the Cartesian and the no-ownershsip theorists are profoundly wrong in holding, as each must, that there are two uses of "I," in one of which it denotes something which it does not denote in the other.

4

The no-ownership theorist fails to take account of all the facts. He takes account of some of them. He implies, correctly, that the unique position or role of a single body in one's experience is not a sufficient explanation of the fact that one's experiences, or states of consciousness, are ascribed to something which *has* them with that peculiar nontransferable kind of possession which is here in question. It may be a necessary part of the explanation, but is not, by itself, a sufficient explanation. The theorist, as we have seen, goes on to suggest that it is perhaps a sufficient explanation of something else: viz., of our confusedly and mistakenly *thinking* that states of consciousness are to be ascribed to something in this special way. But this, as we have seen, is incoherent: for it involves the denial that someone's states of consciousness are anyone's. We avoid the incoherence of this denial, whilst agreeing that the special role of a single body in someone's experience does not suffice to explain why that experience should be ascribed to anyone. The fact of this special role does not, by itself, give a sufficient reason why what *we* think of as a subject of experience should have any use for the conception of himself as such a subject.

When I say that the no-ownership theorist's account fails through not reckoning with all the facts, I have in mind a very simple, but in this question a very central, thought: viz., that it is a necessary condition of one's ascribing states of consciousness, experiences, to oneself, in the way one does, that one should also ascribe them, or be prepared to ascribe them, to others who are not oneself.[3] This means not less than it says. It means, for example, that the ascribing phrases are used in just the same sense when the subject is another as when the subject is oneself. Of course the thought that this is so gives no trouble to the nonphilosopher: the thought, for example, that "in pain" means the same whether one says "I am in pain" or "He is in pain." The dictionaries do not give two sets of meanings for every expression which describes a state of consciousness: a first-person meaning and a second- and third-person meaning. But to the philosopher this thought has given trouble. How could the sense be the same when the method of verification was so different in the two cases—or, rather, when there *was* a method of verification in the one case (the case of others) and not, properly speaking, in the other case (the case of oneself)? Or, again—a more sophisticated scruple—how can it be right to talk of *ascribing* in the case of oneself? For surely there can be a question of ascribing only if there is or could be a question of identifying that to which the ascription is made; and though there may be a question of identifying the one who is in pain when that one is another, how can there be such a question when that one is oneself? But this query answers itself as soon as we remember that we *speak* primarily to others, for the information of others. In one sense, indeed, there is no question of my having to *tell who it is* who is in pain, when I am. In another sense, however, I may have to *tell who it is*, i.e., to let others know who it is.

What I have just said explains, perhaps, how one may properly be said to ascribe states of consciousness to oneself, given that one can ascribe them to others. But how is it that one can ascribe them to others? Now one thing here is certain: that *if* the things one ascribes states of consciousness to, in ascribing them to others, are thought of as a set of Cartesian egos to which only private experiences can, in correct logical grammar, be ascribed, *then* this question is unanswerable and this problem insoluble. If, in identifying the things to which states of consciousness are to be ascribed, private experiences are to be all one has to go on, then, just for the very same reason as that for which there is, from one's own point of view, no question of telling that a private experience is one's own, there is also no question of telling that a private experience is another's. All private experiences, all states of consciousness, will be mine, i.e., no one's. To put it briefly. One can ascribe states of consciousness to oneself only if one can ascribe them to others. One can ascribe them to others only if one can identify other subjects of experience. And one cannot identify others if one can identify them *only* as subjects of experience, possessors of states of consciousness.

It might be objected that this way with Cartesianism is too short. After all, there is no difficulty in distinguishing bodies from one another, no difficulty in identifying bodies. Does not this give us an indirect way of identifying subjects of experience, while preserving the Cartesian mode? Can we not identify such a subject as, for example, "the subject that stands to that body in the same special relation as I stand in to this one," or, in other words, "the subject of those experiences which stand in the same unique causal relation to body N as *my* experiences stand in to body M"? But this suggestion is useless. It requires me to have noted that *my* experiences stand in a special relation to body M, when it is just the right to speak of *my* experiences at all that is in question. That is to say, it requires me to have noted that *my* experiences stand in a special relation to body M; but it requires me to have noted this as a condition of being able to identify other subjects of experiences, i.e., as a condition of my having the idea of myself as a subject of experience, i.e., as a condition of thinking of any experience as *mine*. So long as we persist in talking, in the mode of this explanation, of experiences on the one hand, and bodies on the other, the most I may be allowed to have noted is that experiences, *all* experiences, stand in a special relation to body M, that body M is unique in just this way, that this is what makes body M unique among bodies. (This "most" is perhaps too much—because of the presence of the word "experiences.") The proffered explanation runs: "Another subject of experience is distinguished and identified as the subject of those experiences which stand in the same unique causal relationship to body N as *my* experiences stand in to body M." And the objection is: "But what is the word 'my' doing in this explanation?" It is not as though the explanation could get on without this word. There is a further objection, to which we will recur. It runs: "What right have we, in this explanation, to speak of *the* subject, implying uniqueness? Why should there not be any number of subjects of experience—perhaps qualitatively indistinguishable—each subject and each set of experiences standing in the same unique relation to body N (*or* to body M)? Uniqueness of the body does not guarantee uniqueness of the Cartesian soul."

What we have to acknowledge, in order to begin to free ourselves from these difficulties, is the primitiveness of the concept of a person. What I mean by the concept of a person is the concept of a type of entity such that *both* predicates ascribing states of consciousness *and* predicates ascribing corporeal characteristics, a physical situation etc., are equally applicable to a single individual of that single type. What I mean by saying that this concept is primitive can be put in a number of ways. One way is to return to those two questions I asked earlier: viz., (1) why are states of consciousnes ascribed to anything at all? and (2) why are they ascribed to the very same thing as certain corporeal characteristics, a certain physical situation etc.? I remarked at the beginning that it was not to be supposed that the answers to these questions were independent of each other. Now I shall say that they are connected in this way: that a necessary condition of states of consciousness being ascribed at all is that they should be ascribed to the *very same things* as certain corporeal characteristics, a certain physical situation etc. That is to say, states of consciousness could not be ascribed at all, *unless* they were ascribed to persons, in the sense I have claimed for this word. We are tempted to think of a person as a sort of compound of two kinds of subjects: a subject of experiences (a pure consciousness, an ego) on the one hand, and a subject of corporeal attributes on the other. Many questions arise when we think in this way. But, in particular, when we ask ourselves how we come to frame, to get a use for, the concept of this compound of two subjects, the picture—if we are honest and careful—is apt to change from the picture of two subjects to the picture of one subject and one nonsubject. For it becomes impossible to see how we could come by the idea of different, distinguishable, identifiable subjects of experiences—different consciousnesses—*if this idea is thought of as logically primitive*, as a logical ingredient in the compound-idea of a person, the latter being composed of two subjects. For there could never be any question of assigning an experience, as such, to any subject other than oneself; and therefore never any question of assigning it to oneself either, never any question of ascribing it to a subject at all. So the concept of the pure individual consciousness—the pure ego—is a concept that cannot exist; or, at least, cannot exist as a primary concept in terms of which the concept of a person can be explained or analyzed. It can exist only, if at all, as a secondary, nonprimitive concept, which itself is to be explained, analyzed, in terms of the concept of a person. It was the entity corresponding to this illusory primary concept of the pure consciousness, the ego-substance, for which Hume was seeking, or ironically pretending to seek, when he looked into himself, and complained that he could never discover himself without a perception and could never discover anything but the perception. More seriously—and this time there was no irony, but a confusion, a Nemesis of confusion for Hume—it was this entity of which Hume vainly sought for the principle of unity, confessing himself perplexed and defeated; sought vainly because there is no principle of unity where there is no principle of differentiation. It was this, too, to which Kant, more perspicacious here than Hume, accorded a purely formal ("analytic") unity: the unity of the "I think" that accompanies all my perceptions and therefore might just as well accompany none. Finally it is this, perhaps, of which Wittgenstein spoke, when he said of the subject, first that there is no such thing, and then that it is not a part of the world, but its limit.

So, then, the word "I" never refers to this, the pure subject. But this does not mean, as the no-ownership theorist must think, that "I" in some cases does not refer at all. It refers; because I am a person among others; and the predicates which would, *per impossible* belong to the pure subject if it could be referred to, belong properly to the person to which "I" does refer.

The concept of a person is logically prior to that of an individual consciousness. The concept of a person is not to be analyzed as that of an animated body or of an embodied anima. This is not to say that the concept of a pure individual consciousness might not have a logically secondary existence, if one thinks, or finds, it desirable. We speak of a dead person—a body—and in the same secondary way we might at least think of a disembodied person. A person is not an embodied ego, but an ego might be a disembodied person, retaining the logical benefit of individuality from having been a person.

5

It is important to realize the full extent of the acknowledgment one is making in acknowledging the logical primitiveness of the concept of a person. Let me rehearse briefly the stages of the argument. There would be no question of ascribing one's own states of consciousness, or experiences, to anything, unless one also ascribed, or were ready and able to ascribe, states of consciousness, or experiences, to other individual entities of the same logical type as that thing to which one ascribes one's own states of consciousness. The condition of reckoning oneself as a subject of such predicates is that one should also reckon others as subjects of such predicates. The condition, in turn, of this being possible, is that one should be able to distinguish from one another, to pick out or identify, different subjects of such predicates, i.e., different individuals of the type concerned. The condition, in turn, of this being possible is that the individuals concerned, including oneself, should be of a certain unique type: of a type, namely, such that to each individual of that type there must be ascribed, or ascribable, *both* states of consciousness *and* corporeal characteristics. But this characterization of the type is still very opaque and does not at all clearly bring out what is involved. To bring this out, I must make a rough division, into two, of the kinds of predicates properly applied to individuals of this type. The first kind of predicate consists of those which are also properly applied to material bodies to which we would not dream of applying predicates ascribing states of consciousness. I will call this first kind M-predicates: and they include things like "weighs 10 stones," "is in the drawing-room" and so on. The second kind consists of all the other predicates we apply to persons. These I shall call P-predicates. P-predicates, of course, will be very various. They will include things like "is smiling," "is going for a walk," as well as things like "is in pain," "is thinking hard," "believes in God," and so on.

So far I have said that the concept of a person is to be understood as the concept of a type of entity such that *both* predicates ascribing states of consciousness *and* predicates ascribing corporeal characteristics, a physical situation etc., are equally applicable to an individual entity of that type. All I have said about the meaning of saying that this concept is primitive is that it is not to be analyzed in a certain way or ways. We are not, for example, to think of it as a secondary kind of entity in relation to two primary kinds, viz., a particular consciousness and a particular human body. I implied also that the Cartesian error is just a special case of the more general error, present in a different form in theories of the no-ownership type, of thinking of the designations, or apparent designations, of persons as *not* denoting precisely the same thing or entity for all kinds of predicate ascribed to the entity designated. That is, if we are to avoid the general form of this error, we must *not* think of "I" or "Smith" as suffering from type-ambiguity. Indeed, if we want to locate type-ambiguity somewhere, we would do better to locate it in certain predicates like "is in the drawing-room," "was hit by a stone," etc., and say they mean one thing when applied to material objects and another when applied to persons.

This is all I have so far said or implied about the meaning of saying that the concept of a person is primitive. What has to be brought out further is what the implications of saying this are as regards the logical character of those predicates with which we ascribe states of consciousness. For this purpose we may well consider P-predicates in general. For though not all P-predicates are what we should call "predicates ascribing states of consciousness" (e.g., "going out for a walk" is not), they may be said to have this in common, that they imply the possession of consciousness on the part of that to which they are ascribed.

What then are the consequences of the view as regards the character of P-predicates? I think they are these. Clearly there is no sense in talking of identifiable individuals of a special type, a type, namely, such that they possess both M-predicates and P-predicates, unless there is in principle some way of telling, with regard to any individual of that type, and any P-predicate, whether that individual possesses that P-predicate. And, in the case of at least some P-predicates, the ways of telling must constitute in some sense logically adequate kinds of criteria for the ascription of the P-predicate. For suppose in no case did these ways of telling constitute logically adequate kinds of criteria. Then we should have to think of the relation between the ways of telling and what the P-predicate ascribes, or a part of what it ascribes, always in the following way: we should have to think of the ways of telling as *signs* of the presence, in the individual concerned, of this different thing, viz., the state of consciousness. But then we could only know that the way of telling was a sign of the presence of the different thing ascribed by the P-predicate, by the observation of correlations between the two. But this observation we could each make only in one case, viz., our own. And now we are back in the position of the defender of Cartesianism, who thought our way with it was too short. For what, now, does "our own case" mean? There is no sense in the idea of ascribing states of consciousness to one-self, or at all, unless the ascriber already knows how to ascribe at least some states of consciousness to others. So he cannot argue in general "from his own case" to conclusions about how to do this; for unless he already knows how to do this, he has no conception of *his own case*, or any *case*, i.e., any subject of experiences. Instead, he just has evidence that pain etc., may be expected when a certain body is affected in certain ways and not when others are. If he speculated to the contrary, his speculations would be immediately falsified.

The conclusion here is not, of course, new. What I have said is that one ascribes P-predicates to others on the strength of observation of their behavior; and that the behavior-criteria one goes on are not just signs of the presence of what is meant by the P-predicate, but are criteria of a logically adequate kind for the ascription of the P-predicate. On behalf of this conclusion, however, I am claiming that it follows from a consideration of the conditions necessary for any ascription of states of consciousness to anything. The point is not that we must accept this conclusion in order to avoid skepticism, but that we must accept it in order to explain the existence of the conceptual scheme in terms of which the skeptical problem is stated. But once the conclusion is accepted, the skeptical problem does not arise. So with many skeptical problems: their statement involves the pretended acceptance of a conceptual scheme and at the same time the silent repudiation of one of the conditions of its existence. That is why they are, in the terms in which they are stated, insoluble.

But this is only one half of the picture about P-predicates. For of course it is true of some important classes of P-predicates, that when one ascribes them *to oneself*, one does not do so on the strength of observation of those behavior criteria on the strength of which one ascribes them to others. This is not true of all P-predicates. It is not, in general, true of those which carry assessments of character or capability: these, when self-ascribed, are in general ascribed on the same kind of basis as that on which they are ascribed to others. Even of those P-predicates of which it is true that one does not generally ascribe them to oneself on the basis of the criteria on the strength of which one ascribes them to others, there are many of which it is also true that their ascription is liable to correction by the self-ascriber on this basis. But there remain many cases in which one has an entirely adequate basis for ascribing a P-predicate to oneself, and yet in which this basis is quite distinct from those on which one ascribes the predicate to another. Thus one says, reporting a present state of mind or feeling: "I feel tired, am depressed, am in pain." How can this fact be reconciled with the doctrine that the criteria on the strength of which one ascribes P-predicates to others are criteria of a logically adequate kind for this ascription?

The apparent difficulty of bringing about this reconciliation may tempt us in many directions. It may tempt us, for example, to deny that these self-ascriptions are really ascriptive at all, to *assimilate* first-person ascriptions of states of consciousness to those other forms of behavior which constitute criteria on the basis of which on person ascribes P-predicates to another. This device seems to avoid the difficulty; it is not, in all cases, entirely inappropriate. But it obscures the facts; and is needless. It is merely a sophisticated form of failure to recognize the special character of P-predicates, or, rather, of a crucial class of P-predicates. For just as there is not in general one primary process of learning, or teaching oneself, an inner private meaning for predicates of this class, then another process of learning to apply such predicates to others on the strength of a correlation, noted in one's own case, with certain forms of behavior, so—and equally—there is not in general one primary process of learning to apply such predicates to others on the strength of behavior criteria, and then another process of acquiring the secondary technique of exhibiting a new form of behavior, viz., first-person P-utterances. Both these pictures are refusals to acknowledge the unique logical character of the predicates concerned. Suppose we write "Px" as the general form of propositional function of such a predicate. Then, according to the first picture, the expression which primarily replaces "x" in this form is "I," the first person singular pronoun: its uses with other replacements are secondary, derivative, and shaky. According to the second picture, on the other hand, the primary replacements of "x" in this form are "he," that person," etc., and its use with "I" is secondary, peculiar, not a true ascriptive use. But it is essential to the character of these predicates that they both have first- and third-person ascriptive uses, that they are both self-ascribable otherwise than on the basis of observation of the behavior of the subject of them, and other-ascribable on the basis of behavior criteria. To learn their use is to learn both aspects of their use. In order to *have* this type of concept, one must be both a self-ascriber and an other-ascriber of such predicates, and must see every other as a self-ascriber. In order to *understand* this type of concept, one must acknowledge that there is a kind of predicate which is unambiguously and adequately ascribable *both* on the basis of observation of the subject of the predicate *and* not on this basis, i.e., independently of observation of the subject: the second case is the case where the ascriber is also the subject. If there were no concepts answering to the characterization I have just given, we should indeed have no philosophical problem about the soul; but equally we should not have our concept of a person.

To put the point—with a certain unavoidable crudity—in terms of one particular concept of this class, say, that of depression. We speak of behaving in a depressed way (of depressed behavior) and we also speak of feeling depressed (of a feeling of depression). One is inclined to argue that feelings can be felt but not observed, and behavior can be observed but not felt, and that therefore there must be room here to drive in a logical wedge. But the concept of depression spans the place where one wants to drive it in. We might say: in order for there to be such a concept as that of X's depression, the depression which X has, the concept must cover both what is felt, but not observed, by X, and what may be observed, but not felt, by others than X (for all values of X). But it is perhaps better to say: X's depression *is* something, one and the same thing, which is felt, but not observed, by X, and observed, but not felt, by others than X. (Of course, what can be observed can also be faked or disguised.) To refuse to accept this is to refuse to accept the *structure* of the language in which we talk about depression. That is, in a sense, all right. One might give up talking or devise, perhaps, a different structure in terms of which to soliloquize. What is not all right is simultaneously to pretend to accept that structure and to refuse to accept it; i.e., to couch one's rejection in the language of that structure.

It is in this light that we must see some of the familiar philosophical difficulties in the topic of the mind. For some of them spring from just such a failure to admit, or fully to appreciate, the character which I have been claiming for at least some P-predicates. It is not seen that these predicates could not have either aspect of their use, the self-ascriptive or the nonself-ascriptive, without having the other aspect. Instead, one aspect of their use is taken as self-sufficient, which it could not be, and then the other aspect appears as problematical. So we oscillate between philosophical skepticism and philosophical behaviorism. When we take the self-ascriptive aspect of the use of some P-predicates, say "depressed," as primary, then a logical gap seems to open between the criteria on the strength of which we say that another is depressed, and the actual state of being depressed. What we do not realize is that if this logical gap is allowed to open, then it swallows not only his depression, but our depression as well. For if the logical gap exists, then depressed behavior, however much there is of it, is no more than a sign of depression. But it can only become a sign of depression because of an observed correlation between it and depression. But whose depression? Only mine, one is tempted to say. But if *only* mine, then *not* mine at all. The skeptical position customarily represents the crossing of the logical gap as at best a shaky inference. But the point is that not even the syntax of the premises of the inference exists, if the gap exists.

If, on the other hand, we take the other-ascriptive uses of these predicates as primary or self-sufficient, we may come to think that all there is in the meaning of these predicates, as predicates, is the criteria on the strength of which we ascribe them to others. Does this not follow from the denial of the logical gap? It does not follow. To think that it does is to forget the self-ascriptive use of these predicates, to forget that we have to do with a class of predicates of the meaning of which it is essential that they should be both self-ascribable and other-ascribable to the same individual, where self-ascriptions are not made on the observational basis on which other-ascriptions are made, but on another basis. It is not that these predicates have two kinds of meaning. Rather, it is essential to the single kind of meaning that they do have, that both ways of ascribing them should be perfectly in order.

If one is playing a game of cards, the distinctive markings of a certain card constitute a logically adequate criterion for calling it, say, the Queen of Hearts; but, in calling it this, in the context of the game, one is ascribing to it properties over and above the possession of these markings. The predicate gets its meaning from the whole structure of the game. So with the language in which we ascribe P-predicates. To say that the criteria on the strength of which we ascribe P-predicates to others are of a logically adequate kind for this ascription, is not to say that all there is to the ascriptive meaning of these predicates is these criteria. To say this is to forget that they are P-predicates, to forget the rest of the language-structure to which they belong.

6

Now our perplexities may take a different form, the form of the question: "But how can one ascribe to oneself, not on the basis of observation, the very same thing that others may have, on the basis of observation, reasons of a logically adequate kind for ascribing to one?" This question may be absorbed in a wider one, which might be phrased: "How are P-predicates possible?" or: "How is the concept of a person possible?" This is the question by which we replace those two earlier questions, viz.: "Why are states of consciousness ascribed at all, ascribed to anything?" and "Why are they ascribed to the very same thing as certain corporeal characteristics, etc.?" For the answer to these two initial questions is to be found nowhere else but in the admission of the primitiveness of the concept of a person, and hence of the unique character of P-predicates. So residual perplexities have to frame themselves in this new way. For when we have acknowledged the primitiveness of the concept of a person, and, with it, the unique character of P-predicates, we may still want to ask what it is in the natural facts that makes it intelligible that we should have this concept, and to ask this in the hope of a nontrivial answer, i.e., in the hope of an answer which does not *merely* say: "Well, there are people in the world." I do not pretend to be able to satisfy this demand at all fully. But I may mention two very different things which might count as beginnings or fragments of an answer.

First, I think a beginning can be made by moving a certain class of P-predicates to a central position in the picture. They are predicates, roughly, which involve doing something, which clearly imply intention or a state of mind or at least consciousness in general, and which indicate a characteristic pattern, or range of patterns, of bodily movement, while not indicating at all precisely any very definite sensation or experience. I mean such things as "going for a walk," "coiling a rope," "playing ball," "writing a letter." Such predicates have the interesting characteristic of many P-predicates, that one does not, in general, ascribe them to oneself on the strength of observation, whereas one does ascribe them to others on the strength of observation. But, in the case of these predicates, one feels minimal reluctance to concede that what is ascribed in these two different ways is the same. This is because of the marked dominance of a fairly definite pattern of bodily movement in what they ascribe, and the marked absence of any distinctive experience. They release us from the idea that the only things we can know about without observation or inference, or both, are private experiences; we can know, without telling by either of these means, about the present and future movements of a body. Yet bodily movements are certainly also things we can know about by observation and inference. Among the things that we observe, as opposed to the things we know about without observation, are the movements of bodies similar to that about which we have knowledge not based on observation. It is important that we should understand such movements, for they bear on and condition our own; and in fact we understand them, we interpret them, only by seeing them as elements in just such plans or schemes of action as those of which we know the present course and future development without observation of the relevant present movements. But this is to say that we see such movements as *actions*, that we interpret them in terms of intention, that we see them as movements of individuals of a type to which also belongs that individual whose present and future movements we know about without observation; it is to say that we see others as self-ascribers, not on the basis of observation, of what we ascribe to them on this basis.

These remarks are not intended to suggest how the "problem of other minds" could be solved, or our beliefs about others given a general philosophical "justification." I have already argued that such a "solution" or "justification" is impossible, that the demand for it cannot be coherently stated. Nor are these remarks intended as *a priori* genetic psychology. They are simply intended to help to make it seem intelligible to us, at this stage in the history of the philosophy of this subject, that we have the conceptual scheme we have. What I am suggesting is that it is easier to understand how we can see each other, and ourselves, as persons, if we think first of the fact that we act, and act on each other, and act in accordance with a common human nature. Now "to see each other as persons" is a lot of things, but not a lot of separate and unconnected things. The class of P-predicates that I have moved into the center of the picture are not unconnectedly there, detached from others irrelevant to them. On the contrary, they are inextricably bound up with the others, interwoven with them. The topic of the mind does not divide into unconnected subjects.

I spoke just now of a common human nature. But there is also a sense in which a condition of the existence of the conceptual scheme we have is that human nature should not be common—should not be, that is, a community nature. Philosophers used to discuss the question of whether there was, or could be, such a thing as a "group mind." For some the idea had a peculiar fascination, while to others it seemed utterly absurd and nonsensical and at the same time, curiously enough, pernicious. It is easy to see why these last found it pernicious: they found something horrible in the thought that people should cease to have to individual persons the kind of attitudes that they did have, and instead have attitudes in some way analogous towards groups; and that they might cease to decide individual courses of action for themselves and instead merely participate in corporate activities. But their finding it pernicious showed that they understood the idea they claimed to be absurd only too well. The fact that we find it natural to individuate as persons the members of a certain class of moving natural objects does not mean that such a conceptual scheme is inevitable for any class of beings not utterly unlike ourselves. A technique similar to that which I used . . . to decide whether there was a place in the restricted auditory world for the concept of the self, is available to determine whether we might not construct the idea of a special kind of social world in which the concept of an individual person is replaced by that of a group. Think, to begin with, of certain aspects of actual human existence. Think, for example, of two groups of human beings engaged in some competitive, but corporate activity, such as battle, for which they have been exceedingly well trained. We may even suppose that orders are superfluous, though information is passed. It is easy to suppose that, while absorbed in such activity, the members of the groups make no references to individual persons at all, have no use for personal names or pronouns. They do, however, refer to the groups and apply to them predicates analogous to those predicates as ascribing purposive activity which we normally apply to individual persons. They may *in fact* use in such circumstances the plural forms "we" and "they"; but these are not genuine plurals, they are plurals without a singular, such as occur in sentences like: "We have taken the citadel," "We have lost the game." They may also refer to elements in the group, to members of the group, but exclusively in terms which get their sense from the parts played by these elements in the corporate activity. Thus we sometimes refer to what are in fact persons as "stroke" or "square-leg."

When we think of such cases, we see that we ourselves, over a part of our social lives—not, happily, a very large part—do work with a set of ideas from which that of the individual person is excluded, in which its place is taken by that of the group. But might we not think of communities or groups such that this part of the lives of their members was the dominant part— or was not merely a part, but the whole? It sometimes happens, with groups of human beings, that, as *we* say, their members think, feel, and act "as one." I suggest it is a condition for the existence of the concept of an individual person, that this should happen only sometimes.

It is quite needless to say, at this point: "But all the same, even if it happened, all the time, every member of the group would *have* an individual consciousness, would embody an individual subject of experience." For, once more, there is no sense in speaking of the individual consciousness just as such, of the individual subject of experience just as such; there is no way of identifying with pure entities. It is true, of course, that, in suggesting the fantasy of total absorption in the group, I took our concept of an individual person as a starting point. It is this fact which makes the useless reaction a natural one. But suppose someone seriously advanced the following "hypothesis"; that each part of the human body, each organ and each member, had an individual consciousness, was a separate center of experiences. The "hypothesis" would be useless in the same way as the above remark, only more obviously so. Let us now suppose that there is a class of moving natural objects, divided into groups, each group exhibiting the same characteristic pattern of activity. Within each group there are certain differentiations of appearance accompanying differentiations of function, and in particular there is one member of each group with a distinctive appearance. Cannot one imagine different sets of observations which might lead us in the one case to think of the particular member as the spokesman of the group, as its mouthpiece; and in the other case to think of him as its mouth, to think of the group as a single *scattered* body? The important point is that as soon as we adopt the latter way of thinking, then we abandon the former; we are no longer influenced by the human analogy in its first form, but only in its second; we are no longer tempted to say: Perhaps the members have consciousness. It is helpful here to remember the first startling ambiguity of the phrase, "a body and its members."

7

Earlier, when I was discussing the concept of a pure individual consciousness, I said that though it could not exist as a primary concept to be used in the explanation of a concept of a person (so that there is no mind-body problem, as traditionally conceived), yet it might have a logically secondary existence. Thus, from within our actual conceptual scheme, each of us can quite intelligibly conceive of his or her individual survival of bodily death. The effort of imagination is not even great. One has simply to think of oneself as having thoughts and memories as at present, visual and auditory experiences largely as at present, even, perhaps—though this involves certain complications—some quasi-tactual and organic sensations as at present, whilst (a) having no perceptions of a body related to one's experience as one's own body is, and (b) having no power of initiating changes in the physical condition of the world, such as one at present does with one's hands, shoulders, feet, and vocal chords. Condition (a) mu.st be expanded by adding that no one else exhibits reactions indicating that he perceives a body at the point which one's body would be occupying if one were seeing and hearing in an embodied state from the point from which one is seeing and hearing in a disembodied state. One could, of course, imagine condition (a) being fulfilled, in both its parts, without condition (b) being fulfilled. This would be a rather vulgar fancy, in the class of the table-tapping spirits with familiar voices. But suppose we take disembodiment strictly in the sense that we imagine both (a) and (b) fulfilled. Then two consequences follow, one of which is commonly noted, the other of which is perhaps insufficiently attended to. The first is that the strictly disembodied individual is strictly solitary, and it must remain for him indeed an utterly empty, though not meaningless, speculation, as to whether there are any other members of his class. The other, and less commonly noticed point, is that in order to retain his idea of himself as an individual he must always think of himself as *dis*embodied, as a *former* person. That is to say, he must contrive still to have the idea of himself as a member of a class or type of entities with whom, however, he is now debarred from entering into any of those transactions the past fact of which was the condition of his having any idea of himself at all. Since then he has, as it were, no personal life of his own to lead, he must live much in the memories of the personal life he did lead; or he might, when this living in the past loses its appeal, achieve some kind of attenuated vicarious personal existence by taking a certain kind of interest in the human affairs of which he is a mute and invisible witness—much like that kind of spectator at a play who says to himself: "That's what I should have done (or said)" or "If I were he, I should. . . ." In proportion as the memories fade, and this vicarious living palls, to that degree his concept of himself as an individual becomes attenuated. At the limit of attenuation there is, *from the point of view of his survival as an individual,* no difference between the continuance of experience and its cessation. Disembodied survival, on such terms as these, may well seem unattractive. No doubt it is for this reason that the orthodox have wisely insisted on the resurrection of the body.

NOTES

1. Or at least widely enough supposed to justify our calling it the Cartesian view.

2. The evidence that Wittgenstein at one time held such a view is to be found in Moore's articles in *Mind* on "Wittgenstein's Lectures in 1930–33" (*Mind*, Vol. 64, pp. 13–14). He is reported to have held that the use of "I" was utterly different in the case of "I have a toothache" or "I see a red patch" from its use in the case of "I've got a bad tooth" or "I've got a matchbox." He thought that there were two uses of "I," and that in one of them "I" was replaceable by "this body." So far the view might be Cartesian. But he also said that in the other use (the use exemplified by "I have a toothache" as opposed to "I have a bad tooth"), the "I" *does not denote a possession* and that no Ego is involved in thinking or in having toothache; and referred with apparent approval to Lichtenberg's dictum that, instead of saying "I think," we (or Descartes) ought to say "There is a thought" (i.e., "Es denkt").

The attribution of such a view to Schlick would have to rest on his article, "Meaning and Verification" (see *Readings in Philosophical Analysis*, ed. Feigl and Sellars). Like Wittgenstein, Schlick quotes Lichtenberg, and then goes on to say: "Thus we see that unless we choose to call our body the owner or bearer of the data [the immediate data of experience]—which seems to be a rather misleading expression—we have to say that the data have no owner or bearer." The full import of Schlick's article is, however, obscure to me, and it is quite likely that a false impression is given by the quotation of a single sentence. I shall say merely that I have drawn on Schlick's article in constructing the case of my hypothetical "no-subject" theorist; but shall not claim to be representing his views.

Lichtenberg's anti-Cartesian dictum is, as the subsequent argument will show, one that I endorse, if properly used; but it seems to have been repeated, without being understood, by most of Descartes's critics. (I do not here refer to Wittgenstein and Schlick.)

3. I can imagine an objection to the unqualified form of this statement, an objection which might be put as follows. Surely the idea of a uniquely applicable predicate, i.e., a predicate which belongs to only one individual, is not absurd. And, if it is not, then surely the most that can be claimed is that a necessary condition of one's ascribing predicates of a certain class to one individual, i.e., oneself, is that one should be prepared, or ready, on appropriate occasions, to ascribe them to other individuals, and hence that one should have a conception of what those appropriate occasions for ascribing them would be; but not, necessarily, that one should actually do so on any occasion.

The shortest way with the objection is to admit it, or at least refrain from disputing it; for the lesser claim is all that the argument strictly requires, though it is slightly simpler to conduct it in terms of the larger claim. But it is well to point out further that we are not speaking of a single predicate, or merely of some group or other of predicates, but of the whole of an enormous class of predicates such that the applicability of those predicates or their negations defines a major logical type or category of individuals. To insist, at this level, on the distinction between the lesser and the larger claim is to carry the distinction over from a level at which it is clearly correct to a level at which it may well appear idle and possibly senseless.

The main point here is a purely logical one: the idea of a predicate is correlative with that of a *range* of distinguishable individuals of which the predicate can be significantly, though not necessarily truly, affirmed.

Select Bibliography

Allport, Gordon. *The Person in Psychology* (Boston, 1968).

Anderson, Alan Ross, ed., *Minds and Machines* (Englewood Cliffs, N.J., 1964).

Armstrong, D. M. *Bodily Sensations* (London, 1962).

Ayer, A. J. *The Concept of a Person* (London, 1964).

Bartlett, Sir Frederic. *Thinking* (New York, 1958).

Broad, C. D. *The Mind and Its Place in Nature* (London, 1937). See especially the chapter "The Unity of the Mind."

Bruner, J. S.; Goodnow, J. J.; and Austin, G. A. *A Study of Thinking* (New York, 1956).

Bruner, J. S.; Oliver, R. R.; and Greenfield, P. M., et al. *Studies in Cognitive Growth* (New York, 1966).

Campbell, C. A. *On Selfhood and Godhood* (London, 1957). See Chapter VI, "Self-Consciousness, Self-Identity, and Personal Identity."

Chappell, V. C., ed. *The Philosophy of Mind* (Englewood Cliffs, N.J., 1962).

Crosson, F. J., and Sayre, K. M., eds. *The Modeling of Mind* (South Bend, Ind., 1963).

Fingarette, H. *The Self in Transformation* (New York, 1963).

Flew, Antony, ed. *Body, Mind, and Death* (New York, 1964).

Flugel, J. C. *Studies in Feeling and Desire* (London, 1955).

Geach, Peter. *Mental Acts* (London, 1957).

Gustafson, D. F. *Essays in Philosophical Psychology* (Garden City, N.Y., 1964).

Hampshire, S., ed. *Philosophy of Mind* (New York, 1966).

———. *Thought and Action* (London, 1959).

Hook, Sidney, ed. *Psychoanalysis, Scientific Method and Psychology* (Washington Square, N.Y., 1959).

———. *Dimensions of Mind* (New York, 1961).

Jacobson, E. *The Self and the Object World* (New York, 1964).

James, William. *Principles of Psychology.* (New York, 1950 [originally published, 1890]). See Chapter X, "The Consciousness of Self."

Kenny, A. *Action, Emotion and Will* (London, 1963).

Norbeck, E.; Price-Williams, and Mccord, W. *The Study of Personality* (New York, 1968).

Paton, H. J. *In Defense of Reason* (London, 1951). See the essay titled "Self Identity."

Penelhum, Terence. *Survival and Disembodied Existence* (London, 1970).
Perry, J., ed. *Personal Identity* (Berkeley, Calif., 1975).
Peters, R. S. *The Concept of Motivation* (New York, 1960).
Rorty, Amelie, ed. *The Identities of Persons* (London, 1975). This is a collection of original papers on personal identity.
Russell, Bertrand. *The Analysis of Mind* (London, 1921).
Scher, J. M., ed. *Theories of the Mind* (New York, 1962).
Shoemaker, Sydney. *Self-Knowledge and Self-Identity* (Ithaca, N.Y., 1963).
Stagner, Ross. *Psychology of Personality* (New York, 1961).
Strawson, P. F. *Individuals* (London, 1959).
———. *Studies in Thought and Action* (Oxford, 1968).
Vinacke, W. E. *The Psychology of Thinking* (New York, 1952).
von Leyden, W. *Remembering: A Philosophical Problem* (London, 1961).
Vygotsky, Lev S. *Thought and Language,* edited and translated by E. Hanfmann and G. Vakar, (Cambridge, Mass., 1962).
Wiggins, David. *Identity and Spatio-Temporal Continuity* (Oxford, 1967).
Williams, B. A. O. *Problems of the Self* (Cambridge, England, 1973).
Wylie, Ruth. *The Self-Concept* (Lincoln, Neb., 1961).

Part Four

The Question of Free Will and Agency

Introduction

Of crucial importance to a discussion of agency is the difference between an action and a bodily movement. It is the difference between one raising his finger and his finger merely rising. In the first instance the agent is active, whereas in the latter case he is passive; namely, *he* does not *do* anything. For example, his finger may rise as the result of an electric shock. The issue of active versus passive involvement of the agent concerns both the cause of the happening and whether or not there is any freedom with respect to human action. In other words, does an agent have any control over his actions and, if so, what are the conditions under which he can exercise it? Proponents of determinism argue that since every event has a cause, there can be no free will; any act of will, will itself be caused. There are, then, only two alternatives. Either (a) the cause of one's willing is the willing of the will *ad infinitum* or (b) the cause of one's willing is external to and out of the control of the agent. Option (a) results in absurdity. Option (b) results in determinism. Determinists maintain that human behavior is no different than any other causal sequence, all of which conform to the model of causal necessity: if certain antecedent conditions obtain, then a given consequence is guaranteed to obtain. Such a guarantee automatically rules out free will.

However, the model of causal necessity may not be the only game in town. At the very least an alternative is worth considering and, in so doing, perhaps some sense of free will can be salvaged. What does it mean to say "I can move my finger"? Such a statement means, at minimum, that it is within my power to move my finger. Here there are two important points to consider: (1) the notion of power is obscure, and (2) maintaining that moving one's finger is within one's power does not guarantee the possession of that power. If the determinist is correct, we simply do not have such powers. Therefore, the nature of this power needs to be explored. The claim that it is within my power to move my finger means:

291

(A) Given that there are no sufficient conditions to the contrary, I am able either to move my finger or keep it still.

(A) is a statement of causal contingency. Of course a thorough understanding of (A) requires an analysis of the phrase 'no sufficient conditions to the contrary.'

One sense of 'no sufficient conditions to the contrary' is that there are no physical obstructions external to the agent which would prevent the agent from exercising the option presented in (A) above. This is generally called having the opportunity to act. For example, if the finger referred to in (A) is locked in a cast, then that constitutes a condition external to me so that I cannot move my finger. I do not have the opportunity to move it.

However, an agent may have the opportunity to perform an action but not have the requisite ability. Abilities possess two aspects. (1) They entail that there is no physical obstruction internal to the agent which would prevent him from performing the action in question. (2) They are general in nature. For example, an agent may properly be said to have the ability, say, of throwing a baseball. Suppose, however, that on a particular day he submits to an experiment in which he is injected with a small dose of curare. As a result, he is paralyzed for several hours. We would not say under these conditions that our agent has lost the ability to throw a baseball. Here the important aspect of abilities to note is that if an agent has a given ability, it is understood that his normal physical conditions obtain. This built-in assumption accounts for the general aspect of abilities. If, however, an agent does not have a given ability, it is due to some internal physical obstruction, say, a severed spine resulting in permanent paralysis. The general nature of inabilities is here demonstrated by the permanentness of the situation as opposed to the temporary curare experiment above mentioned.

There may very well be psychological obstructions which are sufficient to prevent an agent from performing an action. One could be in the position to commit hari-kari, that is, have the opportunity and the physical ability to plunge in the knife, but simply not be able psychologically to commit suicide. Such a psychological obstruction may take one of two forms. (1) It may be purely psychological. Acrophobia will prevent a person from seeking heights although he may have the opportunity and the ability to climb. (2) A psychological obstruction may be a result of some external physical obstruction. For example, action under duress has an external physical component such as a threat from a second party. The threat, in turn, has a definite psychological effect upon the agent. In conclusion, for there to be no sufficient conditions to the contrary in order for an agent to be able, that is, to have it within his power to perform an action, means that he must have the opportunity and the ability to perform that action and there must be no psychological obstruction to his performing it.

It should be noted that there is nothing "iffy" about an action being within one's power to perform. The above analysis demonstrated that to say that action

Q is within agent S's power to perform is simply a compact way of claiming facts about a given situation, namely,

(i) S does *in fact* have the opportunity to do $\emptyset$.

(ii) S does *in fact* have the ability to do $\emptyset$.

(iii) There is *in fact* no psychological barrier to the performance by S of $\emptyset$.

[Statements] (i), (ii), and (iii) are the conditions which must obtain in order for action $\emptyset$ to be within S's power to perform.

That it is within one's power to do $\emptyset$ does not entail that he does $\emptyset$ even though there are no sufficient conditions to the contrary. What it does entail is that one does either $\emptyset$ or not-$\emptyset$. This statement of causal contingency says nothing about what the agent will, in fact, do, not to mention how he does what he does.[1]

Some philosophers have argued that the element necessary to determine what an agent will do with respect to those actions which are within his power to perform is wanting. People try to do or get what they want. Wants determine our actions. The issue remains, however, whether or not wants are determined, and, if so, determined by who or what. If they are determined by the agent himself, it would appear that our actions are free.

That actions are not caused, and in that sense free, has been argued on the ground that if the causal sequence is not broken, at least in some sense, no action could ever occur. If, for example, one must first engage in some activity in order to move one's finger whereby that activity functions as the cause of the finger moving, then the agent must do something to cause the activity that is the cause of one's finger moving. This results in an infinite regress the upshot of which is that the agent could never move his finger. Since agents do move their fingers, it must be the case that such activity is uncaused in the manner in which the determinist uses the term. The agent simply moves his finger and is properly the cause of it. Such appears to be a genuine case of free will.

NOTE

1. A. B. Schoedinger, *Wants, Decisions and Human Action: A Proxeological Investigation* (Lanham, Md.: University Press of America, 1978), pp. 107–13.

22

Determinism

Alasdair MacIntyre

I

This paper has two aims. First I shall try to show that certain contemporary solutions offered to that cluster of logical puzzles traditionally known as "the problem of free-will and determinism" not only do not shed light on them, but in some cases engender positive darkness. I shall then go on very tentatively to suggest the outline of a possible solution and to meet the more obvious difficulties that it presents. That this is an important problem no one presumably disputes, but it is perhaps not wholly superfluous to emphasize its precise contemporary importance. For it is paradoxical that refutations of theoretical determinism—of Laplace's dream, for example—which satisfy most contemporary philosophers have been propounded and accepted in a period in which for the first time there has been accomplished what the opponents of classical determinism most feared. The threat of classical determinism did not arise so much from its total programme as from that part of its programme which concerned human action in general and moral action in particular. Consequently it is not the physical sciences which should arouse the apprehension of the anti-determinist, but psychology and the social sciences. Sufficient has been already achieved in these sciences to make it clear that we can expect from them ever increasing success in explaining and predicting human behavior.

From *Mind* 66, no. 261 (January, 1957): 28–41. Reprinted by permission of Oxford University Press.

If one considers, for example, the kind of correlation that Bowlby has claimed to establish between juvenile delinquency of a certain kind and the lack of a mother-figure at certain periods in early childhood (J. Bowlby, *Maternal Care and Mental Health);* or the Freudian hypotheses that certain adult traits are causally dependent on certain childhood failures and achievements; or some of the hypotheses advanced by learning theorists; one can hardly doubt that more and more of behavior will be included in accounts which show such behavior to be causally dependent on antecedent conditions. It does not in the least matter whether the particular hypotheses which I have mentioned turn out to be correct or not. What matters is that this type of explanation is firmly established. This means that the problem of determinism is not purely speculative, arising from philosophical enquiry, but arises from the very nature of the human sciences. Experience compels us to recognize that success in explaining behavior is perhaps Janus-faced. For success in explaining and predicting can never be divorced from success in manipulating and controlling. The traditional cheerleaders of the natural sciences have been wont to emphasize causal explanation as the key to freedom and to offer such examples as medicine and psychotherapy. But successful totalitarian propaganda and social conditioning derive equally from a knowledge of how to predict and manipulate human behavior. *Brave New World* and *1984* are not baseless fantasies.

So there appears a dilemma, either horn of which seems intolerable. The discovery of causal explanations for our actions, preferences and decisions shows that we could not have done other than we have done, that responsibility is an illusion and the moral life as traditionally conceived a charade. It makes praise and blame irrelevant, except in so far as we discover these to be causally effective, and while the moral judgments of agents might therefore retain some point, those of spectators and critics would be pointless. But even the moral judgments of agents would be affected by such discoveries, since in considering what I ought to do my whole assessment of alternatives presupposes that there are alternatives. The gradual establishment of determinism suggests a Spinozistic elimination of distinctively moral terms. Yet we find it difficult to believe that moral praise and blame are appropriate only because and in so far as we are ignorant; or rather, that they are not, but only seem appropriate. But to react against this is to discover that the other horn of the dilemma is equally menacing. For the only possible alternative seems to be a pious hope that psychological and sociological explanation should in fact prove impossible. To believe that human behavior is inexplicable is to offend against all that we have learned from the successive victories of the sciences. Kant was right in seeing in this dilemma a genuine conflict between moral and scientific interests. . . .

III

We call an act "free" when certain criteria are satisfied. Some of these criteria refer to positive features of free acts, and of these only a selection need to be, or indeed can be, satisfied in any one particular case. Thus a free act may be reflective, and that the agent reflected before acting might be part of the evidence that his act was free. But a free act need not be reflective, for it might be impulsive, as jumping in a river to rescue a drowning man can be. In spite of the attempts of legal reformers to use the notion of "acting on impulse" in formulating criteria to decide when a man is or is not responsible for his acts, there is no contradiction in saying that a man on a particular occasion acted freely, responsibly and on impulse. Others of these criteria must always be satisfied for an act to be called "free." These are the criteria which list those features which an act must not possess to be called "free." The resemblances between this list and the list of defenses which an be offered to defeat a claim in the courts as to the existence of a valid contract have been pointed out by Professor [H.L.A.] Hart in his paper on "The Ascription of Responsibility and Rights" *(Logic and Language,* vol. ii, ed. [Antony] Flew). But there is a crucial difference between the two lists. The legal list could in principle be added to, but its items can be enumerated exhaustively. The list of features which must be absent from a free act is indefinitely long. Aristotle gives us some of the most important items on it, but we must go to Freud for others and the neurophysiologists may yet make their additions. The determinist claims that one of these features will always be present in any *prima facie* free act. This is sometimes asserted with a metaphysical generality that is self-condemning, but it need not be. The logically unsophisticated determinist may seek to put his views beyond refutation by asking how we can be certain in any given case that some one of these features will not be discovered or does not go undiscovered. But this question only has force, so long as we use the word "certain" in such a way that we mean by a "certain proposition" a proposition that we can have no reason to doubt; whereas in empirical discourse we mean, or ought to mean, by a "certain proposition," not one that we can have no reason to doubt, but one that we *do* have no reason to doubt. This kind of determinist then can be answered by saying that a given act is free, if on reasonable inspection we find that none of the relevant features are present. To say just this, however, is to betray our weakness in the face of a more moderate determinism. For the case of such a determinism would be that such a reasonable inspection has not yet been made. The sciences of human behavior have so much more to tell us that we must always be prepared for the area of human freedom to be still further delimited.

I want to suggest that we can meet this case by means of a concept which will allow us to admit both the indefinite possibilities of psychological and physiological discovery and the fact that such discoveries may be legitimately added to our list of negative criteria without, however, conceding that we may see the area of human freedom dwindle indefinitely. This is the concept of "rational behavior." Behavior is rational—in this arbitrarily defined sense—if, and only if, it can be influenced, or inhibited by the adducing of some logically relevant consideration. This definition must now be expanded. The expression "logically relevant consideration" is vague, but not, I think, fatally so. What is logically relevant will necessarily vary from case to case. If Smith is about to give generously to someone who appears to be in need, the information that this man is only disguised as a beggar, but has in fact ample means, will be logically relevant. And of course the scope of the concept of rational behavior is far wider than the area of moral choice. The scholar dating a document is behaving rationally in so far as, and only in so far as, he admits only logically relevant considerations. Indeed the task of philosophy might almost be defined as the task of defining "logical relevance." This "can" in the definition of "rational behavior" means "can in principle," for an impulsive action can in this sense be rational. There may in fact be no time to adduce any considerations at all, but we can in principle distinguish the man who would leap in any way from the man who would be stopped by the information that what was in the water was a log and not a man, or that the man was a suicide and that he, the rescuer, had always upheld the right to suicide. Rational behavior is thus by no means coextensive with reflective behavior. Indeed, behavior can be reflective without being, in this sense, rational. For a man may spend a great deal of time thinking about what he should do, and yet refuse to entertain a great many logically relevant considerations. This brings us to what is crucial in the definition. Rational behavior is defined with reference to the possibility of altering it. A man who is behaving rationally will alter his behavior if, and only if, logically relevant considerations are adduced. Thus in principle we can always verify whether or not a man is behaving rationally. But this means that if a man's behavior is rational it cannot be determined by the state of his glands or any other antecedent causal factor. For if giving a man more or better information or suggesting a new argument to him is a both necessary and sufficient condition for, as we say, changing his mind, then we exclude, for this occasion at least, the possibility of other sufficient conditions. All that we need to know is that the other factors in the situation, glandular states and the like, remain more or less constant. We do in fact possess sufficient evidence to be sure enough of this. Thus to show that behavior is rational is enough to show that it is not causally determined in the sense of being the effect of a set of sufficient conditions operating independently of the agent's deliberation or possibility of deliberation. So the discoveries of the physiologist and psychologist may indefinitely increase our knowledge of why men behave irrationally but they could never show that rational behavior in this sense was causally determined . . . .

The arguments that I have so far advanced suggest a sense in which the agent's choice can be called uncaused. But to say that rational behavior is uncaused is misleading. What can be called uncaused is the agent's particular decision, conclusion or deed, in that only the adducing of logically relevant considerations played a part in determining them. But obviously rational behavior is caused in that there are necessary conditions for its occurrence. Thus there is a sense in which the psychologist can rightly be said to provide explanations of rational behavior, and in which nonrational devices may be employed in order that people may behave rationally. This of course is what psychotherapists do, and I have suggested elsewhere that there are important logical differences between those psychotherapeutic methods, such as insulin treatment, which operate solely by means of nonrational, causal devices, and those such as psychoanalysis, in which the treatment extends into the field of rational behavior and in which the adducing of logically relevant considerations plays an essential part. But if these are conditions necessary for rational behavior, there are also conditions sufficient for the fomenting of nonrational behavior. These we have seen created deliberately in Nazi Germany and the Soviet Union. They can also be studied in the techniques of mass advertisement. In an important sense you can be said to *make* men irrational, but you cannot be said to make them rational in the same sense. This is surely the logical ground for the distinction between education and indoctrination.

It should be noted that this analysis of rationality and freedom allows us to speak of complex behavior patterns as more or less free or rational. Distinctively moral behavior enjoys no privileges. Some introspectionists have tried to maintain that over moral behavior the agent could not be deceived as he was elsewhere; but on this analysis we call moral behavior free, in so far as it is a subclass of rational behavior, and we can be deceived or mistaken about it, exactly in the same way as with other kinds of potentially rational behavior.

There is one other sense in which rational behavior can be explained. Because most kinds of rational behavior involve references to principles, and references to principles involves some degree of consistency in acting, rational behavior will often be predictable. This predictability has nothing to do with causal determination. Nowell Smith has pointed out that very often we want to say that an act is both voluntary and predictable; when, for example a good man acts, as we say, "in character." . . . The correct moral is that actions are predictable in two different senses. In the first sense we may predict successfully how a man will behave from knowledge of factors other than and antecedent to his own present and past decisions, preferences and consciously motivated behavior. Such is the prediction that an infant deprived at a certain age of maternal care will prove in later life incapable of genuine love-relationships. But other predictions may be of a kind that can only be made on the basis of data that include knowledge of a man's decisions, preferences and so on. Such, at any rate at the present time, are the predictions as to how votes will be cast at elections. Predictability in this second sense is not only compatible with, but up to a point required by, rational behavior.

IV

Against the case that I have argued so far a powerful counter-attack may be launched by the determinist. This attack may be mounted in three stages and as each is met new and more threatening moves may be developed. The first stage is to point out that in the widest sense of the word "cause" the giving of a reason may function as a cause. This is not to lose sight of the logical distinction between reasons and causes. It is to note that the giving of a reason is not a reason, is always in fact a physical event of a certain kind, the uttering of sounds or the writing of letters, and is therefore admirably adapted to function as a cause. If we allow that this is so, if the giving of reasons is sufficient to alter a man's behavior, then it may be argued we have found causal conditions sufficient to account for rational behavior, and not merely necessary conditions, as I suggested earlier. To meet this first stage of the attack one has only to note that this contention can be made effective only at the cost of being made tautological. For in terms of the concept of rational behavior we can certainly discriminate between a giving of reasons which is causally and a giving of reasons which is rationally effective. You may act as a result of my reasoning with you, but it may be on account of the passion in my tone or as a result of forgotten associations of the words that I used that you were moved to act. A little ingenuity could furnish us with tests for discriminating between such occasions and occasions when you accepted and acted on the reasons I offered you. So that in the sense in which I have maintained it earlier, to act because you were given reasons to act would not necessarily be to act in a causally determined way. It would only be necessarily the case that to act as a result of being given reasons to act was to act as a result of determining causes, if we counted as a cause of behavior anything which influenced behavior at all. If we understood the expression "cause of behavior" in this way, to say that our giving of reasons supplied a sufficient determining cause of behavior would be to utter an empty tautology.

The second stage of the determinist argument would run as follows. It might be suggested that there are empirical grounds for believing that we can always be mistaken about rational behavior, that it may on the surface be influenced by rational considerations and yet be in fact wholly determined by antecedent causes. The evidence for this, it might be suggested, is drawn from an examination of the phenomena of post-hypnotic suggestion. If one suggests to the subject that he shall behave in a particular way—walk out of the room, for example—ten minutes after he has regained normal consciousness, he will not only do this, but he will unhesitatingly produce, if questioned, an ingenious set of reasons to explain why he acts as he does. This is certainly strong evidence that being able to give a rational justification of one's behavior in no way precludes that one's behavior is wholly causally determined. But it provides an opportunity for, rather than a case against, the use of the concept of rational behavior, in the sense defined. If, as a result of post-hypnotic suggestion, a man walked out of the room, producing as he did so a reason for so acting, what would be crucial would be to observe this reaction if we offered him a better reason for staying in the room. If, no matter how good the reasons we offered him, he persisted in leaving it, we should have to say that his behavior was wholly causally determined; but, if the adducing of reasons could change his behavior, we should have to say that the hypnotic suggestion was not a sufficient condition *per se* of his walking out of the room, but was only sufficient in the absence of a good reason for staying in the room. To say this would be to say that in fact the suggestion did not determine his behavior apart from his own rational processes.

It is at this point that the determinist might produce what is certainly his strongest argument. He might suggest that advances in learning theory, for example, might teach us that rational, intelligent behavior was nothing more than well-drilled behavior, of which a complete causal account could be given, only provided that that account was sufficiently complex. Given a detailed knowledge of the subject's learning history and achievements we might be able to predict that when the subject was confronted with the exciting causes of rational behavior that is, the offering of good reasons for behaving in a particular way, we should be able to predict on the basis of laws covering both predisposing and exciting causes how the subject would react. So all rational behavior would be predictable in detail. I find two different kinds of difficulty in this suggestion. The first is that it seems impossible to give this kind of account of rational behavior without misdescribing it. Consider examples from two different fields. If a man confronts a moral problem, weighing up the pros and cons of a situation, to depict his judgment on it as the effect of a causal impact made by the situation would do violence to all our ordinary ways of talking about morality. For we normally want to contrast sharply the irrational reaction of feeling and the carefully scrutinized moral appraisal. It was the error of the emotive theory in ethics to blur this contrast and its restoration has been central to more recent discussion. Likewise someone undergoing psychoanalysis may start by reacting to a particular kind of situation by compulsive and nonrational actions, such as those manifested in claustrophobia or kleptomania. But as his analysis progresses and he becomes aware of unconscious fantasies, desires and motives, he will tend to appraise and to weigh up alternatives and the compulsiveness of his original reaction will fall away. As in moral situations, it must seem that to classify both compulsive and noncompulsive behavior under the heading of reaction to exciting causes determined in its form by certain predisposing causes is to obliterate important distinctions which emerge in simply trying to describe the differences between the two kinds of behavior. Terms such as "appreciation" and "appraisal" and "weighing of pros and cons" which certainly do not express any causal relationship must inevitably find their way into such descriptions.

Secondly, if determinism rests its hopes on this complex pattern of explanation I find it difficult to see how determinism could ever be verified or falsified. For suppose that the determinist is able to supply a complete explanation of my behavior in causal terms. Suppose also that my behavior is rational, that whatever strong reasons are adduced for acting in a certain way I act in that way, that I am infinitely flexible and resourceful in meeting new contingencies. Then no test will be available to decide whether I act as I do because it is the rational way to act or because it is the way in which my deeds are causally determined. For on either supposition I will do the same things. To try and include my reasonableness in a story about causal factors is to try and produce a story about my behavior sufficiently comprehensive to include everything. This means that whereas the contention that my behavior is determined by causal factors is normally taken to mean "determined by causal factors as contrasted with rational appreciaton, etc.," here "causal factors" have nothing to be contrasted with and hence the expression "determined by causal factors" has been evacuated of its customary meaning.

V

What I am trying to argue is easily epitomized. I have claimed in effect that the determinist must either interpret his own thesis in a wide or in a narrow sense. If he interprets it in a narrow sense, then we can contrast "causally determined behavior" and "rational behavior" in such a way that we can in principle enquire of a piece of behavior into which category it falls. Here I would add to what I said above. For there I merely claim that we could in principle draw this distinction. Now I want to add to this the claim that we do in fact in everyday experience find evidence for the occurrence of rational behavior. Constantly, when there are no grounds for believing that there has been any change in causal factors, people decide to act differently because they have adduced reasons for so acting and, if they find that they were mistaken about those reasons, they will once again alter their plans and projects. It is because we so often do experience behavior responsible in that it is rational that we all feel with Dr. Johnson that, no matter how cogent determinist arguments may seem, "We are free and there's an end on 't."

If the determinist, however, interprets his thesis in a wide sense, then he obliterates that contrast between determined behavior and rational, responsible behavior on which his case essentially rests. No doubt the convinced determinist can produce other and better arguments than I have put into his mouth; but I am certain that if the determinist case is to be met at all it must be met in some such way as I have suggested. There is no way out in arguing that determinism and a belief in human responsibility are really compatible. Whatever else is uncertain in this area of argument, of the genuine existence of the conflict that creates the whole problem there can be no doubt whatever.

23

Willing

A. I. Melden

There is a difference between my arm rising and my raising my arm, between my muscles moving and my moving my muscles—in short, between a bodily movement or happening and an action. In this paper I examine one attempt to make out the nature of this difference.

Consider the following. Whenever I raise my arm (deliberately, let us say) I bring to pass certain muscle movements: I make these happen. Hence I raise my arm by moving (contracting and expanding) certain muscles of my arm. This, then, is how I raise my arm.

This of course is a bad argument. We cannot identify what one does with what one makes happen. When I flex the biceps brachii of my arm many things are brought to pass, made to happen. Nerve impulses are transmitted to the muscles, neural circuits in the brain are opened and closed, protein molecules in the brain are set into oscillation, and many more things of which I have not the faintest intimation. But let us consider the conclusion on its own merits. Certainly I can contract certain muscles at will. If someone points to the biceps brachii of my arm and asks me to flex it, this I can easily do. So it is tempting to say that when I raise my arm, I do so by moving certain muscles *just as* when I signal, I do so by raising my arm.

But how do I move certain muscles? There is a difference between my biceps becoming flexed and *my* flexing my biceps, just as there is a difference

From *The Philosophical Review* 68 (1959): 475–84. Copyright © 1959 by The Philosophical Review. Reprinted by permission of the publisher and the author.

between my arm getting raised and my raising my arm. The flexing of my biceps may occur through no doing of mine (someone might raise my arm and in doing so cause my biceps to be flexed), just as my arm getting raised may be something that happens to me through the action of another person who raises my arm and not through anything I do. And what can the difference be between the occurrence of a muscle movement in my arm and my moving that muscle, except that in the latter case it is by doing something that I bring the muscle movement to pass? In short, if it is sensible to say that I raise my arm by moving certain muscles, it is equally sensible to hold that I move those muscles by doing something that brings those muscle movements to pass. And what can this latter doing be that has these muscle movements as effect?

Consider the biceps brachii of my arm. Someone points to it and says, "Flex it!" What must I do in order to comply? Must I say to myself, "Move, muscle, move"? If I do this, nothing will happen. Does nothing happen because I do not mean it? Then how do I mean it? "Meaning what I say"—is this something I do when I say whatever it is that I do say? And how do I do that? Shall we say that I shall mean it only when I *want* my muscle to move? But if I want my biceps to move and stare at it again nothing will happen; I must do something about my want, that is, get what it is that I want. Is it necessary that I set myself—to use H. A. Prichard's expression—to move my biceps?[1] But if "setting myself" means getting ready, putting myself in a state of readiness, again nothing will happen. And if "setting myself to do" means trying to do or exerting myself to do, then I need do nothing of the sort. I do not try to raise my arm unless, for example, it is held down— I simply raise it; and I do not try to flex my biceps unless there is some obstacle to be overcome or some chance of failure.

What then is the difference between my muscles being contracted and my contracting my muscles? A familiar doctrine is that in the latter case I will my muscles to move; in the former case there are causes other than the act of volition. So I move my muscles by performing an act of volition which in turn produces a muscle movement.

Grant for a moment that an event labeled "an act of volition" produces a muscle movement; there is a difference surely between the occurrence of such an event and my producing it. We saw that there is a difference between the occurrence of a muscle movement and my moving that muscle; hence it was that the supposition of acts of volition was invoked. But equally there would seem to be a difference between the occurrence of an act of volition and my performing such an act. Who can say that volitions may not occur through no doing of the subject and in consequence of interior mental events deep within the hidden recesses of the self? If so, willing the muscle movement is not enough; one must will the willing of the muscle movement, and so on ad infinitum. Here someone may retort impatiently: "When I will a muscle movement, *I* will it and that is the end of the matter; there is no other doing by virtue of which this act of volition gets done—I simply will the movement." But even if this reply were correct it would not serve to explain what an action is, as distinguished from a mere happening. It explains the "action" of raising the arm in terms of an internal action of willing, and hence all it does at best is to change the locus of action. Indeed it invites the view argued by Prichard that, strictly speaking and contrary to the notion conveyed by our ordinary ways of speaking, one does not raise one's arm at all: all one does or can do is will and by means of this action produce various effects such as the rising of one's arm. In any case if willing is some sort of doing which one performs not by means of any other doing—one wills and that is the end of the matter—why not say the same with respect to the muscle movement itself, or the tensing of one's biceps? One simply tenses it and there is no doing by virtue of which the tensing gets done. But the troubles involved in the supposition that there are interior acts of willing go even deeper than this; the doctrine, familiar though it may be, is a mare's nest of confusions.

How shall we describe the alleged action of willing? Surely a description of this action independently of the consequence alleged for it—the production of a muscle movement—must be forthcoming. Let us call the act of willing A; then A produces B (a muscle movement), this being taken to be a causal sequence. Now in general if A causes B, a description of A other than that it has the causal property of producing B must be forthcoming; otherwise "A causes B" degenerates into "the thing that produces B produces B." But what description of the act of volition can be offered? If something causes me to jump in fright, jerk my arm, or move my head, "What caused you to . . .?" is intelligible and answerable. It is no good saying, "That which caused me to do it," for this is no answer but a bit of rudeness or a feeble attempt at humor. How then shall one describe the act of willing?

It is at this point that the resort to indefinables appears attractive.[2] Willing is *sui generis,* indefinable, a bit of mental self-exertion in which we engage, an activity not capable of further description but different from the wonderings, thinkings, supposings, expectings, picturings, and so forth, that comprise our mental activities. Yet the appeal to indefinables is a desperate defense that purchases immunity from further attack only at the expense of unintelligibility. If all that can be said about the alleged act of volition by virtue of which a muscle movement is produced is that it is the sort of thing that produces a muscle movement, there is every uncertainty that anyone has understood what is meant by "the act of volition." And if an attmept to rescue this doctrine is made by appealing to something with which, it is alleged, each of us is intimately familiar and hence will have no difficulty in recognizing—the act of volition that produces the muscle movement—the retort must surely be "*What* do I recognize when I recognize an act of volition?" Unless I can recognize this act by having some description in mind that applies to such acts and only to these, it is at best a simple begging of the question to insist that all of us really understand what is being referred to; in fact, it is an implied charge of dishonesty directed at those who refuse to give their assent. And in philosophy, when good manners alone stand in the way of the open parade of charges of this sort, there is something seriously amiss in one's thinking.

But the difficulty in this talk about acts of volition is not merely that some account of acts of volition in general is needed, failing which we can only conclude that the expression "act of volition" can play no role in our discourse, it is equally serious in other respects as well. Let us grant that there is some peculiar mental activity of willing the causal consequence of which is that certain muscles are contracted and others relaxed as we perform our diverse bodily movements, and let us now ask first of all how it is that we are able to learn how to perform these bodily movements. Surely the act of volition involved in the production of one muscle movement must be distinguished from the act of volition involved in the production of any other. There will then be different acts of volition, v_1, v_2, v_3, and so forth, which, respectively, move muscles m_1, m_2, m_3, and so forth. If $v_1 \rightarrow m_1$, $v_2 \rightarrow m_2$, $v_3 \rightarrow m_3$, and so forth, represent causal relations, then just as m_1, m_2, m_3 are distinguishable, so v_1, v_2, v_3 will needs be different in kind. And if I am to learn how to produce m_1 by performing the act of volition v_1, I must not only recognize the difference between v_1 and other acts of volition that have other effects; I must recognize the causal relation holding between v_1 and m_1. Now this would seem to imply at least two things: (1) It must be possible to offer a set of characterizations of these acts of volition each different from the other, corresponding to the set of characterizations that can be given, surely, for the muscle movements m_1, m_2, m_3, m_4, and so forth. (2) I can learn only from experience that m_1 is produced by v_1, m_2, by v_2, m_3 by v_3, and so on. Hence, unless I suppose myself to have been endowed with superhuman prescience, I cannot have been surprised or astonished the first time I performed the act of volition v_1 to discover that muscle movement m_1 occurred, and antecedently I should have no reason for ruling out the possibility that m_2 would not occur; I should have no reason, for example, to suppose that when I performed the act of volition by which in fact my biceps became flexed, my right leg would not have been raised.

Consider the first of these consequences. Now I can certainly distinguish between muscle movements m_1 and m_2, say, the biceps of my right arm from that of my left arm. But how shall I distinguish between the acts of volition v_1 and v_2 by which these distinct muscle movements are produced? If I produce these muscle movements by performing these acts of volition, this at any rate is something I learn to do, an ability I come to acquire. But if I can learn to do this, I must be able to distinguish between the volitions v_1 and v_2. Surely it must be possible to describe the difference. And if this cannot be done, learning to produce m_1 by producing v_1 and learning to produce m_2 by producing v_2 is impossible. How then shall we describe v_1 as distinguished from v_2? Shall we say that not only are volitions in general indefinable, but that the difference between v_1 and v_2 is also something indefinable? At least, however, the difference must be recognizable. Is it that our vocabulary is inadequate? Then let us introduce words that will enable us to mark the distinction. And now that the words have been introduced, explain how they are to be employed! Is it that we can only *point*: v_1 is *this* thing, the one that one finds one performs when m_1 is produced, v_2 is *that* thing, the one that one finds that one performs when m_2 is produced? But this will do the trick only if I already know what sorts of things to look for and only if it is at least possible for me to go on and describe the difference between v_1 and v_2 independently of the considerations that v_1 produces m_1 and v_2 produces m_2. By pointing one can succeed in explaining the meaning of a term or expression, but only if by doing so one can help fill in a gap or supply the links missing in some initial background understanding we have of that term or expression. But here we do not know where to look or what to find. No background understanding is present; we are told that there are certain things—call them "acts of volition"—that they are indefinable, and that nothing more can be said about them at all in explaining how this expression "act of volition" is to be employed. Against this background, how can pointing serve to provide any explanation at all of the difference between act of volition$_1$ (call it mental-muscle-doing$_1$) and act of volition$_2$ (mental-muscle-doing$_2$)? To say at this point that the difference itself is indefinable is, surely, to carry philosophical pretension beyond all limits of credulity.

As far as I know, philosophers are quite unwilling to pile indefinables upon indefinables in this fulsome manner. Prichard for one, despite his characteristic resort to indefinables, is admirable for an equally characteristic subtlety that leads him to reject such simple-minded answers even though, as he himself recognizes, he must accept a conclusion that is open to objections he cannot meet. Consider the second of the two consequences of the doctrine of acts of volition. That v_1 produces m_1 rather than m_2 is a causal fact; but if so, I should have no reason to suppose, when I first performed the act of volition v_1 that m_1 rather than m_2 would follow; for on this view the statement that, for example, I move the biceps brachii of my right arm by performing the act of volition v_1, rather than the biceps brachii of my left arm or the biceps femoris of my right leg, is justified only on the basis of inductive evidence. Now Prichard holds that an act of volition involves a desire to will whatever it is that one wills, and hence some idea of what the volition is likely to produce. This, however, is impossible on the present view since on the first occasions on which I performed v_1 and thereby produced m_1, v_1 would require the thought that I would be doing something that would produce m_1 and by hypothesis I should have no reason to expect what, if anything, v_1 would produce. Prichard is therefore led to the conclusion that an "act of will requires an idea of something which we may cause if we perform the act," a conclusion—indeed a difficulty—he is unable to avoid.[3]

Prichard's predicament involves a matter of central importance which can be stated quite independently of his insistence that if one is to perform an act of volition, one must be moved by a desire to perform that act of volition. The important issue raised by Prichard is whether or not it is intelligible to speak of an act of volition where the very notion of such an act does not involve a reference to the relevant bodily event. Let the act of volition issue in a muscle movement, then, as Prichard himself recognizes, the act must be the willing of that muscle movement; otherwise we should have only inductive grounds for supposing the act to issue in that particular muscle movement. Accordingly we are faced with the following dilemma: If in thinking of v_1 (some particular act of volition) we are of necessity to think of it as the willing of m_1 (some particular muscle movement), then v_1 cannot be any occurrence, mental or physiological, which is causally related to m_1, since the very notion of a causal sequence logically implies that cause and effect are intelligible without any logically internal relation of the one to the other. If, on the other hand, we think of v_1 and m_1 as causally related in the way in which we think of the relation between the movements of muscles and the raising of one's arm, then we must conclude that when first we perform v_1 we should be taken completely by surprise to find that m_1 does in fact ensue. If to avoid this latter consequence we maintain that the thought of the muscle movement enters into the very character of the act of volition (as Prichard puts it, "the *thinking* enters into the character of the *willing*"[4]), no description of the act of volition can be given that does not involve an account of the muscle movement, and hence we must abandon the idea that the act of volition v_1 is a cause that produces m_1, the muscle movement. Prichard's predicament is that his conclusion that "an act of will requires an idea of something which we may cause if we perform the act" is nothing less than self-contradictory.

This then is the logical incoherence involved in the doctrine of acts of volition. Acts of volition are alleged to be direct causes of certain bodily phenomena (whether these be brain occurrences, as Prichard supposed them to be, or muscle movements, as we have been assuming for the sake of argument, is of no matter) just as the latter are causes of the raising of one's arm. For, it is alleged, just as we raise our arms by moving our muscles, so we move our muscles by willing them to move. But no account of the alleged volitions is intelligible that does not involve a reference to the relevant bodily phenomena. And no interior cause, mental or physiological, can have this logical feature of acts of volition. Let the interior event which we call "the act of volition" be mental or physical (which it is will make no difference at all), it must be logically distinct from the alleged effect: this surely is one lesson we can derive from a reading of Hume's discussion of causation. Yet nothing can be an act of volition that is not logically connected with that which is willed; the act of willing is intelligible only as the act of willing whatever it is that is willed. In short, there could not be such an interior event like an act of volition since (here one is reminded of Wittgenstein's famous remark about meaning) nothing of that sort could have the required logical consequences.

Let me review the course of the argument. The doctrine of acts of volition was introduced, it will be remembered, in order to elucidate the distinction between one's arm rising and one's raising one's arm. The former need involve no doing or action performed by the agent; the latter surely does. But instead of rejecting the question "How does one raise one's arm?" by a "One just does" retort, the reply we considered was "One raises one's arm by moving certain muscles." Here the same question arises again: how can one distinguish between "moving certain muscles" and "certain muscles getting moved"? The latter need involve no action on my part at all. And if it makes sense to ask, "How does one raise one's arm?" surely it makes sense to ask, "How does one move certain muscles?" Hence the doing required in order to preserve the distinction between "moving certain muscles" and "certain muscles getting moved" must be a doing other than the doing described as "moving certain muscles." At this point the philosophical doctrine of acts of volition—willings performed by an agent—appears attractive. By willing we move certain muscles; by moving certain muscles we raise our arm. But the acts of volition in question are the ill-begotten offspring of the mating of two quite incompatible ideas: the supposition that such acts are causes, and the requirement that the volitions in question be the willings of the muscle movements. As causes, willings are events on a par with other events including muscle and other bodily movements, with respect to which the inevitable question must arise once more: "How does one perform such an action?" since after all there is the distinction to be preserved between "performing a willing" and "a willing occurring." But if to avoid the threatened regress of "willing a willing" and "willing the willing of a willing" and so on, one rejects the question and questions the intelligibility of such locutions as "willing a willing," the willing in question can only be understood as "the willing of a muscle movement." If so, the willing in question cannot be a cause of the muscle movement, since the reference to the muscle movement is involved in the very description of the willing. In that case to say that one moves certain muscles by willing them to move is not to give any causal account at all. But if this is so, what can it mean to say that one wills a muscle movement—since the willing in question cannot possibly be any interior occurrence in which one engages? If it is intelligible at all it means simply that one moves a muscle. In that case, the alleged elucidation of the statement that one moves certain muscles (in raising ones arm) by willing them to move degenerates into something that is no elucidation at all, namely, that one moves certain muscles by moving them. And if this is so, to say that one wills the movement of certain muscles is not to answer the question "How does one move those muscles?"; it is in fact to reject it. If this is the outcome, why not refuse to plunge into the morass and reject the initial question "How does one raise one's arm?" by saying "One just does"? If, on the other hand, "willing a muscle movement" does not mean "moving a muscle," what on earth can it possibly mean? Surely it is an understatement to say that the philosophical talk about acts of volition involves a mare's nest of confusions!

It is not my contention that the doctrine of volitions is designed to answer only those questions I have raised so far. It is of course true that frequently this doctrine is also invoked in order to give some account of the difference between action that is voluntary and action that is not. Nor do I deny that there is any legitimacy in our familiar use of such locutions as "acting willingly," "doing something of one's own will," "acting willfully," and so on. But these are matters to be examined in their own right and at the proper time.

NOTES

1. Cf. the essay "Duty and Ignorance of Fact" in *Moral Obligation* (Oxford, 1949).

2. Indeed, this is the move made by Prichard in the essay "Acting, Willing, Desiring," written in 1945 and published posthumously in *Moral Obligation* (Oxford, 1949). This essay is worth careful reading; in it Prichard abandons his earlier account of "willing" as setting oneself to do.

3. Ibid., pp. 196–197. See also his second thoughts about his earlier notion of "setting oneself" in the footnotes to his earlier essay, "Duty and Ignorance of Fact," which appear in the same volume (p. 38).

4. Ibid., p. 38.

24

Basic Actions

Arthur C. Danto

"Well, why should we want to know?" said Verity, giving a yawn or causing herself to give one.

I. Compton-Burnett, *Two Worlds and Their Ways*

I

"The man *M* causes the stone *S* to move." This is a very general description of a very familiar sort of episode. It is so general, indeed, that it does not tell us whether or not *M* has performed an action. The description holds in either case; so it *could* have been an action. Without pausing to inquire what further features are required for it definitely to have been an action, let us merely note that *there are* actions that fall under the general description of "causing something to happen." Yet, since this description leaves it unclear whether or not an action has been performed, performing an action cannot be one of the truth conditions for "causing something to happen." And since this description cuts across those two cases, we may assume we are employing the same sense of the expression "causes something to happen" in both. Presumably, we are using "causes" in just the same sense whether we say that the man *M* causes the stone *S* to move *or* we say that the stone *S*

From *American Philosophical Quarterly*, II (April 1965), 141–148. Copyright © 1965. Reprinted by permission of the publisher.

causes the pebble P to move. If it *is* clear from the latter sentence that an action has *not* been performed, this clarity will be due to certain facts about stones rather than to any difference in the concept of causality. It is commonly assumed that stones never perform actions, although men sometimes do. Hence the indefiniteness of our original sentence is not due to any ambiguity in the concept of causality, but rather to certain facts about men, or to certain assumed facts. The concept of causality allows us to ignore differences between men and stones, as well as differences between performing an action and not.

I shall persist in speaking of *individuals* (the man M, the stone S) causing things to happen, even though our concept of causality has been classically analyzed as a relationship between pairs of *events*. According to the classical analysis, the movement of the pebble P is one event, the effect of another event, which I shall, with studied ambiguity, simply designate an S-event, in this case its cause. Comparably, the movement of S in my other example is one event, the effect of another event, similarly and no less ambiguously to be designated an M-event, which is its cause. And this M-event, whether or not it is an action performed by M, is correctly (if rather generally) to be described as *causing something to happen*—namely, the movement of S.

I shall now suppose that my original sentence in fact describes an action performed by M (moving the stone S). Of this particular spatial translation of S we may say three distinct and relevant things: that it is (a) an action, performed by M); that it is (b) something that was *caused* to happen (in this case by M; and that it is (c) the effect of an event distinct from itself (in this case the M-event). That this event can be both (a) and (b) follows from the remarks in the first paragraph. That—disregarding the special information in parentheses—(c) must hold if (b) does—follows from the analysis of causality referred to in the second paragraph. That it is (b) follows, I suppose, from the fact that S is a stone: stones don't *just* start to move without something causing them to move.

We must now look into the M-event itself. Do all three characterizations apply to *it*? This, I fear, cannot be decided without investigation. Let us suppose, however, that the M-event is both (a) and (b), for it might well be. Then it must also be (c), and there must then be yet another event, distinct from it, which is its cause. This may be yet a further M-event, and about it we may raise the same question. It would be rash to claim that we have slid into an infinite regress, damaging or otherwise. But if a given M-event is both (a) and (b) and, hence, (c), then ultimately its being (c) must lead us to a further M-event, which is (a) and *not* (b). And unless some M-events are (a) and not (b), no M-events are ever (a). That is, if there are any actions at all, there must be two distinct *kinds* of actions: those performed by an individual M, which he may be said to have *caused* to happen;

and those actions, also performed by *M*, which he cannot be said to have caused to happen. The latter I shall designate as *basic actions*.

In this paper, I shall defend (and explore the consequences of) four theses which I regard as fundamental to the theory of action:

(1) If there are any actions at all, there are basic actions.

(2) There are basic actions.

(3) Not every action is a basic action.[1]

(4) If *a* is an action performed by *M*, then either *a* is a basic action of *M*, or else it is the effect of a chain of causes the originating member of which is a basic action of *M*.

I wish first to make quite clear the sense in which an individual does not cause his basic actions to happen. When an individual *M* performs a basic action *a*, there is no event distinct from *a* that both stands to *a* as cause to effect *and* is an action performed by *M*. So when *M* performs a basic action, he does nothing first that causes it to happen. It will be convenient to consider two possible objections to this.

It may be objected, first, that there are or may be other senses of "causes" than the sense mentioned above, in accordance with which it would be proper to say that *M* causes his basic actions to happen. Thus, *if* raising an arm were an instance of a basic action, an individual who does this might still be said to cause it to happen in some sense of "cause" other than the sense that I reject in application to basic actions. I accept this objection: there *may be* such other senses of "cause." But (i) we should still require exactly the same distinction that I am urging within the class of actions, and I should therefore be defending the *verbally* distinct thesis that unless there were actions an individual causes to happen in this *new* sense, there would be no actions he caused to happen in the original sense, either. So, unless there were actions of the former sort, causing a stone to move would, for example, never be an *action* that anyone performed (although men might still cause stones to move, since performing an action is not a truth-condition for "causing something to happen"). And (ii) this new sense of "cause" would *not* apply *whether or not* an action had been performed. It should, indeed, be absolutely clear from the sentence "*M* caused *a* to happen"—using this special sense of "cause"—that *M* *had* performed an action. Those who find it convenient to maintain that the concept of causality is invariant to the distinction between performing an action and not, would have as little use for this new sense of "cause" as I do. Neither they nor I would want to say that *stones* cause *anything* to happen in this new sense of "cause." Not that

I wish to restrict the performance of basic actions to men alone. Other individuals may, for all I know, perform them as well. Some theologians have spoken as though everything done by God were a basic action. This would prohibit us, of course, from saying that God caused anything to happen (the making of the Universe would be a basic action). And, for reasons which will soon emerge, this would make the ways of God inscrutable indeed.

It may be objected, second, that if we take the absence of a cause to be the distinguishing mark of a basic action, then we must class as basic actions a great many events that we should be disinclined, on other grounds, to accept as actions at all, e.g., the uniform rectilinear motion of an isolated particle, or perhaps any instance of radioactive decay. This objection is readily deflected. I have not claimed that basic actions are not caused, but only that a man performing one does not cause it by performing some other action that stands to it as cause to effect. Moreover, the absence of a cause would not be a sufficient criterion for a basic action, even if basic actions *were* uncaused. It would serve only to mark off a special class of actions from the rest. Of course, only what is already an action can be a *basic* action. And I have not so much as tried to say what are the general criteria for actions.

II

I have avoided citing unconditional instances of basic actions, in part because any expression I might use, e.g., "moving a limb," could also be used to designate something that was caused to happen or something that was not an action, much less a basic one. I think there is nothing that is always and in each of its instances an unmistakably basic action. This is reflected by language in the fact that from the bare description "M's limb moved," for example, one could not tell whether M had performed a basic action or even an action. Nor could one tell this by observing only the motion of the limb without bringing in differentiating contextual features. I have accordingly contented myself with the neutral expression "M-event," declaring it to be a basic action when I required an instance.

Now I wish to specify some of the differentiating contextual features, and I shall consider four distinct cases, all of which might indifferently be covered by the same description, so that the description alone leaves it unclear whether an action has been performed or not. Of the four cases, three (*C-1, C-2, C-4*) will indeed be actions, and of these one (C-4) will be a basic acion. The four cases together might be termed a *declension* of the description. Not every such description admits of the full declension, for some appear never to be exemplified as basic actions at all. "Moving a stone," I should think, never, or not ordinarily, is exemplified as a basic action, though we have seen that it may be exemplifed by an action. I want to begin with a deliberately controversial example and shall decline the expression "*M* laughs."

C-1. *M* causes himself to laugh.

I am thinking here of cases where someone does something to make himself laugh, and does not simply laugh because of something he happens to do. Thus I may do something ridiculous and laugh because I find it so, but I did not do this ridiculous thing in order to make myself laugh. Again, I sniff a cartridge of nitrous oxide, not knowing it to be nitrous oxide, but just to find out what it is. But, since it is nitrous oxide, I laugh, though I did not sniff to make myself laugh. I wish to include only cases where I do something ridiculous or sniff from a private cartridge of nitrous oxide *in order to* laugh, perhaps because I think laughter good for the liver or because I just enjoy laughing and cannot always wait for someone or something to come along and cause me to laugh. I definitely want to exclude a comedian who laughs at some reruns of his antic films (unless he has them rerun for this special purpose), and definitely want to include someone who deliberately engages in auto-titillation to excite spasmodic laughter. Doubtless, episodes falling under *C-1* are rare in normal adults in our culture, but this is irrelevant. Also irrelevant is the fact that people don't laugh *at* the nitrous oxide they sniff, though they do laugh at the silly faces they pull, for their own delectation, in mirrors.

C-2. Someone or something other than *M* causes *M* to laugh.

This is the typical case for adults and children in our culture. It is for my purposes again irrelevant whether the cause of *M*'s laughter is also its object, or whether it has an object at all (as it does not if he is tickled or submitted to nitrous oxide). Similarly, it is irrelevant whether, in case someone causes *M* to laugh, the former has performed an action or not, whether, that is, he did what he did in order to make *M* laugh. For it is what *M* does that uniquely concerns us here.

C-3. *M* suffers a nervous disorder symptomized by spasmodic laughter.

This is comparable, say, to a tic: *M* laughs unpredictably, and for "no reason." Such laughter is mirthless, of course, but so are some instances falling under the two first cases. It may be argued that the entire case falls under *C-2*, and that in identifying it as the symptom of a nervous disorder, I have marked off a class of causes for *M*'s laughter. Still, the case requires special consideration, in that M's laughing here is never an action, whereas his laughter under *C-2* sometimes *is*.

C-4. *M* has the true power of laughing.

By this I mean that *M* laughs when he wants to without (in contrast with *C-1*) having to cause himself to laugh; without (in contrast with *C-2*) someone or something having to cause him to laugh; without, finally, as in *C-3*, suffering from the relevant nervous disorder. This does not mean that *M* is normal, but only that his abnormality is of a benign sort; i.e., it is by way of a gift. His laughing may have an object: he may, when he wishes, direct a stream of laughter at whom or what he chooses, without the chosen object ever being a *cause* of his laughing.

Instances falling under *C-4* are perhaps rare, but these alone would qualify as basic actions performed by *M* when "*M* laughs" is true. I have identified the case not so much by specifying what differentiating contextual features must be present, but by specifying what differentiating contextual features must be *absent*. Notice that *M*'s laughing here differs markedly from the ability most of us have of making laugh-like noises, e.g., for the sake of politeness, or to save our reputation for seeing a joke when we don't see it, or to play a mocker's role in an amateur theatrical. Most of us can pretend so to laugh: but I speak here of laughing, not of "laughing."

I want now to comment on these four cases.

When *M* laughs under *C-1*, we may say of his laughing three distinct things: that it is (*a*) an action of *M*'s; that it is (*b*) something that *M* causes to happen; and that it is (*c*) the effect of some event, distinct from itself (an *M*-event) which is its cause. *M*'s laughing here is an action in just the same sense in which his causing a stone to move is an action. Causing himself to laugh is the action he performed, though of course the description "*M* caused himself to laugh" leaves it unclear, as in the case of the stone, whether he performed an action at all. One could mark that difference only by bringing in the general differentiating features of action.

In *C-2*, *M* does not cause himself to laugh, and one may find reasons for balking at the claim that his laughing, in such a case, is an action of his at all. For consider this argument. When *M* causes a stone *S* to move, we may agree that the action is *M*'s. But we reject the claim that it is an action of *S*'s. So parity suggests that when someone moves *M* to laughter, this may be an action performed by the former, but not an action of *M*'s.

What I must do is to show that parity is inoperative, and so justify my claim that instances of *C-2* are actions in contrast with instances of *C-3*. Well, I shall somewhat artificially suggest that *M*'s action here requires this description: what he does is to *not not laugh*. The double negative is not, in the language of action, a triviality. Logically, of course, the double negative of a proposition is just that proposition, and from a strictly logical point of view, we could say the same thing, albeit more awkwardly, with "The man *M* causes the stone *S* to not not move" as we straightforwardly say with "the man *M* caused the stone *S* to move." I wish, in fact, to retain that regular inferential feature of double negation which allows us to proceed from not not *A* to *A*, but for the case of action I wish to exclude the reverse inference. For my double negative marks the case of *negligence,* and whether a negligence is to be ascribed to someone is a case for independent investigation. So, pending such investigation, we cannot say, on the basis of knowing that a man laughs, that he is to be charged with negligence. And for this reason we cannot automatically go from "laughs" to "not not laughs." Indeed, since we don't ascribe negligence to stones, it would be invalid, given my convention, to proceed from "the stone moves" to "the stone not not moves."

Do we quite want to say, then, that *C-2* is to be restated thus: *Someone or something other than M causes M to not not laugh?* Perhaps we would, in spite of flaunting usage. What we would be saying, however, is only this: that *M* was excited to laugh and did nothing to inhibit his laughter. And it is our common assumption that men are normally capable of doing something which, in effect, stops the flow of laughter from issuing forth in, say, public guffaws. Whether men are called upon to exercise these inhibitory practices varies from context to context: in the music hall there is license to suspend them, to "let oneself go," but at High Mass there is not. It is in such contexts only that laughter is *pronounced* a negligence, but blaming, surely, does not make of something an action when it would not otherwise have been so. It is only insofar as something is an action already that blaming it, or blaming someone for doing it, is appropriate.

With regard to *C-3,* however, the laughter stands liable to no special charge of negligence: his laughing fails to be a case of not not laughing, for identification of it as a nervous disorder, or in the syndrome of one, locates it beyond the control of the man who is so afflicted. It is, indeed, almost a paradigm case of this: like a hiccough. One *might* blame the man for being in a place where his symptom, easily mistakable as a negligence, might break out unpredictably. Or we might blame him again for a kind of negligence in "not doing something about it," viz., going to a nerve specialist, assuming there is a known cure. At all events, it is plain enough why *C-3* differs from *C-2.* The critical issue, of course, is the matter of *control,* and this brings us to *C-4.* And the rest of this paper is by way of a comment on *C-4.*

Most readers, I think, will resist the suggestion that *C-4* is a case of action. There is good reason for this. For most of us, laughing as a *basic action* is unintelligible. I shall hope to show why this is so, and showing it will involve a demonstration of thesis (2). Meanwhile, the reader might ponder the precise analogue to this in the case of *moving an arm*, which admits of a full declension. Thus *C-1*: M causes his arm to move, i.e., by striking it with his other arm; *C-2*: someone or something other than M causes M's arm to move, e.g., by striking it; *C-3*: M suffers from a nervous disorder, so his arm moves spasmodically and unpredictably, as a kind of tic; and *C-4*: M moves his arm without suffering from a nervous disorder, without someone or something causing it to move, without having to do anything to cause it to move. Here, I am certain, *C-4* is the *typical* case. Moving an arm is one of the standard basic actions. If we now seek to determine in what way this behavior *is* intelligible, we should have no great difficulty in seeing why laughing under *C-4* is *not*.

III

Suppose now that moving a stone is an action performed by M. It is difficult to suppose that *moving a stone* admits of a full declension, largely because it seems to lack cases for *C-3* and *C-4*. In fact, there are difficulties in finding instances for *C-1* and *C-2* unless we change the sense of possession (M's arm, M's stone) from philosophical to legal ownership. But for the moment I shall be concerned only with the fact that we move stones only by causing them to move. This then means that, in order to cause the motion of the stone, something else must be done, or must happen, which is an event distinct from the motion of the stone, and which stands to it as cause to effect. Now this other event may or may not be a basic action of M's. But if it is not, and if it remains nevertheless true that moving the stone *is* an action of his, then there must be something else that M does, which causes something to happen which in turn causes the motion of the stone. And *this* may be a basic action or it may not. But now this goes on forever unless, at some point, a basic action is performed by M. For suppose every action were a case of the agent causing something to happen. This means, each time he does *a*, he must independently do *b*, which causes *a* to happen. But then, in order to do *b*, he must first independently do *a*, which causes *b* to happen. . . . This quickly entails that the agent could perform no action at all. If, accordingly, there are any actions at all of the sort described by "causing something to happen," there must be actions which are *not* caused to happen by the man who performs them. And these are basic actions.

But this argument is perfectly general. If there are any actions at all, there are basic actions. This is a proof of thesis (1). Moreover, if M performs an action describable by "causing something to happen," he must also, as part of what he does, perform an action that he does not cause to happen. And this is a proof of thesis (4). It would be a proof of thesis (2) if in fact there were actions described as "causing something to happen," This would then require us to accept thesis (3) as true: for such an action would not be a basic action, and so not every action is basic.

I do not wish to suggest, however, that the only proof we are entitled to, for the existence of basic actions, is by way of a transcendental deduction, for I believe we all know, in a direct and intuitive way, that there are basic actions, and which actions are basic ones. To show that we do know this will clarify one of the ways in which laughing is a controversial instance of a basic action.

I must make a few preliminary remarks. First, every *normal person* has just the same *repertoire R* of basic actions, and having *R* is what defines a normal person for the theory of action. Second, persons may be *positively abnormal* when their repertoire of basic actions includes actions not included in *R*, and may be *negatively abnormal* when actions included in *R* are not included in their repertoire. Some persons may be both positively and negatively abnormal, e.g., someone who laughs as a basic action but who is paralyzed in one arm. If someone's repertoire is empty, he is capable of no basic actions, and hence of no actions. Such a deprived entity is a *pure patient*, e.g., like a stone. Plainly, our repertoire of actions is greater than our repertoire of basic actions, though a being who performed every possible action and all of whose actions were basic actions may be conceived of: such a being would be a *pure agent*. For the present, however, I am concerned with beings intermediate between pure patients and pure agents, and I want now to say that basic actions are *given* to such beings in two distinct senses, each of which bears a definite analogy to a sense that the term has in the theory of knowledge.[2]

(i) In the theory of knowledge, to say that *p* is *given* is in part to point a contrast: one is saying that *p* is not inferred from some other proposition. Analogously, when I speak of an action as given, I shall mean to say, in effect, that it is a basic action, and point a contrast with actions we *cause* to happen. The notion of givenness is understood this way: *p* is a starting point for an inference to another and (commonly) different proposition *q* for which *p* provides at least part of the evidence. Analogously, an action *a*, if a basic action, is a starting point for the performance of another action *b*, of which it is at least part of the cause. "Is caused by" and "is inferred from" are analogous relations in the theories of knowledge and of action, respectively.

(ii) It has been argued that the distinction between *basic sentences* and sentences of other kinds is not ultimate, that a sentence which, in one context, is indeed a starting point for an inference to another, may, in a different context, itself be inferred to, and hence an end point in an inference.[3] Analogously, an action *a* may, in one context, be a starting point and basic, while it may be caused to happen in a different one. There is some justice in this latter claim: as we have seen, one cannot tell from the bare description "moving an arm" whether a basic action is referred to, or even an action. But, thinking now of sentences, perhaps some restriction can be put on the *kind* of sentence which can be given in sense (i). If *p* is given in one context and inferred in another, there might nevertheless be sentences which are never basic and always are inferred. And a corresponding restriction might hold in the theory of action: even if any action that is ever basic might, under a sufficiently general description, be caused to happen in another context, there might be actions that never are basic under any description. In the theory of knowledge, one such restriction is often defended, namely that basic sentences are those and only those which can be conclusively verified by sense experience, and that no other kind of sentence ever can be given. But within the class of potentially given sentences, a division might be made along the customary lines of sense-modality, i.e., those verified by seeing, or by audition, or by touch, etc. We might then define an *epistemically* normal person as one who experiences in all modes. A negatively abnormal person would then be deficient in at least one such mode, e.g., is blind; and a positively abnormal person then experiences in some mode outside the normal repertoire, e.g., has some "sixth sense." The analogy to the theory of action is obvious. But by means of it we may introduce our second sense of given: the normal modes of experience are "given" in the sense that they constitute the standard cognitive equipment. The normal person has various classes of starting points for inferences as he has various classes of starting points for actions. These are given in the sense that they are not for the most part *acquired*. Thus we speak of the "gift of sight," etc. This does not mean that there need be any sentences in the superstructure to which a negatively abnormal person might not infer; he is deficient only at the base; and then not *totally* deficient (or if he is, then he cannot have any empirical knowledge, is *cognitively impotent*). And similarly, *toutes proportions gardées*, with the negatively abnormal person as defined in the theory of action.

Now when a blind man says that he can know whether a certain object is red or not, there are two senses or uses of "can" that are compatible with his abnormality. He must mean either that he can *infer* to "*x* is red" from other sentences or that his case is not medically hopeless, that by means of a cure he may be restored to that state of normality in which such sentences may be known by him directly and not, as it were, *merely* by means of inference. Yet there is a true and in fact an *analytic* sense in which a blind man cannot know whether a certain object is red, nor, on certain accounts of meaning, so much as know what such a sentence *means* (the nonanalytic senses are usually false). The situation of a *paralyzed* man is perfectly analogous. When he sincerely says that he can move his arm, he must mean either he can *cause* it to move, or that his situation is not medically hopeless. But, in again a true and an analytical sense, he cannot move his arm and does not know, does not so much as understand, what it means to move his arm in the way in which a normal person understands this. For this is the kind of understanding that is alone given to those who have the power to move their arms in the normal, basic way. This kind of understanding cannot so much as be conveyed to a negatively abnormal person while he is so.

Some of the chief difficulties philosophers have encountered in the theory of action are due to their having approached it from the point of view of the negatively abnormal. From *that* point of view, basic action is hopelessly mysterious. There is, however, perhaps no better way of eliciting the quality of our knowledge of these things than to think of endeavoring to remove the mysteriousness surrounding these actions in the thwarted comprehension of the negatively abnormal person. We may achieve some sympathy for his plight by imagining *ourselves* similarly confronting someone who is *positively* abnormal, who can perform, as a basic action, what we at best can cause to happen, and then asking *him* to give us an understanding of his gift. The fact is that we cannot explain to the negatively abnormal, nor can the positively abnormal person explain to us, the way in which the basic action is performed (and this must be appreciated in the same way as the impossibility of explaining to a blind man what red literally looks like, or, if you wish, of our understanding what ultraviolet literally looks like). Suppose—just to take one case—a paralytic asks us what we do *first* when we raise an arm. We should be obliged to say we cannot answer, not because we do not know or understand what we do, but because we know and understand that there is *nothing* we do first. There is no series of steps we must run through, and since the request is implicitly for a *recipe*, we cannot say how we move our arm. A basic action is perfectly simple in the same sense in which the old "simple ideas" were said to be: they were not compounded out of anything more elementary than themselves, but were instead the utlimately simple elements out of which other ideas were compounded.

In one sense, then, we do, and in another we do not, know how we move an arm. But the sense in which we do not know is inappropriate. It is that sense which requires an *account*, and our incapacity for giving any such account is what has induced puzzlement, among philosophers and others, concerning the moving of an arm (and other basic acts generally). But this puzzlement should be dissipated upon the recognition that we have made a grammatical mistake in the inflected language of action. We have taken "moving an arm" as always a case of *C-1*, when *in fact C-4* is the standard case for normal persons moving normal arms normally. But having once committed this mistake, we look for a cause that is not there. And failng to find what we ought never to have expected to find, we complain that we do not know how we do move our arms. But of course we know. It is only that we cannot explain the manner of its doing. For there is no action, distinct from the action itself, to be put into the *explanans*. This is due to what I am terming the *givenness* of basic actions. Reference to basic actions belongs in the explanantia for explaining how things are done. So the paralytic, as long as he remains one, cannot understand: *Just raising the arm is what we do first.*

IV

A paralytic might think there is some *effort* he is not putting forth, by which, if he did or could put it forth, he might as a consequence move his arm. But I want to say that he cannot try to move his arm if moving his arm is not already in his repertoire of basic actions. So in a sense he is right. If he could make the required effort, he could move his arm. But he cannot make that effort, cannot try, for he cannot in the only appropriate sense move his arm.

Consider the analogous situation with someone epistemically abnormal, say a deaf man. To ask a deaf man to try to hear a certain sound is rendered inappropriate by the fact that he is deaf. To try to hear, say, faint and distant music is to make an effortful listening. Only those who can already hear can make this effort. And what would count as trying (listening) in the deaf man's case? He could cup his ear, could place his ear to the ground, could contort his face, and close his eyes. All this, however, is the pantomime of listening. Had he grinned or wagged a finger, it would have been as helpful. For there is no one thing that is better than any other in his situation. It is exactly this way with trying to move an arm. It is appropriate only to ask someone to try to move his arm when something externally inhibits normal movement, e.g., the arms are pinioned, and cannot be moved *freely and without effort*. But the paralytic cannot move his arm at all.

Consider these cases:

(*a*) I am a normal person who has swallowed a drug which gradually takes away the power to move an arm, rendering me, so long as it is in full effect, negatively abnormal. I make tests at five-minute intervals. It gets harder and harder to move my arm. And then I reach a point where I cannot move my arm and cannot *try* to. I have lost the power of trying, together with the power for doing.

(*b*) Someone thinks it would be spectacular to be able to extend and retract his fingernails, the way a cat does with its claws. We tell him it cannot be done, and he retorts that no one has ever tried, and he means to try. But in what should his trying consist? He could shake his fingers hard, could order them to extend, could pray, or draw his soul up into a vast single wish. There is no rational way, for there is no way at all for a normal person. I don't mean that no one is or ever will be able to move his nails and to try to move them (e.g., with tight gloves on). If a man were prepared to suffer some sort of surgery, he might be able to cause his nails to go in and out, but we had not understood that he meant this by "trying." It is after all not the way cats do it. It is more the way we move a loose tooth.

(*c*) I am a normal person, challenged to move a normal stone. I take the challenge to imply the stone is not normal—perhaps it has some incredible density, or is fixed to a shaft driven deeply into the earth. But I decide to try, and the stone moves quite easily, having been a normal stone all along. So I conclude that the challenge was not normal. It turns out I was being asked to move the stone "the way I move my arm." But this is not something I even can try to do. I can, with ridiculous ease, cause the stone to move. So I can try to cause it to move as well. But I cannot try to move it as a basic action—that would be a proper encounter with nothingness.

One can do with effort only what one can do effortlessly; and "trying," the effort of will, is not something apart from the action that stands to it as cause to effect. It is the required action already being performed in untoward circumstances. Doing something gracefully is doing two things. Moving an arm is not then the result of an act of will: it *is* an act of will. But to speak of an act of will when the going is smooth is to behave a little like the dypsomaniac who wants to know what sorts of pink rats ordinary people see.[4]

It should be plain now why laughing, if performed as a basic action, is controversial. It is because whoever could so laugh would be positively abnormal, and we cannot understand what he does. In relation to him, we are in just the same position as the paralytic in relation to us. We lack a kind of gift.

V

It is easy enough to sympathize with those who feel an action is not intelligible unless we can find a causal picture for it. But this is only because they have taken intelligibility to consist in having a causal picture. Dominated by this requirement, they may tend to invent some such picture, populating their inner selves with entities whose job it is to serve the automotive functions demanded by the causal model of intelligibility. But I am asking that we do not strain, and that we use the causal model only where it is natural to use it.

That there are actions, like moving an arm, which do not really require any other action as cause (and so no "inner" action as a cause) entails, I believe, no refutation of dualism. For all the distinctions I am thinking of are reproduced within the mental world, and cut across the distinction between body and mind. If, for instance, we take the description "*M* images *I*" where *I* is a mental image, then it is unclear, as it was in the case of "laughing" or "moves an arm," whether *M* has performed an action or not, or, if an action, then a basic action or not. The whole declension works for, *C-1*: *M* may cause an image to appear in his mind, perhaps by taking a drug; *C-2*: Someone or something other than *M* may cause an image to appear in *M*'s mind; *C-3*: *M* is haunted by an image which appears spontaneously, recurrently, and unpredictably—a symptom, of perhaps a psychic disorder; and *C-4*: *M* simply produces an image, as I and all those with the requisite alpha rhythms are able to do, i.e., as a basic action.[5]

I shall not press for a full parity, though I *am* prepared to defend the view that there is a problem of Other Bodies precisely analogous to the problem of Other Minds. All I wish to empasize is that, whatever disparities there may be between the concept of mind and the concept of body, men may be said to act mentally in much the same way that they may be said to act physically. Among the things I take Descartes to have meant when he said that we are not in our bodies the way a pilot is in a ship, is that we do not always do things, as pilots must with ships, by causing them to happen. We do not turn, as it were, an inner wheel in order, through some elaborate transmission of impulse, to cause an external rudder to shift and, by so doing, get our boat to turn. We act directly. But then neither am I in my *mind* the way a pilot is in a ship. Or rather, I sometimes cause things to happen with my body and with my mind, and I sometimes just act with them directly, as when I perform basic actions. It is best, however, to avoid similes. Any philosophical problems we have with ourselves would only reappear in connection with anything sufficiently similar to us to be a suitable analogue. But if we find ourselves unintelligible, nothing sufficiently similar to us to be helpful is likely to be more clear.

NOTES

1. Thesis (3) is explored in detail in my paper, "What We Can Do," *The Journal of Philosophy* 60 (July 1963): 435–45.

2. The analogy between theory of knowledge and theory of action runs very

deep indeed, almost as though they were isomorphic models for some calculus. Obviously, there are things we can say about actions that do not hold for cognitions, etc., but this means very little. Suppose we have two models M-*i* and M-*j* for a calculus C, and suppose that "star" plays in the same role in M-*i* that "book" plays in M-*j*. It is hardly an argument against their both being models for C that we don't print stars or that books are not centers of solar systems. I shall use theory-of-knowledge features as a guide for structuring the theory of action. When the analogy gives way, it will be interesting to see why it does.

3. Though not always without some awkwardness. Suppose it was held that only sentences can be given which have the form of first-person reports of sense-experience, e.g., "I now see a reddish x. . . ." Such a sentence is not easily rendered as the conclusion of an inference, though it can be so rendered, I suppose, if I both knew that something x had an unmistakable taste and that whatever has this taste is red. Then, by tasting x and seeing only its silhouette, I might feel secure in inferring that I was seeing a reddish x. Of course there are philosophically crucial senses of "see" which would rule this out, and make it, indeed, self-contradictory to say both "I see a reddish x" and "I see the black silhouette of x."

4. It is not difficult to see why it should be thought that there are two distinct things in the case of trying. It is because we often speak of trying and failing. So, if we can try and also succeed, trying is one thing and succeeding is another. And if succeeding consists in raising an arm, *trying* here must be something different, since failing consists in *not*-raising one's arm, and trying then could hardly consist in raising it. But this is not the important sense of the word for the theory of action.

5. But I am not sure whether we are positively abnormal, or those who have no images are negatively abnormal.

25

Causal Power and Human Agency

Richard Taylor

In [my earlier essay] I tried to elicit the idea of power or efficacy that I believe is involved in the concept of causation, limiting myself mostly to causal relationships between inanimate things. We speak, however, not only of the powers of inanimate things such as acids, explosives, and engines, but also in various contexts of the powers of men. The various powers of inanimate things, sometimes also called "capacities," are not generally thought to be particularly problematical, and so it is quite natural for philosophers to suppose that essentially the same idea is operative in statements concerning the powers or capacities of men. Indeed, it is probably fair to say that the commonest thought underlying most philosophical theories of the causal determinism of human behavior is the supposition that the concept of a power or capacity of some object to do something is essentially the same, whether the object in question is an inanimate thing or a man. It is certainly not obvious, however, that one is saying the same sort of thing when he says that it is within his power, say, to wiggle his finger but not his ears, or when he says that a given acid has the power to dissolve a piece of zinc but not a piece of glass. In both cases there is a reference to a power, but perhaps not to powers of the same kind.

Yet there is one thing that powers of both kinds, if they are indeed different, have in common; namely, that in either case we can express the idea of power by the word "can." Thus, to say that it is within my power to move my

From *Action and Purpose* (New York: Humanities Press, 1973), pp. 40–56. Reprinted by permission of the author.

finger, but not my ears, amounts to saying that I *can* do the one but *cannot* do the other. Similarly, to say that a given acid has the power to dissolve zinc but not glass amounts to saying that it can dissolve the one but not the other.

I shall, then, elicit the idea expressed by "can" as it is used in contexts of human agency, but only in such very elementary contexts as imply neither special training, skill, strength, opportunity, position, nor office. I shall not, therefore, be concerned with such meanings as, "I can operate a typewriter" (which requires special training or skill), "I can run for the Senate" (which expresses the idea of opportunity), "I can do forty pushups" (which expresses the idea of strength or endurance), or "I can veto acts of the legislature" (which expresses the idea of a special position or office). Instead I shall restrict myself entirely to the idea expressed in such a simple assertion as "I can move my finger," wherein this is understood to mean that it is within my power to move my finger, and conveys nothing of the idea of special strength, opportunity, skill, training, or position. By thus limiting myself to the simplest possible case, which would otherwise be of no interest whatsoever, I hope to elucidate the simplest and most basic idea of the power of human agency, unencumbered by extraneous notions involved in more interesting and exciting examples. I therefore beg the reader to bear with this otherwise banal example, for while such an action as wiggling one's finger can hold no interest in itself, and is in fact chosen for its lack of significance, it will be used here repeatedly to shed light on one of the gravest and most persistent problems of philosophical thought.

I shall begin with a consideration of certain typical uses of "can" in contexts *not* involving human agency, as these ideas seem much easier to get at. It would, of course, be significant if the ideas of power, with respect both to men and to certain inanimate things, embodied in the notion of *can* turned out to be much the same, but it would be far more significant if the power of agency we ascribe to ourselves turned out to be utterly different from that of any inanimate thing.

THE IDEA OF "CAN" IN CONTEXTS OF INANIMATE THINGS

Let us consider first statements of the form "X can E," wherein X designates some inanimate thing and E some state, event, activity, or property. For example:

1. A triangle can be acute (but not one-sided).

2. (Lucretius thought that) atoms can swerve from their paths.

3. This can be the restaurant we ate in last year.

4. This acid can dissolve a piece of zinc.

Now these four statements seem to express all of the philosophically significant senses of "can" as it is applied to inanimate things. These are, respectively, three senses of *contingency,* which I shall call *logical, causal,* and *epistemic* contingency and, in the case of the fourth statement, the sense of a causal capacity, or better, of *hypothetical possibility.*

What I want most conscientiously and carefully to determine, then, is whether a statement such as

5. I can move my finger,

which embodies the "can" of human agency or power, expresses an idea essentially like that of any of the foregoing. However undramatic such an inquiry might seem in itself, it is nonetheless crucial and laden with grave consequences, for in numberless philosophical discussions, particularly those involving the issue of free will, writers have ineptly fitted the "I can" of agency first to one and then another of these meanings, as best suited whatever doctrine they were endeavoring to uphold, seldom separating these distinctions very well and thus producing more confusion than wisdom.

BASIC MODAL CONCEPTS

All five of the foregoing statements embody modal concepts; that is, in these cases, concepts of what is *possible,* as contrasted with statements of what does happen, what ought to happen, and so on. But the first four, quite obviously, do not express possibilities of the same kind. We must first of all disentangle these.

If we take the idea of impossibility as a generic and undefined one, we can then clearly define the ideas of *necessity, possibility,* and *contingency* in terms of it in this fashion:

E is necessary = ~ E is impossible.

E is possible = ~ (E is impossible).

E is contingent = ~ (~ E is impossible) and ~ (E is impossible).

Thus, more loosely, by these equivalences we can say that it is necessary that something should be such as it is, in case it is impossible that it should be otherwise; that it is possible, in case it is not impossible; and that it is contingent, in case it is neither necessary nor impossible. Now of course there is nothing sacrosanct about using the idea of *impossibility* as our basic and undefined term in defining the others. We could have begun with any of the other three and defined impossibility, together with the other two ideas, in terms of it. But somehow the idea of impossibility seems simpler and intuitively easier for most people to grasp, so we may as well have that as our undefined term.

It should perhaps be noted, however, that the idea of *contingency,* as it is here defined, is not the same as that of *possibility.* Anything which is, in any sense, necessary—such as, that a cube has twelve edges—is in that same sense also possible; but it is not therefore contingent. It is this idea of contingency, as applying to those things that are neither impossible nor necessary, that will be crucial in the development of the ideas which follow.

Since it is the idea of impossibility that is left undefined in the foregoing definitions we can next elicit, without trying to define, three quite distinct and familiar kinds of impossibility. By so doing we can then easily derive, by the foregoing equivalences, three distinct kinds of contingency, and these will correspond exactly with the first three senses of "can" that were illustrated in our first four statements above. The fourth sense of "can," which does not express the idea of contingency at all, will be treated separately.

LOGICAL CONTINGENCY

In the first place, then, and most obviously, a proposition is logically impossible if it is self-contradictory—for example, "A one-sided triangle exists." This is not intended as a definition of logical impossibility, for it is my stated purpose to define logical contingency in terms of logical impossibility; thus the concept of logical impossibility, tolerably clear without definition, is assumed. Now some philosophers have spoken as though this is the only sense in which anything is ever *really* impossible, but we need not involve ourselves in that odd contention. The only thing to note is that something is *contingent* in this logical sense, according to our foregoing equivalences, when it is not logically impossible either that it should or should not exist. It is logically possible for a triangle to be acute, for instance, and just as logically possible for it to be obtuse, an idea that is well expressed by saying that it logically *can* be either, that neither property is logically impossible. This, then, is the first of our four senses of "can."

CAUSAL CONTINGENCY

In the second place something is, in a perfectly familiar sense, *causally* impossible if there exist conditions sufficient, but not logically sufficient, for its nonexistence, or for the existence of something causally incompatible with it. The kind of impossibility here referred to is, then, precisely the causal impossibility introduced in the foregoing [essay], which was not defined there, as it is not defined here. Thus, it is in fact impossible under normal circumstances for a man to live long after ingesting a certain quantity of cyanide, or for gasoline-soaked rags not to ignite when brought into contact with fire under certain conditions—though there are no *logical* impossibilities here involved. To say, then, that something is *contingent* in this causal sense is equivalent, by our definition, to saying that neither its occurrence nor its nonoccurrence is in *this* sense impossible, or that existing conditions are causally sufficient neither for its occurrence nor its nonoccurrence—in short, that it is *uncaused.* Now many philosophers deny that anything in nature *is* contingent, in this causal sense, but this is not to the point. No one would deny that some things are, in this sense, impossible; our purpose is merely to give content to the *idea* of contingency, defined in terms of this perfectly familiar sense of impossibility. Moreover, some theoretical physicists believe, as did Lucretius, that some things in nature *are* causally contingent. Again the correctness of their opinion is irrelevant, but there can at least be no doubt about what they mean.

This, of course, is the second sense of "can" that was illustrated above. If it were *true* of a given particle that its behavior was not causally determined, then we could say that it can, for instance, swerve, and also that it can fail to swerve, expressing exactly the idea of causal contingency.

EPISTEMIC CONTINGENCY

In the third place, something is sometimes spoken of as impossible when it is only known to be false, though this is admittedly a philosophically odd, though nonetheless common, sense of "impossible." Someone might say, for example, "But that man *can't* be my father," meaning only that he knows he is not, or, "It is impossible for her to have been at the theater," again meaning that it is known that she was not. We can call this an epistemic sense of impossibility, and an epistemically contingent state or event is therefore one concerning which it is not *known* whether it occurred, or will occur, or not. This is the third sense of "can" that was illustrated and it is, in fact, exceedingly common. Thus, a man might say of a familiar-looking place that it *can* be the restaurant he ate in a year ago, at the same time realizing that it can be entirely new to him. Similarly I might say, after tossing a normal coin but before looking to see what came up, that it can be heads and it can be tails, even though knowing that in the *causal* sense one or the other of these speculations is impossible. Or one might even say of a column of figures that its sum can be 720, or it can be 721, meaning only that he does not yet know which, even though he knows that one or the other of these is *logically* impossible.

CAPACITIES

Now the fourth sense of "can" illustrated above is perhaps the most common of all. Unlike the other three, however, it expresses no idea of contingency at all, but the very opposite. "Can" is, in other words, in this sense, an expression of a *capacity,* or of what *does* happen—indeed, what *must* happen—in case certain conditions are met. It thus conveys the idea of a *causal connection* between certain states or events. For example, the statement "This acid can dissolve a piece of zinc" does not mean merely that it is logically contingent whether a piece of zinc would dissolve in it (though it is), nor, manifestly, that if some zinc were to dissolve in it, the dissolving would be *uncaused,* nor, equally obviously, that we do not *know* what would happen to a piece of zinc in that acid. It means that if some zinc *were* dropped in the acid, it would dissolve—that the chemical composition of the acid is sufficient, assuming certain other conditions to hold, for a lump of zinc's dissolving in it. And this, far from suggesting that the behavior of the zinc in those conditions is *contingent,* entails the very opposite; namely, that this behavior is causally necessitated by those conditions, or that any other behavior of the zinc under those conditions is causally impossible.

"MIGHT AND MIGHT NOT"

It should be noted next, then, that the first three senses of "can," but emphatically not the fourth, can be conveyed equally by the expression "might," so understood as to mean "might *and* might not." Thus, I could say of a red ball that it might be black, expressing the idea that its color is logically (though perhaps neither causally nor epistemically) contingent. Similarly, if I tossed a coin whose behavior was, let us suppose, causally undetermined, I could say that it might come heads and it might come tails, expressing the idea that the outcome is causally contingent. And finally, I could say of a familiar-looking restaurant that I might have eaten there before, and I might not have, only making the point that I do not know which.

But note that if I say of a jar of acid that is before me that it can dissolve a piece of zinc, I do *not* mean that a piece of zinc dropped into it might dissolve and might not. On the contrary, my whole point is that it *would* dissolve, or that, under those conditions, could not *but* dissolve, and I mean to *deny* that it might not.

THE "CAN" OF HUMAN AGENCY

Let us now turn to the idea expressed by "can" as it figures in certain contexts of human agency, such as our fifth statement, to see whether it is essentially the same as any one of the above, or whether it is, as I believe, an idea different from any of these.

The statement "I can move my finger," as well as the statement "I can hold my finger still," are *both* true (though their joint truth obviously does not entail that I can do both *at once*). This I take to be quite certain, and if anyone should doubt the truth of either, then I could show him in the most direct manner possible that he should not have doubted it. If, then, there is any philosophical theory which entails that one or the other of these statements must be false—and I believe there have been many such theories—then that theory is most doubtful.

What, then, do I mean by "can" in such statements? Obviously, I do not mean merely that it is *logically contingent* whether I move my finger, (although it is). If a physician were to ask me whether I can move it, he would not be inquiring whether it would be self-contradictory to suppose that I do, or that I do not. He already knows that it would not, without asking.

Nor do I mean merely that it is *epistemically contingent,* although perhaps it is. That is, when I say I can move my finger, the point I am making is plainly not that I do not happen to *know* whether I am going to move it, (though I may not). If a physician were to ask me whether I can move it, he would not be asking me to guess, speculate, or hazard a prediction concerning whether I am apt to move it.

It follows, therefore, that if "can," in this context, expresses an idea essentially like any I have elicited, then it expressed either the idea of *causal contingency,* the second sense of "can" illustrated, or of *hypothetical possibility* or *capacity,* the fourth sense. The remainder of this [essay] will be devoted to showing that it embodies neither of these ideas, but has a totally different meaning; while this meaning entails that the event in question—a finger motion, in this case—is causally contingent (and hence, that one important version of the doctrine of free will is true), it is not equivalent to that.

HYPOTHETICAL POSSIBILITY

Let us consider first, then, the suggestion, very commonly found in philosophical literature, that statements like our fifth one, "I can move my finger," express the idea of a causal capacity or hypothetical possibility, and are thus like our fourth statement, "This acid can dissolve a piece of zinc." If this is so, then statements expressing the "can" of human agency must, like this latter one, embody the idea that *if* an event of a certain kind were to happen, then something quite different—a finger motion, in the case we are considering— would follow as a result.

Now the statement about the acid and zinc expresses, we noted, the idea of a capacity, or better, the idea of a *causal relationship* between different events or states—a piece of zinc being dropped into a certain volume of acid, on the one hand, and its dissolving, on the other. It is thus equivalent to a hypothetical in the subjunctive, or a statement about what would happen, in case something else happened. If, accordingly, the statement about my finger expresses essentially the same idea, then it too must be equivalent to some subjunctive hypothetical expressing the idea of a causal relationship between different events or states—some as yet unnamed event or state, presumably within me, on the one hand, and a finger motion, on the other. Or, to put the same point more vividly, if I am asked by the physician whether I can move my finger, and I reply that I *can,* then what I am telling him, if "can" here (as in the acid and zinc case) expresses a hypothetical possibility, is that *if* there should occur within me a certain (unnamed) event or state, then the finger motion would at once follow as a causal consequence.

Now that is certainly *not* what is expressed by "can" in this context. This can be seen very clearly from the fact that such hypotheticals as do undoubtedly express a genuine causal relationship between some antecedent occurrent state or event and some bodily change—such as a motion of my finger—regarded as its effect, do not even appear to convey the idea of "can" that we are seeking. There is the concomitant observation that such hypotheticals as do express this idea of "can" are mere grammatical equivalences, and far from conveying the idea of any discovered or discoverable causal relationships, state purely logical relationships between concepts; these are thereby ruled out *ab initio* as causal statements. We find, in short, that there is no hypothetical statement or set of such statements which, as in the acid and zinc case, *both* (a) expresses the idea of a causal relationship between events or states, *and* (b) expresses the idea of "can" that we are after. It has been one of the most persistent errors of philosophy to suppose that, since it is not hard to find hypotheticals that express the one idea or the other, and since both kinds *are* hypotheticals and thus grammatically and logically similar, then *some* one or more of them must somehow express both ideas at once.

Thus, it is very easy to supply subjunctive hypotheticals expressing a genuine causal relationship between some event or state within me, say, and the motion of my finger, which do not, however, convey anything like the idea of "can" that we are seeking, but which nevertheless express precisely the idea of "can" involved in the acid and zinc case. We can say, for instance, that if a certain muscle, well known to anatomists, were to contract, then my finger would move; but this might still be true, even if *I cannot* move my finger—for example, in case I cannot move the muscle in question. Again, if I happen to be subject to spasms of a certain kind, we can say that if a nerve impulse of such and such a kind were to occur, perhaps in my brain, then my finger would twitch. But this is not equivalent to saying that *I* can move my finger, for I might have no control over the occurrence of those impulses. Nor, let it be noted, does it approach any closer to saying that I can, if someone arbitrarily baptizes such an empirically discoverable nerve impulse, say, a "volition." A physician would not conclude that I can move my finger merely upon learning that I am subject to spasms of that sort. He might, in fact, reasonably regard it as evidence to the contrary.

We must, then, rule out these inappropriate hypotheticals—not because they do not express the idea of a causal relationship (for manifestly they do), and not because they do not express the idea of "can" as it is embodied in the acid and zinc case (for they do express that idea exactly), but because they do not express the idea of *I can.*

"VOLITIONS"

It might be tempting at this point to suggest that "I can" expresses the idea of a genuine causal relationship in which a special kind of event fills the role of the cause—namely, a certain internal or *mental* occurrence, introspectively discoverable, and known to philosophers as an *act of will* or (synonymously) a *volition.* Thus, to be specific, the statement "I can move my finger" must express the idea that if there were to occur somewhere within me or perhaps "within my mind" a particular one of these special events—namely, a motion-of-this-finger volitional event—I would find that event to be at once followed by a motion of the finger in question, which I might then reasonably conclude was its effect.

But if we refuse to be beguiled by the profundity of such a description, and just look at the picture it brings forth, how absurd it becomes! Surely when I say I can move my finger, and know that what I am saying is true, I am not expressing the idea of a causal connection between the behavior of my finger and some such internal hocus-pocus as this, the occurrence of which I can seriously doubt. Besides, even if this picture were not quite fantastic from the standpoint of ordinary experience, we can wonder whether I *can* bring about such an internal mental cause, and in particular, whether I can perform inwardly the elaborate and complicated set of such causes evidently needed in order to make my finger move in a similarly elaborate and complicated way, and if so, what "can" might mean in *this* case. If I *can,* then to what further internal events are *these* causally related? And if I *cannot,* how can we still say that I can move my finger after all?

NONCAUSAL HYPOTHETICALS

Not having found quite what we want in this direction, we turn more hopefully to those hypotheticals which in common usage do express just the idea of "can" that we are after, to see whether they might *also* be construed as expressing the idea of a causal relationship. But here we find that those usually proposed as substitutes are merely conventional equivalences of meaning rather than expressions of discovered causal connections. We also find that not only do we have no reason whatever for supposing that they express causal relationships between occurrent events or states, but that they simply cannot express such a connection; in fact, if so interpreted, they yield the same kind of absurdity as our previous example.

It is generally supposed, for example, that such a statement as, "I can move my finger," is equivalent to the hypothetical, "I will move my finger if I want to." And so it is—but this second statement surely does not express a causal relationship between occurrent events or states. If it did, we would have to understand it to mean that the occurrence within me of a certain state or event of a rather special kind, namely, of a certain wanting or craving for finger motions, would set my finger in motion, which is at best a doubtful picture, such "wantings" as this having every semblance of fiction. If we asked someone who had just moved his finger, *why* he had done so, and got the reply that he did so because he wanted to, we would be no wiser, recognizing that an explanation had been refused rather than given, only the fact itself being repeated that he had jolly well moved it. "I will move my finger if I want to" is essentially no different from "I'll have one more drink if I want to," uttered in a tone of defiance. Such a hypothetical can hardly, in justice to common sense, be construed as expressing any discoverable causal connections between events or states, whether these be "internal" or "external," "mental" or "physical."

For this and other reasons we must reject the other hypothetical renditions of "I can" that suggest themselves, such as "I will if I try," "if I intend," "if I wish," "if I choose," "if it suits my purpose," "if there's any point to it," and so on. Now all these hypotheticals can, let it be noted, be regarded as equivalent *in meaning* to the categorical, "I can." But being each of them equivalent in meaning to the same thing, they are equivalent in meaning to each other—which by itself sufficiently shows that they are not expressions of a causal relationship between occurrent events or states. For the events or states properly called "trying," "wishing," "intending," "having as one's purpose," and so on, if these be regarded as events or states that might actually occur within me, are *not* the same. Hypotheticals embodying these concepts, then, if they were interpreted as referring to such occurrent states or events, could not be equivalent in meaning. They are vastly more like such a pair of hypotheticals as, "You may have orange juice if you like" and "You may have orange juice if you choose," which are surely exactly equivalent, and neither of which means anything like "You may have orange juice if there is any." Both, in fact, mean no more than "You may have orange juice."

If, moreover, we ask, in the case of *any* such hypothetical that is seriously proposed as an expression of the relation between a cause and its effect, what might be the criterion for deciding whether it is *true,* we find this criterion to be the very occurrence of that event which is supposed to be regarded as the effect, rendering the relationship embodied in the hypothetical, not the empirically discoverable one of a cause to its effect, but the logical one of entailment between concepts. The fact, however, that a given event occurs, can never *entail* that another wholly different one will occur, or has occurred, if the relation between them is that of cause to effect. The fact, for example, that a piece of zinc is dropped into a volume of a certain acid cannot *entail* that it dissolves, nor vice versa, and if there were such entailment, the relation embodied in the hypothetical expressing that fact could not at the same time be regarded as one of causation. Suppose, then, that someone moves his finger, and we propose as a *causal* explanation for this, that he *wanted* to move it. How shall we, or the agent himself, decide whether this was in fact the cause? How do we, or how does he, know that this motion was not caused by, say, his wanting to move a different finger, or even his wanting to move his toe? Has anyone had numerous occasions to observe within himself this particular *want,* and then come to the realization that it is in fact always soon followed by that particular motion, until he has finally come to expect the one upon finding the occurrence of the other? Plainly not. Our entire *criterion* for saying what he *wanted* (or tried, or intended, or whatnot) to do, is what he in fact *did;* we do not infer the former from the latter, on the basis of what we have in fact found, but we regard the former as something *entailed* by what we now find, namely, just his moving that finger. This by itself shows that the relation expressed in the hypothetical, "I will move my finger if I want to," is, if the hypothetical is true at all, a logical relationship between concepts, resting only on an equivalence of meaning, and as such *cannot* be a causal relationship between states or events.

SIMPLE CAUSAL CAPACITIES AND SIMPLE POWERS

One final consideration, though a fairly technical one, will serve to show further the dissimilarity between the "can" of agency and that of causal capacity; namely, that while in the case of the latter a certain type of subjunctive inference is not destroyed by the supposition that it is physically impossible for the capacity in question to be realized, such an inference is not always possible in the case of an agent.

Let us suppose, for example, that a given volume of acid has at a certain time the power to dissolve a given piece of zinc. Suppose further, however, that conditions are such as to render it physically impossible that it should then do so. We can suppose, for instance, that the piece of zinc in question is in a vault, heavily guarded, and so on, such that it is physically impossible for the acid then to dissolve it. We can nevertheless affirm that the acid still has the capacity to dissolve it, meaning by this, of course, that if (contrary to fact) that piece of zinc were then in the acid, under easily specifiable conditions, the acid would then be dissolving it.

But now suppose that conditions are such as to render it causally impossible for me to move my finger. We can suppose, for instance, that my hand is encased in a strong and tight cast, rendering any manual movement whatever impossible. Now here we *cannot* affirm that it is nevertheless within my power to move my finger. Unlike the capacity or power of the acid, my power is cancelled by the physical impossibility of exercising it. We cannot say that if (contrary to fact) the cast were not now on my hand, then I *would* move my finger. The most we can say is that, were it not for the cast, I *could* move it, that it would be within my power to move it. A looser way of expressing this difference is to say that when every impediment to the realization of an ordinary causal capacity of an inanimate thing is removed, then that capacity is forthwith realized, whereas when every impediment to the exercise of a simple human power is removed, then that power *can* be exercised. It is still up to the agent in question whether that power is in fact exercised or not.

CAUSAL CONTINGENCY

We may conclude, then, that "can," in the context we are considering, does not, unlike the zinc and acid case, express the idea of causal capacity, or hypothetical possibility. The only thing left, therefore, if we are to suppose that it expresses a meaning similar to any of the first four I elicited, is to see if it expresses the idea of *causal contingency*.

In this case, the statement, "I can move my finger," means that my finger might move and it might not, where "might and might not" expresses the idea that the event in question is, not merely epistemically, but *causally* contingent, or that there are no conditions either causally sufficient for or causally incompatible with my finger's moving.

It is easy to show, however, that this is *not* the meaning of "can" in this case, for it is quite possible that the statement "I can move my finger" is false, even in a situation in which "My finger might move and it might not," understood in the sense of causal contingency, is true. Suppose, for example, that I am paralyzed, so that I cannot, by hypothesis, move my finger. It is nevertheless imaginable that, despite this circumstance, my finger *does* move from time to time, and that its motions are uncaused. No doubt this never happens, but the point is that if it were to happen it would not warrant us to say that I can move my finger; it just moves, in this case, without my having anything to do with it.

One other possibility remains, and that is to insist that there is an essential difference between *my* moving my finger, and my finger merely *moving,* and hence, that "I can move my finger" expresses, not simply the idea that any motions of my finger are causally contingent, but, more significantly, that it is causally contingent whether *I* produce them.

That there is this essential difference seems beyond question, for my moving my finger is not even materially equivalent to my finger's moving, the first always entailing but never being entailed by the latter. To concede this, however, is already to abandon the possibility of understanding human agency according to the model of inanimate behavior, for in the case of the latter *no* such distinction ever need be made. The tree's waving its branches *is* equivalent to its branches waving, and the acid's dissolving the zinc *is* equivalent to the zinc's dissolving in the acid, assuming no other solvent to be present. Even in the case of robots and computing machines, we can describe completely what they *do* merely by describing what *happens* (in their wires, vacuum tubes, etc.), without any reference to their *doing* anything at all.

Quite apart from this, however, it can be shown that while the statement "I can move my finger" together with the statement "I can hold my finger still" *entails* that my moving my finger is causally contingent, and hence, that the motions of my finger are themselves causally contingent, it is not *equivalent* to that. If this is so, then the meaning of "can," in this context, evidently does not correspond to *any* familiar meaning it has in contexts involving only inanimate things.

The statements "I can move my finger" and "I can hold my finger still" are, I said, normally both true, though their joint truth does not entail that I can do both at once. If, however, existing conditions are causally sufficient for my moving my finger, then it follows that it is causally impossible for me not to move it. If, on the other hand, existing conditions are causally sufficient for my holding it still, then it is causally impossible for me to move it. Since, however, it is true both that I can move it and that I can hold it still, it follows that neither is causally impossible.

That the statement "I can move my finger" does not express *just* this idea, however—that is, is not equivalent to saying that I might move it and I might not, understanding this in the sense of causal contingency—follows from the fact that this latter might be true in circumstances in which the former is not. That is, it might be true that it is causally contingent whether I move my finger (and not merely whether my finger moves), and yet false that I both can move it, and can hold it still. Suppose, for example, that I have a roulette wheel whose behavior is really causally contingent—for example, one whose end state is no exact function of the force with which it is spun. Suppose, further, that I resolve to move my finger if it stops on an odd number, and to hold it still if it stops on an even one, and that there are conditions (the certainty of death if I fail, for instance) sufficient for my not changing my resolve. Now in this situation it is certainly true that I might move my finger and I might not, understanding "might and might not" to express causal contingency. Until the wheel stops there are no conditions sufficient for my doing the one, and none sufficient for my doing the other. Yet it is not true that I *can* move it, and *also* that I *can* hold it still, assuming that my resolve *cannot* change. I know that I might move it, and that I might not, but not only do I not know whether I will move it—I do not even know, until the wheel stops, and assuming that I *cannot* change my resolve, whether I *can* move it. I just have to wait and see. What I do, in this situation, is no longer *up to me,* but entirely dependent on the behavior of a wheel over which I have no control.

"POWER"

I conclude, then, that "can" in the statement "I can move my finger" does not *ever* mean what it means when applied to inanimate things, although it *entails* what is meant by that word as it might be applied to some extraordinary inanimate thing, namely, one whose behavior is uncaused. What *else* is meant by "can," in this case, in addition to meaning that my moving my finger is causally contingent, is suggested by what was just said; namely, that whether or not I *do* move my finger is "up to me" or, to use a more archaic expression, is something "within my power." And this is certainly a philosophically baffling expression which I feel sure no one can ever analyze; yet it *is* something that is well understood. One can sometimes know perfectly, for example, that it is up to him, or in his power, to move his finger, and one can sometimes— as in the sort of example just considered—know that it is not up to him, but up to something else, even if it should nevertheless be contingent. We therefore understand what it *is* for something to be in our power, and the fact that no one can *say* what it is is no disconfirmation of this. This notion, however, is *never* embodied in the meaning of "can" as it is used with reference to physical things; for it never makes sense to say that it is up to a volume of acid whether it dissolves a lump of zinc, or up to a tree whether it waves its branches, or that it is within the power even of a causally undetermined roulette wheel whether it picks an odd number or an even one.

26

Actions, Reasons, and Causes

Donald Davidson

What is the relation between a reason and an action when the reason explains the action by giving the agent's reason for doing what he did? We may call such explanations *rationalizations,* and say that the reason *rationalizes* the action.

In this paper I want to defend the ancient—and common-sense—position that rationalization is a species of ordinary causal explanation. The defense no doubt requires some redeployment, but not more or less complete abandonment of the position, as urged by many recent writers.[1]

I

A reason rationalizes an action only if it leads us to see something the agent saw, or thought he saw, in his action—some feature, consequence, or aspect of the action the agent wanted, desired, prized, held dear, thought dutiful, beneficial, obligatory, or agreeable. We cannot explain why someone did what he did simply by saying the particular action appealed to him; we must indicate what it was about the action that appealed. Whenever someone does something for a reason, therefore, he can be characterized as (a) having some sort of pro attitude toward actions of a certain kind, and (b) believing (or knowing, perceiving, noticing, remembering) that his action is of that kind.

From the *Journal of Philosophy* 60 (1963): pp. 685–700. Copyright © 1963 by Journal of Philosophy, Inc. Reprinted by permission of the author and the publisher.

Under (a) are to be included desires, wantings, urges, promptings, and a great variety of moral views, aesthetic principles, economic prejudices, social conventions, and public and private goals and values in so far as these can be interpreted as attitudes of an agent directed toward actions of a certain kind. The word "attitude" does yeoman service here, for it must cover not only permanent character traits that show themselves in a lifetime of behavior, like love of children or a taste for loud company, but also the most passing fancy that prompts a unique action, like a sudden desire to touch a woman's elbow. In general, pro attitudes must not be taken for convictions, however temporary, that every action of a certain kind ought to be performed, is worth performing, or is, all things considered, desirable. On the contrary, a man may all his life have a yen, say, to drink a can of paint, without ever, even at the moment he yields, believing it would be worth doing.

Giving the reason why an agent did something is often a matter of naming the pro attitude (*a*) or the related belief (*b*) or both; let me call this pair the *primary reason* why the agent performed the action. Now it is possible to reformulate the claim that rationalizations are causal explanations, and give structure to the argument as well, by stating two theses about primary reasons:

1. For us to understand how a reason of any kind rationalizes an action it is necessary and sufficient that we see, at least in essential outline, how to construct a primary reason.

2. The primary reason for an action is its cause.

I shall argue for these points in turn.

II

I flip the switch, turn on the light, and illuminate the room. Unbeknownst to me I also alert a prowler to the fact that I am home. Here I do not do four things, but only one, of which four descriptions have been given.[2] I flipped the switch because I wanted to turn on the light, and by saying I wanted to turn on the light I explain (give my reason for, rationalize) the flipping. But I do not, by giving this reason, rationalize my alerting of the prowler nor my illuminating of the room. Since reasons may rationalize what someone does when it is described in one way and not when it is described in another, we cannot treat what was done simply as a term in sentences like "My reason for flipping the switch was that I wanted to turn on the light"; otherwise we would be forced to conclude, from the fact that flipping the switch was identical with alerting the prowler, that my reason for alerting the prowler was that I wanted to turn on the light. Let us mark this quasi-intentional[3] character of action descriptions in rationalizations by stating a bit more precisely a necessary condition for primary reasons:

C_1. R is a primary reason why an agent performed the action A under the description d only if R consists of a pro attitude of the agent toward actions with a certain property, and a belief of the agent that A, under the description d, has that property.

How can my wanting to turn on the light be (part of) a primary reason, since it appears to lack the required element of generality? We may be taken in by the verbal parallel between "I turned on the light" and "I wanted to turn on the light." The first clearly refers to a particular event, so we conclude that the second has this same event as its object. Of course it is obvious that the event of my turning on the light can't be referred to in the same way by both sentences, since the existence of the event is required by the truth of "I turned on the light" but not by the truth of "I wanted to turn on the light." If the reference were the same in both cases, the second sentence would entail the first; but in fact the sentences are logically independent. What is less obvious, at least until we attend to it, is that the event whose occurrence makes "I turned on the light" true cannot be called the object, however intentional, of "I wanted to turn on the light." If I turned on the light, then I must have done it at a precise moment, in a particular way—every detail is fixed. But it makes no sense to demand that my want be directed at an action performed at any one moment or done in some unique manner. Any one of an indefinitely large number of actions would satisfy the want, and can be considered equally eligible as its object. Wants and desires often are trained on physical objects. However, "I want that gold watch in the window" is not a primary reason, and explains why I went into the store only because it suggests a primary reason—for example, that I wanted to buy the watch.

Because "I wanted to turn on the light" and "I turned on the light" are logically independent, the first can be used to give a reason why the second is true. Such a reason gives minimal information: it implies that the action was intentional, and wanting tends to exclude some other pro attitudes, such as a sense of duty or obligation. But the exclusion depends very much on the action and the context of explanation. Wanting seems pallid beside lusting, but it would be odd to deny that someone who lusted after a woman or a cup of coffee wanted her or it. It is not unnatural, in fact, to treat wanting as a genus including all pro attitudes as species. When we do this and when we know some action is intentional, it is empty to add that the agent wanted to do it. In such cases, it is easy to answer the question "Why did you do it?" with "For no reason," meaning not that there is no reason but that there is no *further* reason, no reason that cannot be inferred from the fact that the action was done intentionally; no reason, in other words, besides wanting to do it. This last point is not essential to the present argument, but it is of interest because it defends the possibility of defining an intentional action as one done for a reason.

A primary reason consists of a belief and an attitude, but it is generally otiose to mention both. If you tell me you are easing the jib because you think that will stop the main from backing, I don't need to be told that you want to stop the main from backing; and if you say you are biting your thumb at me because you want to insult me, there is no point in adding that you think that by biting your thumb at me you will insult me. Similarly, many explanations of actions in terms of reasons that are not primary do not require mention of the primary reason to complete the story. If I say I am pulling weeds because I want a beautiful lawn, it would be fatuous to eke out the account with "And so I see something desirable in any action that does, or has a good chance of, making the lawn beautiful." Why insist that there is any *step,* logical or psychological, in the transfer of desire from an end that is not an action to the actions one conceives as means? It serves the argument as well that the desired end explains the action only if what are believed by the agent to be means are desired.

Fortunately, it is not necessary to classify and analyze the many varieties of emotions, sentiments, moods, motives, passions, and hungers whose mention may answer the question "Why did you do it?" in order to see how, when such mention rationalizes the action, a primary reason is involved. Claustrophobia gives a man's reason for leaving a cocktail party because we know people want to avoid, escape from, be safe from, put distance between themselves and, what they fear. Jealousy is the motive in a poisoning because, among other things, the poisoner believes his action will harm his rival, remove the cause of his agony, or redress an injustice, and these are the sorts of things a jealous man wants to do. When we learn a man cheated his son out of greed, we do not necessarily know what the primary reason was, but we know there was one, and its general nature. Ryle analyzes "he boasted from vanity" into "he boasted on meeting the stranger and his doing so satisfies the lawlike proposition that whenever he finds a chance of securing the admiration and envy of others, he does whatever he thinks will produce this admiration and envy" (*The Concept of Mind,* 89). This analysis is often, and perhaps justly, criticized on the ground that a man may boast from vanity just once. But if Ryle's boaster did what he did from vanity, then something entailed by Ryle's analysis is true: the boaster wanted to secure the admiration and envy of others, and he believed that his action would produce this admiration and envy; true or false, Ryle's analysis does not dispense with primary reasons, but depends upon them.

To know a primary reason why someone acted as he did is to know an intention with which the action was done. If I turn left at the fork because I want to get to Katmandu, my intention in turning left is to get to Katmandu. But to know the intention is not necessarily to know the primary reason in full detail. If James goes to church with the intention of pleasing his mother, then he must have some pro attitude toward pleasing his mother, but it needs more information to tell whether his reason is that he enjoys pleasing his mother, or thinks it right, his duty, or an obligation. The expression "the intention with which James went to church" has the outward form of a description, but in fact it is syncategorematic and cannot be taken to refer to an entity, state, disposition, or event. Its function is context is to generate new descriptions of actions in terms of their reasons; thus "James went to church with the intention of pleasing his mother" yields a new, and fuller, description of the action described in "James went to church." Essentially the same process goes on when I answer the question "Why are you bobbing around that way?" with "I'm knitting, weaving, exercising, sculling, cuddling, training fleas."

Straight description of an intended result often explains an action better than stating that the result was intended or desired. "It will soothe your nerves" explains why I pour you a shot as efficiently as "I want to do something to soothe your nerves," since the first in the context of explanation implies the second; but the first does better, because, if it is true, the facts will justify my choice of action. Because justifying and explaining an action so often go hand in hand, we frequently indicate the primary reason for an action by making a claim which, if true, would also verify, vindicate, or support the relevant belief or attitude of the agent. "I knew I ought to return it," "The paper said it was going to snow," "You stepped on *my* toes," all, in appropriate reason-giving contexts, perform this familiar dual function.

The justifying role of a reason, given this interpretation, depends upon the explanatory role, but the converse does not hold. Your stepping on my toes neither explains nor justifies my stepping on your toes unless I believe you stepped on my toes, but the belief alone, true or false, explains my action.

III

In the light of a primary reason, an action is revealed as coherent with certain traits, long- or short-termed, characteristic or not, of the agent, and the agent is shown in his role of Rational Animal. Corresponding the the belief and attitude of a primary reason for an action, we can always construct (with a little ingenuity) the premises of a syllogism from which it follows that the action has some (as Miss Anscombe calls it) "desirability characteristic."[4] Thus there is a certain irreducible—though somewhat anemic—sense in which every rationalization justifies: from the agent's point of view there was, when he acted, something to be said for the action.

Noting that nonteleological causal explanations do not display the element of justification provided by reasons, some philosophers have concluded that the concept of cause that applies elsewhere cannot apply to the relation between reasons and actions, and that the pattern of justification provides, in the case of reasons, the required explanation. But suppose we grant that reasons alone justify in explaining actions; it does not follow that the explanation is not also—and necessarily—causal. Indeed our first condition for primary reasons (C_1) is designed to help set rationalizations apart from other sorts of explanation. If rationalization is, as I want to argue, a species of causal explanation, then justification, in the sense given by C_1, is at least one differentiating property. How about the other claim: that justifying is a kind of explaining, so that the ordinary notion of cause need not be brought in? Here it is necessary to decide what is being included under justification. Perhaps it means only what is given by C_1: that the agent has certain beliefs and attitudes in the light of which the action is reasonable. But then something essential has certainly been left out, for a person can have a reason for an action, and perform the action, and yet this reason not be the reason why he did it. Central to the relation between a reason and an action it explains is the idea that the agent performed the action *because* he had the reason. Of course, we can include this idea too in justification; but then the notion of justification becomes as dark as the notion of reason until we can account for the force of that "because."

When we ask why someone acted as he did, we want to be provided with an interpretation. His behavior seems strange, alien, outré, pointless, out of character, disconnected; or perhaps we cannot even recognize an action in it. When we learn his reason, we have an interpretation, a new description of what he did which fits it into a familiar picture. The picture certainly includes some of the agent's beliefs and attitudes; perhaps also goals, ends, principles, general character traits, virtues or vices. Beyond this, the redescription of an action afforded by a reason may place the action in a wider social, economic, linguistic, or evaluative context. To learn, through learning the reason, that the agent conceived his action as a lie, a repayment of a debt, an insult, the fulfillment of an avuncular obligation, or a knight's gambit is to grasp the point of the action in its setting of rules, practices, conventions, and expectations.

Remarks like these, inspired by the later Wittgenstein, have been elaborated with subtlety and insight by a number of philosophers. And there is no denying that this is true: when we explain an action, by giving the reason, we do redescribe the action; redescribing the action gives the action a place in a pattern, and in this way the action is explained. Here it is tempting to draw two conclusions that do not follow. First, we can't infer, from the fact that giving reasons merely redescribes the action and that causes are separate from effects, that therefore reasons are not causes. Reasons, being beliefs and attitudes, are certainly not identical with actions; but, more important, events are often redescribed in terms of their causes. (Suppose someone was injured. We could redescribe this event "in terms of a cause" by saying he was burned.) Second, it is an error to think that, because placing the action in a larger pattern explains it, therefore we now understand the sort of explanation involved. Talk of patterns and contexts does not answer the question of how reasons explain actions, since the relevant pattern or context contains both reason and action. One way we can explain an event is by placing it in the context of its cause; cause and effect form the sort of pattern that explains the effect, in a sense of "explain" that we understand as well as any. If reason and action illustrate a different pattern of explanation, that pattern must be identified.

Let me urge the point in connection with an example of Melden's. A man driving an automobile raises his arm in order to signal. His intention, to signal, explains his action, raising his arm, by redescribing it as signalling. What is the pattern that explains the action? Is it the familiar pattern of an action done for a reason? Then it does indeed explain the action, but only because it assumes the relation of reason and action that we want to analyze. Or is the pattern rather this: the man is driving, he is approaching a turn; he knows he ought to signal; he knows how to signal, by raising his arm. And now, in this context, he raises his arm. Perhaps, as Melden suggests, if all this happens, he does signal. And the explanation would then be this: if, under these conditions, a man raises his arm, then he signals. The difficulty is, of course, that this explanation does not touch the question of why he raised his arm. He had a reason to raise his arm, but this has not been shown to be the reason why he did it. If the description "signalling" explains his action by giving his reason, then the signalling must be intentional; but, on the account just given, it may not be.

If, as Melden claims, causal explanations are "wholly irrelevant to the understanding we seek" of human actions (184) then we are without an analysis of the "because" in "He did it because . . . ," where we go on to name a reason. Hampshire remarks, of the relation between reasons and action, "In philosophy one ought surely to find this . . . connection altogether mysterious" (166). Hampshire rejects Aristotle's attempt to solve the mystery by introducing the concept of wanting as a causal factor, on the grounds that the resulting theory is too clear and definite to fit all cases and that "There is still no compelling ground for insisting that the word 'want' *must* enter into every full statement of reasons for acting" (168). I agree that the concept of wanting is too narrow, but I have argued that, at least in a vast number of typical cases, some pro attitude must be assumed to be present if a statement of an agent's reasons in acting is to be intelligible. Hampshire does not see how Aristotle's scheme can be appraised as true or false, "for it is not clear what could be the basis of assessment, or what kind of evidence could be decisive" (167). Failing a satisfactory alternative, the best argument for a scheme like Aristotle's is that it alone promises to give an account of the "mysterious connection" between reasons and actions.

IV

In order to turn the first "and" to "because" in "He exercised *and* he wanted to reduce and thought exercise would do it," we must, as the basic move,[5] augment condition C_1 with:

C_2. A primary reason for an action is its cause.

The considerations in favor of C_2 are by now, I hope, obvious; in the remainder of this paper I wish to defend C_2 against various lines of attack and, in the process, to clarify the notion of causal explanation involved.

A. The first line of attack is this. Primary reasons consist of attitudes and beliefs, which are states or dispositions, not events; therefore they cannot be causes.

It is easy to reply that states, dispositions, and conditions are frequently named as the causes of events: the bridge collapsed because of a structural defect; the plane crashed on take-off because the air temperature was abnormally high; the plate broke because it had a crack. This reply does not, however, meet a closely related point. Mention of a causal condition for an event gives a cause only on the assumption that there was also a preceding event. But what is the preceding event that causes an action?

In many cases it is not difficult at all to find events very closely associated with the primary reason. States and dispositions are not events, but the onslaught of a state or disposition is. A desire to hurt your feelings may spring up at the moment you anger me; I may start wanting to eat a melon just when I see one; and beliefs may begin at the moment we notice, perceive, learn, or remember something. Those who have argued that there are no mental events to qualify as causes of actions have often missed the obvious because they have insisted that a mental event be observed or noticed (rather than an observing or a noticing) or that it be like a stab, a qualm, a prick or a quiver, a mysterious prod of conscience or act of the will. Melden, in discussing the driver who signals a turn by raising his arm, challenges those who want to explain actions causally to identify "an event which is common and peculiar to all such cases" (87), perhaps a motive or an intention, anyway "some particular feeling or experience" (95). But of course there is a mental event: at some moment the driver noticed (or thought he noticed) his turn coming up, and that is the moment he signalled. During any continuing activity, like driving, or elaborate performance, like swimming the Hellespont, there are more or less fixed purposes, standards, desires, and habits that give direction and form to the entire enterprise, and there is the continuing input of information about what we are doing, about changes in the environment, in terms of which we regulate and adjust our actions. To dignify a driver's awareness that his turn has come by calling it an experience, much less a feeling, is no doubt exaggerated, but whether it deserves a name or not, it had better be the reason why he raises his arm. In this case, and typically, there may not be anything we would call a motive, but if we mention such a general purpose as wanting to get to one's destination safely, it is clear that the motive is not an event. The intention with which the driver raises his arm is also not an event, for it is no thing at all, neither event, attitude, disposition, nor object. Finally, Melden asks the causal theorist to find an event that is common and peculiar to all cases where a man intentionally raises his arm, and this, it must be admitted, cannot be produced. But then neither can a common and unique cause of bridge failures, plane crashes, or plate breakings be produced.

The signalling driver can answer the question "Why did you raise your arm when you did?" and from the answer we learn the event that caused the action. But can an actor always answer such a question? Sometimes the answer will mention a mental event that does not give a reason: "Finally I made up my mind." However, there also seem to be cases of intentional action where we cannot explain at all why we acted when we did. In such cases, explanation in terms of primary reasons parallels the explanation of the collapse of the bridge from a structural defect: we are ignorant of the event or sequence of events that led up to (caused) the collapse, but we are sure there was such an event or sequence of events.

B. According to Melden, a cause must be "logically distinct from the alleged effect" (52); but a reason for an action is not logically distinct from the action; therefore, reasons are not causes of actions.[6]

One possible form of this argument has already been suggested. Since a reason makes an action intelligible by redescribing it, we do not have two events, but only one under different descriptions. Causal relations, however, demand distinct events.

Someone might be tempted into the mistake of thinking that my flipping of the switch caused my turning on of the light (in fact it caused the light to go on). But it does not follow that it is a mistake to take "My reason for flipping the switch was that I wanted to turn on the light" as entailing, in part, "I flipped the switch, and this action is further describable as having been caused by my wanting to turn on the light." To describe an event in terms of its cause is not to identify the event with its cause, nor does explanation by redescription exclude causal explanation.

The example serves also to refute the claim that we cannot describe the action without using words that link it to the alleged cause. Here the action is to be explained under the description: "my flipping the switch," and the alleged cause is "my wanting to turn on the light." What possible logical relation is supposed to hold between these phrases? It seems more plausible to urge a logical link between "my turning on the light" and "my wanting to turn on the light," but even here the link turned out, on inspection, to be grammatical rather than logical.

In any case there is something very odd in the idea that causal relations are empirical rather than logical. What can this mean? Surely not that every true causal statement is empirical. For suppose "A caused B" is true. Then the cause of $B = A$; so, substituting, we have "The cause of B caused B," which is analytic. The truth of a causal statement depends on *what* events are described; its status as analytic or synthetic depends on *how* the events are described. Still, it may be maintained that a reason rationalizes an action only when the descriptions are appropriately fixed, and the appropriate descriptions are not logically independent.

Suppose that to say a man wanted to turn on the light *meant* that he would perform any action he believed would accomplish his end. Then the statement of his primary reason for flipping the switch would entail that he flipped the switch—"straightway he acts," as Aristotle says. In this case there would certainly be a logical connection between reason and action, the same sort of connection as that between "It's water-soluble and was placed in water" and "It dissolved." Since the implication runs from description of cause to description of effect but not conversely, naming the cause still gives information. And, though the point is often overlooked, "Placing it in water caused it to dissolve" does not entail "It's water-soluble"; so the latter has additional explanatory force. Nevertheless, the explanation would be far more interesting if, in place of solubility, with its obvious definitional connection with the event to be explained, we could refer to some property, say a particular crystalline structure, whose connection with dissolution in water was known only through experiment. Now it is clear why primary reasons like desires and wants do not explain actions in the relatively trivial way solubility explains dissolvings. Solubility, we are assuming, is a pure disposition property: it is defined in terms of a single test. But desires cannot be defined in terms of the actions they may rationalize, even though the relation between desire and action is not simply empirical; there are other, equally essential criteria for desires— their expression in feelings and in actions that they do not rationalize, for example. The person who has a desire (or want or belief) does not normally need criteria at all—he generally knows, even in the absence of any clues available to others, what he wants, desires, and believes. These logical features of primary reasons show that it is not just lack of ingenuity that keeps us from defining them as dispositions to act for these reasons.

C. According to Hume, "we may define a cause to be an object, followed by another, and where all the objects similar to the first are followed by objects similar to the second." But, Hart and Honoré claim, "The statement that one person did something because, for example, another threatened him, carries no implication or covert assertion that if the circumstances were repeated the same action would follow" (52). Hart and Honoré allow that Hume is right in saying that ordinary singular causal statements imply generalizations, but wrong for this very reason in supposing that motives and desires are ordinary causes of actions. In brief, laws are involved essentially in ordinary causal explanations, but not in rationalizations.

It is common to try to meet this argument by suggesting that we do have rough laws connecting reasons and actions, and these can, in theory, be improved. True, threatened people do not always respond in the same way; but we may distinguish between threats and also between agents, in terms of their beliefs and attitudes.

The suggestion is delusive, however, because generalizations connecting reasons and actions are not—and cannot be sharpened into—the kind of law on the basis of which accurate predictions can reliably be made. If we reflect on the way in which reasons determine choice, decision, and behavior, it is easy to see why this is so. What emerges, in the *ex post facto* atmosphere of explanation and justification, as *the* reason frequently was, to the agent at the time of action, one consideration among many, *a* reason. Any serious theory for predicting action on the basis of reasons must find a way of evaluating the relative force of various desires and beliefs in the matrix of decision; it cannot take as its starting point the refinement of what is to be expected from a single desire. The practical syllogism exhausts its role in displaying an action as falling under one reason; so it cannot be subtilized into a reconstruction of practical reasoning, which involves the weighing of competing reasons. The practical syllogism provides a model neither for a predictive science of action nor for a normative account of evaluative reasoning.

Ignorance of competent predictive laws does not inhibit valid causal explanation, or few causal explanations could be made. I am certain the window broke because it was struck by a rock—I saw it all happen; but I am not (is anyone?) in command of laws on the basis of which I can predict what blows will break which windows. A generalization like "Windows are fragile, and fragile things tend to break when struck hard enough, other conditions being right" is not a predictive law in the rough—the predictive law, if we had it, would be quantitative and would use very different concepts. The generalization, like our generalizations about behavior, serves a different function: it provides evidence for the existence of a causal law covering the case at hand.

We are usually far more certain of a singular causal connection than we are of any causal law governing the case; does this show that Hume was wrong in claiming that singular causal statements entail laws? Not necessarily, for Hume's claim, as quoted above, is ambiguous. It may mean that "*A* caused *B*" entails some particular law involving the predicates used in the descriptions "*A*" and "*B*," or it may mean that "*A* caused *B*" entails that there exists a causal law instantiated by some true descriptions of *A* and *B*.[7] Obviously, both versions of Hume's doctrine give a sense to the claim that singular causal statements entail laws, and both sustain the view that causal explanations "involve laws." But the second version is far weaker, in that no particular law is entailed by a singular causal claim, and a singular causal claim can be defended, if it needs defense, without defending any law. Only the second version of Hume's doctrine can be made to fit with most causal explanations; it suits rationalizations equally well.

The most primitive explanation of an event gives its cause; more elaborate explanations may tell more of the story, or defend the singular causal claim by producing a relevant law or by giving reasons for believing such exists. But it is an error to think no explanation has been given until a law has been produced. Linked with these errors is the idea that singular causal statements necessarily indicate, by the concepts they employ, the concepts that will occur in the entailed law. Suppose a hurricane, which is reported on page 5 of Tuesday's *Times,* causes a catastrophe, which is reported on page 13 of Wednesday's *Tribune.* Then the event reported on page 5 of Tuesday's *Times* caused the event reported on page 13 of Wednesday's *Tribune.* Should we look for a law relating events of these *kinds?* It is only slightly less ridiculous to look for a law relating hurricanes and catastrophes. The laws needed to predict the catastrophe with precision would, of course, have no use for concepts like hurricane and catastrophe. The trouble with predicting the weather is that the descriptions under which events interest us—"a cool, cloudy day with rain in the afternoon"—have only remote connections with the concepts employed by the more precise known laws.

The laws whose existence is required if reasons are causes of actions do not, we may be sure, deal in the concepts in which rationalizations must deal. If the causes of a class of events (actions) fall in a certain class (reasons) and there is a law to back each singular causal statement, it does not follow that there is any law connecting events classified as reasons with events classified as actions—the classifications may even be neurological, chemical, or physical.

D. It is said that the kind of knowledge one has of one's own reasons in acting is not compatible with the existence of a causal relation between reasons and actions: a person knows his own intentions in acting infallibly, without induction or observation, and no ordinary causal relation can be known in this way. No doubt our knowledge of our own intentions in acting will show many of the oddities peculiar to first-person knowledge of one's own pains, beliefs, desires, and so on; the only question is whether these oddities prove that reasons do not cause, in any ordinary sense at least, the actions that they rationalize.

You may easily be wrong about the truth of a statement of the form "I am poisoning Charles because I want to save him pain," because you may be wrong about whether you are poisoning Charles—you may yourself be drinking the poisoned cup by mistake. But it also seems that you may err about your reasons, particularly when you have two reasons for an action, one of which pleases you and one which does not. For example, you do want to save Charles pain; you also want him out of the way. You may be wrong about which motive made you do it.

The fact that you may be wrong does not show that in general it makes sense to ask you how you know what your reasons were or to ask for your evidence. Though you may, on rare occasions, accept public or private evidence as showing you are wrong about your reasons, you usually have no evidence and make no observations. Then your knowledge of your own reasons for your actions is not generally inductive, for where there is induction, there is evidence. Does this show the knowledge is not causal? I cannot see that it does.

Causal laws differ from true but nonlawlike generalizations in that their instances confirm them; induction is, therefore, certainly a good way to learn the truth of a law. It does not follow that it is the only way to learn the truth of a law. In any case, in order to know that a singular causal statement is true, it is not necessary to know the truth of a law; it is necessary only to know that some law covering the events at hand exists. And it is far from evident that induction, and induction alone, yields the knowledge that a causal law satisfying certain conditions exists. Or, to put it differently, one case is often enough, as Hume admitted, to persuade us that a law exists, and this amounts to saying that we are persuaded, without direct inductive evidence, that a causal relation exists.[8]

E. Finally I should like to say something about a certain uneasiness some philosophers feel in speaking of causes of actions at all. Melden, for example, says that actions are often identical with bodily movements, and that bodily movements have causes; yet he denies that the causes are causes of the actions. This is, I think, a contradiction. He is led to it by the following sort of consideration: "It is futile to attempt to explain conduct through the causal efficacy of desire—all *that* can explain is further happenings, not actions performed by agents. The agent confronting the causal nexus in which such happenings occur is a helpless victim of all that occurs in and to him" (128, 129). Unless I am mistaken, this argument, if it were valid, would show that actions cannot have causes at all. I shall not point out the obvious difficulties in removing actions from the realm of causality entirely. But perhaps it is worth trying to uncover the source of the trouble. Why on earth should a cause turn an action into a mere happening and a person into a helpless victim? Is it because we tend to assume, at least in the arena of action, that a cause demands a causer, agency an agent? So we press the question; if my action is caused, what caused it? If I did, then there is the absurdity of infinite regress; if I did not, I am a victim. But of course the alternatives are not exhaustive. Some causes have no agents. Primary among these are those states and changes of state in persons which, because they are reasons as well as causes, make persons voluntary agents.

NOTES

1. Some examples: G. E. M. Anscombe, *Intention,* Oxford, 1959; Stuart Hampshire, *Thought and Action* (London, 1959); H. L. A. Hart and A. M. Honoré, *Causation in the Law* (Oxford, 1959); William Dray, *Laws and Explanation in History* (Oxford, 1957); and most of the books in the series edited by R. F. Holland, *Studies in Philosophical Psychology,* including Anthony Kenny, *Action, Emotion and Will* (London, 1963), and A. I. Melden, *Free Action* (London, 1961). Page references in parentheses will all be to these works.

2. We would not call my unintentional alerting of the prowler an action, but it should not be inferred from this that alerting the prowler is therefore something different from flipping the switch, say just its consequence. Actions, performances, and events not involving intention are alike in that they are often referred to or defined partly in terms of some terminal stage, outcome, or consequence.

The word "action" does not very often occur in ordinary speech, and when it does it is usually reserved for fairly portentous occasions. I follow a useful philosophical practice in calling anything an agent does intentionally an action, including intentional omissions. What is really needed is some suitably generic term to bridge the following gap: suppose "*A*" is a description of an action, "*B*" is a description of something done voluntarily, though not intentionally, and "*C*" is a description of something done involuntarily and unintentionally: finally, suppose *A* = *B* = *C*. Then *A, B,* and *C* are the same—what? "Action," "event," "thing done," each have, at least in some contexts, a strange ring when coupled with the wrong sort of description. Only the question "Why did you (he) do A?" has the true generality required. Obviously, the problem is greatly aggravated if we assume, as Melden does (*Free Action,* 85), that an action ("raising one's arm") can be identical with a bodily movement ("one's arm going up").

3. "Quasi-intensional" because, besides its intensional aspect, the description of the action must also refer in rationalizations; otherwise it could be true that an action was done for a certain reason and yet the action not have been performed. Compare "the author of *Waverley*" in "George IV knew the author of *Waverley* wrote *Waverley*."

4. Miss Anscombe denies that the practical syllogism is deductive. This she does partly because she thinks of the practical syllogism, as Aristotle does, as corresponding to a piece of practical reasoning (whereas for me it is only part of the analysis of the concept of a reason with which someone acted), and therefore she is bound, again following Aristotle, to think of the conclusion of a practical syllogism as corresponding to a judgment, not merely that the action has a desirable characteristic, but that the action is desirable (reasonable, worth doing, etc.).

5. I say "as the basic move" to cancel the suggestion that C_1 and C_2 are jointly *sufficient* to define the relation of reasons to the actions they explain. I believe C_2 can be strengthened to make C_1 and C_2 sufficient as well as necessary conditions, but here I am concerned only with the claim that both are, as they stand, necessary.

6. This argument can be found, in one or more versions, in Kenny, Hampshire, and Melden, as well as in P. Winch, *The Idea of a Social Science* (London, 1958), and R. S. Peters, *The Concept of Motivation* (London, 1958). In one of its forms, the argument was of course inspired by Ryle's treatment of motives in *The Concept of Mind*.

7. We could roughly characterize the analysis of singular causal statements hinted at here as follows: "*A* caused *B*" is true if and only if there are descriptions of *A* and *B* such that the sentence obtained by putting these descriptions for "*A*" and "*B*" in "*A* caused *B*" follows from a true causal law. This analysis is saved from triviality by the fact that not all true generalizations are causal laws; causal laws are distinguished (though of course this is no analysis) by the fact that they are inductively confirmed by their instances and by the fact that they support counterfactual and subjunctive singular causal statements.

8. My thinking on the subject of this section, as on most of the topics discussed in this paper, has been greatly influenced by years of talk with Professor Daniel Bennett.

27

Intentional Action

Alvin I. Goldman

WANTS AND BELIEFS AS CAUSES OF ACTS

In defining basic act-types I said that there is a causal connection between wanting to do a basic act A and the actual performance of a token of type A. This fact, however, does not exhaust the topic of the causal relation between wanting and acting. First, in defining basic act-types I assumed that S's want to do A was the only want he had at the time, or the only relevant want. We must now worry about what happens if S has competing wants. Secondly, an agent usually does a basic act A not because he wants to do A (*per se*) but because he wants to do A' and believes that A will generate A'. In the normal situation, some cluster of wants *and* beliefs cause[es] the performance of a basic act. Thirdly, from the fact that basic act-tokens are caused by an agent's wants, or by his wants and beliefs, it may not be apparent that acts which are *generated* by this basic act-token are caused by those wants and beliefs. These topics require further discussion.

I want to say first that, to my knowledge, no precise, predictively adequate law is known that correlates wants and beliefs with the performance of acts. I think that there are commonsense generalizations which can be formulated and which can sometimes be used for predictive purposes. But nothing has been formulated that compares favorably with certain laws in

From *A Theory of Human Action* by Alvin I. Goldman. (Englewood Cliffs, N.J.: Prentice–Hall, Inc., 1970), pp. 72–85. Reprinted by permission of the author.

the physical sciences. It is most important to recognize, however, that knowledge of precise laws is not necessary to justify the statement that wants and beliefs *cause* acts. Most of our knowledge of singular causal propositions is not based on knowledge of precise, universal laws.[1] I know that on various occasions flying rocks cause windows to break, but I could not formulate any universal, predictively adequate law that relates the occurrence of rocks flying with windows breaking. Similarly, many centuries before precise measurements for temperature were developed, it was known that cold weather often causes water to freeze. But at that time no one was able to state a universal law that gives precise conditions under which water would freeze. People could have said that water freezes if it gets cold *enough*, but they could not have said how cold is cold enough.

We are in a similar situation, I think, with respect to wants, beliefs, and acts. We certainly know that wants and beliefs result in acts. Indeed, this is part of our conception of wanting and believing. But although we can formulate very rough generalizations about wants, beliefs, and acts, we cannot state precise universal laws, using concepts for which we have precise measurement techniques. The absence of measuring techniques is one of the largest obstacles in the way of a precise universal law. Obviously the relative strengths of desires are very important in determining what acts a person performs. But in the absence of fully adequate techniques for measuring these strengths, reliable predictions cannot be made. Perhaps the identification of neurophysiological states that correlate with wanting and believing might help us achieve techniques for measuring wants and beliefs,[2] but certainly at the present time we do not have this information. The important point for present purposes, however, is that the justification of the belief that wants and beliefs cause acts does not await the discovery of a precise universal law. Many people know that too much water often causes plants to die, but hardly any of these people could state the precise conditions under which a specifiable amount of water will cause a plant to die. Of course, one can be sure that a certain very large amount of water will cause a certain plant to die. But similarly, one can often be sure that a certain very strong desire (and strong belief) will cause a certain agent to perform a certain act. The problem in the plant case is that one cannot predict whether a certain moderate amount of water will cause a plant to die, though *ex post facto* one can say that it did cause the plant to die. Similarly, although we can say *ex post facto* that certain desires and beliefs caused a particular act *A*, we could not have *predicted* that that act would be performed.

Let us look at the vague, rough generalizations about wants, beliefs, and acts that can be constructed from our commonsense knowledge. One such generalization would be *L*.

> *L: If any agent* S *wants to do* A' *(at* t) *more than any other act, and if* S *believes that basic act* A_1 *is more likely to generate* A' *than any other (incompatible) basic act, and if* S *is in standard conditions with respect to* A_1 *(at* t*), then* S *does* A_1 *(at* t*).*

L gives us some idea of the relationship between wants, beliefs, and acts, but it has several failings. First, there are cases in which S believes that A_1 would generate some act which he very much dislikes, in addition to generating A'. Hence, even though he believes that A_1 is the basic act most likely to generate the desired act A', he will refrain from doing A_1. Secondly, suppose that S wants to do A' (at t) more than he wants to do A^* (at t). However, he does not believe that there is any basic act very likely to generate A'. He thinks that A_1 is more likely to generate A' than any other basic act, but not really very likely. On the other hand, he is sure there is a basic act which would generate his doing A^*. Here, even though he wants A' more than A^*, he may refrain from doing A_1. Thirdly, suppose that S believes that basic act A_2 has quite a good chance of generating A', though not quite as good as A_1. On the other hand, A_2 would generate acts he desires in addition to generating A', while A_1 would only generate A' and not these other desired acts. Then S might choose to do A_2 instead of A_1.

To avoid these difficulties, we might formulate generalization L'.

> *L': If any agent* S *believes that hypothetical act-tree** A_1, A_2 . . ., A_n *(to be performed at* t*) is more likely, all in all, to achieve more of his desires than any other act-tree (that could be performed at* t*), and if* S *is in standard conditions with respect to each of the basic acts of this act-tree (at* t*), then* S *performs each of these basic acts (at* t*).*

L' is an improvement over L, because it takes into account more than one of S's wanted and unwanted acts, and secondly, because it combines the probability factor with the amount-of-desirability factor. But while it is more comprehensive than L, L' suffers from even greater vagueness. The main vagueness of L' lies in the combination of probability and amount-of-desirability. If there are two hypothetical act-trees under consideration, one having a higher probability of achieving lesser desires and the other having a smaller probability of achieving greater desires, which will S choose? This depends in part on what sort of decision "criterion" the agent employs, but L' tells us nothing about this. Moreover, it cannot be assumed that all people employ the same criterion, nor even that the same person employs the

---

*See note 1 of selection 28 for an explanation of "act-tree."—*Ed.*

same criterion on all occasions. When this sort of problem is compounded with our inability to make precise measurements of intensities of desire, or to add these intensities, it becomes clear that L' cannot be used to make predictions in all cases. It does not mean that L' can *never* be used predictively. There are some cases in which one course of action is *clearly* more attractive to S than any other course of action, for it clearly combines greater probability of success with greater desirability. Here we can make predictions with substantial confidence. But in the hard cases, L' will not be of much help.

Until now I have said that wants and beliefs cause basic act-tokens, but I wish also to contend that acts which are generated by basic act-tokens are caused by these wants and beliefs. This point seems fairly obvious to me. If something causes S's moving his hand, and if S's moving his hand generates S's closing the door, then that same thing is a cause of S's closing the door. Again, if something causes S's extending his arm, and if S's extending his arm generates S's signaling for a turn, then that same thing is a cause of S's signaling for a turn. Admittedly, the causation of S's closing the door may involve more factors than are involved in the causation of S's moving his hand. But whatever is the cause of S's moving his hand is at least a *partial* cause of S's closing the door.

One might think that those generational conditions that enable a basic act token to generate a higher act-token might be counted among the causes of the higher act. But usually it is inappropriate to call these conditions "causes" of the act. Where S's extending his arm generates S's signaling for a turn, for example, it would be odd to regard the existence of the rule about signaling as a "cause" of S's signaling for a turn. Similarly, where S's jumping six feet three inches generates S's outjumping George, it would be odd to regard George's having jumped six feet as a "cause" of S's outjumping George (though it might be a cause in *certain* cases we could imagine). Even in causal generation, this does not seem natural. The light's going on, for example, can hardly be considered a "cause" of S's turning on the light. And even the position of the switch, the condition of the wiring system, etc. would not ordinarily be called "causes" of S's turning on the light. In all of these cases, however, the generational conditions are *causally relevant* to the performance of the higher act, even if they would not ordinarily be called "causes" of the higher act. Their role might be compared to that of "standing conditions" in various causal processes. We would not ordinarily call the presence of oxygen a "cause" of a particular combustion, but it is a causally relevant condition. Similarly, the condition of the wiring system, the position of the switch, etc., are *causally relevant conditions* of S's turning on the light. In general, then, wants and beliefs which cause a certain basic act also cause anything that is generated by that basic act. But these generated acts will always have some causally relevant conditions that were not causally relevant with respect to the basic act.

Some philosophers have sought to deny that what I call "higher-level" or "generated" acts can be governed by causal laws, because they are irreducible to physical movements. P. F. Strawson, for example, writes:

> . . . there are no effective correlations between the two vocabularies for talking about what goes on, the vocabulary of human action and the vocabulary of physical science. If, for example, every case of someone's telling a lie were an instance of one physically specifiable class of sets of physical movements (and vice versa), and every instance of someone's jilting his girl friend were an instance of another such class (and vice versa), then the reign of law in the field of physical movement would mean that lying and jilting could be deterministically explained. There would, as far as lying and jilting were concerned, be physical laws of human action as well as physical laws of physical movement. But there is no question of any such correlations ever being established.[3]

Strawson seems to think that in order for S's lying (at t) to be caused, there must be a correlation between *all* instances of lying and some specific set of physical movements—e.g., bodily-movement acts. Unless lying can be *reduced* to physical movements, he seems to be saying, there is a gulf between acts of lying and physical movements. And hence, although the physical movements may be caused, the acts of lying are not caused. This position is wholly indefensible. There is no reason whatever for requiring *all* instances of lying to be correlated with, or reduced to, some one set of physical movements or bodily-movement acts. Each distinct act-token of lying may be generated by a different bodily-movement act. But if each of these bodily-movement acts is caused, then each act-token of lying would also be caused.

A slightly different reason for thinking that higher-level acts are not caused is that there are no laws dealing with many (perhaps all) of the properties of which higher-level act-tokens are instances. There are no laws saying, "Whenever x, y, and z, then a person checkmates his opponent," or saying "Whenever x, y, and z, then a person turns on a light." It is a mistake to think, however, that an act-token is caused only if the property of which it is an instance is a dependent variable of some universal law. It would indeed be foolish of psychologists or social scientists to try to formulate or discover laws for every act-property, including checkmating one's opponent, turning on a light, or, to take an even more extreme case, pitching one's sixth straight shut-out. But the absence of such laws does not imply that tokens of these properties are uncaused. If John's moving his hand is caused, and if, given the circumstances, this generates John's checkmating his opponent, then we can say that John's checkmating his opponent is caused, despite the absence of laws dealing with checkmates. Similarly, if a baseball's curving in a certain direction is caused, and if, in the circumstances, this generates the baseball's curving *foul*, then we can say that the baseball's curving foul is caused, despite the fact that there are no laws dealing with foul territory. Surely it would be absurd to assert that the ball's curving foul is *uncaused*.

REASONS AND CAUSES

Purposive behavior is closely connected with the concept of "reasons." One might, indeed, with Miss Anscombe,[4] define an intentional act as one which the agent does *for a reason*. But what is it to do something for a reason? When we explain an act in terms of the agent's reason, what kind of explanation is this? In particular, is this a species of causal. explanation, or is it an explanation of quite a different sort? Many recent philosophers claim that reasons-explanations, or motive-explanations, are not species of causal explanations, and some have even claimed that they preclude causal explanations.[5] But I wish to contend that reasons-explanations *are* a species of causal explanations.[6]

To say that S's reason for doing act A was A' is equivalent to saying that S did A in order to do A'. In saying that S's reason for extending his arm was to signal for a turn we are saying that S extended his arm in order to signal for a turn. And when we say that his reason for flipping the switch was to turn on the light we are saying that S flipped the switch in order to turn on the light. What, then, is the force of an "in order to" explanation?

When we say that S flipped the switch in order to turn on the light, the explanandum event is obviously S's flipping the switch. But what does the explanans consist of? What events, states of affairs, or facts are being cited as the explanatory factors of S's flipping the switch? At first glance it may seem that the explanans refers to another act of S—viz., his act of turning on the light. A little reflection will show, however, that this is not the case. First, the assertion that S turned on the light cannot be the whole of the explanans. For the fact that S turned on the light is not a sufficient condition for saying that S flipped the switch *in order to* turn on the light. The fact that S *did* turn on the light by flipping the switch does not imply that the *point* of flipping the switch was to turn on the light. He may have had quite a different reason for flipping the switch. Secondly, the fact that S turned on the light is not even a component of the *in order to* explanation, for the *in order to* explanation can be perfectly correct though S did not turn on the light at all. Suppose S wanted to turn on the light and believed that he would turn it on by flipping the switch. But suppose that, in fact, the switch in question operates the exhaust fan rather than the light. Thus, S does not succeed in performing the act of turning on the light. Nevertheless, it is correct to say that S flipped the switch *in order to* turn on the light.

What, then, is implied by saying that S flipped the switch "in order to" turn on the light? Evidently, this explanation implies that S *wanted* to turn on the light, and it also implies that he *believed* (at least to some degree) that he would turn on the light *by* flipping the switch. Does the *whole* of the explanans consist in the assertion that S wanted to turn on the light and that he believed that his flipping the switch would generate his turning on the light? Clearly not. The statement that S had this want and had this belief is compatible with the statement that he flipped the switch *for some other reason*, or *not for any reason at all, i.e., accidentally*. Suppose S wanted to turn on the light, but decided to fetch his pipe first. While reaching for the pipe, however, he accidentally flipped the switch and thereby accidentally turned on the light. Here it is true to say that S wanted to turn on the light and that he believed that he would turn it on by flipping the switch. But it is false to say that he flipped the switch in order to turn on the light, or that his reason for flipping the switch was to turn on the light. Thus, the statement that S flipped the switch *in order to* turn on the light implies more than that S *had* the indicated want and *had* the indicated belief. It also implies that his having this want and his having this belief *caused* or *resulted in*, his flipping the switch. Such an explanation not only implies that he *had* an action-plan that included the indicated want and belief, but also implies that this action-plan *caused* (in the characteristic way) the act of flipping the switch.

Talk about an agent's *reason* for action, we see, can be analyzed in terms of the *action-plans* which *cause* his action. When I ask why S did A—i.e., for what reason he did A—I presuppose that he had some action-plan that included A and that caused his performance of A. Of course, that presupposition could be wrong. There may have been no action-plan that both included A and caused the performance of A. If there was no such action-plan, then S's doing A was not intentional; and hence there is no answer to the question *why* (i.e., for what reason) he did A. But if there was an action-plan that both included A and that caused the performance of A, then act A *was* done for a reason. And the point of my inquiry is to find out what that reason was. In other words, the point of my inquiry is to ascertain *what* act it was that S both *wanted* to perform and *believed* would be generated by (or on the same level as) act A.

In his book *Free Action*, A. I. Melden contends that when we explain a man's action in terms of his motives or reasons, we are simply "*redescribing*" his action. Melden says that "citing a motive is giving a fuller characterization of the action."[7] This statement is potentially quite misleading, however.

It is true that in answer to the question, "Why was he extending his arm?" we might reply, "He was signaling for a turn." And this reply is properly construed as giving the agent's *reason* for extending his arm. It is a mistake, however, to think that this answer is simply a way of saying *that* the agent signaled for a turn, of saying that he actually performed that action. We have already seen that the mere performance of such an act does not imply that it was the man's *reason* for acting. It is possible that he performed the act of signaling for a turn without its having been his *reason* for extending his arm. (He might not have known that extending one's arm counts as signaling.) Thus, in the context, the reply "He was signaling for a turn" means "He was *aiming* at signaling for a turn" or "His *goal* was to signal for a turn," and not merely "He exemplified the act-property of signaling for a turn." The statement is not concerned with the act-tokens actually occurring, but with the agent's aims or purposes, in short, his action-plan. Normally, when we say "What are you doing?" we are not interested in being told what things the agent is actually doing; we want to know the desires or purposes out of which he is acting. Hence, an answer to such a question is normally taken as a specification of his *desires* or *goals*, not as a description of his actual act-tokens.

This point is underlined by the fact that the performance of *certain* acts implies, or presupposes, that the agent is acting out specific desires or purposes. The performance of such an act as *hiding from George*, or *hunting rabbits*, or *trying to repair one's watch* implies that the agent has certain goals or purposes, in other words, that he is acting out of certain specific desires. If we want to explain *S*'s reason for crouching behind a car, therefore, we can ascribe to him the further act of hiding from George. The ascription of this act implies that *S* is crouching behind the car *out of a desire* to prevent George from seeing him—that is, that his act of crouching behind the car is caused by a desire to prevent George from seeing him. Similarly, if we want to explain why *S* is playing with certain springs, we can ascribe to him the act of trying to repair his watch. The ascription of this act implies that he is playing with the springs in order to repair his watch—that is, out of a desire to repair his watch. In these cases the performance of the indicated act *presupposes* the presence of a certain desire and its causal role in the agent's behavior. Just as the performance of the act of *re*marrying presupposes that the agent has been married before, so the performance of the act of hiding from George presupposes that the agent has a certain desire, and is acting *from* that desire. Hence, although the agent's action can be explained by referring to these acts, the force of the explanation rests on an appeal to *wants* of the agent and the *causal* force of those wants.

There are many reasons why philosophers have felt that explanations in terms of reasons are not a species of causal explanation. Many of these arguments are connected with the view that wants, or motives, are not causally related to acts. . . . [L]et me mention two other points.

First, it is important to notice that, from the point of view of the agent himself, practical reasoning does not appear as a causal process. When an agent is trying to decide what action to perform, he is trying to select the "best" course of action. A decision of this sort usually requires attention to the probable consequences of alternative acts, and sometimes requires attention to moral principles, etc. Now considerations such as these seem very far from any question concerning the causation of his action. "What will be the consequences of my doing A?" is a very different matter from "What will cause my doing A?" or "Will anything cause my doing A?" Nevertheless, although the agent, while deliberating, does not normally worry about the causes of his action, the process of weighing alternatives, of noticing their probable consequences, etc.—this process itself *constitutes* a causal process culminating in his action. Although the agent's reasoning does not focus on its own causal efficacy, it *has* causal efficacy *vis-àvis* his action.

Another source of the rejection of the view that human action is explainable by reference to causes is the tendency to assimilate causation in general to *mechanical* causation. In the minds of some philosophers, talk of causation calls up a picture of billiard balls propelling one another or levers pushing and pulling. All causation is assimilated to blind mechanism, to relations between "colorless movements," and this is taken to be incompatible with reasons or rationality. But why should causal relations obtain only between "colorless movements"? Why should all causality imply blind, unreasoning mechanism? Why can't states having intentional objects—e.g., beliefs, thoughts, intentions, desires, etc.—be involved in causal relations?

The notion of reasons and reasoning is intimately tied, I believe, to intentionalistic states. Thus, if intentionalistic states are involved in causal relations, the notion of causation should not be inimical to the notion of reason, should not imply blind, unreasoning mechanism. But from a commonsense point of view, some of the clearest cases of causality involve intentionalistic states. Among the most certain causal propositions we know may be the proposition that S's desire for sleep was caused, at least in part, by his having stayed awake for 35 hours, and that S's thinking of Vienna was caused by his wife reminding him of their trip. Similarly, I think we know that intentionalistic states are sometimes causes of other effects, including acts. One cannot say, therefore, that causality is incompatible with reasons or reasoning. Perhaps some philosophers' attempts to analyze causality have this consequence, but so much the worse, I think, for those analyses.

CAUSALITY AND AGENCY

The view that acts are caused has often been opposed from another quarter, a line of opposition that centers around the concept of agency. An agent is an entity that originates activity, that makes things happen instead of passively suffering external causes to operate through him. In this sense stones and pieces of wood are not agents, but human beings are; for human beings are the sources or originators of their own activities.

The idea of universal causation, however, seems to be incompatible with this notion of human agency. If every event is caused by prior events, then a person's acts must be caused by events that occurred prior to the agent's birth. But if his acts were caused by such events, how can the *agent* be considered their cause, their source, or their originator? My contention that acts are caused by wants and beliefs opens the door to this dilemma, for it opens the door to causes of acts other than the agent himself. To be sure, I have not yet claimed that every event is caused, nor is this implied by anything said in this [essay]. I believe that universal causation is a real possibility, however. Thus, I must confront the question of how to reconcile universal causation with the concept of agency.

The problem is twofold. First, there is the problem of agent-causation versus want-and-belief causation. If the acts of an agent are caused by his wants and beliefs, how can *he*, the agent, be considered their cause? Secondly, if an agent's acts are caused by events that preceded his birth, how can we consider *him* to be their source or originator?

In addressing these problems, I wish first to draw a distinction between *event-causation* and *object-causation*, and to contend that these are not *rival* candidates in the search for causes. There is clearly a difference between an *object* (a thing, a substance), causing *x* and an event or state causing *x*. Since Hume, philosophers have paid comparatively little attention to the role of *objects* in causal talk (though Hume himself often used the term "object" in his discussion of causality). Carrying on the Humean tradition, philosophers have reiterated the claim that causes are things that figure in laws or regularities. But it doesn't make any sense to try to place objects in a regularity, even to consider them as "factors" which, together with others, fulfill the antecedent of a causal law. It makes no sense to say "Whenever Smith, Jones, and Brown, then . . . " or "Whenever this rock, this shoe, and this door, then. . . ." Of course, we might say "Whenever Smith *eats seafood*, then . . ." or "Whenever Smith *has a fever*, then . . . ," but these sentences would correlate something with an *event involving Smith*, or a *state of Smith*, not with *Smith*.

I believe that whenever we say that an *object, O,* is a cause of *x*, this presupposes that there is a *state of O* or an *event involving O* that causes, or was a partial cause, of *x*. This seems fairly clear for physical objects. We say that the *brick* was the cause of the broken window when the *impact* of the brick on the window caused the window to break. We say that the *water* caused the building to collapse when the *pressure* of the water on its walls caused its collapse. And when we say that *the masked figure* caused so-and-so to jump, we presuppose that the masked figure's *being seen* by so-and-so caused him to jump, or that the *appearance* of the masked figure caused so-and-so to jump. In none of these cases is there an *incompatibility* between the event-causation and the object-causation. If we accept the proposition that the impact of the brick on the window caused it to break, we are not obliged to *deny* the proposition that the *brick* caused it to break. If we accept the proposition that the pressure of the water caused the building to collapse, we are not obliged to *deny* that the *water* caused it to collapse.

Now agent-causation, I believe, is simply a special case of object-causation, since an agent is simply a particular kind of object or substance. And I contend that in the case of agents, as in the case of other objects, there is no incompatibility between saying that a certain agent was the (object-)cause of a certain event and saying that an event or state involving the agent was the (event-)cause of the same effect. I do not claim that agents are called the cause of an event under the same circumstances that bricks or bodies of water are called causes. I simply wish to assert that there is not always an incompatibility between saying that an agent caused *x* and saying that some event (or state) *of* the agent caused *x*. There is room for both assertions because there is room for both object-causes and event-causes; there need be no rivalry between them.

In at least one kind of case the above contention should be uncontroversial. Suppose that the light's going on was caused by an event *of* John, or *involving* John—viz., John's flipping the switch. The fact that this is the event-cause of the light's going on is clearly not incompatible with the fact that *John* is the agent-cause of the light's going on. We can say, without contradiction, *both* that *John's flipping the switch* caused the light to go on and that *John* caused the light to go on. Similarly, I think, when an act of John's is caused by John's *wants and beliefs*, it would not be correct to say that *John* caused his act. (In ordinary language we do not say that people "cause" their own acts, but I see no objection to introducing this locution.) The fact that *John's wanting to turn on the light* caused John's flipping the switch does not preclude the fact that *John* caused John's flipping the switch. There is no contradiction in saying both, since John's having that want is just an *event-* (or *state-*)cause of the act while John is the *agent-*cause of the act.

Richard Taylor writes:

It is plain that, whatever I am, I am never identical with any such event, process, or state as is usually proposed as the "real cause" of my act, such as some intention or state of willing. Hence, if it is really and unmetaphorically true, as I believe it to be, that I sometimes cause something to happen, this would seem to entail that it is *false* that any event, process, or state not identical with myself should be the real cause of it.[8]

This is precisely the point I am denying. Of course, I am not asserting that wants and beliefs are the "real" causes of acts, as *opposed* to the agent. (I don't know what Taylor means here by "real" cause, anyway.) I am merely asserting that it may be literally and unmetaphorically true that *I* am the cause—the agent-cause—of my act, and *also* true that *my-wanting-such-and-such* and *my-believing-such-and-such* are causes—event-causes—of my act. *I* am not identical with my wants and beliefs, but nevertheless both I *and* these states of mine can be causes of my act.

There are at least two possible reasons why someone might think that *my* being the cause of an act is incompatible with my *wants* or *beliefs* being causes of my acts. First, one might simply fail to draw the distinction between event-causation and object-causation, and therefore fail to see that they are not incompatible. Secondly, one might be led into this error by thinking of mental events or mental states as agents in their own right, like little people ensconced in the heads of regular-sized people. Since there can't be two agent-causes of the same (individual) act—so the argument would run—*I* could not be the cause of an act if my *wants* and *beliefs* were causes of it. But of course wants and beliefs are not little agents or little entities of any sort, so this second line of argument is wholly misguided.

Recently I have been arguing that want-and-belief causation of acts is *compatible* with agent-causation of acts, but I also believe that agent-causation is *explicable* in terms of want-and-belief causation. The idea of performing an *act* (in the fullest sense), as I have argued, is explicable in terms of want-and-belief causation. Similarly, the idea of something being *up to me*, or *within my power*, is connected with the idea of something being dependent on *my desires*. It is up to *me* whether or not there will be a light on in this room, for the light's being on or off is dependent on *my desires*. But it is not up to *me* whether De Gaulle is reelected, since my desires have no effect in the matter whatsoever.

A further test of the relationship between agency and wants-and-beliefs is found in the comparison of the class of things we are inclined to call "agents" or think of as "agents," and the class of things whose behavior is a function of wants and beliefs, or can be interpreted, more or less analogically, as a function of wants and beliefs. These classes are virtually co-extensive. After human beings, they include the higher animals and perhaps some sophisticated machines. The behavior of dogs, for example, is easily interpretable in terms of desires and expectations, so it is not surprising that many people treat dogs as agents almost on a par with humans. The behavior of computers also bears certain resemblances of behavior that is caused by wants and beliefs, and this accounts for the fact that predicates are sometimes applied to them which are typically reserved for human agents. By contrast, it would be almost impossible seriously to regard a rock as an agent, since rocks have no properties which incline us to attribute desires and beliefs to them.

Authors like Taylor, Chisholm,[9] and C. A. Campbell[10] apparently believe that there are occasions on which agents cause acts without any state or event of the agent being an event-cause of these acts. But it is difficult for me to see how, if they were right, we could ever *tell* that there are such occasions. On my view, a case of grimacing done as an act is distinguishable from grimacing which occurs as a mere reflex because the-agent's-wanting-to-grimace precedes the act but does not ordinarily precede the mere reflex. But on their view, how could the distinction be made? How do I distinguish my grimacing *as an act* from my grimacing *as a reflex*? Or, to pose a slightly different problem, how do I tell that *I* am causing my grimacing and that my grimacing is not totally uncaused? On Taylor's view, acts are not *uncaused*; they are caused by *agents*. But how are we to distinguish absence of causation from causation by agents? Normally we identify causes with the help of regularities, but regularities obtain with respect to events, states, processes, and the like, which are precluded *ex hypothesi* by Taylor's view. Thus, the notion of agent-causation *unconnected* with event-causation is bound to be a mysterious and obscure notion. It will be replied that the notion of event-causation is equally mysterious, since it has long eluded philosophical analysis. But the point about *analysis* is not pertinent to my argument here. I admit that I cannot *analyze* the notion of event-causation any more than Taylor can analyze *his* notion of agent-causation. At least in the case of event-causation, however, we have *some* idea of what it comes to since we have *some* idea of the conditions under which certain events can be said to cause others. Mill's methods, for example, are *some* help in this direction. But we have *no* indication, if we use Taylor's notion of agent-causation, of the conditions under which an agent causes an act.

I turn now to the problem raised by the possibility that a person's acts are caused by events which occurred prior to his birth. This would seem to imply that the agent is not the author, source, or originator of his own acts; it looks as if the source of the acts must be traced to quite different things, things which were in existence before the agent himself came into existence. But if I am right in tracing the idea of agency to causation by wants and beliefs, this picture is unwarranted. As long as the act is caused by the wants and beliefs of the agent, then *he* is the author, the source, the originator of the act. The fact that these wants and beliefs were themselves caused by much earlier events does not affect the matter. There is no limit to the number of (event-)causes that a given event may have. Thus, the fact that the act was caused by events of seventy years ago does not vitiate the fact that the act was also caused by the current wants and beliefs of the agent. The events of seventy years ago had their effect on the act only *via* the wants and beliefs, and therefore only *via* the agency of the person who performed it. To paraphrase Hobart's classic discussion of the issue,[11] the past finished its business when it produced the agent as he is, with his wants and beliefs; it does not stretch out a ghostly hand to *compete* with these wants and beliefs in causing the agent's acts. Nor does it compete with the agent himself, as if it were some *other* agent, trying to overpower the agent in an attempt to achieve its own goals and objectives.

NOTES

1. See, for example, Davidson, "Actions, Reasons, and Causes," *The Journal of Philosophy* 60 (1963): 697 [see selection number 26 of this volume]; Michael Scriven, "Causes, Connections and Conditions in History," in W. Dray, ed., *Philosophical Analysis and History* (New York, 1966), section 4, and J. L. Mackie, "Causes and Conditions," *American Philosophical Quarterly* 2, no. 4 (1965), sections 4, 5, and 9.

2. See chapter five [of *A Theory of Human Action*].

3. In D. F. Pears, ed., *Freedom and the Will* (New York: St. Martins Press, 1963), p. 66.

4. *Intention* (Ithaca: Cornell University Press, 1958), p. 9.

5. Proponents of the view that explanations in terms of reasons or motives are not a species of causal explanations include the following: G. E. M. Anscombe, *Intention* (Ithaca: Cornell University Press, 1958); Isaiah Berlin, "The Concept of Scientific History," in W. Dray, ed., *Philosophical Analysis and History* (New York: Harper & Row, Publishers, 1966); William Dray, *Laws and Explanation in History* (Oxford· Oxford University Press, 1957); Philippa Foot, "Free Will as Involving Determinism," *The Philosophical Review* 66 (1957): 439–50; D. W. Hamlyn, "Behavior," *Philosophy* 27 (1953): 132–45; H. L. A. Hart and A. M. Honore, *Causation in the Law* (Oxford: Oxford University Press, 1959): A. I. Melden, *Free Action* (London: Routledge & Kegan Paul Ltd., 1961; New York: Humanities Press Inc.); R. S. Peters, *The Concept of Motivation* (London, 1958); Charles Taylor, *The Explanation of Behavior* (London: Routledge & Kegan Paul Ltd., 1964; New York: Humanities Press Inc.); Richard Taylor, *Action and Purpose* (Englewood Cliffs, N.J.: Prentice-Hall, Inc., 1966); Gilbert Ryle, *The Concept of Mind* (London: Hutchinson and Company Ltd., 1949); J. O. Urmson, "Motives and Causes," *Procedures of the Aristotelian Society*, Supplementary Volume 26 (1952): 179–94.

6. A good defense of this position is Davidson's article, "Actions, Reasons, and

Causes," *loc. cit.*, to which I am much indebted. Also see William P. Alston, "Wants, Actions, and Causal Explanations," in H. N. Castaneda, ed., *Minds, Intentionality, and Perception* (Detroit: Wayne State University Press, 1967).

7. Melden, *Free Action*, p. 88.

8. Richard Taylor, *Action and Purpose*, p. 111.

9. "Freedom and Action," in K. Lehrer, ed., *Freedom and Determinism* (New York: Random House, 1966), pp. 19–20.

10. "Is 'Free Will' a Pseudo-Problem?" *Mind* 60 (1951): 446–65; and *On Selfhood and Godhood* (London: The MacMillan Company, 1957).

11. "Free Will as Involving Determination and Inconceivable Without It," *Mind* 43, no. 169 (1934): 1–27.

28

Beliefs, Wants, and Decisions

Andrew B. Schoedinger

In most theories of action in which wants function as causes of behavior, beliefs play an integral role . . . . Goldman offers the following general formula:

> If any agent believes that hypothetical act-tree, A_1, A_2, . . . A_n (to be performed at t) is more likely, all in all, to achieve more of his desires than any other act-tree (that could be perfromed at t), and if S is in standard conditions with respect to each of the basic acts of this act-tree (at t), then S performs each of these basic acts (at t).[1]

This formula is deceiving because it claims, on the one hand, that an agent will perform that action (which is within his power to perform) which be believes will satisfy the greatest number of his wants. In this case, the degree of difficulty in performing that action appears to play no part. On the other hand, it could be taken to mean that given two or more *ways* of obtaining that which an agent wants (and if those ways are within his power to perform), he will perform that action which he believes will most likely satisfy his wants. In this case, ease of obtaining what one wants plays a role. I will argue that in either case, beliefs need not necessarily play a role in the causal process of the performance of actions. This is not to say that beliefs never play such

From *Wants, Decisions and Human Action: A Praxeological Investigation* (Lanham, Md.: University Press of America, 1978), pp. 193-201. Reprinted by permission of the publisher.

a role. The point is that they are not a necessary element in the causal process as Goldman seems to think.

Let us examine the view that an agent will perform that action (among those which are within his power to perform) which he *believes* will satisfy the greatest number of the wants he possesses at the time he makes his decision. There are undoubtedly cases which conform to such a model, but not necessarily so. Take, for example, the plausible case of an athlete who at time t has three desires. He wants to break the 100-yard-dash record, and he wants to eat and rest because he has been practicing all day long. His continued attempt at the record 100 yard dash is mutually exclusive of his eating and resting. In other words, he would satisfy more of his desires if he stopped practicing and instead ate and rested. Furthermore, even if he believes that more of his wants could be satisfied if he stopped practicing, such a belief may make very little difference in determining what the athlete decides to do. It would be highly probable that he would deny himself food and rest so that he could try to satisfy that single desire to break the 100-yard-dash record. What Goldman's formula fails to take into account is intensity of competing wants. It is not always simply a case of an agent doing what he believes will satisfy the greatest number of wants. If an agent wants something badly enough, he will try to get it even at the expense of other wants which be believes could be satisfied in greater number. Hence, intensity of wants is the crucial aspect of the above example and the belief that a given course of action will satisfy the greatest number of wants plays no role in the causal process. Therefore, Goldman's formula is inadequate.

Let us turn to the second way of interpreting Goldman's formula; namely, that given two wants (and those wants are within an agent's power to perform), he will perform that action which he believes will most likely satisfy his wants. This interpretation is itself ambiguous. (a) It may be understood to mean that an agent will always perform that action which he believes will most *easily* satisfy his wants. (b) It may be taken to mean simply that an agent will perform that action which he believes will *ultimately* satisfy his wants. If this interpretation of Goldman's formula is construed in sense (a), then it is not necessarily the case. There are undoubtedly instances where it does obtain in that sense, but again, not necessarily so. Suppose, for example, that an agent has two ways of making a billiards shot, one more difficult than the other. Furthermore, suppose that he is aware of the difference in difficulty. It is perfectly plausible that the agent might try to make the more difficult of the two shots. He might do this for no other reason than to prove to himself (or others) that he possesses the skill to make such a shot. In such a case it is clear that the agent does not engage in that action which he believes will most easily satisfy his want. One way to approach this counterexample is to argue that what, in fact, the agent wants is not simply to make the shot, but to make the more difficult shot of the two. Hence, he will try to make that shot which will most easily satisfy the want. In other words, the difficulty of the shot becomes incorporated into the want thus clearing the way for one to rest on the original claim that an agent will most easily satisfy his want. Two problems arise by making such a move. It is not at all clear what it means to claim that the agent would try what he believes to be the easiest way of making the more difficult of the two shots. (1) If it means that the agent will, for example, bridge his hand in one way rather than another because he believes that is the easiest *method* by which he can make the more difficult shot of the two, it is clear that the door is open to an infinite regress for then the issue becomes whether or not he makes the easiest bridge in the easiest way possible for the purpose of making the more difficult shot of the two. (2) A second interpretation of the situation results in an outright contradiction. If the agent wants to make the more difficult shot of the two, then he cannot try to make it in the way he believes it to be most easily made because that would lessen the difficulty of the shot. By so lessening the difficulty of the shot the possibility arises that that shot which the agent believes to be the easier of the two becomes the more difficult of the two if the agent were to try to make the easier of the two shots in the most difficult possible way. So it matters not whether the difficulty of the shot becomes incorporated into the want or remains external to it. In either case, there remain difficulties with respect to any model of human action which asserts that an agent will attempt to satisfy his wants in those ways he believes to be most *easily* obtained.

If the second interpretation of Goldman's formula is construed in sense (b), namely, that an agent will perform that action (among those which are within his power to perform) which he believes will *ultimately* satisfy his want, the following results. This claim is clearly false if the agent believes that there is more than one action (among those within his power to perform) which will ultimately satisfy his want. If the ultimate satisfaction of the want is the only criterion for choosing between alternative courses of action which the agent believes will satisfy the want, then there is no telling which action the agent will perform. There needs be a third element present in the decision-making process. A likely third element would be the ease of satisfaction of the want, namely, the agent will choose that course of action (among those which he believes will ultimately satisfy his want) which he believes will most easily satisfy his want. This case, therefore, reduces to the first interpretation of the second way of interpreting Goldman's formula. And the problems with that interpretation have already been made evident.

The second manner of construing the second way of interpreting Goldman's formula only makes sense if the agent believes that there is only one alternative action (among those within his power to perform) which will ultimately satisfy his want. Such a claim, although reasonable, is noninformative. It is obvious that if an agent believes that there is only one way to ultimately satisfy his want, then he will pursue that course of action. He certainly will not pursue a course of action which he believes will not satisfy his want.

It is this writer's contention that beliefs are construed as a necessary part of causal models of action because there is a confusion between the wanting of $\emptyset$ and the means of achieving $\emptyset$. The latter is strictly methodological. It has to do with how one attempts to do or get that which one wants. The major purpose for discussing the above problems is to demonstrate that in a decision-making model of human action, beliefs play a role only in the choice of method or means of obtaining that which is wanted. The methodology of obtaining what one wants is secondary because until one decides upon what one wants, any decision with respect to *how* one will obtain it is vacuous. As demonstrated above, if one wants $\emptyset$ badly enough one will try to do or get it. However, one may argue that a consideration of the difficulty of obtaining what one wants will have an influence on the agent deciding which of the objects of his wants he will try to obtain. Here the implication is that given competing wants, the agent will try to obtain that object of want which he believes will be most easily obtained. But this is not the case, as argued above.

There may very well be another reason why beliefs often appear as a necessary element in causal models of human action. While formulating such models, it is tempting to suppose that agents always act in the most rational manner possible. On the surface, it does not appear very rational for an agent to choose that action (among those which are within his power to perform) which he believes would not (1) satisfy the greatest number of his wants or (2) most easily satisfy his wants. The point is, though, that agents simply do not always act in the most rational way possible. When this fundamental fact of human nature is recognized, it then becomes evident that beliefs do not play a *necessary* role in the causal sequence of human action.

Some will criticize the above analysis on the basis that the very difference between wanting and merely wishing is that the former entails believing a given action in question is within one's power. There are problems, however, with this line of reasoning. For example, it entails that if an agent wants to make a difficult pool shot, he must believe that it is within his power to make that shot. But this is clearly not the case. I may know full well that such a shot is not within my power and try and try again to make that shot as demonstration of my wanting to make it. The critic can attack this example in one of two ways. (a) He can argue that the agent must at least believe that he will be able to make the shot if he practices long enough. But it should be noted that if this is the case the belief involved once again reduces to one concerning the methodology as to how one's want is to be achieved and in this case it is via practice. (b) One can argue that although the agent need not believe that it is within his power to make the pool shot, he must at least believe that it is within his power to attempt to make the shot, e.g., he must believe that it is within his power to pick up the pool cue, bridge his hand, stroke the cue in such a way as to strike the cue ball in an attempt to succeed in making the shot. This alternative, however, is no better that (a) since the belief involved here also involves the methodology of making shots, namely, what is involved in *attempting* to make the pool shot.

Others would counter the above analysis by conceding that while beliefs do not play a necessary role in a causal model of action in the specific ways set out above, they are nevertheless necessary in a more general cognitive sense. After all, one must believe that one is not hallucinating otherwise one's wants would be rendered vacuous. In other words, it is claimed that it is necessary for an agent to believe that the general context within which his specific actions are performed is "real" otherwise there would be no basis for wanting. I would like to suggest that this sense of believing, if it does in fact constitute believing at all, does not conform to what we normally maintain as believing. Rather, this general cognitive sense of the notion in question can be more adequately understood by the concept of *Lebenswelt*. Heidegger used the notion in explaining a primordial sense of intentionality. This primordial or "operative" intentionality refers to prepredicative experiences, ones that occur before any subject-object split. Such a notion is the very heart of a phenomenology of perception. It simply means that human beings function within a very general framework of consciousness *qua* perception by which they confront objects in the external world *before* any explicit analysis of them.[2] . . .

NOTE

1. Goldman, *A Theory of Human Action* (Englewood Cliffs, N.J.: Prentice-Hall, Inc., 1970), p. 74 [see selection 27 of this volume]. An act-tree is a diagram of the relevant actions generated by the performance of a basic art. The term 'relevant' is important for it is logical to maintain that the performance of a basic act results in an infinite number of (unknown and/or undesired) actions. The phrase 'standard conditions' essentially means that the basic acts referred to are within the agent's power to perform in accordance with the above analysis of that power (see the Introduction to Part Four of this volume). For another causal account of human action generated by wants in conjunction with beliefs see C. J. Ducasse, "Explanation, Mechanism and Teleology," in H. Feigl and W. Sellars, ed., *Readings in Philosophical Analysis* (New York: Appleton-Century-Crofts, Inc., 1949), pp. 540–44.

Select Bibliography

GENERAL

D'Arcy, E. *Human Acts* (London, 1963)

Hampshire, S., *Thought and Action* (London, 1959), esp. chs. 2–3.

———. *Freedom of the Individual* (London, 1965).

Kenny, A. *Action, Emotion and Will* (London, 1963).

Louch, A.R. *Explanation and Human Action,* (Los Angeles, 1969).

Melden, A. I. *Free Action* (London, 1961).

Morris, H., ed. *Freedom and Responsibility* (Stanford, 1961).

Pears, D. F., ed. *Freedom and the Will* (London, 1963).

Schoedinger, A. B. *Wants, Decisions, and Human Action: A Praxeological Investiga-tion* (Lanham, Md., 1978).

Taylor, C. *The Explanation of Behaviour* (London, 1964).

THE NATURE OF ACTION

Ackrill, J. L. "Aristotle's Distinction between Energia and Kinesis," *New Essays on Plato and Aristotle,* edited by R. Bambrough (London, 1965).

Aristotle. see *Index Aristotelicus,* edited by H. Bonitz (Graz, 1955) under Energia, Kinesis, Pathos, Poiesis, Praxis.

Austin, J. *Lectures on Jurisprudence* (London, 1863): Lectures XVIII-XIX.

Baier, K. "Acting and Producing," *Journal of Philosophy* 62 (1965): 645–48.

———. "Action and Agent," *Monist* 49 (1965): 183–95.

Chisholm, R. M. "The Descriptive Element in the Concept of 'Action,' " *Journal of Philosophy* 61 (1964): 613–24.

Danto, A. C. "What We Can Do," *Journal of Philosophy* 60 (1963): 435–45.

Daveney, T. F. "Choosing," *Mind* 73 (1964): 515–26.

Dias, R. W. M. *Jurisprudence* (London, 1964), ch. 10.

Ewing, A. C. "What Is Action?" *Proceedings of the Aristotelian Society Supplementary* 17 (1938): 86–101.

Feinberg, Joel. "Action and Responsibility," from *Philosophy in America,* edited by M. Black (London, 1965), pp. 134–60.

Fitzgearld, P. J. "Voluntary and Involuntary Acts," from *Oxford Essays in Jurisprudence,* edited by A. G. Guest (London, 1961), pp. 1–28.

Franks, O. S. "What Is Action?" *Proceedings of the Aristotelian Society, Supplementary* 17 (1938): 102–20.

Geach, P. T. "Ascriptivism," *The Philosophical Review* 69 (1960): 221–25.

Hamlyn, D. W. "Behaviour," *Philosophy* 28 (1953): 132–45.

Hart, H. L. A. "The Ascription of Responsibility and Rights," *Proceedings of the Aristotelian Society* 49 (1949): 171–94.

Hobbes, J. *Leviathan* (1651), esp. part 1, ch. 6.

Holmes, O. W. *The Common Law* (London, 1911), ch. 2.

Hume D. *An Enquiry Concerning Human Understanding* (1748), #vii–viii.

———. *A Treatise of Human Nature* (1738), esp. Book II, part iii, ##1–4.

Kotarbinski, T. "Concept of Action," *Journal of Philosophy* 57 (1960): 215–22.

Ladd, J. "The Ethical Dimensions of the Concept of Action," *Journal of Philosophy* 62 (1965): 633–45.

Locke, J. *An Essay Concerning Human Understanding* (1690), Book II, ch. xxi.

MacMurray, J. "What Is Action?" *Proceedings of the Aristotelian Society, Supplementary* 17 (1938): 69–85.

Mill, J. S. *System of Logic* (1843), Book III, ch. v, #11.

O'Shaughnessy, B. "The Limits of the Will," *The Philosophical Review* 65 (1956): 443–90.

Palmer, F. R. *A Linguistic Study of the English Verb* (London, 1965).

Parsons, T., and Shils, E. A. (eds.), *Towards a General Theory of Action* (Cambridge, Mass., 1951).

Pennock, J. R. "The Problem of Responsibility," in *Responsibility, Nomos III,* edited by C. J. Friedrich (New York, 1960): 3–27.

Pitcher, G. "Hart on Action and Responsibility," *The Philosophical Review* 69 (1960): 226–35.

Potts, T. C. "States, Activities and Performances," *Proceedings of the Aristotelian Society, Supplementary* 39 (1965): 65–84.

Ryle, G. *The Concept of Mind,* (London, 1949), chs. 3–4.

Sachs, D. "A Few Morals about Acts," *The Philosophical Review* 75 (1966): 91–98.

Silber, J. R. "Human Action and the Language of Volitions," *Proceedings of the Aristotelian Society* 64 (1964): 199–220.

Taylor, C. C. W. "States, Activities and Performances," *Proceedings of the Aristotelian Society, Supplementary* 39 (1965): 85–102.

Taylor, R. "I Can," *The Philosophical Review* 69 (1960): 78–89.

Vendler, Z. "Verbs and Times," *The Philosophical Review* 66 (1957): 143–60.

Vesey, G. N. A. "Volition," *Philosophy* 36 (1961): 352–65.

Williams, G. L. *Criminal Law: The General Part* (London, 1961), ch. 1.

Wittgenstein, L. *Philosophical Investigations* (Oxford, 1953), #611–60.

DESCRIPTIONS OF ACTION

Anscombe, G. E. M. "On Brute Facts," *Analysis* 18 (1958): 69–72.
Austin, J. L. *How to Do Things with Words* (Oxford, 1962).
Bennett, J. "Whatever the Consequences," *Analysis* 26 (1966): 83–102.
Benson, J. "The Characterization of Actions and the Virtuous Agent," *Proceedings of the Aristotelian Society* 63 (1963): 251–66.
Bentham, J. *The Principles of Morals and Legislation* (Oxford, 1789), esp. chs. vii–x.
Chopra, Y. N. "The Consequences of Human Actions," *Proceedings of the Aristotelian Society* 65 (1965): 147–66.
Donnellan, K. S. "Knowing What I Am Doing," *Journal of Philosophy* 60 (1963): 401–409.
Griffin, J. "Consequences," *Proceedings of the Aristotelian Society* 65 (1965): 167–82.
Meiland, J. W. "Are There Unintentional Actions?" *The Philosophical Review* 72 (1963): 377–81.
Will, F. L. "Intention, Error, and Responsibility," *Journal of Philosophy* 61 (1964): 171–79.

EXPLANATIONS OF ACTION

Anscombe, G. E. M. *Intention* (Oxford, 1957).
Austin, J. L., "A Plea for Excuses," *Proceedings of the Aristotelian Society* 57 (1957): 1–30.
———. "Three Ways of Spilling Ink," *The Philosophical Review* 75 (1966): 427–40.
Ayer, A. J. *Man as a Subject for Science,* Auguste Comte Memorial Lecture 6 (London, 1964).
Baier, K. "Reasons for Doing Something," *Journal of Philosophy* 61 (1964): 198–203.
Beck, L. W. "Agent, Actor, Spectator, and Critic," *Monist* 49 (1965): 167–82.
———. "Conscious and Unconscious Motives," *Mind* 75 (1966): 155–79.
Bennett D. "Action, Reason, and Purpose," *Journal of Philosophy* 62 (1965): 85–96.
Berofsky, B. "Determinism and the Concept of a Person," *Journal of Philosophy* 61 (1964): 461–75.
Brandt, R., and J. Kim. "Wants as Explanations of Actions," *Journal of Philosophy* 60 (1963): 425–35.
Brodbeck, May. "Meaning and Action," *Philosophy of Science* 30 (1963): 309–24.
Brown, R. "The Explanation of Behaviour," *Philosophy* 40 (1965): 344–48.
Goldberg, B. "Can a Desire Be a Cause?" *Analysis* 25 (1965): 70–72.
Hamlyn, D. W. "Causality and Human Behaviour," *Proceedings of the Aristotelian Society, Supplementary* 38 (1964): 125–42.
Hart, H. L. A. "Acts of Will and Responsibility," *Jubilee Lectures at Sheffield,* edited by O. R. Marshall (London, 1960), pp. 115–44.
Hart, H. L. A., and Honoré, A. M. *Causation in the Law* (Oxford, 1959).
Heath, P. L. "Intentions," *Proceedings of the Aristotelian Society, Supplementary* 29 (1955): 147–64.

Jenkins, J. S. "Motives and Intention," *The Philosophical Quarterly* 15 (1965): 155–64.

Louch, A. R. "Science and Psychology," *British Journal for the Philosophy of Science* 12 (1962): 314–27.

MacIntyre, A. C. "The Antecedents of Action," *British Analytical Philosophy,* edited by Williams and Montefiore, (London, 1966) 205–25.

———. "A Mistake about Causality in Social Science," *Philosophy, Politics and Sociology,* II, edited by P. Laslett and W. G. Runciman (Oxford, 1962), 48–70.

Meiland, J. W. *The Nature of Intention* (London, 1970).

Passmore, J. A. "Intentions," *Proceedings of the Aristotelian Society, Supplementary* 29 (1955): 131–46.

Peters, R. S. *The Concept of Motivation* (London, 1958).

Peters, R. S., and Tajfel, H., "Hobbes and Hull—Metaphysicians of Behaviour," *British Journal for the Philosophy of Science* 7 (1957): 30–44.

Prichard, H. A. "Acting, Willing, Desiring," from *Moral Obligation* (Oxford, 1949), 187–98.

Scheffler, I. *The Anatomy of Inquiry* (New York, 1963), 88–123.

Smart, J. J. C. "Causality and Human Behaviour," *Proceedings of the Aristotelian Society Supplementary* 38 (1964): 143–48.

Sutherland, N. S. "Motives as Explanations," *Mind* 68 (1959): 145–59.

Urmson, J. O. "Motives and Causes," *Proceedings of the Aristotelian Society, Supplementary* 26 (1952): 179–94.

Teichmann, J. "Mental Cause and Effect," *Mind* 70 (1961): 36–52.

White, A. R. *The Philosophy of Mind* (New York, 1967), ch. 6.

Part Five

The Question of
Artificial Intelligence

Introduction

Although the age of cybernetics is in its infancy, the issue as to whether or not human beings are machines is quite old. Descartes argued that the difference between human beings and animals was that the former possess thoughts and feelings whereas the latter do not. He was attempting to establish mind *qua* consciousness as the essential difference between the two. Here there are two important points. (1) There is the assumption that animal behavior can be explained mechanistically and (2) that consciousness provides the basis for teleological behavior.

With respect to (1), Julien LaMettrie, in his book *L'Homme Machine* (1747), attempted to turn the tables on Descartes by arguing that human beings are a species of animal and that therefore their behavior is as mechanistic as the remainder of the biosphere. LaMettrie's thesis did not go unnoticed. Several nineteenth-century theorists, most notably T. H. Huxley, argued that man was nothing other than conscious automation. This line of reasoning has extended itself into the twentieth century in the form of extreme behaviorism manifested by the writings of C. L. Hull and B. F. Skinner.

(2) During the latter part of the nineteenth century, William James disputed the claims of mechanistic psychology, contending that machines were incapable of purposive or self-adapted movement. Somehow it is felt that the essential difference between human beings and "hardware" is that the former engage in goal-oriented behavior. How, pray tell, could any (hardware) machine achieve by its own accord some self-determined goal? This issue of teleology has created a sizable stumbling block for those who believe in the viability of artificial intelligence. Nevertheless, the possibility (and probability) that human beings are programmed should seriously be taken into account. If we are programmed and manifest teleological behavior, then we may be forced to maintian that automata are teleogically oriented as well. However, the issue is not so simple. Does goal-oriented behavior entail thinking? If

so, there is a problem since machines can solve a myriad of problems, from complicated chess moves to medical diagnostics.

At some point or other the disputants in this discussion concerning the viability of artificial intelligence must determine whether the issue is an empirical one or a matter of semantics. This distinction is very important since much of the literature concerning artificial intelligence has been concerned with just this conflict. Some argue that by definition a human being cannot be a machine; namely, that there are *a priori* concerns that make the two classes of entity mutually exclusive. Others maintain that the *a priori* position is closed-minded and that it's really an empirical question; namely, that the only reason machines have not been able to reproduce human activity to date is due to a lack of technological sophistication. At a certain point there must be some agreement on both sides of the issue as to what properly constitutes "intelligence." In a 1950 article titled "Computing Machinery and Intelligence," A. M. Turing argued that there are ontological criteria that can be satisfied and therefore used to distinguish humans from machines. If under highly sophisticated conditions a (hardware) machine could simulate a human response, then we would be forced to admit that there is artificial intelligence. As the technology in cybernics becomes progressively more sophisticated, it appears that (a) we are capable of producing very complex decision-making machines and that the potential is limitless, and (b) human beings are highly complex machines.

In light of the conflict between the *a priori* and empirical points of view it is important to ask the following questions: (1) Can a machine think? If so, what are the criteria that constitute thinking? (2) Can a machine feel? Descartes ambiguously maintained that animals do not feel. In what sense do they not feel? Might machines feel? In what sense is this a pertinent question? The problem of criteria is of utmost importance: to a great extent it determines whether or not there can be any meaningful discussion about artificial intelligence at the outset.

29

Elements of a Theory
of Human Problem Solving

Allen Newell, J. C. Shaw, and Herbert A. Simon

In this paper we shall set forth the elements of a theory of human problem solving, together with some evidence for its validity drawn from the currently accepted facts about the nature of problem solving. What questions should a theory of problem solving answer? First, it should predict the performance of a problem solver handling specified tasks. It should explain how human problem solving takes place: what processes are used, and what mechanisms perform these processes. It should predict the incidental phenomena that accompany problem solving, and the relation of these to the problem-solving process. For example, it should account for "set" and for the apparent discontinuities that are sometimes called "insight." It should show how changes in the attendant conditions—both changes "inside" the problem solver and changes in the task confronting him—alter problem-solving behavior. It should explain how specific and general problem-solving skills are learned, and what it is that the problem solver "has" when he has learned them.

INFORMATION-PROCESSING SYSTEMS

Questions about problem-solving behavior can be answered at various levels and in varying degrees of detail. The theory to be described here explains

From *Psychological Review* 65 (1958): 151–66.

problem-solving behavior in terms of what we shall call *information processes.* If one considers the organism to consist of effectors, receptors, and a control system for joining these, then this theory is mostly a theory of the control system. It avoids most questions of sensory and motor activities. The theory postulates:

1. A control system consisting of a number of *memories,* which contain symbolized information and are interconnected by various ordering relations. The theory is not at all concerned with the physical structures that allow this symbolization, nor with any properties of the memories and symbols other than those it explicitly states.

2. A number of *primitive information processes,* which operate on the information in the memories. Each primitive process is a perfectly definite operation for which known physical mechanisms exist. (The mechanisms are not necessarily known to exist in the human brain, however—we are only concerned that the processes be described without ambiguity.)

3. A perfectly definite set of rules for combining these processes into whole *programs* of processing. From a program it is possible to deduce unequivocally what externally observable behaviors will be generated.

At this level of theorizing, *an explanation of an observed behavior of the organism is provided by a program of primitive information processes that generates this behavior.*

A program viewed as a theory of behavior is highly specific: it describes one organism in a particular class of situations. When either the situation or the organism is changed, the program must be modified. The program can be used as a theory—that is, as a predictor of behavior—in two distinct ways. First, it makes many precise predictions that can be tested in detail regarding the area of behavior it is designed to handle. For example, the theory considered in this paper predicts exactly how much difficulty an organism with the specified program will encounter in solving each of a series of mathematical problems: which of the problems it will solve, how much time (up to a proportionality constant) will be spent on each, and so on.

Second, there will be important qualitative similarities among the programs that an organism uses in various situations, and among the programs used by different organisms in a given situation. The program that a human subject uses to solve mathematical problems will be similar in many respects to the program he uses to choose a move in chess: the program one subject uses for any such task will resemble the programs used by other subjects possessing similar training and abilities. If there were no such similarities, if each subject and each task were completely idiosyncratic, there could be no theory of human problem solving. Moreover, there is some positive evidence, as we shall see, that such similarities and general characteristics of problem-solving processes do exist.

In this paper we shall limit ourselves to this second kind of validation of our theory of problem solving. We shall predict qualitative characteristics of human problem-solving behavior and compare them with those that have already been observed and described. Since all of the available data on the psychology of human problem solving are of this qualitative kind, no more detailed test or a program is possible at present. The more precise validation must wait upon new experimental work.[1]

In succeeding sections we shall describe an information-processing program for discovering proofs for theorems in logic. We shall compare its behavior qualitatively with that of human problem solvers. In general, the processes that compose the program are familiar from everyday experience and from research on human problem solving: searching for possible solutions, generating these possibilities out of other elements, and evaluating partial solutions and cues. From this standpoint there is nothing particularly novel about the theory. It rests its claims on other considerations:

1. It shows specifically and in detail how the processes that occur in human problem solving can be compounded out of elementary information processes, and hence how they can be carried out by mechanisms.

2. It shows that a program incorporating such processes, with appropriate organization, can in fact solve problems. This aspect of problem solving has been thought to be "mysterious" and unexplained because it was not understood how sequences of simple processes could account for the successful solution of complex problems. The theory dissolves the mystery by showing that nothing more need be added to the constitution of a successful problem solver.

RELATION TO DIGITAL COMPUTERS

The ability to specify programs precisely, and to infer accurately the behavior they will produce, derives from the use of high-speed digital computers. Each specific theory—each program of information processes that purports to describe some human behavior—is coded for a computer. That is, each primitive information process is coded to be a separate computer routine, and a "master" routine is written that allows these primitive processes to be assembled into any system we wish to specify. Once this has been done, we can find out exactly what behavior the purported theory predicts by having the computer "simulate" the system.

We wish to emphasize that we are not using the computer as a crude analogy to human behavior—we are not comparing computer structures with brains, nor electrical relays with synapses. Our position is that the appropriate way to describe a piece of problem-solving behavior is in terms of a program: a specification of what the organism will do under varying environmental circumstances in terms of certain elementary information processes it is capable of performing. This assertion has nothing to do—directly—with computers. Such programs could be written (now that we have discovered how to do it) if computers had never existed.[2] A program is no more, and no less, an analogy to the behavior of an organism than is a differential equation to the behavior of the electrical circuit it describes. Digital computers come into the picture only because they can, by appropriate programming, be induced to execute the same sequences of information processes that humans execute when they are solving problems. Hence, as we shall see, these programs describe both human and machine problem solving at the level of information processes.[3]

With this discussion of the relation of programs to machines and humans behind us, we can afford to relax into convenient, and even metaphoric, uses of language without much danger of misunderstanding. It is often convenient to talk about the behavior implied by a program as that of an existing physical mechanism doing things. This mode of expression is legitimate, for if we take the trouble to put any particular program in a computer, we have in fact a machine that behaves in the way prescribed by the program. Similarly, for concreteness, we will often talk as if our theory of problem solving consisted of statements about the ability of a comptuer to do certain things.

THE LOGIC THEORIST

We can now turn to an example of the theory. This is a program capable of solving problems in a particular domain—capable, specifically, of discovering proofs for theorems in elementary symbolic logic. We shall call this program the Logic Theorist (LT).[4] We assert that the behavior of this program, when the stimulus consists of the instruction that it prove a particular theorem, can be used to predict the behavior of (certain) humans when they are faced with the same problem in symbolic logic.

The program of LT was not fashioned directly as a theory of human behavior: it was constructed in order to get a program that would prove theorems in logic. To be sure, in constructing it the authors were guided by a firm belief that a practicable program could be constructed only if it used many of the processes that humans use. The fact remains that the program was not devised by fitting it directly to human data. As a result, there are many details of LT that we would not expect to correspond to human behavior. For example, no particular care was exercised in choosing the primitive information processes to correspond, point by point, with elementary human processes. All that was required in writing the program was that the primitive processes constitute a sufficient set and a convenient set for the type of program under study.

Since LT has been described in detail elsewhere (6, 8),* the description will not be repeated here. It will also be unnecessary to describe in detail the system of symbolic logic that is used by LT. For those readers who are not familiar with symbolic logic, we may remark that problems in the sentential calculus are at about the same level of difficulty and have somewhat the same "flavor" as problems in high school geometry.[5]

Design of the Experiments

First we will describe the overt behavior of LT when it is presented with problems in elementary symbolic logic. In order to be concrete, we will refer to an experiment conducted on a digital computer. We take an ordinary general-purpose digital computer,[6] and store in its memory a program for interpreting the specifications of LT. Then we load the program that specifies LT. The reader may think of this program as a collection of techniques that LT has acquired for discovering proofs. These techniques range from the ability to read and write expressions in symbolic logic to general schemes for how a proof might be found.

Once we have loaded this program and pushed the start button, the computer, to all intents and purposes, *is* LT. It already knows how to do symbolic logic, in the sense that the basic rules of operation of the mathematics are already in the program (analogously to a human's knowing that "equals added to equals give equals" in elementary algebra).

We are now ready to give LT a task. We give it a list of the expressions (axioms and previously proved theorems) that it may take as "given" for the task at hand. These are stored in LT's memory. Finally, we present LT with another expression and instruct it to discover a proof for this expression.

From this point, the computer is on its own. The program plus the task uniquely determines its behavior. It attempts to find a proof—that is, it tries various techniques, and if they don't work, it tries other techniques. If LT finds a legitimate proof, it prints this out on a long strip of paper. There is, of course, no guarantee that it will find a proof; after working for some time, the machine will give up—that is, it will stop looking for a proof.

Now the experimenters know exactly what is in the memory of LT when

---

*See the numbered reference list following the notes to this selection—*Ed.*

it starts—indeed, they created the program. This, however, is quite different from saying that the experimenters can predict everything LT will do. In principle this is possible; but in fact the program is so complex that the only way to make detailed predictions is to employ a human to simulate the program by hand. (A human can do anything a digital computer can do, although it may take him considerably longer.)

1. As the initial experiment, we stored the axioms of *Principia Mathematica*, together with the program, in the memory of LT, and then presented to LT the first 52 theorems in chapter 2 of *Principia* in the sequence in which they appear there. LT's program specified that as a theorem was proved it was stored in memory and was available, along with the axioms, as material for the construction of proofs of subsequent theorems. With this program and this order of presentation of problems, LT succeeded in proving 38 (73 percent) of the 52 theorems. About half of the proofs were accomplished in less than a minute each; most of the remainder took from one to five minutes. A few theorems were proved in times ranging from 15 minutes to 45 minutes. There was a strong relation between the times and the lengths of the proofs—the time increasing sharply (perhaps exponentially) with each additional proof step.

2. The initial conditions were now restored by removing from LT's memory the theorems it had proved. (Translate: "A new subject was obtained who knew how to solve problems in logic but was unfamiliar with the particular problems to be used in the experiment.") When one of the later theorems of chapter 2 (Theorem 2.12) was presented to LT, it was not able to find a proof, although when it had held the prior theorems in memory, it had found one in about ten seconds.

3. Next, an experiment was performed intermediate between the first two. The axioms and Theorem 2.03 were stored in memory, but not the other theorems prior to Theorem 2.21, and LT was again given the task of proving the latter. Now, using Theorem 2.03 as one of its resources, LT succeeded— in fifteen minutes—where it had failed in the second experiment. The proof required three steps. In the first experiment, with all prior theorems available, the proof required only one step.

Outcome of the Experiments

From these three series of experiments we obtain several important pieces of evidence that the program of LT is qualitatively like that of a human faced with the same task. The first, and most important, evidence is that LT does in fact succeed in finding proofs for a large number of theorems.

Let us make this point quite clear. Since LT can actually discover proofs for theorems, its program incorporates a *sufficient* set of elementary processes arranged in a sufficiently effective strategy to produce this result. Since no other program has ever been specified for handling successfully these kinds of problem-solving tasks, no definite alternative hypothesis is available. We are well aware of the standard argument that "similarity of function does not imply similarity of process." However useful a caution this may be, it should not blind us to the fact that specification of a set of mechanisms sufficient to produce observed behavior is strong confirmatory evidence for the theory embodying these mechanisms, especially when it is contrasted with theories that cannot establish their sufficiency.

The only alternative problem-solving mechanisms that have been completely specified for these kinds of tasks are simple algorithms that carry out exhaustive searches of all possibilities, substituting "brute force" for the selective search of LT. Even with the speeds available to digital computers, the principal algorithm we have devised as an alternative to LT would require times of the order of hundreds or even thousands of years to prove theorems that LT proves in a few minutes. LT's success does not depend on the "brute force" use of a computer's speed, but on the use of heuristic processes like those employed by humans.[7] This can be seen directly from examination of the program, but it also shows up repeatedly in all the other behavior exhibited by LT.

The second important fact that emerges from the experiments is that LT's success depends in a very sensitive way upon the order in which problems are presented to it. When the sequence is arranged so that before any particular problem is reached some potentially helpful intermediate results have already been obtained, then the task is easy. It can be made progressively harder by skipping more and more of these intermediate stepping-stones. Moreover, by providing a single "hint," as in the third experiment (that is, "Here is a theorem that might help"), we can induce LT to solve a problem it had previously found insoluble. All of these results are easily reproduced in the laboratory with humans. To compare LT's behavior with that of a human subject, we would first have to train the latter in symbolic logic (this is equivalent to reading the program into LT), but without using the specific theorems of chapter 2 of *Principia Mathematica* that are to serve as problem material. We would then present problems to the human subject in the same sequence as to LT. For each new sequence we would need naive subjects, since it is difficult to induce a human subject to forget completely theorems he has once learned.

PERFORMANCE PROCESSES IN THE LOGIC THEORIST

We can learn more about LT's approximation to human problem solving by instructing it to print out some of its intermediate results—to work its problems on paper, so to speak. The data thus obtained can be compared with data obtained from a human subject who is asked to use scratch paper as he works a problem, or to think aloud.[8] Specifically, the computer can be instructed to print out a record of the subproblems it works on and the methods it applies, successfully and unsuccessfully, while seeking a solution. We can obtain this information at any level of detail we wish, and make a correspondingly detailed study of LT's processes.

To understand the additional information provided by this "thinking aloud" procedure, we need to describe a little more fully how LT goes about solving problems. This description has two parts: (*a*) specifying what constitutes a proof in symbolic logic; (*b*) describing the methods that LT uses in finding proofs.

Nature of a Proof

A proof in symbolic logic (and in other branches of logic and mathematics) is a sequence of statements such that each statement: (*a*) follows from one or more of the others that precede it in the sequence, or (*b*) is an axiom or previously proved theorem.[9] Here "follows" means "follows by the rules of logic."

LT is given four rules of inference:

Substitution. In a true expression (for example, "[p or p] implies p") there may be substituted for any variable a new variable or expression, provided that the substitution is made throughout the original expression. Thus, by substituting p or q for p in the expression "(p or p) implies p," we get: "[p or q] or [p or q]) implies (p or q)" but *not:* "([p or q] or p) implies p."

Replacement. In a true expression a connective ("implies," etc.) may be replaced by its definition in terms of other connectives. Thus "A implies B" is defined to be "not-A or B"; hence the two forms can be used interchangeably.

Detachment. If "A" is a true expression and "A implies B" is a true expression, then B may be written down as a true expression.

Syllogism (Chaining). It is possible to show by two successive applications of detachment that the following is also legitimate: If "a implies b" is a true expression and "b implies c" is a true expression, then "a implies c" is also a true expression.

Proof Methods

The task of LT is to construct a proof sequence deriving a problem expression from the axioms and the previously proved theorems by the rules of inference listed above. But the rules of inference, like the rules of any mathematical system or any game, are permissive, not mandatory. That is, they state what sequences *may* legitimately be constructed, not what particular sequence should be constructed in order to achieve a particular result (i.e., to prove a particular problem expression). The set of "legal" sequences is exceeding large, and to try to find a suitable sequence by trial and error alone would almost always use up the available time or memory before it would exhaust the set of legal sequences.[10]

To discover proofs, LT uses *methods* which are particular combinations of information processes that result in coordinated activity aimed at progress in a particular direction. LT has four methods (it could have more): *substitution, detachment, forward chaining,* and *backward chaining.* Each method focuses on a single possibility for achieving a link in a proof.

The substitution method attempts to prove an expression by generating it from a known theorem employing substitutions of variables and replacements of connectives.

The detachment method tries to work backward, utilizing the rule of detachment to obtain a new expression whose proof implies the proof of the desired expression. This possibility arises from the fact that if B is to be proved, and we already know a theorem of the form "A implies B," then proof of A is tantamount to proof of B.

Both chaining methods try to work backward to new problems, using the rule of syllogism, analogously to the detachment method. Forward chaining uses the fact that if "a implies c" is desired and "a implies b" is already known, then it is sufficient to prove "b implies c." Backward chaining runs the argument the other way: desiring "a implies c" and knowing "b implies c" yields "a implies b" as a new problem.

The methods are the major organizations of processes in LT, but they are not all of it. There is an executive process that coordinates the use of the methods, and selects the subproblems and theorems upon which the methods operate. The executive process also applies any learning processes that are to be applied. Also, all the methods utilize common subprocesses in carrying out their activity. The two most important subprocesses are the *matching* process, which endeavors to make two given subexpressions identical, and the *similarity test,* which determines (on the basis of certain computed descriptions) whether two expressions are "similar" in a certain sense (for details, cf. 8).

LT can be instructed to list its attempts, successful and unsuccessful, to use these methods, and can list the new subproblems generated at each stage by these attempts. We can make this concrete by an example:

Suppose that the problem is to prove "p implies p." The statement "(p or p) implies p" is an axiom; and "p implies (p or p)" is a theorem that has already been proved and stored in the theorem memory. Following its program, LT first tries to prove "p implies p" by the substitution method, but fails because it can find no similar theorem in which to make substitutions.

Next, it tries the detachment method. Letting B stand for "p implies p," several theorems are found of the form "A implies B." For example, by substitution of not-p for q, "p implies (q or p)" becomes "p implies (not-p or p)"; this becomes, in turn, by replacement of "or" by "implies": "p implies (p implies p)." Discovery of this theorem creates a new subproblem: "Prove A"—that is, "prove p." This subproblem, of course, leads nowhere, since p is not a universally true theorem, hence cannot be proved.

At a later stage in its search LT tries the chaining method. Chaining forward, it finds the theorem "p implies (p or p)" and is then faced with the new problem of proving that "(p or p) implies p." This it is able to do by the substitution method, when it discovers the corresponding axiom.

All of these steps, successful and unsuccessful, in its proof—and the ones we have omitted from our exposition, as well—can be printed out to provide us with a complete record of how LT executed its program in solving this particular problem.

SOME CHARACTERISTICS OF THE PROBLEM-SOLVING PROCESS

Using as our data the information provided by LT as to the methods it tries, the sequence of these methods, and the theorems employed, we can ask whether its procedure shows any resemblance to the human problem-solving process as it has been described in psychological literature. We find that there are, indeed, many such resemblances, which we summarize under the following headings: set, insight, concept formation, and structure of the problem-subproblem hierachy.

Set

The term "set," sometimes defined as "a readiness to make a specified response to a specified stimulus" (4. p. 65), covers a variety of psychological phenomena. We should not be surprised to find that more than one aspect of LT's behavior exhibits "set," nor that these several evidences of set correspond to quite different underlying processes.

1. Suppose that after the program has been loaded in LT, the axioms and a sequence of problem expressions are placed in its memory. Before LT undertakes to prove the first problem expression, it goes through the list of axioms and computes a description of each for subsequent use in the "similarity" tests. For this reason, the proof of the first theorem takes an extra interval of time amounting, in fact, to about twenty seconds. Functionally and phenomenologically, this computation process and interval represent a *preparatory set* in the sense in which that term is used in reaction-time experiments. It turns out in LT that this preparatory set saves about one third of the computing time that would otherwise be required in later stages of the program.

2. *Directional set* is also evident in LT's behavior. When it is attempting a particular subproblem, LT tries first to solve it by the substitution method. If this proves fruitless, and only then, it tries the detachment method, then chaining forward, then chaining backward. Now when it searches for theorems suitable for the substitution method, it will not notice theorems that might later be suitable for detachment (different similarity tests being applied in the two cases). It attends single-mindedly to possible candidates for substitution until the theorem list has been exhausted: then it turns to the detachment method.

3. Hints and the change in behavior they induce have been mentioned earlier. Variants of LT exist in which the order of methods attempted by LT, and the choice of units in describing expressions, depend upon appropriate hints from the experimenter.

4. Effects from directional set occur in certain learning situations—as illustrated, for example, by the classical experiments of Luchins. Although LT at the present time has only a few learning mechanisms, these will produce strong effects of directional set if problems are presented to LT in appropriate sequences. For example, it required about 45 minutes to prove Theorem 2.48 in the first experiment because LT, provided with all the prior theorems, explored so many blind alleys. Given only the axioms and Theorem 2.16, LT proved Theorem 2.48 in about 15 minutes because it now considered a quite different set of possibilities.

The instances of set observable in the present program of LT are natural and unintended by-products of a program constructed to solve problems in an efficient way. In fact, it is difficult to see how we could have avoided such effects. In its simplest aspect, the problem-solving process is a search for a solution in a very large space of possible solutions. The possible solutions must be examined in *some* particular sequence, and if they are, then certain possible solutions will be examined before others. The particular rule that induces the order of search induces thereby a definite set in the ordinary psychological meaning of that term.

Preparatory set also arises from the need for processing efficiency. If certain information is needed each time a possible solution or group of solutions is to be examined, it may be useful to compute this information, once and for all, at the beginning of the problem-solving process, and to store it instead of recomputing it each time.

The examples cited show that set can arise in almost every aspect of the problem-solving process. It can govern the sequence in which alternatives are examined (the "method" set), it can select the concepts that are used in classifying perceptions (the "viewing" set), and it can consist in preparatory processes (the description of axioms).

None of the examples of set in LT relate to the way in which information is stored in memory. However, one would certainly expect such set to exist, and certain psychological phenomena bear this out—the set in association experiments, and so-called "incubation" processes. LT as it now stands is inadequate in this respect.

Insight

In the psychological literature, "insight" has two principal connotations: (*a*) "suddenness" of discovery, and (*b*) grasp of the "structure" of the problem, as evidenced by absence of trial and error. It has often been pointed out that there is no necessary connection between the absence of overt trial-and-error behavior and grasp of the problem structure, for trial and error may be perceptual or ideational, and no obvious cues may be present in behavior to show that it is going on.

In LT an observer's assessment of how much trial and error there is will depend on how much of the record of its problem-solving processes the computer prints out. Moreover, the amount of trial and error going on "inside" varies within very wide limits, depending on small changes in the program.

The performance of LT throws some light on the classical debate between proponents of trial-and-error learning and proponents of "insight," and shows that this controversy, as it is usually phrased, rests on ambiguity and confusion. LT searches for solutions to the problems that are presented it. This search must be carried out in some sequence, and LT's success in actually finding solutions for rather difficult problems rests on the fact that the sequences it uses are not chosen casually but do, in fact, depend on problem "structure."

To keep matters simple, let us consider just one of the methods LT uses proof by substitution. The number of valid proofs (of *some* theorem) that the machine can construct by substitution of new expressions for the variables in the axioms is limited only by its patience in generating expressions. Suppose now that LT is presented with a problem expression to be proved by substitution. The crudest trial-and-error procedure we can imagine is for the machine to generate substitutions in a predetermined sequence that is independent of the expression to be proved, and to compare each of the resulting expressions with the problem expression, stopping when a pair are identical (cf. 7).

Suppose, now, that the generator of substitutions is constructed so that it is *not* independent of the problem expression—so that it tries substitutions in different sequences depending on the nature of the latter. Then, if the dependence is an appropriate one, the amount of search required on the average can be reduced. A simple strategy of this sort would be to try in the axioms only substitutions involving variables that actually appear in the problem expression.

The actual generator employed by LT is more efficient (and hence more "insightful" by the usual criteria) than this. In fact, it works backward from the problem expression, and takes into account necessary conditions that a substitution must satisfy if it is to work. For example, suppose we are substituting in the axiom "p implies (q or p)," and are seeking to prove "r implies (r or r)." Working backward, it is clear that *if* the latter expression can be obtained from the former by substitution at all, then the variable that must be substituted for p is r. This can be seen by examining the first variable in each expression, without considering the rest of the expression at all (cf. 7).

Trial and error is reduced to still smaller proportions by the method for searching the list of theorems. Only those theorems are extracted from the list for attempted substitution which are "similar" in a defined sense to the problem expression. This means, in practice, that substitution is attempted in only about ten percent of the theorems. Thus a trial-and-error search of the theorem list to find theorems similar to the problem expression is substituted for a trial-and-error series of attempted substitutions in each of the theorems.

In these examples, the concept of proceeding in a "meaningful" fashion is entirely clear and explicit. Trial-and-error attempts take place in some "space" of possible solutions. To approach a problem "meaningfully" is to have a strategy that either permits the search to be limited to a smaller subspace, or generates elements of the space in an order that makes probable the discovery of one of the solutions early in the process.

We have already listed some of the most important elements in the program of LT for reducing search to tolerable proportions. These are: (*a*) the description programs to select theorems that are "likely" candidates for substitution attempts; (*b*) the process of working backwards, which uses information about the goal to rule out large numbers of attempts without actually trying them. In addition to these, the executive routine may select the sequence of subproblems to be worked on in an order that takes up "simple" subproblems first.

Concepts

Most of the psychological research on concepts has focused on the processes of their formation. The current version of LT is mainly a performance program, and hence shows no concept formation. There is in the program, however, a clearcut example of the use of concepts in problem solving. This is the routine for describing theorems and searching for theorems "similar" to the problem expression or some part of it in order to attempt substitutions, detachments, or chainings. All theorems having the same description exemplify a common concept. We have, for example, the concept of an expression that has a single variable, one argument place on its left side, and two argument places on its right side: "p implies (p or p)" is an expression exemplifying this concept; so is "q implies (q implies q)."

The basis for these concepts is purely pragmatic. Two expressions having the same description "look alike" in some undefined sense; hence, if we are seeking to prove one of them as a theorem, while the other is an axiom or theorem already proved, the latter is likely construction material for the proof of the former.

Hierarchies of Processes

Another characteristic of the behavior of LT that resembles human problem-solving behavior is the hierarchical structure of its processes. Two kinds of hierarchies exist, and these will be described in the next two paragraphs.

In solving a problem, LT breaks it down into component problems. First of all, it makes three successive attempts: a proof by substitution, a proof by detachment, or a proof by chaining. In attempting to prove a theorem by any of these methods, it divides its task into two parts: first, finding likely raw materials in the form of axioms or theorems previously proved; second, using these materials in matching. To find theorems similar to the problem expression, the first step is to compute a description of the problem expression: the second step is to search the list of theorems for expressions with the same description. The description-computing program divides, in turn, into a program for computing the number of levels in the expression, a program for computing the number of distinct variables, and a program for computing the number of argument places.

LT has a second kind of hierarchy in the generation of new expressions to be proved. Both the detachment and chaining methods do not give proofs directly but, instead, provide new alternative expressions to prove. LT keeps a list of these subproblems, and, since they are of the same type as the original problem, it can apply all its problem-solving methods to them. These methods, of course, yield yet other subproblems, and in this way a large network of problems is developed during the course of proving a given logic expression. The importance of this type of hierarchy is that it is not fixed in advance, but grows in response to the problem-solving process itself, and shows some of the flexibility and transferability that seem to characterize human higher mental processes.

The problem-subproblem hierarchy in LT's program is quite comparable with the hierarchies that have been discovered by students of human problem-solving processes, and particularly by de Groot in his detailed studies of the thought methods of chess players (2, pp. 78–83, 105–111). Our earlier discussion of insight shows how the program structure permits an efficient combination of trial-and-error search with systematic use of experience and cues in the total problem-solving process.

SUMMARY OF THE EVIDENCE

We have now reviewed the principal evidence that LT solves problems in a manner closely resembling that exhibited by humans in dealing with the same problems. First, and perhaps most important, it is in fact capable of finding proofs for theorems—hence incorporates a system of processes that is sufficient for a problem-solving mechanism. Second, its ability to solve a particular problem depends on the sequence in which problems are presented to it in much the same way that a human subject's behavior depends on this sequence. Third, its behavior exhibits both preparatory and directional set. Fourth, it exhibits insight both in the sense of vicarious trial and error leading to "sudden" problem solution, and in the sense of employing heuristics to keep the total amount of trial and error within reasonable bounds. Fifth, it employs simple concepts to classify the expressions with which it deals. Sixth, its program exhibits a complex organized hierarchy of problems and subproblems.

COMPARISON WITH OTHER THEORIES

We have proposed a theory of the higher mental processes, and have shown how LT, which is a particular exemplar of the theory, provides an explanation for the processes used by humans to solve problems in symbolic logic. What is the relation of this explanation to others that have been advanced?

Associationism

The broad class of theories usually labelled "associationist" share a generally behaviorist viewpoint and a commitment to reducing mental functions to elementary, mechanistic neural events. We agree with the associationists that the higher mental processes can be performed by mechanisms—indeed, we have exhibited a specific set of mechanisms capable of performing some of them.

We have avoided, however, specifying these mechanisms in neurological or pseudoneurological terms. Problem solving—at the information-processing level at which we have described it—has nothing specifically "neural" about it, but can be performed by a wide class of mechanisms, including both human brains and digital computers. We do not believe that this functional equivalence between brains and computers implies any structural equivalence at a more minute anatomical level (e.g., equivalence of neurons with circuits). Discovering what neural mechanisms realize these information-processing functions in the human brain is a task for another level of theory construction. Our theory is a theory of the information processes involved in problem solving, and not a theory of neural or electronic mechanisms for information processing.

The picture of the central nervous system to which our theory leads is a picture of a more complex and active system than that contemplated by most associationists. The notions of "trace," "fixation," "excitation," and "inhibition" suggest a relatively passive electrochemical system (or, alternatively, a passive "switchboard"), acted upon by stimuli, altered by that action, and subsequently behaving in a modified manner when later stimuli impinge on it.

In contrast, we postulate an information-processing system with large storage capacity that holds, among other things, complex strategies (programs) that may be evoked by stimuli. The stimulus determines what strategy or strategies will be evoked; the content of these strategies is already largely determined by the previous experience of the system. The ability of the system to respond in complex and highly selective ways to relatively simple stimuli is a consequence of this storage of programs and this "active" response to stimuli. The phenomena of set and insight that we have already described and the hierarchical structure of the response system are all consequences of this "active" organization of the central processes.

The historical preference of behaviorists for a theory of the brain that pictured it as a passive photographic plate or switchboard, rather than as an active computer, is no doubt connected with the struggle against vitalism. The invention of the digital computer has acquainted the world with a device—obviously a mechanism—whose response to stimuli is clearly more complex and "active" than the response of more traditional switching networks. It has provided us with operational and unobjectionable interpretations of terms like "purpose," "set," and "insight." The real importance of the digital computer for the theory of higher mental processes lies not merely in allowing us to realize such processes "in the metal" and outside the brain, but in providing us with a much profounder idea than we have hitherto had of the characteristics a mechanism must possess if it is to carry out complex information-processing tasks.

Gestalt Theories

The theory we have presented resembles the associationist theories largely in its acceptance of the premise of mechanism, and in few other respects. It resembles much more closely some of the Gestalt theories of problem solving, and perhaps most closely the theories of "directed thinking" of Selz and de Groot. A brief overview of Selz's conceptions of problem solving, as expounded by de Groot, will make its relation to our theory clear.

1. Selz and his followers describe problem solving in terms of processes or "operations" (2, p. 42). These are clearly the counterparts of the basic processes in terms of which LT is specified.

2. These operations are organized in a strategy, in which the outcome of each step determines the next (2, p. 44). The strategy is the counterpart of the program of LT.

3. A problem takes the form of a "schematic anticipation." That is, it is posed in some such form as: Find an X that stands in the specified relation R to the given element E (2, pp. 44–46). The counterpart of this in LT is the problem: Find a *sequence of sentences* (X) that stands in the relation of *proof* (R) to the given *problem expression* (E). Similarly, the subproblems posed by LT can be described in terms of schematic anticipations: for example, "Find an expression that is 'similar' to the expression to be proved." Many other examples can be supplied of "schematic anticipations" in LT.

4. The method that is applied toward solving the problem is fully specified by the schematic anticipation. The counterpart in LT is that, upon receipt of the problem, the executive program for solving logic problems specifies the next processing step. Similarly, when a subproblem is posed—like "prove the theorem by substitution"—the response to this subproblem is the initiation of a corresponding program (here, the method of substitution).

5. Problem solving is said to involve (*a*) finding means of solution, and (*b*) applying them (2, pp. 47–53). A counterpart in LT is the division between the similarity routines, which find "likely" materials for a proof, and the matching routines, which try to use these materials. In applying means, there are needed

both *ordering* processes (to assign priorities when more than one method is available) and *control* processes (to evaluate the application) (2, p. 50).

6. Long sequences of solution methods are coupled together. This coupling may be *cumulative* (the following step builds on the result of the preceding) or *subsidiary* (the previous step was unsuccessful, and a new attempt is now made) (2, p. 51). In LT the former is illustrated by a successful similarity comparison followed by an attempt at matching; the latter by the failure of the method of substitution, which is then followed by an attempt at detachment.

7. In cumulative coupling, we can distinguish *complementary* methods from *subordinated* methods (2, p. 52). The former are illustrated by successive substitutions and replacements in successive elements of a pair of logic expressions. The latter are illustrated by the role of matching as a subordinate process in the detachment method.

We could continue this list a good deal further. Our purpose is not to suggest that the theory of LT can or should be translated into the language of "directed thinking." On the contrary, the specification of the program for LT clarifies to a considerable extent notions whose meanings are only vague in the earlier literature. What the list illustrates is that the processes that we observe in LT are basically the same as the processes that have been observed in human problem solving in other contexts.

PERFORMANCE AND LEARNING

LT is primarily a performance machine. That is to say, it solves problems rather than learning how to solve problems. However, although LT does not learn in all the ways that a human problem solver learns, there are a number of important learning processes in the program of LT. These serve to illustrate some, but not all, of the forms of human learning.

Learning in LT

By learning, we mean any more or less lasting change in the response of the system to successive presentations of the same stimulus. By this definition— which is the customary one—LT does learn.

1. When LT has proved a theorem, it stores this theorem in its memory. Henceforth, the theorem is available as material for the proof of subsequent theorems. Therefore, whether LT is able to prove a particular theorem depends, in general, on what theorems it has previously been asked to prove.

2. LT remembers, during the course of its attempt to prove a theorem, what subproblems it has already tried to solve. If the same subproblem is obtained twice in the course of the attempt at a proof, LT will remember and will not try to solve it a second time if it has failed a first.

3. In one variant, LT remembers what theorems have proved useful in the past in conjunction with particular methods and tries these theorems first when applying the method in question. Hence, although its total repertory of methods remains constant, it learns to apply particular methods in particular ways.

These are types of learning that would certainly be found also in human problem solvers. There are other kinds of human learning that are not yet represented in LT. We have already mentioned one—acquiring new methods for attacking problems. Another is modifying the descriptions used in searches for similar theorems, to increase the efficiency of those searches. The latter learning process may also be regarded as a process for concept formation. We have under way a number of activities directed toward incorporating new forms of learning into LT, but we will postpone a more detailed discussion of these until we can report concrete results.

What Is Learned

The several kinds of learning now found in LT begin to cast light on the pedagogical problems of "what is learned?" including the problems of transfer of training. For example, if LT simply stored proofs of theorems as it found these, it would be able to prove a theorem a second time very rapidly, but its learning would not transfer at all to new theorems. The storage of *theorems* has much broader transfer value than the storage of *proofs,* since, as already noted, the proved theorems may be used as stepping stones to the proofs of new theorems. There is no mystery here in the fact that the transferability of what is learned is dependent in a very sensitive way upon the form in which it is learned and remembered. We hope to draw out the implications, psychological and pedagogical, of this finding in our subsequent research on learning.

CONCLUSION

We should like, in conclusion, only to draw attention to the broader implications of this approach to the study of information-processing systems. The heart of the approach is describing the behavior of a system by a well specified program, defined in terms of elementary information processes. In this approach, a specific program plays the role that is played in classical systems of applied mathematics by a specific system of differential equations.

Once the program has been specified, we proceed exactly as we do with traditional mathematical systems. We attempt to deduce general properties of the system from the program (the equations): we compare the behavior predicted from the program (from the equations) with actual behavior observed in experimental or field settings: we modify the program (the equations) when modification is required to fit the facts.

The promise of this approach is several-fold. First, the digital computer provides us with a device capable of realizing programs, and hence, of actually determining what behavior is implied by a program under various environmental conditions. Second, a program is a very concrete specification of the processes, and permits us to see whether the processes we postulate are realizable, and whether they are sufficient to produce the phenomena. The vaguenesses that have plagued the theory of higher mental processes and other parts of psychology disappear when the phenomena are described as programs.

In the present paper we have illustrated this approach by beginning the construction of a thoroughly operational theory of human problem solving. There is every reason to believe that it will prove equally fruitful in application to the theories of learning, of perception, and of concept formation.

NOTES

1. Several studies of individual and group problem-solving behavior with logic problems have been carried out by O. K. Moore and Scarvia Anderson (5). The problems Moore and Anderson gave their subjects are somewhat different from those handled by our program, and hence a detailed comparison of behavior is not yet possible. We are now engaged, with Peter Houts, in replicating and extending the experiments of Moore and Anderson with human subjects and at the same time modifying our program to predict the human laboratory behavior in detail.

2. We can, in fact, find a number of attempts in the psychological literature to explain behavior in terms of programs—or the prototypes thereof. One of the most interesting, because it comes relatively close to the modern conception of a computer program, is Adrian de Groot's analysis of problem solving by chess players (2). The theory of de Groot is based on the thought-psychology of Selz, a somewhat neglected successor to the Wurzburg school. Quite recently, and apparently independently, we find the same idea applied by Jerome S. Bruner and his associates to the theory of concept formation (1). Bruner uses the term "strategy," derived from economics and game theory, for what we have called a program.

3. For a fuller discussion of this point see (9).

4. In fact, matters are a little more complicated, for in the body of this paper we will consider both the basic program of LT and a number of variants on this

program. We will refer to all of these variants, interchangeably, as "LT." This will not be confusing, since the exact content of the program we are considering at any particular point will always be clear from the context.

5. LT employs the sentential calculus as set forth in chapters 1 and 2 of A. N. Whitehead and Bertrand Russell, *Principia Mathematica* (10)—the "classic" of modern symbolic logic. A simple introduction to the system of *Principia* will be found in (3).

6. The experiments described here were carried out with the RAND JOHNNIAC computer. The JOHNNIAC is an automatic digital computer of the Princeton type. It has a word length of 40 bits, with two instructions in each word. Its fast storage consists of 4,096 words of magnetic cores, and its secondary storage consists of 9,216 words on magnetic drums. Its speed is about 15,000 operations per second. The programming techniques used are described more fully in (6). The experiments are reported in more detail in (7).

7. A quantitative analysis of the power of the heuristics incorporated in LT will be found in (7).

8. Evidence obtained from a subject who thinks aloud is sometimes compared with evidence obtained by asking the subject to theorize introspectively about his own thought processes. This is misleading. Thinking aloud is just as truly behavior as is circling the correct answer on a paper-and-pencil test. What we infer from it about other *processes* going on inside the subject (or the machine) is, of course, another question. In the case of the machine, the problem is simpler than in the case of the human, for we can determine exactly the correspondence between the internal processes and what the machine prints out.

9. The axioms of symbolic logic and the theories that follow from them are all tautologies, true by virtue of the definitions of their terms. It is their tautological character that gives laws of logic their validity, independent of empirical evidence, as rules of inductive inference. Hence the very simple axioms that we shall use as examples here will have an appearance of redundancy, if not triviality. For example, the first axiom of *Principia* states, in effect, that "if any particular sentence (call it p) is true, or if that same sentence (p) is true, then that sentence (p) is, indeed, true"— for example, "if frogs are fish, or if frogs are fish, then frogs are fish." The "if— then" is trivially and tautologically true irrespective of whether p is true, for in truth frogs are not fish. Since our interest here is in problem solving, not in logic, the reader can regard LT's task as one of manipulating symbols to produce desired expressions, and he can ignore the material interpretations of these symbols.

10. See (7). The situation here is like that in chess or checkers where the player knows what moves are legal but has to find in a reasonable time a move that is also "suitable")—that is, conducive to winning the game.

REFERENCES

1. Bruner, J. S., Goodnow, J., and Austin, G. *A Study of Thinking*. New York: Wiley, 1956.

2. De Groot, A. *Het Denken van den Schaker.* Amsterdam: Noord-Hollandsche Uitgevers Maatschappij, 1946.

3. Hilbert, D., and Ackermann, W. *Principles of Mathematical Logic.* New York: Chelsea, 1950.

4. Johnson, D. M. *The Psychology of Thought and Judgment.* New York: Harper, 1955.

5. Moore, O. K., and Anderson, S. B. "Search Behavior in Individual and Group Problem Solving." *American Sociological Review* 19 (1955): 702–714.

6. Newell, A., and Shaw, J. C. "Programming the Logic Theory Machine." *Proceedings Western Joint Computer Conference* (Institute of Radio Engineers), 1957, pp. 230–40.

7. Newell, A., Shaw, J. C. and Simon, H. A. "Empirical Explorations with the Logic Theory Machine." *Proceedings Western Joint Computer Conference* (Institute of Radio Engineers), 1957, pp. 218–30.

8. Newell, A., and Simon, H. A. "The Logic Theory Machine: A Complex Information Processing System." *Transactions on Information Theory* (Institute of Radio Engineers), 1956, Vol. IT-2, No. 3, pp. 61–79.

9. Simon, H. A., and Newell, A. "Models, Their Uses and Limitations." In L. D. White (Ed.), *The State of the Social Sciences.* Chicago: University of Chicago Press, 1956, pp. 66–83.

10. Whitehead, A. N., and Russell, B. *Principia Mathematica.* Vol. I. (2nd ed.) Cambridge: Cambridge University Press, 1925.

30

The Compleat Robot: A Prolegomena to Androidology

Michael Scriven

INTRODUCTION

The day was when men sought to discover the secrets of the demigods, the elixirs, spells, and potions of the supernaturally endowed. Perhaps the day will yet come when we, having promoted ourselves to the leading role by discovering there is no one above us, will find ourselves in the role of the magician, the possessor of mysterious powers, and snapping at our heels will be the machines. The question in our mind, and on their tapes, will be: "What is the secret of consciousness?" If they are sufficiently well programmed in the language of mythology, ancient and contemporary, it is perhaps even conceivable that they will refer to their search as the Quest for the Thinking Man's Philtre. In this paper I shall consider what, if any, unique essence characterizes the human brain, what, if any, human property prevents a super-computer from saying "Anything you can do, I can do better."

THE MEANING OF "MACHINE"

There are many important terms in our language which cannot be explicitly defined, for various reasons, yet can be correctly applied in typical cases. One

From *Dimensions of Mind*, edited by Sidney Hook (New York: New York University Press, 1960), pp. 113–33. Reprinted by permission of the publisher.

of these is "machine," another is "science," and there are others such as "truth" and "toothache." We can readily apply such terms in some cases, while in other cases it is hard to decide whether they apply, and there are likely to arise new cases of both sorts. It is possible to introduce some artificial definition—e.g., by requiring that a science be concerned with prediction or experimentation, which will be approximately correct and sometimes convenient. But when dealing with a logical problem, couched in terms which include these words, we can only employ a stipulative definition like this if we can prove in advance that we are not presupposing an answer to the question. For example, if we define "machine" as an inanimate artifactual device, we cannot go on to ask whether machines might one day be conscious. Yet it is not at all obvious that the answer *is* trivially negative in the usual sense of "machine." This definition has other drawbacks: to define a machine in such a way as to require that it be manufactured is both imprecise (why can't a human mother be regarded as manufacturing her offspring?) and too restrictive, since a spontaneously-generated adding machine, complete even to the Marchant label, would present a problem that might leave the physicist and the theologian at a loss for words but not the comptometer operator, who would not hesitate to call it a machine. Similar criticisms apply to requirements about inorganic constituents (which would rule out airplanes and cranes with wooden pulley-blocks) and about predictable behavior (which would rule out roulette wheels or radium-driven randomizers).

I shall confine myself to enquiring whether something that *is* manufactured from the usual electronic and mechanical components found in a computer workshop, with possible future refinements and substitutes, must forever lack certain capacities possessed by the brain. I think we can safely say that this would be a machine, without having to commit ourselves to any dubious propositions about what would *not* be a machine. (Whenever possible, I shall try to make the points in terms of an even narrower kind of machine —e.g., contemporary computers.) And in these terms the phrase "thinking machine" is not a trivial contradiction. Incidentally, our answers will leave us uncommitted about the question of whether a biophysicist can produce living creatures from inorganic elements. Although at the moment this appears to be only a technical problem, it is certainly a different problem, since he has a narrower choice of materials and an easier goal than the roboticist in his task of duplicating the brain functions of higher vertebrates. We shall return to the problem of constituents in the next section.

MOVING AND REPRODUCING

A simple question arises immediately. May it not be true that the particular substances of which the brain is composed are enormously more efficient for its tasks than anything we could expect to find in the inventory of a computer workshop? This might be true to a degree that would render machines with powers comparable to men so gigantic that they would be incapable of incorporation in a self-propelling unit comparable to that which the human brain inhabits.

Three comments are in order. First, this is not a very exciting point even if true, since there would be, under this hypothesis, few, if any, human tasks that could not be done by putting mechanical sensors and effectors where the human being would be, and using relays to feed data to and commands from the machine. Even if there are any such tasks, they are not ones that the human can do by virtue of his brain or mind, but by virtue of his body size. Second, there are no very strong reasons for thinking the point valid. Mechanical effectors and sensors can be made both smaller and better than human ones. For instance, they can be ultraviolet sensitive. The use of magnetic imprinting, crystal orientation, subminiaturization, and fail-safe circuitry, has already reduced or will reduce the required volume by several orders of magnitude and there seems no barrier except cost to further progress. Third, if we find that, for example, protein molecules provide the best storage medium, their employment would not necessarily mean we were no longer constructing a machine. Naturally, transplanting a human brain into a robot body is cheating, but the use of some of the same *substances,* either synthesized or extracted from dead tissue, is hardly enough to disqualify the product from being a machine. Our task is to see whether we can make a pseudobrain—something with performance the same as or better than that of a human brain, but made in a different way, i.e., with largely different components and "wiring." There would still be considerable interest in the question of whether we can make a synthetic brain, no holds barred, but there would be less general agreement that it should be called a machine. (Would one call a synthetic flower a machine? A synthetic jellyfish?) I shall restrict our attention to the more difficult task of constructing a mechanical pseudobrain, which utilizes at most some of the same substances or "wiring" as the human brain, and thus retains a clearer title to the adjective "mechanical." There is a certain tension between the term "mechanical" and the term "living," so that the more inclined we are to call it alive because of the things it does, the less inclined we shall be to call it a machine. I shall continue to assume that these terms are logically marriageable, although they are uneasy bedfellows, but the substance of my points can be expressed in other ways if this assumption is not granted.

Having thus dealt with very simple behavioral and constitutional considerations, we may proceed to some of the traditionally more favored obstacles to the functional duplication of human mentality by mechanical means.

PREDICTING AND CHOOSING

It is a standard sarcasm amongst computer technicians that, contrary to the popular opinion, they are dealing with some of the most unpredictable and unreliable entities known. There are several causes of this. First, there are the errors of inadequate programming, which cannot be dismissed as mere operator errors, since a program often involves tens of thousands of characters in the "machine language," not all the consequences of which can be foreseen by the programmer any more than Euclid foresaw all the consequences of his axioms. Secondly, there are mechanical breakdowns within the machine— by no means uncommon, though to some extent their seriousness can be overcome by duplication, fail-safe wiring, and alarm arrangements. Thirdly, there are variations due to uncertainty-principle effects in junctions, relays, thermionic valves, etc. The importance of these variations is commonly slight, but over a long haul they guarantee "individuality" to a computer. Fourthly, there is the cumulative inaccuracy possible with analogue computers. Fifthly, there is the possibility of deliberately using a randomizer in the circuitry, important in learning circuits. Sixthly, there is the rapidity of operation that makes the fastest computer unpredictable in fact.

It is thus highly unsatisfactory to suggest that computer output behavior is predictable. Even if the addition of "in principle" will get you past some of these objections, it is such a slippery password that its users often find themselves in the wrong camp. Here, I think the only safe conclusion is that some computers are "in principle" unpredictable in a way essentially similar to the way human beings are.

The argument that "free-will" is (a) possessed by humans, and (b) implies a unique unpredictability different from that mentioned above, requires both clarification and substantiation, especially its second assertion. I would say it is now readily provable that the kind of free will required to make sense of the idea of responsibility and punishment is perfectly compatible with determinism and third-person predictability, and there is no evidence for any other kind. Hence, even if machines were predictable it would be possible for them to have free will. Since neither they nor human beings are in practice entirely predictable, the argument that only one of the two species has free will needs further grounds, several of which we shall examine under other headings, but none of which appears to provide insuperable differences.

The converse problem to the one just considered is also of relevance to the free-will issue, and serves to clarify the meaning of "predictable in principle." This is the problem of whether a computer can in principle predict everything. If, for the moment, one supposes that a computer can in principle be error-free, the answer is still negative, and thus a further element of similarity with the human being possessing free will is preserved—the limitation in the power *to* predict. The standard example is the computer with total data and unbounded speed which is connected to a photo-electric cell and phosphor lamp in a certain way and then programmed to predict whether the lamp will be alight five minutes later. The photo-electric cell is focused on the output tape and the lamp so connected that if the output tape reads "yes," the lamp switches off, and if it reads "no," the lamp switches on. The prediction is thus self-invalidating. The other standard case is the prediction of one computer's state by another which is trying to do the same to it; the necessity for a finite time-lag, however brief, between input and output can be shown to produce gross errors under suitable circumstances.

Now these cases have analogues in human experience. The realization that one can do "just the opposite," no matter what prediction is announced about one's choice, in trivial matters such as the closing of an eye is a powerful element in the support for free will. (It corresponds, as we shall see, to the first case just described.) One might say that all that is in fact shown by such feelings and freedom is that certain events are not *publicly* predictable. For the prediction can still be made as long as it is not announced to the individual to which it refers. But not only does this remark make less sense in the case of the computer, it also underestimates the importance of the point. For the possibility of falsifying any announced prediction does show that the feeling of free choice is not an "illusion" in any useful sense. "Illusions" can be dispelled, but dispelling a man's "illusion" that his choice is not yet made, that it is still "up to him," is often logically impossible since any announcement about his choice will immediately be falsified. But it is essential to remember that predictability does not eliminate freedom. A virtuous man is no less virtuous because we know he is and hence can guess what he'll do. We are not wrong to praise a man simply because we foresee his actions—we would be wrong only if they were actions over which he had no control.[1]

The predictability issue, taken either way, is deeply involved in philosophical puzzles of some interest, but it again provides no grounds for supposing the machine to be inferior to the brain, either because its powers of prediction are too great, or because they are too small.

Creating and Discovering

"Machines only do what we tell them to do. They are incapable of genuinely original thought." As in nearly all these claims, two importantly different points are run together here. These are what I shall call the "performatory" element and the "personality" element. The performatory problem here is whether a computer can produce results which, when translated, provide what would count as an original solution or proof *if it came from a man.* The personality problem is whether we are entitled to call such a result a solution or proof, despite the fact that it did *not* come from a man. The logical trap is this: no *one* performatory achievement will be enough to persuade us to apply the human-achievement vocabulary, but if we refuse to use this vocabulary in each case separately, on this ground, we will, perhaps wrongly, have committed ourselves to avoiding it even when *all* the achievements are simultaneously attained.[1] I shall, for convenience, use the human-achievement vocabulary, but without thereby prejudging the issue. If it transpires that there are *no* essential performatory differences at all, we shall then consider whether we are entitled to apply the terms in their full sense. No single simple property of an object suffices to guarantee that it is an apple, but several *sets* of such properties are sufficient.

The originality point has some sting when we are considering very simple computers, but the moment we have a learning circuit and/or a randomizer for generating trial-and-error runs, the picture is different. We will discuss the learning point in the next section, but I here wish to carry on with the consequences of the randomizer mentioned in the last section, which provides a simple kind of originality. For example, a computer using a randomizer may come up with a solution to a differential equation that no one else has been able to obtain. Is this to count as being original or not (observationally speaking—we ignore for the moment the fact that the result is mechanical in origin)? Certainly we "built in" the instructions to use the randomizer, but this does not enable us to foretell what results will come out. This is another exercise in the trustworthiness of the "in principle" notion. I shall make only two comments.

First, the randomizer may be of two kinds. If it is a classical randomizer (i.e., of the "roulette-wheel" type), there is some point to the remark that its outcome is in principle predictable, but none at all to the suggestion that we could ever in practice predict it. Now Euler was an original man, but was he original in any stronger sense than that no one did *in fact* think of his results before him? How could any further claim be supported? Even if it can, there is a stronger source of originality possible for a computer— the use of a quantum randomizer. And to argue that it is in principle possible to predict the outcome of a radium-driven randomizer is even less feasible, because, (a) taken at face value, it is denied by most contemporary physicists, (b) if it means that a deterministic theory might conceivably someday be found, then this is always true, and so the alleged distinction between the man and the machine, in terms of the "in principle" predictability of the latter, becomes vacuous, since one cannot rationally deny the *possibility* of an exact psychological predictive theory.

Of course, more is involved in producing solutions to equations than in producing random numbers, these must have been put through the test of satisfying the equation. But this involves only a routine calculation by the computer. There thus appears to be no reason why a computer cannot produce solutions to problems that are original in the sense of being (a) historically novel, and (b) in no useful sense predictable. Nevertheless, we feel that originality of this trial-and-error kind is relatively uninteresting. The important kind of originality is that which produces new theories, new conceptual schemes, new works of art. How could a machine possibly do this?

The key notion in the design of a creative machine would be the use of analogy. It has been argued by MacKay that in fact such a machine would have to be of the species referred to as analogue computers (as opposed to digital computers). I shall give some reasons for disagreeing with this in the section on understanding. But whatever type of computer is involved, there is no doubt that it must possess means for the *weighted comparison* of different descriptions. Thus, if it is fed data about the notion of a satellite around a planet, while on a theory-building program, it will register the formal similarity between this kind of motion and the motion of a body attached by a string to a fixed point and given a certain initial tangential velocity. It will, noting no better analogy, examine the consequences of the "theory" that an *invisible* connection exists between the planet and its satellite, the idea of invisibility being well-established in its data banks in connection with magnetic fields, sound waves, etc. Deduction of the consequences of such a hypothesis proves satisfactory of a certain value of the force in the invisible string, a value which depends on its "length" in a simple way. The analogy with magnetic fields now registers strongly and the computer formulates and successfully tests the law of gravitational attraction.

The crucial difference from the trial-and-error method we first discussed lies not in the absence of trial and error, but in the origin of the candidates for trial; instead of randomly selected elements of a previously obvious class— e.g., the integers—it is necessary to provide a means for electing candidates from the indefinite class of possible hypotheses and then for improving them by adding modifications themselves selected in a similar way. The selection is no longer wholly random, because some candidates have better qualifications than others. What makes them better can be called their antecedent probability, but is perhaps better called the extent of the analogy between their known properties and those required in the situation under study. Any idea of an exact weighting of such analogies, which is perhaps suggested by referring to probabilities, is quite unjustified; the best one can expect is a partial ordering, and since this is all the human brain employs it is clearly adequate.

How would one go about giving the computer data of this kind? A simple beginning would be with curve-fitting problems where loose estimates of the importance of errors of a given magnitude, as against the value of simplicity for computation and theoretical fertility, can be given. The procedure can then be made more complicated in a way involving learning-circuits of the kind to be mentioned in the next section, enabling the computer to adjust the relative weighting of errors and complexity.

The procedure of *trial* is comparatively simple. The definition of the problem (say, the proof of Goldbach's Hypothesis, or the production of an adequate theory for the behavior of liquid helium) itself gives the tests that the successful candidate must pass. The application of these tests is, in the sciences, perfectly routine. There is still the possible difficulty of dealing with cases where several candidates pass the test. Here selection of the best will involve a decision similar to that involved in selecting the best candidates for the tests. This will, for example, occur where ideas such as simplicity are involved, and these make us think of creativity in the arts, where it is clear that we do not have very precise standards for judging the merits of works of art. But the computer's memory banks can with ease be indoctrinated with the canons of free verse, iambic pentameters, or nursery rhymes, and instruction to exploit low-level analogies as if they were high-level ones, and to adjust the result in certain ways by reference to ease of comprehension, richness of associations, and onomatopoeic force, would provide poetry of any acceptable kind. There is no doubt that the subtlety of poetic metaphor and the emotive effect of various rhyme-schemes will not *easily* be compressed into a computer; but they are not easily learned by human beings, and human beings are remarkably disunited about the kind of scaling that would be correct in comparing these virtues (cf. simplicity and fertility of scientific theories). The net effect of these considerations is that there is much less chance that computer verse will be detectable by a literary critic than there was that paintings by chimpanzees would be identifiable by art-critics.

Summing up the discussion of originality, the simplest kind is readily obtainable by a machine and the more complicated kind is obtainable subject to the (feasible but difficult) development of analogy-assessing procedures. Connected with the assessment of analogies is the whole question of mechanical learning, to which we now turn.

LEARNING

The usual contemporary computer is essentially a complex instrument, a close relative to the comptometer, and the idea that it does only what we tell it to do is well founded. This idea is more precisely put by saying that it cannot modify its own programming, more loosely by saying it cannot learn by experience. But there are already a few computers, among them modified versions of the IBM 704 and 709, which are more advanced than this. Professor Wiener has referred to them as having "higher-order programming," i.e., as being programmed to modify their basic procedure in certain ways depending on the results obtained from earlier trials. Such machines are already capable of playing a good game of chess, proving theorems in geometry, and so on. The two special features of their design are the provision of assessment rules whereby they can judge the success of various procedures in various situations, and a special kind of instruction. In the chess case, we provide them with the set of possible moves by every chessman, they calculate the results of applying all applicable ones at a particular stage of the game and, using the assessment rules, decide which offers the best option.

A simple assessment rule, used during early stages of a game, would be one which gives greater credit for a position according to the number of pieces deployed, the "openness" of the position, possibly measured by the number of squares covered. More complex, and more essential, rules will involve assessing a move in terms of its consequences in the light of possible moves by the opponent, the ideal being a move which can be inevitably (i.e., whatever the opponent does) converted into checkmate, less ideal ones resulting in the capture of favorable exchange of pieces. Thus we instruct the machine to proceed in such a way as to maximize the expectation of checkmate; and we provide certain suggestions as to reliable indicators of a good move, since no computer can actually compute all possible future outcomes of a given move except in some parts of the end game. So far, simple enough; but the special feature of the instructions is that we program the computer to continually reevaluate the suggested *indicators* in the light of its experience in using them to obtain checkmate. It is thus considering hypotheses at two levels. Within a game, it asks: "Is this a good move as far as my current standards of good moves go?"; and after each game, it asks whether a different weighting of the standards would have been more likely to produce success—and if so, it readjusts the weights for future use.

At this stage we have a model of learning by experience. Its application to a chess-playing machine is simpler than to a theory-building machine because the possible moves in chess are a precisely defined family, unlike possible theories. It is true that in computer design it is more difficult to achieve con-trolled imprecision than precision, whereas the converse might be said to be characteristic of adult humans; and it is the imprecise methods of analogy and suggestion that produce new theories. But the proper analogy to computer design is human education from infancy, not the generation of free associations in adults, and the learner, like the computer, finds it much simpler to follow the exact rules of the syllogism than to evaluate complex analogies. Despite the difficulties, there can be no grounds for radical pessimism about the possibility of combining the devices of originality with those of learning to produce a machine that is cognitively a match for the human being—so far as we have considered the differences between them.

UNDERSTANDING AND INTERPRETING

There is a special kind of cognitive barrier that we have not so far considered and which involves a novel difficulty. Naturally, we shall not speak of a machine as "understanding" a theorem simply because it can type out a proof of it on command. What must it *do* in order to be doing what human beings do who are said to understand a theorem? (Even if it does this, it does not—as we have previously stressed—follow that we should say it understands, for apart from what it *does* there is the question of what it *is;* and it may be argued that such predicates as "understanding" are inapplicable to machines. But we shall have removed one further *ground* for this argument.) It seems clear to me that the performatory element in the concept of understanding is the capacity to *relate* whatever is said to be understood to a variety of other material in the correct way. Understanding the special theory of relativity involves knowing the relation between its components, the relation of it to other theories, and the relation of it to its applications. Understanding is knowing, but it is knowing certain things. Knowing something is not *ipso facto* understanding something (one knows the date of one's birthday, or the composition of polyurethane, without understanding anything [except a language]). But there is a very large slice of personality in the concept of understanding; we are much more reluctant to apply it to a machine than such a term as "compute." About this slice we cannot dispute; we can only point out that the theory that understanding is a mental sensation, a theory which is heavily ingrained in us, no doubt contributes to our reluctance, but does so illicitly. The point is well, though briefly, discussed in Wittgenstein's *Philosophical Investigations.*

A special difficulty of the concept of understanding arises in connection with the idea of understanding the concept of an irrational number. We here run into the apparent obstacle of the Lowenheim-Skolem Theorem. According to this theorem, it is not possible to give a unique characterization of the reals and hence the irrationals, at least in the following sense: any attempted strict formalization of the real numbers can be shown to be ambiguous in that it can be given at least one interpretation in the rational numbers, i.e., every formalization we produce can be legitimately interpreted in a way contrary to that intended, a way that omits any reference to the irrationals. Now it seems plausible to say that the description of the reals that we give to a computer will be subject to the same irreducible ambiguity, and hence that we shall never be sure that it has actually "grasped" the *proper* idea of real number, which includes the irrationals, rather than one of the other strictly permissible interpretations. A similar suggestion is made by Nagel and Newman in *Gödel's Proof* when they argue that the Gödel incompleteness theorem presents a serious obstacle to the construction of comprehensive theorem-proving computers; we shall return to this suggestion in a moment. The error in these arguments, as I see it, lies in the idea that the tests of understanding in mathematics are purely syntactical, that the intrasystemic transformations are the only defining properties of the concepts—of number, or proof, or truth. In fact, we can perfectly well regard it as a crucial test of comprehension of the concept of irrational number on the part of man or machine, that he or it immediately identify the square root of two, and π, and the base of natural logarithms as examples of irrational numbers. If this is required, then consideration of the formal properties will guarantee the correct field of entities (other simple requirements on the interpretation of the logical operators would also suffice).

It seems to me that the point is akin to the one arising when we ask whether a blind man can be said fully to understand the meaning of the word "red" when he has mastered (a) the syntactical rules governing color words, and (b) a device which correlates color-differences with musical tones so that he can indirectly differentiate (but not identify) colors reliably. This would *almost* locate the term "red" in the semantic space, but not completely; his interpretation would be invariant under transformations that did not offend current idioms or hue-separation. For example, he could get the color of a particular dahlia wrong although not the natural color of a ripe lemon. (There would be a *series* of tests—linked comparisons—which would uncover the dahlia's color, but he couldn't recognize it immediately.) We are somewhat undecided whether to say that his *comprehension* (of the term "red") is incomplete, or merely his *experience*. Certainly he is not capable of using the term properly in normal circumstances, but neither is a man who has lost his sight—yet the latter understand perfectly well what "red" means. Similarly, the axioms of a formal system provide much but not all of the meaning of "irrational number"; the clincher is the link with examples, the capacity to apply the language correctly in paradigm cases. In certain areas of mathematics, this is guaranteed by the formal rules, but in others the concepts are not merely formal shorthand, but refer to aspects of a complex construction that can readily be *perceived* but not exhaustively eliminated by substituting other, equivalent concepts. (A related difficulty arises in trying to treat the Peano postulates as defining the integers.) In sum, then, I do not find the existence of a residual ambiguity in an axiomatization of mathematics a good reason for supposing that computers can never understand mathematical concepts.

Similarly, the limitations imposed by the Gödel incompleteness theorem on the formalization of mathematics are, so far as I can see, no more of an obstacle to a mechanical mathematician. As is well known, given any Gödel sentence G which is provably true but undecidable within a system S, it is easy to construct an S^2 within which it is derivable—the uninteresting way being to add G to the system S. Now, Nagel and Newman are struck by the fact that whatever axioms and rules of inference one might give a computer, there would apparently be mathematical truths, such as G, which it could never "reach" from these axioms by the use of these rules. This is true, but their assumption that we could suppose ourselves to have given the machine an adequate idea of mathematical truth when we gave it the axioms and rules of inference is not true. This would be to suppose the formalists were right, and they were shown by Gödel to be wrong. The Gödel theorem is no more an obstacle to a computer than to ourselves. One can only say that mathematics would have been easier if the formalists had been right, and it would in that case be comparatively easy to construct a mechanical mathematician. They weren't and it isn't. But just as we can recognize the truth of the unprovable formula by comparing what it says with what we know to be the case, so can a computer do the same.

It is appropriate here to mention another formal theorem, one which an enthusiastic roboticist might think supports his cause. Craig's theorem has been invoked on occasions to support the view that theories, and hence the necessity for understanding theoretical terms, are dispensable. It does indeed demonstrate the eliminability of certain terms from a given vocabulary under certain conditions. If it is supposed that these conditions correspond to the relationship between theoretical terms and observational terms, the conclusion might follow. But one of the conditions is that there be an absolutely sharp separation between terms of these two kinds. Now, it seems clear that it is part of the nature of theoretical terms that they should sometimes—for example, by progress in techniques of observation—become observable. Another condition requires that the only logically interesting effects of theoretical terms lie in their deduced consequences in the observation vocabulary. Even if deduction were in fact the only vehicle for generating the consequences of theories, this would not be a satisfactory position. The reasons for this require support from a general theory of meaning, but they can be condensed into the comment that part of the meaning of a theory lies in its relation to other theories, and part in its internal logical structure, so that understanding a theory is by no means the same as understanding its empirical consequences. Finally, Craig's theorem has the awkward result that the elimination of theoretical terms is achieved only at the expense of adding an infinite number of axioms in the observation language.

ANALYZING

At the practical level, some of the above considerations are already highly relevant. There is a great deal of work now proceeding on the mechanization of translation, abstraction, and indexing. A few words on each topic will perhaps serve to indicate the present situation and its consequences for our inquiry.

Translation

It is simple enough to build a mechanical *decoder* (or encoder) and they have been in use for many years. If translation were the same as decoding, there would be no special problem. Unfortunately, there are great differences. A code is a way of rendering portions of a single language obscure; decoding consists of applying the key in reverse. But French, except when used by certain people one knows, is not a way of rendering English obscure. It is a way of doing what English also does—describing, explaining, exhorting, ordering, promising, praising, and so on. Since they are both universal languages, and their relation is thus unlike that of mathematics to music, it is reasonable to expect that a *fairly* satisfactory equivalent exists in each for any natural unit in the other. Now, a word or a sentence is not what I have in mind when talking of a natural unit—a word or a sentence is a *phonetically,* or *calligraphically,* or *psychologically* convenient unit. A natural unit is a description, an explanation, an exhortation, etc., produced in a particular context. (Of course, a translation of this depends to some extent on a personal impression of the context, and the linguistic element usually does not fully describe the context.) If we were to suppose that the existence of workable translations of *natural units* implied the existence of workable translations of the *spoken or written* units (i.e., the words and sentences), then a mechanical translator would be a relatively simple problem for the programmer. The discovery that this supposition is unsound is, it seems to me, the chief ground for the present pessimism amongst workers in this area.

But there is no absolute barrier here. In the first place, there are actually many words or groups of words, especially in Western languages, which allow a very general and straightforward translation into corresponding units in other such languages, partly because they are used in only one kind of context. This is especially true in the vital area of technical vocabularies. Secondly, although the language is not always descriptive of a context, it often affords clues to it, so that by taking large enough sections, a translation can be made highly accurate at least for informational purposes. But the translation of poetry is an example of the opposite extreme where a one-many relation holds between a context and associated language complexes. And it is a useful warning, since this is not altogether unlike the situation of theoretical propositions. Finally, provision once being made for the sensory equipment of a robot—a point shortly to be discussed—we would possess a system whose linguists would be of the same kind as our own, and whose translations would therefore be potentially better, their memory being better.

Abstracting

Mechanical abstractors have already been built in response to the desperate need for systematizing scientific work and publication. They operate on a word (or phrase) frequency count, retaining those words of four letters, or more, that occur most often. This is the most primitive possible device for abstraction and all one can say is that it is surprising how often it nearly does a fair job. (It is not very often.) There are really no short-cuts of this kind that are worth much trouble; we shall not be able to rely—and we need to be able to rely—on abstracting done by someone lacking a first-rate comprehension of the subject being treated. Unfortunately, using such rare individuals for such purposes is intellectually and economically inefficient. The natural solution is mechanization. It is less of a solution than might appear at first sight, since, although the comprehension is feasible as I have argued above, the difficulties are so formidable that the initial cost of such a device will enormously outweigh the cost of discovering and training extra humans for the task. We may indeed find that the super computers of the future will need human servants because they can't afford mechanical aides—a nice twist to the present argument for automation, although perhaps it ranges a little too far into the future to convince the unions today.

Indexing

Essentially similar problems arise over indexing. Under what headings should an article be referenced or a paragraph be indexed? A simple machine can index an article or passage under all the words in it, or under the most frequent. Both are clearly quite unsatisfactory. The crucial concepts here are those of *relevance* and *importance*. To know which topics an article is relevant to requires more than an understanding of the article—it requires knowledge of all potentially relevant fields. Worse, as our theories change, relevance changes and continual reindexing from scratch is necessary, i.e., all references must be scanned for deletion *and* amplification. It is a tall order to build a machine with the kind of knowledge and speed required for these tasks, but it is increasingly beyond the powers of man to perform such tasks himself, and an increasingly large amount of work is being "lost" in the technical literature, or expensively duplicated because of the inefficiency of indexing (and cataloguing—a special case). There is really no satisfactory alternative to the machines and we shall have to try them, there being no reason for supposing we cannot succeed but every reason for supposing we shall find it very difficult. It may not be impossible "in principle," but we sometimes abandon our "in principles."

DECIDING

In the indexing problem, that matter of relevance is crucial but only half the problem. A particular passage in the *American Journal of Physics* will be relevant to some degree to an uncountable number of topics. If an index is to be useful at all, a subset of these topics must suffice and a decision must be made by the indexer as to the most important of these. If this is to be done sensibly it requires some estimate of importance and some value for a "cutting score," i.e., a level of importance beyond which inclusion in the index is guaranteed and below which it is precluded. As we have suggested earlier, it is a mistake to suppose that a full arithmetization is possible, and partial ordering is all that we need. The issue is really the same as that associated with choosing likely hypotheses and raises no new difficulties for the programmer. The difficulties are bad enough even if not new. The procedure of governing the cutting score by estimates of the maximum permissible size of the index, the seriousness of errors of omission versus excessive bulk, corresponds to the procedure for deciding what hypotheses to consider in a given situation, or, in problem solving, what maneuvers to try out, if any— e.g., which premises to try out as bases for a mathematical proof.

PERCEIVING

The performatory aspect of perception is differentiation of the responses to differentiated stimuli. This is the aim of good scientific instrument design and a computer with its own temperature-recording devices is easily made. The human brain, however, is rather good at detecting similarities and differences of a kind which it would be tremendously difficult to arrange to detect mechanically. For example, the visual recognition of a female acquaintance when she is wearing different clothes, is at varying distances, in varying light and from varying angles, wearing various expressions, hairstyles, and makeup, requires configurational comparison of great sensitivity and complexity. It is clear enough how one would go about developing a machine with the capacity to perform such tasks, which we do so casually. Here again we would face the "degrees of similarity" problem, and "matching" problems probably best solved by the use of an optical comparator using rapidly varying magnification. A start will have to be made in connection with star-mapping programs using the photomultiplier tubes, and automatic navigation for unmanned interstellar rockets. The recognition of star patterns, regardless of orientation, should not prove too difficult, and the more complex gestalts may be attacked piecemeal.

Extrasensory Perceiving

Turing apparently thought that telepathy was the one impossibility for the machine. I am not clear whether he thought this because of skepticism about telepathy in humans or because of a "direct-mental-contact" theory of telepathy, or for some other reason. Neither of the suggested reasons seems altogether satisfactory. The evidence for telepathy in humans is hard to dismiss fairly, but there is no ground for thinking it cannot be regarded as a brain function of a new kind, analogous to the generation of the alpha- and beta-rhythms. We are completely ignorant of the forms of energy or the physical features of the brain that are responsible for telepathy, although intensive work with the electroencephalograph is continuing at Duke and in London. In this respect, ESP represents a more difficult problem for the roboticist than any of the preceding ones, and forms a natural link to the problem of feeling. If it should transpire that no brain elements are responsible for ESP, then it will present a special philosophical problem; but until then, we must assume the contrary and continue the search. We are not at all clear how the memory works, but we do not doubt its existence. It is quite unreasonable to argue as some have done, that because the ESP function has not been localized in the brain, it follows that we should doubt its existence. What I have said about telepathy applies, a fortiori, to the less well-supported phenomena of precognition and psychokinesis.

FEELING

The most difficult problem of all those that face the roboticist trying to match human capacity is that of inducing the phenomena of sensation. The difficulty lies not with the outward signs—we have already indicated the way in which these can be achieved. It is the doubt whether there is any actual sensation associated with the wincing, gasping, sighing, and snapping that we succeed in building in for manifestation in "appropriate" circumstances. A radical behaviorist will not of course be troubled by such doubts, but even the identity theorists would not share his equanimity. We all know what it is to feign feelings and we thus know what it is to behave as if one had a certain feeling although one lacks it—and we wonder if the robot is merely "going through the motions." (It is not, of course, correctly described as "feigning," since this entails an understanding of the nature of not feigning—and we are disputing even this possibility.)

Turing argued[3] that if a robot could be so built that remote interrogation could not distinguish it from a human being we would have to agree that it had feelings. This is oversimple, not only because verbal stimuli are too limited for satisfactory proof, but because it seems to make perfectly good sense to say: "It says it is in love because we built [it] to say so—but is it? It says it is fond of A. E. Housman and thinks Keats is sickly, but does it really *enjoy* Housman?" In making these points in a reply to Turing,[4] I overlooked two points which now seem to me important and which improve the chances of a decision, although they do not support Turing's view.

In the first place, one must reject the "argument from design" (android-ological version), the argument that because the machine is designed to say it is in love it cannot be supposed that it is *really* in love. For the design may, and perhaps must, have achieved both ends. (To assume the opposite is to adopt a naïve interactionism.) Performatory evidence is not decisive (contra Turing), but neither is it negligible. It fulfills a necessary condition, in a sense which is amplified in my paper in the symposium on "Criteria" in the *Journal of Philosophy,* November 1959. What is a sufficient condition? The answer must be that there is no *logically* sufficient condition statable in terms that can be verified by an external observer. Even a telepath who declares that he directly perceives sensations in the robot exactly as in humans may merely be reacting to brain emanations that are similar. But there are conditions which make doubt profitless although not meaningless—e.g., doubts about the origin of the universe. These conditions are, for the most part, readily imaginable, consisting in the indefinitely sustained and effortless performance and description of emotional conditions, the development of new art forms, the prosecution of novel moral causes (Societies for the Prevention of Cruelty to Robots, etc.), in brief the maintenance and extrapolation of the role of a sensitive man, with dreams and feelings. However, I have thought of a less obvious further test which perhaps merits a separate section.

LYING

Remembering that, strictly speaking, to refer to an entity as lying commits one to the personality component as well as the performatory one, I shall use the term to refer to the performatory element for the moment. Now, the substance of my disagreement with Turing was that a machine *might* be made to duplicate sensation-behavior without having the sensation, i.e., the designer could fool the interrogator. But suppose our aim as a designer is not to pass the Turing test, since that is inconclusive, but actually to determine whether robots can be built that have feelings. I suggest that we construct a series of robots called R. George Washington I, II, II [sic.], etc. (using Asimov's convention of the R for "Robot" before name), with the following characteristics. They should be taught to use English in the strictest way. They would refer to human beings as being in pain under the usual circumstances, but under what appear to be corresponding circumstances with robots they would use behaviorist language, saying that R. Einstein XI had produced the words "I am in pain," etc. And they would use the same care when describing their own states, saying for example: "R. George Washington I has been subject to overload current" or ". . . has received a potentially damaging stimulus of unknown origin"—it being the named robot speaking. In teaching them to speak in this way, we make it quite clear that other descriptions of themselves may also be appropriate, including those applied to human beings, but we do not assert that they do apply. We also introduce the robot to the concept of truth and falsity and explain that to lie is to utter a falsehood when the truth is known, a practice of value in some circumstances but usually undesirable. We then add a circuit to the robot, at a special ceremony at which we also christen it, which renders lying impossible regardless of conflict with other goals it has been told are important. This makes the robot unsuitable for use as a personal servant, advertising copywriter, or politician, but renders it capable of another service. Having equipped it with all the performatory abilities of humans, fed into its banks the complete works of great poets, novelists, philosophers, and psychologists, we now ask it whether it has feelings. And it tells us the truth since it can do no other. If the answer is "No," we construct further robots on different principles. If the answer is "Yes," we have answered our original question. To the objection that we cannot be sure it understands the question, it seems to me we can reply that we have every good reason for thinking that it does understand, as we have for thinking this of other *people*.

The logical structure of the argument thus consists in standing on a performatory analysis of understanding to reach a conclusion about the nonperformatory issue of sensations. If, with Brentano, one believes there is an irreducible nonbehavioral element in such concepts as belief and understanding, and that these, rather than sensations, are the hallmark of mind, my maneuver will not be convincing because it does not refer to that element which his followers translate as intentionality. But one may accept the irreducibility thesis, as I do, and regard the missing element as a compound of the possession of sensations and the possession of personality. This element is not the only one responsible for the irreducibility which also derives from the complexity of the mental-activity concepts in the same way as that which renders theoretical terms not reducible to observational ones. Then we get half of the missing element from the first R. George Washington to say "Yes," and there remains only the question of personality.

BEING

What is it to be a person? It can hardly be argued that it is to be human since there can clearly be extraterrestrials of equal or higher culture and intelligence who would qualify as people in much the same way as the people of Yucatan and Polynesia. Could an artifact be a person? It seems to me the answer is now clear; and the first R. George Washington to answer "Yes" will qualify. A robot might do many of the things we have discussed in this paper and not qualify. It could not do them all and be denied the accolade. We who must die salute him.

NOTES

1. It is interesting to compare this with the view that none of the arguments for the existence of God are logically sound, but taken all together they are convincing.
2. See D. M. MacKay, *On the Logical Indeterminacy of a Free Choice*, Proceedings of the Twelfth International Congress of Philosophy (Venice: 1958).
3. "Computing Machinery and Intelligence," *Mind* (1950).
4. "The Mechanical Concept of Mind," *Mind* (1953).

31

The Imitation Game

Keith Gunderson

I

Disturbed by what he took to be the ambiguous, if not meaningless, character of the question "Can machines think?" the late A. M. Turing in his article "Computing Machinery and Intelligence" sought to replace that question in the following way. He said:

> The new form of the problem can be described in terms of a game which we call the "imitation game." It is played with three people, a man (A), a woman (B), and an interrogator (C) who may be either sex. The interrogator stays in a room apart from the other two. The object of the game for the interrogator is to determine which of the other two is the man and which is the woman. He knows them by labels X and Y, and at the end of the game he says either "X is A and Y is B" or "X is B and Y is A." The interrogator is allowed to put questions to A and B thus:
>
> C: "Will X please tell me the length of his or her hair?"
> Now suppose X is actually A, then A must answer. It is A's object in the game to try to cause C to make the wrong identification. His answer might therefore be
> "My hair is shingled, and the longest strands are about nine inches long."

From *Mind* 73 (NS), no. 290 (April 1964). Copyright © 1964. Reprinted by permission of the author and Oxford University Press.

In order that tones of voice may not help the interrogator the answers should be written, or better still, typewritten. The ideal arrangement is to have a teleprinter communicating between the two rooms. Alternatively the question and answers can be repeated by an intermediary. The object of the game for the third player (B) is to help the interrogator. The best strategy for her is probably to give truthful answers. She can add such things as "I am the woman, don't listen to him!" to her answers, but it will avail nothing as the man can make similar remarks. We now ask the question, "What will happen when a machine takes the part of A in this game?" Will the interrogator decide wrongly as often as when the game is played between a man and a woman? These questions replace our original, "Can machines think?"

And Turing's answers to these latter questions are more or less summed up in the following passage: "I believe that in fifty years' time it will be possible to program computers, with a storage capacity of about 10^9, to make them play the imitation game so well that an average interrogator will not have more than 70 percent chance of making the right identification after five minutes of questioning." And though he goes on to reiterate that he suspects that the original question "Can machines think?" is meaningless, and that it should be disposed of and replaced by a more precise formulation of the problems involved (a formulation such as a set of questions about the imitation game and machine capacities), what finally emerges is that Turing does answer the "meaningless" question after all, and that his answer is in the affirmative and follows from his conclusions concerning the capabilities of machines which might be successfully substituted for people in the imitation-game context.

It should be pointed out that Turing's beliefs about the possible capabilities and capacities of machines are not limited to such activities as playing the imitation game as successfully as human beings. He does not, for example, deny that it might be possible to develop a machine which would relish the taste of strawberries and cream, though he thinks it would be "idiotic" to attempt to make one, and confines himself on the whole in his positive account to considerations of machine capacities which could be illustrated in terms of playing the imitation game.

So we shall be primarily concerned with asking whether or not a machine, which could play the imitation game as well as Turing thought it might, would thus be a machine which we would have good reasons for saying was capable of thought and what would be involved in saying this.

Some philosophers[1] have not been satisfied with Turing's treatment of the question "Can machines think?" But the imitation game itself, which indeed seems to constitute the hub of his positive treatment, has been little more than alluded to or remarked on in passing. I shall try to develop in a somewhat more detailed way certain objections to it, objections which, I believe, Turing altogether fails to anticipate. My remarks shall thus in the main be critically oriented, which is not meant to suggest that I believe there are no plausible lines of defense open to a supporter of Turing. I shall, to the contrary, close with a brief attempt to indicate what some of these might be and some general challenges which I think Turing has raised for the philosopher of mind. But these latter I shall not elaborate upon.

II

Let us consider the following question: "Can rocks imitate?" One might say that it is a question "too meaningless to deserve discussion." Yet it seems possible to reformulate the problem in relatively unambiguous words as follows:

> The new form of the problem can be described in terms of a game which we call the "toe-stepping game." It is played with three people, a man (A), a woman (B), and an interrogator (C) who may be of either sex. The interrogator stays in a room apart from the other two. The door is closed, but there is a small opening in the wall next to the floor through which he can place most of his foot. When he does so, one of the other two may step on his toe. The object of the game for the interrogator is to determine, by the way in which his toe is stepped on, which of the other two is the man and which is the woman. He knows them by labels X and Y, and at the end of the game he says either "X is A and Y is B" or "X is B and Y is A." Now the interrogator—rather the person whose toe gets stepped on—may indicate before he puts his foot through the opening, whether X or Y is to step on it. Better yet, there might be a narrow division in the opening, one side for X and one for Y (one for A and one for B).
>
> Now suppose C puts his foot through A's side of the opening (which may be labeled X or Y on C's side of the wall). It is A's object in the game to try to cause C to make the wrong identification. His step on the toe might therefore be quick and jabbing like some high-heeled woman.
>
> The object of the game for the third player (B) is to help the person whose toe gets stepped on. The best strategy for her is probably to try to step on it in the most womanly way possible. She can add such things as a slight twist of a high heel to her stepping, but it will avail nothing as the man can step in similar ways, since he will also have at his disposal various shoes with which to vary his toe-stepping.

We now ask the question: "What will happen when a rock-box (a box filled with rocks of varying weights, sizes, and shapes) is constructed with an electric eye which operates across the opening in the wall so that it releases a rock which descends upon C's toe whenever C puts his foot through A's side of the opening, and thus comes to take the part of A in this game?" (The situation can be made more convincing by constructing the rock-box so that there is a mechanism pulling up the released rock shortly after its descent, thus avoiding telltale noises such as a rock rolling on the floor, etc.) Will then the interrogator—the person whose toe gets stepped on—decide wrongly as often as when the game is played between a man and a woman? These questions replace our original, "Can rocks imitate?"

I believe that in less than fifty years' time it will be possible to set up elaborately constructed rock-boxes, with large rock-storage capacities, so that they will play the toe-stepping game so well that the average person who would get his toe stepped on would not have more than 70 percent chance of making the right identification after about five minutes of toe-stepping.

The above seems to show the following: what follows from the toe-stepping game situation surely is not that rocks are able to imitate (I assume no one would want to take that path of argument) but only that they are able to be rigged in such a way that they could be substituted for a human being in a toe-stepping game without changing any essential characteristics of that game. And this is claimed in spite of the fact that if a human being were to play the toe-stepping game as envisaged above, we would no doubt be correct in saying that that person was imitating, etc. To be sure, a digital computer is a more august mechanism than a rock-box, but Turing has not provided us with any arguments for believing that its role in the imitation game, as distinct from the net results it yields, is any closer a match for a human being executing such a role, than is the rock-box's execution of its role in the toe-stepping game a match for a human being's execution of a similar role. The parody comparison can be pushed too far. But I think it lays bare the reason why there is no contradiction involved in saying, "Yes, a machine can play the imitation game, but it can't think." It is for the same reason that there is no contradiction in saying, "Of course a rock-box of such-and-such a sort can be set up, but rocks surely can't imitate." For thinking (or imitating) cannot be fully described simply by pointing to net results such as those illustrated above. For if this were not the case it would be correct to say that a piece of chalk could think or compose because it was freakishly blown about by a tornado in such a way that it scratched a rondo on a blackboard, and that a phonograph could sing, and that an electric-eye could see people coming.

People may be let out of a building by either an electric-eye or a doorman. The end result is the same. But though a doorman may be rude or polite, the electric-eye neither practices nor neglects etiquette. Turing brandishes net results. But I think the foregoing at least indicates certain difficulties with any account of thinking or decision as to whether a certain thing is capable of thought which is based primarily on net results. And, of course, one could always ask whether the net results were really the same. But I do not wish to follow that line of argument here. It is my main concern simply to indicate where Turing's account, which is cast largely in terms of net results, fails because of this. It is not an effective counter to reply: "But part of the net results in question includes intelligent people being deceived!" For what would this add to the general argument? No doubt people could be deceived by rock-boxes! It is said that hi-fidelity phonographs have been perfected to the point where blindfolded music critics are unable to distinguish their "playing" from that of, let us say, the Budapest String Quartet. But the phonograph would never be said to have performed with unusual brilliance on Saturday, nor would it ever deserve an encore.

III

Now perhaps comparable net results achieved by machines and human beings is all that is needed to establish an analogy between them, but it is far from what is needed to establish that one sort of subject (machines) can do the same thing that another sort of subject (human beings or other animals) can do. Part of what things do is how they do it. To ask whether a machine can think is in part to ask whether machines can do things in certain ways.

The above is relevant to what might be called the problem of distinguishing and evaluating the net results achieved by a machine as it is touched on by Scriven in his discussion of what he calls "the performatory problem" and "the personality problem." In "The Compleat Robot: A Prolegomena to Androidology," he writes:

> The performatory problem here is whether a computer can produce results which, when translated, provide what would count as an original solution or proof *if it came from a man*. The personality problem is whether we are entitled to call such a result a solution or proof, despite the fact that it did *not* come from a man.

And continues:

The logical trap is this: no *one* performatory achievement will be enough to persuade us to apply the human-achievement vocabulary, but if we refuse to use this vocabulary in each case separately, on this ground, we will, perhaps wrongly, have committed ourselves to avoiding it even when *all* the achievements are simultaneously attained.

My concern is not however, with what is to count as an original solution or proof. Scriven, in the above, is commenting on the claims: "Machines only do what we tell them to do. They are incapable of genuinely original thought." He says that two "importantly different points are run together." The above is his attempt to separate these points. But it seems that there are at least three, and not just two, points which are run together in the just-mentioned claims. The third point, the one not covered by Scriven's distinction between the performatory and personality problems, is simply the problem, mentioned above, of discerning when one subject (a machine) has *done the same thing* as another subject (a human being). And here "doing the same thing" does not simply mean "achieved similar end result." (Which is not to suggest that the phrase can never be used in that way in connection with thinking.) This is of interest in respect to Scriven's discussion, since it might be the case that all the achievements were simultaneously attained by a machine, as Scriven suggests, and that we had decided on various grounds that they should count as original proofs and solutions and thus surmounted the personality problem, but yet felt unwilling to grant that the machines were capable of "genuinely original thought." Our grounds for this latter decision might be highly parallel to our grounds for not wanting to say that rocks could imitate (even though rock-boxes had reached a high level of development). Of course our grounds might not be as sound as these. I am simply imagining the case where they are, which is also a case where all the achievements are attained in such a way that they count as original solutions or proofs. In this case we would see that answers to questions about originality and performance and the logical trap mentioned by Scriven would be wholly separate from whatever answers might be given to the question whether or not the machines involved thought, and would thus be unsuitable as answers to the question whether or not they were capable of "genuinely original thought." In other words, questions as to originality and questions as to thinking are not the same, but this dissimilarity is left unacknowledged in Scriven's account.

IV

But let us return to the imitation game itself. It is to be granted that if human beings were to participate in such a game, we would almost surely regard them as deliberating, deciding, wondering—in short, "thinking things over"—as they passed their messages back and forth. And if someone were to ask us for an example of Johnson's intellectual prowess or mental capabilities, we might well point to this game which he often played, and how he enjoyed trying to outwit Peterson and Hanson who also participated in it. But we would only regard it as one of the many examples we might give of Peterson's mental capacities. We would ordinarily not feel hard pressed to produce countless other examples of Peterson deliberating, figuring, wondering, reflecting, or what in short we can call thinking. We might, for example, relate how he works over his sonnets or how he argues with Hanson. Now, I do not want to deny that it is beyond the scope of a machine to do these latter things. I am not, in fact, here concerned with giving an answer to the question, "Can machines think?" What I instead want to emphasize is that what we would say about Peterson in countless other situations is bound to influence what we say about him in the imitation game. A rock rolls down a hill and there is, strictly speaking, no behavior or action on the part of the rock. But if a man rolls down a hill we might well ask if he was pushed or did it intentionally, whether he's enjoying himself, playing a game, pretending to be a tumbleweed, or what. We cannot think of a man as simply or purely rolling down a hill—unless he is dead. A fortiori, we cannot understand him being a participant in the imitation game apart from his dispositions, habits, etc., which are exhibited in contexts other than the imitation game. Thus we cannot hope to find any decisive answer to the question as to how we should characterize a machine which can play (well) the imitation game, by asking what we would say about a man who could play (well) the imitation game. Thinking, whatever positive characterization or account is correct, is not something which any one example will explain or decide. But the part of Turing's case which I've been concerned with rests largely on one example.

V

The following might help to clarify the above. Imagine the dialogue below:

> Vacuum Cleaner Salesman: Now here's an example of what the all-purpose Swish 600 can do. (He then applies the nozzle to the carpet and it sucks up a bit of dust.)
> Housewife: What else can it do?
> Vacuum Cleaner Salesman: What do you mean "What else can it do?" It just sucked up that bit of dust, didn't you see?
> Housewife: Yes, I saw it suck up a bit of dust, but I thought it was all-purpose. Doesn't it suck up larger and heavier bits of straw

or paper or mud? And can't it get in the tight corners? Doesn't
it have other nozzles? What about the cat hair on the couch?
Vacuum Cleaner Salesman: It sucks up bits of dust. That's what
vacuum cleaners are for.
Housewife: Oh, that's what it does. I thought it was simply an example of what it does.
Vacuum Cleaner Salesman: It is an example of what it does. What
it does is to suck up bits of dust.

We ask: Who's right about examples? We answer: It's not perfectly clear
that anyone is lying or unjustifiably using the word "example." And there's
no obvious linguistic rule or regularity to point to which tells us that if S
can only do x, then S's doing x cannot be an example of what S can do
since being an example presupposes or entails or whatnot that other kinds
of examples are forthcoming (sucking up mud, cat hair, etc.). Yet, in spite
of this, the housewife has a point. One simply has a right to expect more
from an all-purpose Swish 600 than what has been demonstrated. Here clearly
the main trouble is with "all-purpose" rather than with "example," though there
may still be something misleading about saying, "Here's an example . . . ,"
and it would surely mislead to say, "Here's *just* an example. . . ," followed
by ". . . of what the all-purpose Swish 600 can do." The philosophical relevance of all this to our own discussion can be put in the following rather
domestic way: "thinking" is a term which shares certain features with "all-purpose" as it occurs in the phrase "all-purpose Swish 600." It is not used to
designate or refer to one capability, capacity, disposition, talent, habit, or feature of a given subject any more than "all-purpose" in the above example
is used to mark out one particular operation of a vacuum cleaner. Thinking,
whatever positive account one might give of it, is not, for example, like swimming or tennis playing. The question as to whether Peterson can swim or
play tennis can be settled by a few token examples of Peterson swimming
or playing tennis. (And it might be noted it is hardly imaginable that the question as to whether Peterson could think or not would be raised. For in general
it is not at all interesting to ask that question of contemporary human beings,
though it might be interesting for contemporary human beings to raise it in
connection with different anthropoids viewed at various stages of their evolu-
tion.) But if we suppose the question were raised in connection with Peterson
the only appropriate sort of answer to it would be one like, "Good heavens,
what makes you think he can't?" (as if anticipating news of some horrible
brain injury inflicted on Peterson). And our shock would not be at his perhaps
having lost a particular talent. It would not be like the case of a Wimbledon
champion losing his tennis talent because of an amputated arm.
    It is no more unusual for a human being to be capable of thought than

it is for a human being to be composed of cells. Similarly, "He can think" is no more an answer to questions concerning Peterson's mental capacities or intelligence, than "He's composed of cells" is an answer to the usual type of question about Peterson's appearance. And to say that Peterson can think is not to say there are a few token examples of thinking which are at our fingertips, any more than to say that the Swish 600 is all-purpose is to have in mind a particular maneuver or two of which the device is capable. It is because thinking cannot be identified with what can be shown by any one example or type of example; thus Turing's approach to the question "Can a machine think?" via the imitation game is less than convincing. In effect he provides us below with a dialogue very much like the one above:

> Turing: You know, machines can think.
> Philosopher: Good heavens! Really? How do you know?
> Turing: Well, they can play what's called the imitation game. (This is followed by a description of same.)
> Philosopher: Interesting. What else can they do? They must be capable of a great deal if they can really think.
> Turing: What do you mean, "What else can they do?" They play the imitation game. That's thinking, isn't it?
> Etc.

But Turing, like the vacuum cleaner salesman, has trouble making his sale. Nonetheless, I will indicate shortly why certain of our criticisms of his approach might have to be modified.

VI

But one last critical remark before pointing to certain shortcomings of the foregoing. As indicated before, Turing's argument benefits from his emphasizing the fact that a machine is being substituted for a human being in a certain situation, and does as well as a human being would do in that situation. No one, however, would want to deny that machines are able to do a number of things as well as or more competently than human beings, though surely no one would want to say that every one of such examples provided further arguments in support of the claim that machines can think. For in many such cases one might, instead of emphasizing that a machine can do what a human being can do, emphasize that one hardly needs to be a human being to do such things. For example: "I don't even have to think at my job; I just seal the jars as they move along the belt," or, "I just pour out soft drinks one after the other like some machine." The latter could hardly be construed as suggesting "My, aren't soft-drink vending machines clever," but rather suggests, "Isn't my job stupid; it involves little or no mental effort at all." Furthermore, as Professor Ryle has suggested to me, a well-trained bank cashier can add, subtract, multiply, and divide without having to think about what he is doing and while thinking about something else, and can't many of us run through the alphabet or a popular song without thinking? This is not meant to be a specific criticism of Turing as much as it is meant as a reminder that being able to do what human beings can do hardly implies the presence of intellectual or mental skills real or simulated, since so many things which human beings do involve little if any thinking. Those without jobs constitute a somewhat different segment of the population from those without wits.

VII

But the following considerations seem to temper some of the foregoing criticisms. A defender of Turing might emphasize that a machine that is able to play the imitation game is also able to do much more: it can compute, perhaps be programed to play chess, etc., and consequently displays capacities far beyond the "one example" which has been emphasized in our criticisms. I shall not go into the details which I think an adequate reply to this challenge must take into account. But in general I believe it would be possible to formulate a reply along the lines that would show that even playing chess, calculating, and the performance of other (most likely computational) operations provide us with at best a rather narrow range of examples and still fails to satisfy our intuitive concept of thinking. The parallel case in respect to the Housewife and Vacuum Cleaner Salesman would be where the Housewife still refused to accept the vacuum cleaner as "all-purpose" even though it had been shown to be capable of picking up scraps somewhat heavier than dust. Nonetheless, even if our reply were satisfactory, the more general question would remain unanswered: what range of examples would satisfy the implicit criteria we use in our ordinary characterization of subjects as "those capable of thought"?

A corollary: If we are to keep the question "Can machines think?" interesting, we cannot withhold a positive answer simply on the grounds that it (a machine) does not duplicate human activity in every respect. The question "Can a machine think if it can do everything a human being can do?" is not an interesting question, though it is somewhat interesting to ask whether there would not be a logical contradiction in supposing such to be, in fact, a machine. But as long as we have in mind subjects which obviously are machines, we must be willing to stop short of demanding their activities to fully mirror human ones before we say they can think, if they can. But how far short? Again the above question as to the variety and extent of examples required is raised.

Furthermore, it might be asserted that with the increasing role of machines in society the word "think" itself might take on new meanings, and that it is not unreasonable to suppose it changing in meaning in such a way that fifty years hence a machine which could play the imitation game would in ordinary parlance be called a machine which could think. There is, however, a difference between asking whether a machine can think given current meanings and uses of "machine" and "think" and asking whether a machine can think given changes in the meanings of "machine" and "think." My own attention has throughout this paper been centered on the first question. Yet there is a temporal obscurity in the question "Can machines think?" For if the question is construed as ranging over possible futures, it may be difficult to discuss such futures without reference to changing word meanings and uses. But this raises an entire family of issues which there is not space to discuss here. To some extent Turing's own views are based on certain beliefs he has about how we will in the future talk about machines. But these are never discussed in any detail, and he does not address himself to the knotty problems of meaning which interlace with them.

VIII

A final point: the stance is often taken that thinking is the crowning capacity or achievement of the human race, and that if one denies that machines can think, one in effect assigns them to some lower level of achievement than that attained by human beings. But one might well contend that machines can't think, for they do much better than that. We could forever deny that a machine could think through a mathematical problem, and still claim that in many respects the achievement of machines was on a higher level than that attained by thinking beings, since machines can almost instantaneously and infallibly produce accurate and sometimes original answers to many complex and difficult mathematical problems with which they are presented. They do not need to "think out" the answers. In the end the steam drill outlasted John Henry as a digger of railway tunnels, but that didn't prove the machine had muscles; it proved that muscles were not needed for digging railway tunnels.

NOTE

1. See Michael Scriven, "The Mechanical Concept of Mind," pp. 31ff., and "The Compleat Robot: A Prolegomena to Androidology" in *Dimensions of Mind,* Sidney Hook, ed. (New York: New York University Press, 1960). [See selection 30 in the present volume.] Also a remark by Paul Ziff in "The Feelings of Robots," pp. 98ff. [see selection 33 in the present volume], and others—for example, C. E. Shannon and J. McCarthy in their preface to *Automata Studies* (Princeton: Princeton University Press, 1956).

32

On Consciousness in Machines

Arthur C. Danto

Suppose all the physical discrepancies between the human brain and the currently most highly developed servomechanisms were someday overcome, and that the machine turned out to be conscious. What then would happen with the old quarrel between dualists and anti-dualists regarding the mind-body problem? I venture to say that nothing would happen with that quarrel: partisans of each position would doubtless applaud the great feat in technology, but the machine would nonetheless leave the basic philosophical disagreements where it found them. For, by hypothesis, the machine will have been brought to an order of functional complexity comparable with that of the human brain, and the quarrel has all along been concerned with relations, one term of which consists in mechanisms of just this order of complexity. And since the problems have always arisen in connection with human beings, the more the machines can be changed to resemble human beings, the more, philosophically, *c'est la même chose*. So the empirical crux of the controversy, if it exists at all, is not to be breached in this manner. The best that might be shown would be a certain correlation between consciousness and mechanisms of a certain order of complexity, independent of the causal provenance of the latter. But the empirical hypothesis thus confirmed is compatible with all main positions on the mind-body problem.

But what about my initial supposition regarding the construction of a

From *Dimensions of Mind*, edited by Sidney Hook (New York: New York University Press, 1960), pp. 165–71. Reprinted by permission of the publisher.

conscious machine: is this a sheer exercise in science fiction or a wild anticipation of the shape of things to come? This is not for me to answer, but I do wish to distinguish two different questions which the supposition raises: (a) can machines be brought to this required degree of complexity, and (b) would they then be conscious? It lies outside the competence of the philosopher to pronounce on (a): the answer to it is wholly a matter of the progress of science, and has to do with the correctness of neuron theory, of proposed analogies between nerve-cells and switches, and on the solution to a host of intricate problems concerning circuitry, cooling, and the like. But about (b) the philosopher may say a word or two. Is the proposition "A machine M becomes conscious when it reaches a point p of complexity" of the same kind as "Water boils at $100°$ C"? If so, the only answer to (b) is: *wait and see.* But philosophers might temporize, on the grounds that while we are reasonably clear about the predicate "is boiling" we are far from clear on "is conscious," so that until a bit of philosophical lexicography has been done, we will hardly know what to look for when M has been brought to p. This would be my response to (b). But other philosophers have a readier answer: there is no point in waiting and seeing, for there will be nothing to look for. We are indeed not clear on the predicate "is conscious," but we *are* clear on the entities to which it appropriately applies when it applies at all. And the predicate does not apply to machines. Some such premise as this seemed to underlie the remarks of a number of persons at our conference, their statements being enthymenmatic conclusions to a near-relative of a Paradigm Case Argument. But this short way with (b) seems to me to raise problems of its own, if not about machines at least about language, and I would like to spell some of these out.

I

Dr. Scriven was concerned to specify a set of crucial properties of the human brain, properties such that if mechanical brains lacked them, we would be obliged to concede that mechanical brains belong to an order essentially different from human brains. Consciousness was one such property, perhaps the critical one. Now it can be argued that even human brains are not conscious: *persons* are, and persons have brains. But this only calls for rephrasing on Scriven's part. It has become a natural idiom to speak of certain machines as "brains" (e.g., "giant brains"), but we could as easily speak of them as having brains, the question being whether machines are conscious the way persons are in virtue of their mutual possession of comparable brains. Scriven went on to sketch an experiment, the positive outcome of which would yield an affirmative answer to this query. We construct a machine (of a kind I shall henceforward refer to as a Scriven Machine) which (1) is programmed in such wise as to have command of the full resources of the English language and (2) furnishes only true answers to questions asked it when it can furnish any answer at all. Now we simply ask the machine whether it is conscious or, perhaps, whether it feels it when we send through an unduly high number of volts. If the answer is affirmative, we can conclude from (1) that the answer is linguistically correct and from (2) that it is true, and that *Scriven* Machines, at least, are conscious.

But if the "short way" with (b) rests on a sound argument, we can readily predict the outcome of the experiment without going to the trouble and expense of building a Scriven Machine. For given the conventions of English which the argument invokes, and given that these conventions are built into the machine in accordance with (1), it immediately follows that the Scriven Machine must answer "No" to the critical question. And the reason it would give (if it could give reasons) would be "I am a machine and machines are not conscious." The programming of it in accordance with (1) has made the machine an unwitting master of Paradigm Case analysis. But I begin to feel just here that (1) conflicts with (2), except in the sense that in view of (1) the truth in question is so trivial as to eliminate the value of the experiment. Adherence to the presumed conventions of English disqualifies the Scriven Machine from giving a nontrivial answer to the question, just in the same way that the conventions of some Eastern European country in the old days, which ruled that peasants have no feelings, disqualifies a nontrivial answer to the question "Did that hurt?" asked of a peasant under the knout.

The question I would ask then, consistently with my view on (b), is when and at what point would we be prepared to *change* the conventions and so allow the Scriven Machine at least the option of a nontrivial answer to questions regarding its inner states? But in fact, I contend, the very existence of a Scriven Machine would force *some* change in language whether we liked it or not. Thus, to refuse to make a change at one point would automatically be to allow a change elsewhere (I take my cue here from some comments of Professor Hilary Putnam). Not to change our language would be perforce to change our language. The Scriven Machine, indeed, is so designed as to force a change in the rules governing its own construction. Here is another instance of mechanical treachery of the sort to which Prof. Wiener likes to call to our attention.

II

For, notice that, given (1), the Scriven Machine would be obliged to give a negative answer to any question Q which made essential use of any predicate f which, in ordinary usage, is not correctly applied to machines. As a special case, the machine would have to refuse self-application of any predicate f, application of which presupposes correct application of the predicate "is conscious." In particular, "is thinking," "is feeling," "is wanting to," etc. For consciousness, as defined in the OED, is "The state of fact of being conscious, as a condition and concomitant of all thought, feeling, and volition." All such predicates I shall tern non-M. From remarks made in our discussion, I gather "gets the meaning of Q" (where Q is a question) is non-M. So while it is true that we can ask and get answers to questions from the Scriven Machine, we cannot say the machine gets the meaning of the questions we ask. With this restriction in mind, I want to construct a dialogue between the Scriven Machine and a human interlocutor.

> I: Here are some rather complicated instructions. I am going to ask you a question Q, but before you give me an answer to Q, I want you first to give answers to a series of other questions. Then give me an answer to Q. Now, Q is: how much is three times four? The first thing I want you to answer is: do you get the meaning of Q?
>
> M: No.
>
> I: Do you know the answer to Q?
>
> M: No.
>
> I. Do you recall what Q asked?
>
> M: No.
>
> I: Fine. Now what is the answer to Q?
>
> M: Twelve.
>
> I: Do you believe that to be the correct answer?
>
> M: No.
>
> I: *Is* it the correct answer?
>
> M: Yes.
>
> I: Then why don't you believe it's the correct answer?
>
> M: I'm a machine, and machines don't have beliefs. So I don't have beliefs.
>
> I: I suppose that's why you answered "No" when I asked whether you got the meaning, knew the answer, and recalled the question?
>
> M: That's right.
>
> I: Suppose you weren't a machine: how would you answer those questions?
>
> M: That's a counterfactual, I'm afraid.

It is hard to make out from this dialogue whether greater violence is being done to English or to truth, quite apart from the matter of injustice to the Scriven Machine—as though it were being denied the *right* to apply predicates to itself which we would have thought descriptive but which turn out also to be honorific. And one begins to feel that in fairness both to truth and the Scriven Machine, we had better relax some conventions of language.

For in fact some conventions of language have already been relaxed. As Moore recognized, one cannot say and disbelieve a proposition, one cannot correctly use "I don't believe p" together with "p is correct." One might get out of this by insisting that neither "believes p" nor "does not believe p" applies to machines. But this way out is at best prompted by a certain prejudice, and still leaves us with the fact that, in ordinary English, to answer at $t +_\Delta t$ a question Q asked at t is to recall Q. And I should think that it follows from the fact that something is recalled by x that x is conscious. So either we must allow that the Scriven Machine is conscious, or change the meaning of certain important mental terms. Of course, one can always avail oneself of Duhem-Quine maneuvers, and make changes "elsewhere in the system." I should like to consider another alternative myself. We might (A) decide that Scriven Machines are human and (B) persist in saying that non-M predicates are to be withheld from application to machines. But (A) reflects the sort of mentality which finds it congenial to deny that black swans are swans, to retain empirical generalizations only at the price of making them analytic and hence no longer empirical generalizations. And it continues to solve the problem of consciousness in machines by such trivial devices as insisting that whenever something is conscious it is not a machine. (B), meanwhile, imposes upon us the task of finding other terms which will do the work non-M predicates would do if non-M predicates could be applied to machines. For the whole language of action must go by the board: as Prof. Toulmin pointed out, we could not even speak of machines playing checkers.

So let us construct a special language, L_m to be exclusively applied to machines. We might save ourselves a great deal of labor by just affixing subscripts to the appropriate English words, e.g., "recalls$_m$" or "plays$_m$ checkers." But the subscripted terms of L_m must designate movements of mechanical parts, or dispositions of mechanical parts to move in certain ways, or functions of integrated motions of mechanical parts. But just which movements, dispositions or functions are to be designated with "recalls$_m$"? Surely those which are related to whatever machines do which corresponds to what humans do when "recalls" is true of humans. Otherwise why use "recalls$_m$" and not just some arbitrary word? But even arbitrary terms in L_m require translation into English if the machines are to be used in any significant way. So, (1) L_m is parasitic on English roughly as sense-datum language is parasitic on physical-object language; (2) we are still left with a problem whether to include a term "conscious$_m$" in L_m, and a further problem as to what "conscious$_m$" would designate if it *were* included in L_m—since, after all, we are not clear on what properties "conscious" connotes in English; finally, (3) there would be cold comfort in saying that machines are conscious$_m$ but not conscious, since there is a major problem as yet to be seriously faced in our discussion—namely, how are we to distinguish between the class of entities to be spoken of with "m" subscripts and humans? Granted that L_m applies exclusively to machines, the question remains how machines are to be distinguished from human beings. And this, I gather, is far less easy to make clear than once it was thought to be. Indeed, it is likely to grow more difficult in the future. And how strange it would be to insist that machines are not conscious, and yet be unable to single out machines.

Well, we could try another experiment. We could program the Scriven Machine with the full resources of English *and* L_m, but refuse to tell it which language is appropriate to itself. And when we asked it to find out, which comes to asking it "Are you a machine?" I don't know what the answer would be: perhaps the Scriven Machine would produce answers in unsubscripted English, and what would we say then? After all, the language it employs is bound to reflect whatever vaguenesses exist in our language, and it would have the same problems in the face of indefinite criteria which all of us have. So in the end it is up to us to decide. The Scriven Machine has only our conventions to work with.

III

But suppose we just *decided* that Scriven Machines are conscious! Would this really make its answer to the critical question any less trivially predictable than it now is—i.e., "I am a Scriven Machine, and Scriven Machines are conscious. So I am conscious"? I say it all depends on what basis the decision was made. If it was simply a *fiat* on our part, or perhaps just a trouble-saving reaction to the linguistic tensions the Scriven Machine precipitates, then the issue remains trivialized and there is no special gain. If it was made on the basis of differential behavioral criteria, then it depends upon whether the Scriven Machine satisfied these. "But which behavioral criteria?" I do not know. And that is why I gave a temporizing answer to (b).

But someone is apt to be discontented with this. "Satisfaction of differential behavioral criteria doesn't *prove* that something is conscious. At best it still reflects a decision you have made concerning when and when not to bestow the predicate 'is conscious.' Whether or not something is conscious, however, is a matter independent of your tests. So just because something has passed all the tests doesn't guarantee that it is conscious. Even if Scriven Machines *are* conscious, other machines might not be and still pass all the tests!" True. But this is a problem we face amongst ourselves. René Descartes, that arch-doubter, would cheerfully have taken you and me to be automata, differential behavioral criteria notwithstanding. So let's not ask the impossible.

33

The Feelings of Robots

Paul Ziff

Could a robot have feelings? Some say of course.[1] Some say of course not.[2]

1. I want the right sort of robots. They must be automata and without doubt machines.

I shall assume that they are essentially computing machines, having microelements and whatever micromechanisms may be necessary for the functioning of these engineering wonders. Furthermore, I shall assume that they are powered by microsolar batteries: instead of having lunch they will have light.

And if it is clear that our robots are without doubt machines then in all other respects they may be as much like men as you like. They may be the size of men. When clothed and masked they may be virtually indistinguishable from men in practically all respects: in appearance, in movement, in the utterances they utter, and so forth. Thus except for the masks any ordinary man would take them to be ordinary men. Not suspecting they were robots nothing about them would make him suspect.

But unmasked the robots are to be seen in all their metallic lustre. What is in question here is not whether we can blur the line between a man and a machine and so attribute feelings to the machine. The question is whether

---

From *Analysis* 19, no. 3 (1959). Reprinted by permission of the author and the publisher.

we can attribute feelings to the machine and so blur the line between a man and a machine.

2. Could robots have feelings? Could they, say, feel tired, or bored?

Ex hypothesi robots are mechanisms, not organisms, not living creatures. There could be a broken-down robot but not a dead one. Only living creatures can literally have feelings.

If I say "She feels tired" one can generally infer that what is in question is (or was or will be in the case of talk about spirits)[3] a living creature. More generally, the linguistic environment ". . . feels tried" is generally open only to expressions that refer to living creatures. Suppose you say "The robot feels tired." The phrase "the robot" refers to a mechanism. Then one can infer that what is in question is not a living creature. But from the utterance of the predicative expression ". . . feels tired" one can infer that what is in question is a living creature. So if you are speaking literally and you say "The robot feels tired" you imply a contradiction. Consequently one cannot literally predicate ". . . feels tired" of "the robot."

Or again: no robot will ever do everything a man can. And it doesn't matter how robots may be constructed or how complex and varied their movements and operations may be. Robots may calculate but they will not literally reason. Perhaps they will take things but they will not literally borrow them. They may kill but not literally murder. They may voice apologies but they will not literally make any. These are actions that only persons can perform: *ex hypothesi* robots are not persons.

3. "A dead robot" is a metaphor but "a dead battery" is a dead metaphor: if there were a robot around it would put its metaphor to death.

What I don't want to imply I need not imply. An implication can be weakened. The sense of a word can be widened or narrowed or shifted. If one wishes to be understood then one mustn't go too far: that is all. Pointing to one among many paintings, I say "Now *that* one is a *painting*." Do I mean the others are not? Of course not. Yet the stress on "that" is contrastive. So I say "The robot, that mechanism, not of course a living creature but a machine, it feels tired": you cannot infer that what is in question here is a living creature.

If I say of a person "He feels tired," do you think I am saying that he is a living creature and only that? If I say "The robot feels tired" I am not saying that what is in question is a living creature, but that doesn't mean that nothing is being said. If I say "The robot feels tired," the predicate ". . . feels tired" means whatever it usually means except that one cannot infer that what is in question is a living creature. That is the only difference.

And what has been said about "The robot feels tired" could be said equally well about "The robot is conscious," "The robot borrowed my cat," and so forth.

4. Could robots feel tired? Could a stone feel tired? Could the number 17 feel tired? It is clear that there is no reason to believe that 17 feels tired. But that doesn't prove anything. A man can feel tired and there may be nothing, there need be nothing at all, that shows it. And so with a robot or a stone or the number 17.

Even so, the number 17 could not feel tired. And I say this not because or not simply because there are no reasons to suppose that 17 does feel tired but because there are good reasons not to suppose that 17 feels tired and good reasons not to suppose that 17 ever feels anything at all. Consequently it is necessary to consider whether there are any reasons for supposing that robots feel tired and whether there are good reasons for not supposing that robots ever feel anything at all.

5. Knowing George and seeing the way he looks I say he feels tired. Knowing Josef and seeing the way he looks I don't say he feels tired. Yet if you don't know either of them then to you George and Josef may look alike.

In one sense they may look alike to me too, but not in another. For George but not Josef will look tired. If you ask me to point out the difference there may be nothing relevant, there need be nothing relevant, to point to. For the relevant difference may be like that between looking at an unframed picture and looking at it framed. Only the frame here is provided by what I know about them: you cannot see what I know.

(Speaking with the robots, one can say that the way things look to me, my present output, will not be the same as yours, the way things look to you, even though at present we may both receive the same input, the same stimuli, and this is because your mechanism was not in the same initial state as mine, owing either to a difference in structure or to a difference in previous inputs.)

If we say of a person that he feels tired, we generally do so not only on the basis of what we see then and there but on the basis of what we have seen elsewhere and on the basis of how what we have seen elsewhere ties in with what we see then and there. And this is only to say that in determining whether or not a person feels tired both observational and theoretic considerations are involved and, as everywhere, are inextricably interwoven.

6. Suppose you and I visit an actor at home. He is rehearsing the role of a grief-stricken man. He ignores our presence as a grief-stricken man might. His performance is impeccable. I know but you do not know that he is an actor and that he is rehearsing a role. You ask "Why is he so miserable?" and I reply "He isn't." "Surely," you say, "he is grief-stricken. Look at him!

Show me what leads you to say otherwise!" and of course there may be nothing then and there to show.

So Turing[4] posed the question whether automata could think, be conscious, have feelings, etc., in the following naïve way: what test would an automaton fail to pass? MacKay[5] has pointed out that any test for mental or any other attributes to be satisfied by the observable activity of a human being can be passed by automata. And so one is invited to say what would be wrong with a robot's performance.

Nothing need be wrong with either the actor's or a robot's performance. What is wrong is that they are performances.

7. Suppose K is a robot. An ordinary man may see K and not knowing that K is a robot, the ordinary man may say "K feels tired." If I ask him what makes him think so, he may reply "K worked all day digging ditches. Anyway, just look at K: if he doesn't look tired, who does?"

So K looks tired to the ordinary man. That doesn't prove anything. If I know K is a robot, K may not look tired to me. It is not what I see but what I know. Or it is not what I see then and there but what I have seen elsewhere. Where? In a robot psychology laboratory.

8. If I say "The robot feels tired," the predicate ". . . feels tired" means whatever it usually means except that one cannot infer that what is in question is a living creature. That is the only difference.

To speak of something living is to speak of an organism in an environment. The environment is that in which the behavior of the organism takes place. Death is the dissolution of the relation between an organism and its environment. In death I am pluralized, converted from one to many. I become my remains. I merge with my environment.

If we think of robots being put together, we can think of them being taken apart. So in our laboratory we have taken robots apart, we have changed and exchanged their parts, we have changed and exchanged their programs, we have started and stopped them, sometimes in one state, sometimes in another, we have taken away their memories, we have made them seem to remember things that were yet to come, and so on.

And what we find in our laboratory is this: no robot could sensibly be said to feel anything. Why not?

9. Because there are not psychological truths about robots but only about the human makers of robots. Because the way a robot acts (in a specified context) depends primarily on how we programed it to act. Because we can program a robot to act in any way we want it to act. Because a robot could be programed to act like a tired man when it lifted a feather and not when it lifted a ton. Because a robot couldn't mean what it said any more than

a phonograph record could mean what it said. Because we could make a robot say anything we want it to say. Because coveting thy neighbor's robot wife would be like coveting his car and not like coveting his wife. Because robots are replaceable. Because robots have no individuality. Because one can duplicate all the parts and have two virtually identical machines. Because one can exchange all the parts and still have the same machines. Because one can exchange the programs of two machines having the same structure. Because . . . .

Because no robot would act tired. Because a robot could only act like a robot programed to act like a tired man. For suppose some robots are programed to act like a tired man after lifting a feather while some are so programed that they never act like a tired man. Shall we say "It is a queer thing but some robots feel tired almost at once while others never feel tired"? Or suppose some are programed to act like a tired man after lifting something blue but not something green. Shall we say "Some robots feel tired when they lift blue things but not when they lift green things"? And shall we conclude "Some robots find blue things heavier than green things"? Hard work makes a man feel tired: what will make a robot act like a tired man? Perhaps hard work, or light work, or no work, or anything at all. For it will depend on the whims of the man who makes it (though these whims may be modified by whatever quirks may appear in the robot's electronic nerve network, and there may be unwanted and unforeseen consequences of an ill-conceived program). Shall we say "There's no telling what will make a robot feel tired"? And if a robot acts like a tired man then what? Some robots may be programed to require a rest, others to require more work. Shall we say "This robot feels tired so put it back to work"?

What if all this were someday to be done with and to human beings? What if we were someday to break down the difference between a man and his environment? Then someday we would wake and find that we are robots. But we wouldn't wake to a mechanical paradise or even an automatic hell: for then it might not make sense to talk of human beings having feelings just as it now doesn't make sense to talk of robots having feelings.

A robot would behave like a robot.

NOTES

1. Cf. D. M. MacKay, "The Epistemological Problem for Automata," in *Automata Studies* (Princeton: Princeton University Press, 1956), pp. 235ff.

2. Cf. M. Scriven, "The Mechanical Concept of Mind" (see [*Analysis* 19, no. 3 (1959):] pp. 31ff.).

3. I shall henceforth omit the qualification.

4. Cf. [Turing,] "Computing Machinery and Intelligence" [*Analysis* 19, no. 3 (1959):].

5. Cf. "Mentality in Machines," *Proceedings of the Aristotelian Society*, Supp. Vol. 26 (1952): 61ff.

34

Minds and Machines

Hilary Putnam

The various issues and puzzles that make up the traditional mind-body problem are wholly linguistic and logical in character: whatever few empirical "facts" there may be in this area support one view as much as another. I do not hope to establish this contention in this paper, but I hope to do something toward rendering it more plausible. Specifically, I shall try to show that all of the issues arise in connection with any computing system capable of answering questions about its own structure, and have thus nothing to do with the unique nature (if it *is* unique) of human subjective experience.

To illustrate the sort of thing that is meant one kind of puzzle that is sometimes discussed in connection with the "mind-body problem" is the puzzle of *privacy*. The question "How do I know I have a pain?" is a *deviant*[1] ("logicaly odd") question. The question "How do I know Smith has a pain?" is not at all deviant. The difference can also be mirrored in impersonal questions: "How does anyone ever know he himself has a pain?" is deviant; "How does anyone ever know that someone else is in pain?" is nondeviant. I shall show that the difference in status between the last two questions is mirrored in the case of machines: if T is any *Turing machine* (see below), the question "How does T ascertain that it is in state A?" is, as we shall see, "logically odd" with a vengeance; but if T is capable of investigating its neighbor

From *Dimensions of Mind*, edited by Sidney Hook (New York: New York University Press, 1960), pp. 138–50. Reprinted by permission of the publisher.

machine T' (say, T has electronic "sense-organs" which "scan" T'), the question "How does T ascertain that T' is in state A?" is not at all odd.

* * *

It is instructive to note that the traditional argument for dualism is not at all a conclusion from "the raw data of direct experience" (as is shown by the fact that it applies just as well to nonsentient machines), but a highly complicated bit of reasoning which depends on (A) the reification of universals[2] (e.g., "properties," "states," "events"); and on (B) a sharp analytic-synthetic distinction.

I may be accused of advocating a "mechanistic" world-view in pressing the present analogy. If this means that I am supposed to hold that machines think,[3] on the one hand, or that human beings are machines, on the other, the charge is false. If there is some version of mechanism sophisticated enough to avoid these errors, very likely the considerations in this paper support it.[4]

TURING MACHINES

The present paper will require the notion of a *Turing machine*[5]. . . .

Briefly, a Turing machine is a device with a finite number of internal configurations, each of which involves the machine's being in one of a finite number of *states*,[6] and the machine's scanning a tape on which certain symbols appear.

* * *

PRIVACY

Let us suppose that a Turing machine T is constructed to do the following. A number, say "3000," is printed on T's tape and T is started in T's "initial state." Thereupon T computes the 3000th (or whatever the given number was) digit in the decimal expansion of π prints this digit on its tape, and goes into the "rest state," (i.e., turns itself off). Clearly the question "How does T 'ascertain" [or 'compute,' or 'work out'] the 3000th digit in the decimal expansion of π?" is a sensible question. And the answer might well be a complicated one. In fact, an answer would probably involve three distinguishable constituents:

(i) A description of the sequence of states through which T passed in arriving at the answer, and of the appearance of the tape at each stage in the computation.

(ii) A description of the *rules* under which T operated (these are given by the "machine table" for T).

(iii) An explanation of the *rationale* of the entire procedure.

Now let us suppose that someone voices the following objection: "In order to perform the computation just described, T must pass through states A, B, C, etc. But how can T ascertain that it is in states A, B, C, etc?"

It is clear that this is a silly objection. But what makes it silly? For one thing, the "logical description" (machine table) of the machine describes the states only in terms of their *relations* to each other and to what appears on the tape. The "physical realization" of the machine is immaterial, so long as there *are* distinct states A, B, C, etc., and they succeed each other as specified in the machine table. Thus one can answer a question such as "How does T ascertain that X?" (or "compute X," etc.) only in the sense of describing the *sequence of states* through which T must pass in ascertaining that X (computing X, etc.), the rules obeyed, etc. But there is no "sequence of states" through which T must pass to be in a single state!

Indeed, suppose there were—suppose T could not *be* in state A without first *ascertaining* that it was in state A (by first passing through a sequence of other states). Clearly a vicious regress would be involved. And one "breaks" the regress simply by noting that the machine, in ascertaining the 3000th digit in π *passes through* its states—but it need not in any significant sense "ascertain" that it is passing through them . . . .

Let us modify our case, however, by supposing that whenever the machine is in one particular state (say, "state A") it prints the words "I am in state A." Then someone might grant that the machine does not in general ascertain what state it is in, but might say in the case of state A (after the machine printed "I am in state A"): "The machine ascertained that it was in state A."

Let us study this case a little more closely. First of all, we want to suppose that when it is in state A the machine prints "I am in state A" without first passing through any other states. That is, in every row of the column of the table headed "state A" there appears the instruction: *print[7] "I am in State A."* Secondly, by way of comparison, let us consider a human being, Jones, who says "I am in pain" (or "Ouch!" or "Something hurts") whenever he is in pain. To make the comparison as close as possible, we will have to suppose that Jones's linguistic conditioning is such that he simply says "I am in pain" "without thinking," i.e., without passing through any introspectible mental states other than the pain itself. In Wittgenstein's terminology, Jones simply *evinces* his pain by saying "I am in pain"—he does not first reflect on it (or heed it, or note it, etc.) and then consciously describe it. (Note that this simple possibility of uttering the "proposition," "I am in pain" without first performing any mental "act of judgment" was overlooked by traditional epistemologists from Hume to Russell!) Now we may consider the parallel questions "Does the machine 'ascertain' that it is in state A?" and "Does Jones 'know' that he is in pain?" and their consequences.

Philosophers interested in semantical questions have, as one might expect, paid a good deal of attention to the verb "know." Traditionally, three elements have been distinguished: (1) "X knows that p" implies that p is *true* (we may call this the *truth* element); (2) "X knows that p" implies that X believes that p (philosophers have quarreled about the word, some contending that it should be "X is *confident* that p," or "X *is in a position to assert* that p"; I shall call this element the *confidence* element); (3) "X knows that p" implies that X has evidence that p (here I think the word "evidence" is definitely wrong,[8] but it will not matter for present purposes; I shall call this the *evidential* element). Moreover, it is part of the meaning of the word "evidence" that nothing can be literally evidence for itself: if X is evidence for Y, then X and Y must be different things.

In view of such analyses, disputes have arisen over the propriety of saying (in cases like the one we are considering) "Jones knows that he is in pain." On the one hand, philosophers who take the common-sense view ("When I have a pain I *know* I have a pain") argue somewhat as follows: It would be clearly false to say Jones does *not* know he has a pain; but either Jones knows or he does not; hence, Jones knows he has a pain. Against these philosophers, one might argue as follows: "Jones does not know X" implies Jones is not in a position to assert that X; hence, it is certainly wrong to say "Jones does not know he has a pain." But the above use of the Law of the Excluded Middle was fallacious: words in English have *significance ranges,* and what is contended is that it is not semantically correct to say *either* "Jones knows that he has a pain" *or* "Jones does not know he has a pain" (although the former sentence is certainly less misleading than the latter, since *one* at least of the conditions involved in knowing is met—Jones is in a position to assert he has a pain. (In fact the *truth* and *confidence* elements are both present; it is the evidential element that occasions the difficulty.)

I do not wish to argue this question here;[9] the present concern is rather with the similarities between our two questions. For example, one might decide to accept (as "nondeviant," "logically in order," "nonselfcontradictory," etc.) the two statements:

(a) The machine ascertained that it was in state A,

(b) Jones knew that he had a pain,

or one might reject both. If one rejects (a) and (b), then one can find alternative formulations which are certainly semantically acceptable: e.g., [for (a)] "The machine was in state A, and this caused it to print: 'I am in state A;' " [for (b)] "Jones was in pain, and this caused him to say 'I am in pain' " (or, "Jones was in pain, and he evinced this by saying 'I am in pain' ").

On the other hand, if one accepts (a) and (b), then one must face the questions (a¹) "*How* did the machine ascertain that it was in state A?" and (b¹) "*How* did Jones know that he had a pain?"

And if one regards these questions as having answers at all, then they will be degenerate answers—e.g., "By being in state A" and "By having the pain."

At this point it is, I believe, very clear that the difficulty has in both cases the same cause. Namely, the difficulty is occasioned by the fact that the "verbal report" ("I am in state A," or "I am in pain") issues directly from the state it "reports": no "computation" or additional "evidence" is needed to arrive at the "answer." And the philosophic disagreements over "how to talk" are at bottom concerned with finding a terminology for describing cognitive processes in general that is not misleading in this particular case. [Note that the traditional epistemological answer to (b¹)—namely, "by introspection"—is false to the facts of this case, since it clearly implies the occurrence of a mental event (the "act" of introspection) distinct from the feeling of pain.]

Finally, let us suppose that the machine is equipped to "scan" its neighbor machine T^1. Then we can see that the question "How does T ascertain that T^1 is in state A?" may be a perfectly sensible question, as much so as "How does T ascertain that the 3000th digit of π is so-and-so?" In both cases the answer will involve describing a whole "program" (plus explaining the *rationale* of the program, if necessary). Moreover, it will be necessary to say something about the physical context linking T and T^1 (arrangement of sense organs, etc.), and not just to describe the internal states of T: this is so because T is now answering an *empirical* and not a mathematical question. In the same way "How did Sherlock Holmes know that Jones was in pain?" may be a perfectly sensible question, and may have quite a complicated answer.

"MENTAL" STATES AND "LOGICAL" STATES

Consider the two questions:

(1) How does Jones know he has a pain?

(2) How does Jones know he has a fever?

The first question is, as we saw in the preceding section, a somewhat peculiar one. The second question may be quite sensible. In fact, if Jones says "I have a pain" no one will retort "You are mistaken." (One *might* retort

"You have made a slip of the tongue" or "You are lying," but not "You are *mistaken.*") On the other hand, if Jones says "I have a fever," the doctor who has just taken Jones's temperature may quite conceivably retort "You are mistaken." And the doctor need not mean that Jones made a linguistic error, or was lying, or confused.

It might be thought that, whereas the difference between statements about one's own state and statements about the state of others has an analogue in the case of machines, the difference, just touched upon, between statements about one's "mental" state and statements about one's "physical" state, in traditional parlance, does not have any analogue. But this is not so. Just what the analogue is will now be developed.

First of all, we have to go back to the notion of a Turing machine. When a Turing machine is described by means of a "machine table," it is described as something having a tape, a printing device, a "scanning" device (this may be no more than a point of the machine which at any given time is aligned with just one square of the tape), and a finite set (A, B, C, etc.) of "states." (In what follows, these will be referred to at times as *logical states* to distinguish them from certain other states to be introduced shortly.) Beyond this it is described only by giving the deterministic rules which determine the order in which the states succeed each other and what is printed when.

In particular, the "logical description" of a Turing machine does not include any specification of the *physical nature* of these "states"—or indeed, of the physical nature of the whole machine. (Shall it consist of electronic relays, of cardboard, of human clerks sitting at desks, or what?) In other words, a given "Turing machine" is an *abstract* machine which may be physically realized in an almost infinite number of different ways.

As soon as a Turing machine is physically realized, however, something interesting happens. Although the machine has from the logician's point of view only the states A, B, C, etc., it has from the engineer's point of view an almost infinite number of additional "states" (though not in the same sense of "state"—we shall call these *structural states.*) For instance, if the machine consists of vacuum tubes, one of the things that may happen is that one of its vacuum tubes may fail—this puts the machine in what is from the physicist's if not the logician's point of view a different "state." Again, if the machine is a manually operated one built of cardboard, one of its possible "nonlogical" or "structural" states is obviously that its cardboard may buckle. And so on.

A physically realized Turing machine may have no way of ascertaining its own structural state, just as a human being may have no way of ascertaining the condition of his appendix at a given time. However, it is extremely convenient to give a machine electronic "sense organs" which enable it to scan itself and to detect minor malfunctions. These "sense organs" may be visualized as causing certain symbols to be printed on an "input tape" which the machine "examines" from time to time. (One minor difficulty is that the "report" of a sense organ might occupy a number of squares of tape, whereas the machine only "scans" one square at a time—however this is unimportant, since it is well known that the effect of "reading" any finite number of squares can be obtained using a program which only requires one square to be scanned at a time.)

(By way of a digression, let me remark that the first actually constructed digital computers did not have any devices of the kind just envisaged. On the other hand, they *did* have over 3000 vacuum tubes, some of which were failing at any given time! The need for "routines" for self-checking therefore quickly became evident.)[10]

A machine which is able to detect at least some of its own structural states is in a position very analogous to that of a human being, who can detect some but not all of the malfunctions of his own body, and with varying degrees of reliability. Thus, suppose the machine "prints out": "Vacuum tube 312 has failed." The question "How did the machine ascertain that vacuum tube 312 failed?" is a perfectly sensible question. And the answer may involve a reference to both the physical structure of the machine ("sense organs," etc.) and the "logical structure" (program for "reading" and "interpreting" the input tape).

If the machine prints: "Vacuum tube 312 has failed" when vacuum tube 312 is in fact functioning, the mistake may be due to a miscomputation (in the course of "reading" and "interpreting" the input tape) or to an incorrect signal from a sense organ. On the other hand, if the machine prints: "I am in state A," and it does this simply because its machine table contains the instruction: *Print: "I am in state A when in state A,"* then the question of a miscomputation cannot arise. Even if some accident causes the printing mechanism to print: "I am in state A" when the machine is *not* in state A, there was not a "miscomputation" (only, so to speak, a "verbal slip").

It is interesting to note that just as there are two possible descriptions of the behavior of a Turing machine—the engineer's structural blueprint and the logician's "machine table"—so there are two possible descriptions of human psychology. . . .

The analogy which has been presented between logical states of a Turing machine and mental states of a human being, on the one hand, and structural states of a Turing machine and physical states of a human being, on the other, is one that I find very suggestive. In particular, further exploration of this analogy may make it possible to further clarify the notion of a "mental state" that we have been discussing. This "further exploration" has not yet been undertaken, at any rate by me, but I should like to put down, for those who may be interested, a few of the features that seem to distinguish logical and mental states respectively from structural and physical ones:

(1) The functional organization (problem solving, thinking) of the human being or machine can be described in terms of the sequences of mental or logical states respectively (and the accompanying verbalizations), without reference to the nature of the "physical realization" of these states.

(2) The states seem intimately connected with *verbalization.*

(3) In the case of rational thought (or computing), the "program" which determines which states follow which, etc., is open to rational criticism.

MIND-BODY "IDENTITY"

The last area in which we have to compare human beings and machines involves the question of *identifying* mental states with the corresponding physical states (or logical states with the corresponding structural states). As indicated at the beginning of this paper, all of the arguments for and against such identification can perfectly well be discussed in terms of Turing machines.

For example, in the 1930s Wittgenstein used the following argument: If I observe an after-image, and observe at the same time my brain state (with the aid of a suitable instrument) I observe *two* things, not one. (Presumably this is one argument *against* identification.) But we can perfectly well imagine a "clever" Turing machine "reasoning" as follows: "When I print 'I am in state A,' I do not have to use my 'sense organs.' When I do use my 'sense organs' and compare the occasions upon which I am in state A with the occasions upon which flip-flop 36 is on, I am comparing *two* things and not one." And I do not think that we would find the argument of this mechanical Wittgenstein very convincing!

By contrast, Russell once carried the "identity" view to the absurd extreme of maintaining that all we ever *see* is portions of our own brains. Analogously, a mechanical Russell might "argue" that "all I ever observe is my own vacuum tubes." Both "Russells" are wrong—the human being observes events in the outside world, and the process of "observation" involves events in his brain. But we are not therefore forced to say that he "really" observes his brain. Similarly, the machine T may "observe," say, cans of tomato soup (if the machine's job is sorting cans of soup), and the process of "observation" involves the functioning of vacuum tubes. But we are not forced to say that the machine "really" observes its own vacuum tubes.

*   *   *

NOTES

1. By "deviant" utterance is here meant one that deviates from a semantical regularity (in the appropriate natural language). The term is taken from (8).

2. This point was made by Quine in (4).

3. Cf. Ziff's paper (7) and the reply (4) by Smart. Ziff has informed me that by a "robot" he did not have in mind a "learning machine" of the kind envisaged by Smart, and he would agree that the considerations brought forward in his paper would not necessarily apply to such a machine (if it can properly be classed as a "machine" at all). On the question of whether "this machine thinks (feels, etc.)" is *deviant* or not, it is necessary to keep in mind the point raised by Ziff (that the important question is not whether or not the utterance is deviant, but whether or not it is deviant for nontrivial reasons). . . .

4. In particular, I am sympathetic with the general standpoint taken by Smart in (5) and (6).

5. For further details, cf. (1) and (2).

6. This terminology is taken from (2) and differs from that of Davis and Turing.

7. Here it is necessary to suppose that the entire sentence "I am in state A" counts as a single symbol in the machine's alphabet.

8. For example, I know that the sun is 93 million miles from the earth, but I have no *evidence* that this is so. In fact, I do not even remember where I learned this.

9. In fact, it would be impossible to decide whether "Jones knows he has a pain" is deviant or not without first reformulating the evidential condition so as to avoid the objection in note 7 (if it can be reformulated so as to save anything of the condition at all). However the discussion above will indicate, I believe, why one might *want* to find that this sentence is deviant.

10. Actually, it was not necessary to add any "sense organs"; existing computers check themselves by "performing crucial experiments with themselves" (i.e., carrying out certain test computations and comparing the results with the correct results which have been given).

REFERENCES

1. Davis, Martin. *Computability and Unsolvability.* New York: McGraw-Hill Book Co., 1958.
2. Kleene, Stephen Cole. *Introduction to Metamathematics.* New York: Von Nostrand, 1952.
3. Quine, Willard Van Orman. "The Scope and Language of Science," British Journal for the Philosophy of Science, 8 (1957).
4. Smart, J. J. C. "Professor Ziff on Robots," *Analysis* 19 (1959): 117–18.
5. ———. "Incompatible Colors," *Philosophical Studies* 10 (1959): 39–42.

6. Smart, J. J. C. "Sensations and Brain Processes," *Philosophical Review* 168 (1959): 141–56.
7. Ziff, Paul. "The Feelings of Robots," *Analysis* 19 (1959): 64–68.
8. ———. *Semantic Analysis.* Ithaca: Cornell University Press, n.d.

35

Love in a Machine Age

Paul Weiss

[Many] suppose, without question or examination, that one never knows other minds—or, to put it better, other selves with their minds, wills, emotions, etc.—directly. They resolutely put aside the suggestion that there may be an immediate intuition, sympathy, love, or other way of penetrating beyond the outward forms men exhibit. They take it for granted that no one can even reach the edge of another's privacy, that one cannot possibly get below his surface. Most of them speak as if there were no "below"; they are phenomenalists, differing amongst themselves as to whether or not they want to stress language, behavior, perception, process, or some other horizontally-structured way of dealing with the world. One need remark only that there are other reputable philosophic positions besides phenomenalism —metaphysical theories which insist that there are substances, existentialisms with their acknowledgment of radical privacies, and the like—to know that the common position is open to question. It is surely unwarranted. I think it is mistaken.

For the moment let us put that matter aside. The question then before us would seem to be fourfold:

1. Do or can machines act in ways which in principle duplicate all the acts of men?

From *Dimensions of Mind*, edited by Sidney Hook (New York: New York University Press, 1960), pp. 177–80. Reprinted by permission of the publisher.

2. If machines could not duplicate all men's actions, would such behavior testify to the presence in men of some inward nature or power?

3. If machines could duplicate all men's actions, would that testify to the presence in the machines of some inward nature or power?

4. Would the incapacity to distinguish the behavior of men from that of machines show that men were indistinguishable from machines?

1. Behavior occurs in space and time. There is no path or rhythm which one can antecedently claim is closed to some machine or other. It seems clear, then, that the behavior of men can in principle be duplicated by machines.

2. Were a man to behave in ways machines could not, this would show only that he was more flexible, had a wider range, than those artifacts had. It would not necessarily show that he had a private nature, mind, or will, and that the machines did not.

3. Were a machine to behave just as men do, it would have to be credited with a mind, if minds are accredited to men; or the men must be denied to have minds, if this is denied to the machine.

4. When I see others I see them from the outside. If this is the only source of my knowledge of them I cannot know whether or not they have minds. Attending only to *other* men, and observing only their behaviors, I cannot find a way of distinguishing them in principle from all possible machines. But if there be another source of knowledge regarding at least one man, which is not grounded on observable public behavior, then men and machines can be distinguished, despite a lack of difference in their behaviors.

I know myself not only from the outside but from within. Others may not know that I have a mind. Since I can see in the mirror, and in other ways, that I behave somewhat like other men, I conclude that they have minds similar to mine, or that I, being alone in having a mind, am a distinct type of being. And if I cannot distinguish men from machines, I must go on to say that the machines too have minds, or that once again I am distinct in type from them.

To say that I am a distinct type of being is to make an ontological claim. To say that I am like others but have a source of information regarding myself which they do not have, is, in contrast, to make an epistemological claim. The former insists on a difference in natures despite all publicly available evidence that can be produced to the contrary. It goes beyond what the facts warrant. The fact that others are not sure that I have a mind does not make me conclude that I do not have one. Rather, I conclude that they are not privy to all my sources of information. . . . The only warranted conclusion to be drawn is the epistemological one that though I am of the same type as they are, as evidenced by our behavior, I have a source of evidence they do not have regarding the existence of my own mind. Since behaviorally they are of the same type as I am, I must credit each of them with a mind as well, and with the capacity to draw on direct evidence showing that he has one.

When machines behave as men do, I ought to say of those artifacts what I now say of those men: that they too have minds. Furthermore, I ought to say that they have wills as well, that they have private selves, secret feelings, a damning conscience, foolish hopes, good and bad intensions, justified and unjustified beliefs. I ought to grant that they have aesthetic sensitivity, the power to speculate, and that they may even have a religious faith. I ought to say of them, as I say of myself, that they are responsible, they are guilty, they are human—all too human. In short, I ought to say that the kind of mind I know I have, must be attributed to all beings which behave as I do, no matter what their origin or appearance—providing behavior is the only criterion for determining whether or not beings are of the same type.

If we now withdraw the supposition and affirm that through love and sympathy we can penetrate beneath the forms men exhibit in public, and can therefore directly reach their private beings, we will still be able to say that, on the basis of bodily behavior alone, we rightly can attribute minds, wills, feelings, etc., to machines, as well as to other men. But we will also be able to say that we cannot love those machines. There will perhaps be some men we will not love, and some machines to which we will become attached. If we find a being which looks and behaves like other men and is beyond our capacity ever to love, we must say of it that it is only a machine, to be placed outside the society where only men can be. Should we find a machine which we can love, we must say of it that it has a human nature and human powers. We will, in short, divide beings, all of whom behave in the same way, into two classes, calling "men" those which are in principle within our powers to love, and calling "machines" those which we cannot possibly love.

Alternatively, I may find that I am unable to love what other men or even machines may report that they can love. If I cannot show that they are in error, I must conclude that they are superior to me. If it is the case that I not only do not, but cannot possibly, love Nazis, or Israelis, or Japanese, or whatever, while others, whether they be machines or men, *can* love them, it is *I* who must be said not to be human. I preserve my humanity only so far as I am one who is intrinsically able to love whatever can be loved.

Both what cannot be loved by one who can love, and what cannot love what can be loved, are less than human, no matter how much they look like and behave like men. Machines fail on both counts. They are not on a footing with me. They are, in short, not human, and thus cannot be said to have selves or minds, rights or responsibilities. The conclusion is not surprising, for we all know that a machine is an artifact whose parts are united so as to enable them to act together, whereas a man is a unity in which the whole governs the behavior of the parts. Only such a unity has a self, with feelings, mind, will, and the rest.

Phenomenalism may reach the point where men and machines are indistinguishable. It must then conclude that machines, like men, have minds, or conversely, that men, like machines, have no minds. The results are equivalent. But love and pity, hate and contempt, will then show how limited phenomenalism is.

Phenomenalism may—indeed must—stop short with behavior. It may fail to see but cannot make nonexistent what love discerns. In a machine age, as in any other, it is love that marks the man.

Select Bibliography

Anisimov, S. F. "Man and Machine," in *Philosophical Problems of Cybernetics*. Report No. JPRS 1990-N. Washington, D.C.: Joint Publications Research Service, 1959.

Armer, P. "Attitudes Toward Intelligent Machines," in E. Feigenbaum and J. Feldman, eds., *Computers and Thought* (New York, 1963).

Ashby, W. F. *Design for a Brain* (New York, 1954).

———. "Can an Mechanical Chess Player Outplay Its Designer?" *British Journal for the Philosophy of Science* 3 (1952): 44–47.

Benacerraf, P. "God, the Devil and Godel," *The Monist* 51 (1967): 9–32.

Blake, D. V., and Uttley, A. M., eds. *Proceedings of a Symposium on Mechanization of Thought Processes,* 2 vols. (London, 1959).

Borko, H., ed. *Computer Applications in the Behavioral Sciences,* Englewood Cliffs, N.J., 1962.

Burks, Arthur W. "Computation, Behaviors, and Structure in Fixed and Growing Automata," *Behavioral Science* 6, no. 1 (1961): 5–22.

Butler, Samuel. *Erewhon,* chaps. 23–25.

Carnap, Rudolf. "The Interpretation of Physics," in *Readings in the Philosophy of Science,* H. Feigl and M. Brodbeck, eds. (New York, 1953), pp. 309–18.

———. "The Methodological Character of Theoretical Concepts," in *Foundations of Science and the Concepts of Psychology and Psychoanalysis,* H. Feigl and M. Scriven, eds., Vol. I, (Minneapolis, 1956), Minnesota Studies in the Philosophy of Science, pp. 38–76.

Chappell, V. C., ed. *The Philosophy of Mind* (Englewood Cliffs, N.J., 1962).

Chomsky, Noam, *Syntactic Structures.* The Hague, 1957.

Church, Alonzo. *Introduction to Mathematical Logic.* Princeton, N.J., 1956.

———. "An Unsolvable Problem of Elementary Number Theory," *American Journal of Mathematics* 58 (1936): 345–63.

Cohen, Jonathan. "Can There Be Artificial Minds?" *Analysis* 16 (1955): 36–41.

Copi, I. M., Elgot, C. C., and Wright, J. B. "Realization of Events by Logical Nets," *Journal for the Association of Computing Machinery* 5 (1958): 181–96.

Davis, Martin. *Computability and Unsolvability* (New York, 1958).

Descartes, René. *Philosophical Works,* trans. E. Haldane and G. R. T. Ross, (New York, 1955).

Driesch, H., *The History and Theory of Vitalism* (New York, 1914).

Dreyfus, H., *Alchemy and Artificial Intelligence* (RAND Publication P-3244, Santa Monica, Calif., 1965).

Feigenbaum, E., and Feldman, J., eds. *Computers and Thought* (New York, 1963).

Feldman, J. "Computer Simulation of Cognitive Processes," in H. Borko, ed., *Computer Applications in the Behavioral Sciences* (Englewood Cliffs, N.J., 1962), pp. 337–56.

Fodor, J., and Katz, J., eds. *The Structure of Language: Readings in the Philosophy of Language,* Englewood Cliffs, N.J., 1964.

Friedberg, R. M. "A Learning Machine," Part 1, *IBM Journal of Research and Development* 11 (1958): 2–13.

Gelernter, H. L. "Realization of a Geometry-Proving Machine," *Proceedings of the International Conference on Information Processing.* Paris, 1959.

George, F. H., "Logic and Behavior," *Science News* 45 (1957): 46–60.

Godel, Kurt. "Uber Formal Unentscheidbare Satze der *Principia Mathematica* und verwanter Systeme," Part I, *Monatshefte fur Mathematik und Physik* 38 (1931): 173–89.

Gunderson, K. "Asymmetries and Mind-Body Perplexities," in S. Winokut and M. Radner, eds., *Minnesota Studies in the Philosophy of Science,* Vol. 4, Minneapolis, 1970, 273–309.

————. "Cybernetics," in P. Edwards, ed., *Encyclopedia of Philosophy* (New York, 1967).

————. "Cybernetics and Mind-Body Problems," *Inquiry* 12 (1969): 406–19.

————. "Interview of a Robot," *Analysis* 23 (1963): 136–42.

————. "Minds and Machines: A Survey," in R. Klibansky, ed., *Contemporary Philosophy: A Survey* (Florence, 1968).

Haldane, J. B. S. "The Mechanical Chess-Player," *British Journal for the Philosophy of Science* 3 (1952): 189–91.

Hanson, Norwood Russell. *Patterns of Discovery* (London, 1958).

Hartree, D. R., *Calculating Instruments and Machines* (Urbana, 1949).

Hook, S., ed. *Dimensions of Mind* (New York, 1960).

Huxley, T. H. "On the Hypothesis that Animals Are Automata, and Its History," in *Essays, Vol. 1: Methods and Results* (New York, 1911).

Jefferson, G. "The Mind of Mechanical Man," Lister Oration for 1949, *British Medical Journal* 1 (1949): 1105–21.

Kleene, Stephen Cole. *Introduction to Metamathematics* (Princeton, N.J., 1952).

————. "General Recursive Functions of Natural Numbers," *American Journal of Mathematics* 57 (1935): 153–73, 219–44.

Lacey, A. R. "Men and Robots," *Philosophical Quarterly* 10 (1960): 61–72.

La Mettrie, J. *Man a Machine,* trans. by G. Bussey (Chicago, 1953).

Lange, F. A. *The History of Materialism,* trans. by E. C. Thomas, ed., (London, 1950).

Lovelace, Mary Caroline. *Scientific Memoirs,* R. Taylor, ed., Vol. III, 1842, pp. 691–731.

Lucas, J. R., "The Lesbian Rule," *Philosophy* 30 (1955): 195–213.

———. "Minds, Machines, and Godel," *Philosophy* 36 (1961): 112–27.

———. "On Not Worshipping Facts," *Philosophical Quarterly* 8 (1958): 144–56.

MacKay, D. M. "The Epistemological Problem for Automata," in *Automata Studies* (Princeton, N.J., 1956), pp. 235–251.

———. "Mentality in Machines," *Proceedings of the Aristotelian Society, Supplementary* 26 (1952): 61–86.

———. "Mind-Like Behaviour in Artifacts," *British Journal for the Philosophy of Science* 2 (1951): 110.

———. "Operational Aspects of Intellect," in *Proceedings of the Symposium on Mechanization of Thought Processes,* D. V. Blake and A. M. Uttley, eds., (London, 1959).

Mays, W. "The Hypothesis of Cybernetics," *British Journal for the Philosophy of Science* 2 (1951): 249–50.

McCulloch, W. S. "The Brain as a Computing Machine," *Electrical Engineering,* 68 (1949): 492–97.

McCulloch, W. S., and Pfeiffer, J. E., "Of Digital Computers Called Brains," *Scientific Monthly* 69 (1949): 368–76.

McDougall, W. *An Introduction to Social Psychology* (London, 1908; New York, 1961).

Miller, G., Galanter, E., and Pribram, K., *Plans and the Structure of Behavior* (New York, 1960).

Minsky, Marvin L. "Heuristic Aspects of the Artificial Intelligence Problem," Group Report 34–35; Massachusetts Institute of Technology, Lincoln Laboratory, Lexington, (December 1956).

———. "A Selected Descriptor-Indexed Bibliography to the Literature on Artificial Intelligence," *IRE Transactions on Human Factors in Electronics* (1961): 39–55.

———. "Steps Toward Artificial Intelligence," *Proceedings of the IRE* 49 (1961): 8–30.

Nagel, Ernest and Newman, J. R., *Godel's Proof* (New York, 1958).

Newell, A., and Simon, H., "Computers in Psychology," in R. Luce, R. Bush, and E. Galanter, eds., *Handbook to Mathematical Psychology* (New York, 1963).

———. *The Simulation of Human Thought* (The RAND Corporation, Report No. P-1734, Santa Monica, Calif., 1959).

Oppenheim, Paul, and Putnam, Hilary. "Unity of Science as a Working Hypothesis," in *Concepts, Theories, and the Mind-Body Problem,* H. Feigl, G. Maxwell, and M. Scriven, eds., Minnesota Studies in the Philosophy of Science, Vol. II. (Minneapolis, 1958).

Parkinson, G. H. "The Cybernetic Approach to Aesthetics," *Philosophy* 36 (1961): 49–61.

Pitts, W., and McCulloch, W. S., "How We Know Universals," *Bulletin for Mathematical Biophysics* 9 (1947): 127–47.

Popper, K. R. "Indeterminism in Quantum Physics and Classical Physics," *British Journal for the Philosophy of Science* 1 (1951): 179–88.

Puccetti, R. "On Thinking Machines and Feeling Machines," *British Journal for the Philosophy of Science* 18 (1967): 39–51.

Putnam, Hilary. "The Analytic and the Synthetic," in *Scientific Explanation, Space, and Time,* H. Feigl and G. Maxwell, eds., Minnesota Studies in the Philosophy of Science, Vol. III. (Minneapolis, 1962).

———. "The Mental Life of Some Machines," in H. N. Castaneda, ed., *Intentionality, Minds, and Perception* (Detroit, 1967), pp. 177–200.

———. "Robots: Machines or Artificially Created Life?" *Journal of Philosophy* 61 (1964): 668–91.

Quine, Willard Van Orman. "The Scope and Language of Science," *British Journal for the Philosophy of Science* 8 (1957): 1–17.

Rashevsky, N. "Is the Concept of an Organism as a Machine a Useful One?" *Scientific Monthly* 80 (1955): 32–35.

Reitman, W. *Cognition and Thought* (New York, 1966).

Richards, P. I. "On Game-Learning Machines," *Scientific Monthly* 74 (1959): 201–205.

Rogers, H. *Theory of Recursive Functions and Effective Computability* (mimeographed), Massachusetts Institute of Technology, 1957.

Rorty, Amelie O., "Slaves and Machines," *Analysis* 22 (1962): 118–20.

Rosenbloom, Paul C. *Elements of Mathematical Logic* (New York, 1951).

Rosenfield, L. *From Beast-Machine to Man-Machine: Animal Soul in French Letters from Descartes to La Mettrie* (New York, 1941).

Ross, T. "The Synthesis of Intelligence—Its Implications," *Psychological Review* 45 (1938): 87–91.

Rosser, B. "Extensions of Some Theorems of Godel and Church," *Journal of Symbolic Logic* 1 (1936): 87–91.

Ryle, Gilbert. *The Concept of Mind* (London 1949).

Samuel, A. L. "Some Studies in Machine Learning Using the Game of Checkers," *IBM Journal of Research and Development* 3 (1959): 210–29.

Sayre, K. *Recognition: A Study in the Philosophy of Artificial Intelligence* (Notre Dame, Ind., 1965).

Selfridge, O. G. "Pandemonium: A Paradigm for Learning," Massachusetts Institute of Technology, Lincoln Laboratory (Lexington, 1960).

Shannon, C. E. "A Chess-Playing Machine," *Scientific American* 182 (1950): 48–51.

Shannon, C. E., and McCarthy, J., eds., *Automata Studies* (Princeton, N.J., 1956).

Shaw, R., Halwes, T., and Jenkins, J., *The Organism as a Mimicking Automaton,* Center for Research in Human Learning, University of Minnesota (in mimeograph), 1966.

Simmons, P. L., and Simmons, R. F., *The Simulation of Cognitive Behavior, II: An Annotated Bibliography* (Santa Monica, Calif., System Development Corporation, SP-590/002/00, 1961).

———. "The Simulation of Cognitive Processes: An Annotated Bibliography," *IRE Transactions on Electronic Computers,* EC-10, No. 3 (1961): 462–83.

Smart, J. J. C. "Godel's Theorem, Church's Theorem and Mechanism," *Synthese* 13 (1961): 105–110.

———. "Incompatible Colors," *Philosophical Studies* 10 (1959): 39–42.

———. "Sensations and Brain Processes," *The Philosophical Review* 68 (1959): 141–56.

Travis, L. E. "Observing How Humans Make Mistakes to Discover How to Get Computers to Do Likewise," Santa Monica, Calif., System Development Corporation, SP-776, 1962.

Turing, A. M. "Computing Machinery and Intelligence," in A. Anderson, ed., *Minds and Machines* (Englewood Cliffs, N.J., 1964), pp. 4–30.

———. "On Computable Numbers, with an Application to the Entscheidungsproblem," *Proceedings of the London Mathematical Society* 42 (1937): 230–65.

von Neumann, John. *The Computer and the Brain* (New Haven, Conn., 1958).

———. "The General and Logical Theory of Automata," *Cerebral Mechanisms in Behavior*, L. A. Jeffries, ed., The Hixson Symposium (New York, 1951), pp. 1–31.

Vartanian, A. *Diderot and Descartes: A Study of Scientific Naturalism in the Enlightenment* (Princeton, N.J., 1953).

White, B. "Studies of Perception, in H. Borko, ed., *Computer Applications in the Behavioral Sciences* (Englewood Cliffs, N.Y., 1962), pp. 280–305.

Wilkes, M. V. "Can Machines Think?" *Proceedings of the IRE* 41 (1953): 1230–34.

Wisdom, J. O. "The Hypothesis of Cybernetics," *British Journal of the Philosophy of Science* 2 (1951–52): 1–24.

———. "A New Model for the Mind-Body Relationship," *British Journal for the Philosophy of Science* 2 (1951–52): 295–301.

Wisdom, J. O., Spilsbury, R. J., and MacKay, D. M., "Symposium: Mentality in Machines," *Proceedings of the Aristotelian Society Supplementary* 26 (1952): 1–61.

Wittgenstein, L., *Philosophical Investigations,* trans., G. E. M. Anscombe, (New York, 1953).

Wright, M. A. "Can Machines Be Intelligent?" *Process Control and Automation* 6 (1959): 2–6.

Ziff, Paul. *Semantic Analysis* (Ithaca, N.Y., 1960).